D0171771

EYEWITNESS *TRAVEL GUIDES*

SEVILLE
& ANDALUSIA

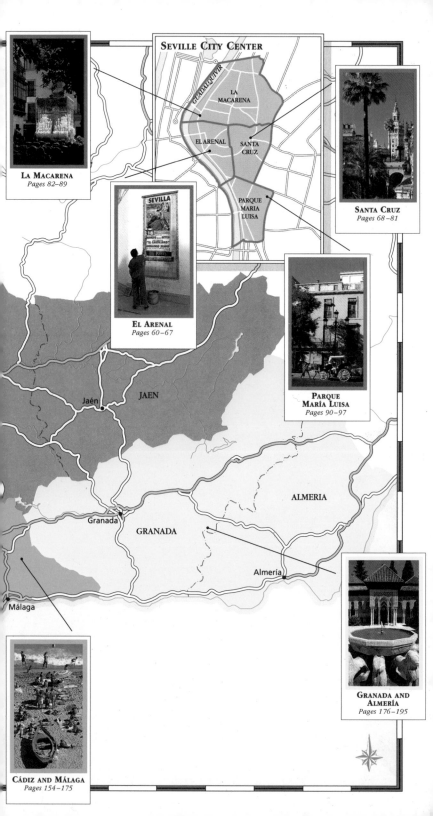

SEVILLE CITY CENTER

GUADALQUIVIR

LA MACARENA

EL ARENAL

SANTA CRUZ

PARQUE MARIA LUISA

LA MACARENA
Pages 82–89

SANTA CRUZ
Pages 68–81

EL ARENAL
Pages 60–67

PARQUE MARÍA LUISA
Pages 90–97

JAEN

Jaén

Granada

GRANADA

ALMERIA

Almería

Málaga

GRANADA AND ALMERÍA
Pages 176–195

CÁDIZ AND MÁLAGA
Pages 154–175

EYEWITNESS *TRAVEL GUIDES*

SEVILLE
& ANDALUSIA

DK

DORLING KINDERSLEY

LONDON • NEW YORK • STUTTGART • MOSCOW

DK

A DK PUBLISHING BOOK

PROJECT EDITOR Anna Streiffert
ART EDITOR Robert Purnell
EDITORS Marcus Hardy, Jane Oliver
US EDITORS Mary Sutherland, Kathleen Kent
DESIGNERS Malcolm Parchment, Katie Peacock
MAP COORDINATORS Michael Ellis, David Pugh

MANAGING EDITORS Vivien Crump, Helen Partington
MANAGING ART EDITOR Stephen Knowlden
DEPUTY EDITORIAL DIRECTOR Douglas Amrine
SENIOR MANAGING ART EDITOR Gillian Allan

PRODUCTION David Proffit
PICTURE RESEARCH Monica Allende, Naomi Peck
DTP DESIGNER Sarah Martin

MAIN CONTRIBUTORS
David Baird, Martin Symington, Nigel Tisdall

MAPS
Gary Bowes, Anna Nilsson, Richard Toomey
(ERA-Maptec Ltd, Dublin, Ireland),
Jennifer Skelley (Lovell Johns Ltd, Oxford, UK)

PHOTOGRAPHERS
Neil Lukas, John Miller, Linda Whitwam

ILLUSTRATORS
Richard Draper, Isidoro González-Adalid Cabezas
(Acanto Arquitectura y Urbanismo S.L.), Steven Gyapay,
Claire Littlejohn, Maltings, Chris Orr, John Woodcock
•
Film outputting bureau Cooling Brown (London)
Reproduced by Colourscan (Singapore)
Printed and bound by G. Canale & C. (Italy)

First American Edition, 1996
2 4 6 8 10 9 7 5 3 1

Published in the United States by
DK Publishing, Inc.,
95 Madison Avenue, New York, New York 10016

Library of Congress Cataloging-in-Publication Data
Seville and Andalusia. -- 1st American ed.
      p.   cm. -- (Eyewitness travel guides)
Includes index.
Cover title: Seville & Andalusia.
ISBN 0-7894-0427-3
1. Seville (Spain) -- Guidebooks.   2. Andalusia (Spain)
-- Guidebooks.   I. Title: Seville and Andalusia.   II. Series.
DP402.S38S4 1996   95-4500
914.6' 80483 -- dc20   CIP

Every effort has been made to ensure that the information in this book is as up-to-
date as possible at the time of going to press. However, details such as telephone
numbers, opening hours, prices, gallery hanging arrangements, and travel
information are liable to change. The publishers cannot accept responsibility
for any consequences arising from the use of this book.
We would be delighted to receive any corrections and suggestions for incorporation
in the next edition. Please write to the Deputy Editorial Director, Eyewitness Travel
Guides, Dorling Kindersley, 9 Henrietta Street, London WC2E 8PS.
THROUGHOUT THIS BOOK, FLOORS ARE REFERRED TO IN ACCORDANCE WITH EUROPEAN USAGE.
I.E, "FIRST FLOOR" IS ONE FLIGHT UP.

Previous pages: Torre del Oro in Seville by night

CONTENTS

HOW TO USE
THIS GUIDE 6

**Bible illustration in Moorish style
dating from the 10th century**

INTRODUCING
SEVILLE AND
ANDALUSIA

PUTTING SEVILLE
AND ANDALUSIA ON
THE MAP 10

A PORTRAIT OF
ANDALUSIA 14

ANDALUSIA THROUGH
THE YEAR 32

THE HISTORY
OF SEVILLE AND
ANDALUSIA 38

**Horse and carriage at Plaza de
España, Parque María Luisa**

Zahara de la Sierra, one of Andalusia's traditional *pueblos blancos* (white towns)

The Generalife

HOW TO USE THIS GUIDE

THIS GUIDE HELPS you to get the most from your stay in Seville and Andalusia. It provides expert recommendations and detailed practical information. *Introducing Seville and Andalusia* maps the region and sets a historical and cultural context. *Seville Area by Area* and

Andalusia Area by Area describe the important sights, with maps, pictures, and detailed illustrations. Suggestions on what to eat and drink, accommodations, shopping, and entertainment are in *Travelers' Needs*, and the *Survival Guide* has tips on everything from transportation to using the telephone.

SEVILLE AREA BY AREA

The center of Seville has been divided into four sightseeing areas. *Across the River* makes up a fifth area. Each area has its own chapter, which opens with a list of the sights described. All the sights are numbered and plotted on an Area Map. The detailed information for each sight is presented in numerical order, thereby making it easy to locate within the chapter.

Sights at a Glance lists the chapter's sights by category: Churches, Museums and Galleries, Historic Buildings, Streets and Plazas, etc.

2 Street-by-Street Map
This gives a bird's-eye view of the heart of each sight-seeing area.

A suggested route for a walk covers the more interesting streets in the area.

All pages relating to central Seville have red thumb tabs.

A locator map shows where you are in relation to other areas of the city center.

1 Area Map
For easy reference, the sights are numbered and located on a map. The sights are also shown on the Street Finder on pages 108–13.

Stars indicate the sights that no visitor should miss.

3 Detailed information on each sight
All the sights in Seville are described individually. Addresses and practical information are provided. The key to the symbols used in the information block is shown on the back flap.

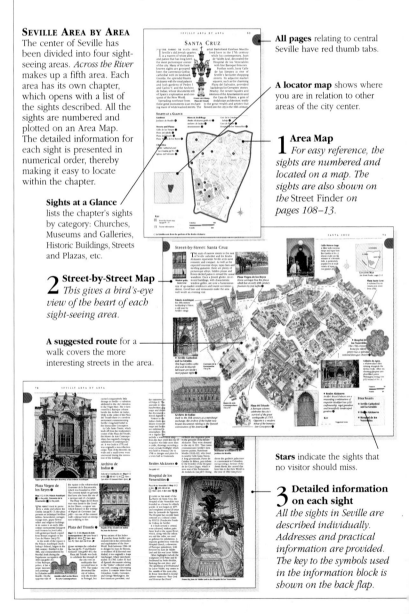

1 Introduction
The landscape, history, and character of each region is described here, showing how the area has developed over the centuries and what it offers the visitor today.

ANDALUSIA AREA BY AREA
In this book, Andalusia has been divided into four distinct regions, each of which has a separate chapter. The most interesting sights to visit have been numbered on a Pictorial Map.

Each area of Andalusia has color-coded thumb tabs.

2 Pictorial Map
This shows the main road network and provides an illustrated overview of the whole region. All entries are numbered, and there are also some useful tips on getting around the region by car, bus, and train.

3 Detailed information on each entry
All the important towns and other places to visit are dealt with individually. They are listed in order, following the numbering given on the Pictorial Map. Within each town or city, there is detailed information on important buildings and other sights.

Features give information on topics of particular interest.

The Visitors' Checklist provides a summary of the practical information you need to plan your visit.

4 The top sights
These are given two or more full pages. Historic buildings are dissected to reveal their interiors; museums and galleries have color-coded floor plans to help you locate the most interesting exhibits.

Stars indicate the best features and important works of art.

INTRODUCING
SEVILLE AND
ANDALUSIA

Putting Seville and Andalusia on the Map

A NDALUSIA IS SPAIN'S SOUTHERNMOST REGION, bordered by
Extremadura and Castilla-La Mancha to the north and
Murcia to the northwest. Its long coastline faces the Atlantic
to the west and the Mediterranean to the south and east. One
of Spain's largest regions, it covers an area of 87,267 sq km
(33,693 sq miles) and has a population of 6.8 million. Partly
as a result of Expo '92 *(see pp54–5)*, communications
have improved greatly with new highways and the
fast-track AVE train linking Seville and Córdoba with
Madrid. Several international airports serve the area,
Seville and Málaga being the most important.

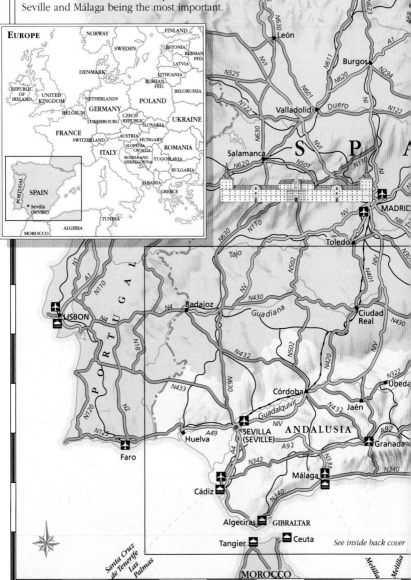

See inside back cover

◁ **Painting of the Feria de Abril in Seville by Dominguez Becquer (1885)**

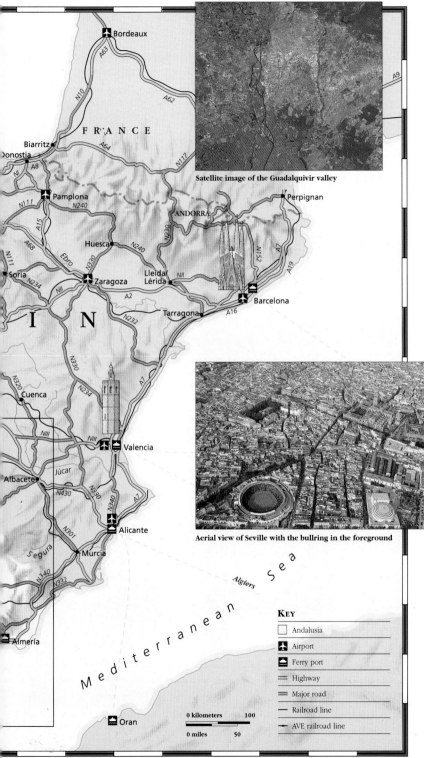

Satellite image of the Guadalquivir valley

Aerial view of Seville with the bullring in the foreground

KEY

	Andalusia
✈	Airport
⛴	Ferry port
=	Highway
	Major road
	Railroad line
	AVE railroad line

Seville City Center and Greater Seville

SEVILLE CITY CENTER is a compact maze of old, narrow streets, with most sights within walking distance. A couple of wide, busy avenues cut through the center, dividing it into separate areas. This book focuses on these areas, starting with the historic neighborhoods on each side of Avenida de la Constitución. To the west, along the river, is El Arenal with the Plaza de Toros; and to the east lies the old Jewish quarter of Santa Cruz, dominated by the massive cathedral and the Reales Alcázares. In the north lies La Macarena with its many churches, and the Parque María Luisa stretches out beyond the Universidad, south of the historic center.

El Arenal: Plaza de Toros de la Maestranza and Torre del Oro

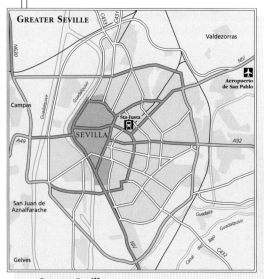

Greater Seville

West of the Guadalquivir River lies the site of Expo '92 and the picturesque Triana quarter. Sprawling industrial zones and modern residential areas surround the town center.

Parque María Luisa: the Plaza de España, built for the 1929 Exposition

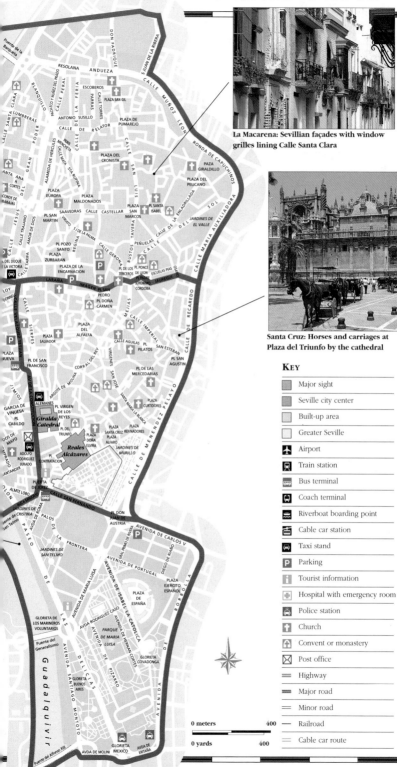

La Macarena: Sevillian façades with window grilles lining Calle Santa Clara

Santa Cruz: Horses and carriages at Plaza del Triunfo by the cathedral

KEY

	Major sight
	Seville city center
	Built-up area
	Greater Seville
✈	Airport
🚆	Train station
🚌	Bus terminal
🚍	Coach terminal
⛴	Riverboat boarding point
🚠	Cable car station
🚕	Taxi stand
P	Parking
ℹ	Tourist information
✚	Hospital with emergency room
🚓	Police station
✝	Church
⛪	Convent or monastery
✉	Post office
═	Highway
═	Major road
═	Minor road
—	Railroad
═	Cable car route

0 meters   400

0 yards   400

A PORTRAIT OF ANDALUSIA

ANDALUSIA IS WHERE *all Spain's stereotypes appear to have come together. Bullfighters, flamenco dancers, white villages, and harsh* sierras *are all there in abundance. But they form only part of an intricate tapestry. Beneath the surface, expect to find many contradictions. Wherever you travel, particularly when you escape from the tourist-engulfed coast, you will come across the unexpected, whether it is a local* fiesta *or a breathtaking view.*

Until the 1950s Andalusia had changed scarcely at all since the middle of the 19th century, when the English traveler, Richard Ford, described it as "a land bottled for antiquarians" – almost a feudal society, with attendant rigid social strata.

A basket of newly-harvested olives

Today, four-lane highways stretch from horizon to horizon where not so long ago there were only dirt tracks. Children whose parents are illiterate play with computers and plan their university careers. Agriculture is still important, but there are also factories turning out cars and aircraft. As in most other European countries, the service industries, tourism especially, predominate. In 1991 they accounted for 63 percent of the region's GNP as compared with 8.7 percent for agriculture and fishing. Yet the seven million inhabitants of Andalusia retain their characteristic love of talk and folklore, their indifference to time, and their abundant hospitality.

THE MOORISH LEGACY

The Andalusian character is complex because it reflects a complex history. Successive invaders, including the Phoenicians, Romans, Visigoths, and Moors, have all left their indelible mark. Although the Christian rulers of Spain ejected both Jews and Moors

Musicians, singers, and dancers continuing a flamenco tradition that dates from the 18th century *(see p26)*

◁ **Bullfighters *(see pp24–5)* in traditional costumes, preparing for the *corrida***

from their kingdom, they could not remove their influences on the country – let alone on Andalusia. Look at the face of an Andalusian man or woman and you will catch a glimpse of North Africa. Centuries of Moorish occupation *(see pp44–5)* and the inevitable mingling of blood have created a race and culture different from any in Europe.

Sevillanos **enjoying a predinner drink and some tapas** *(see pp222–3)*

As you travel around the region, you will find abundant physical evidence of the Moorish legacy: in the splendor of the Alhambra *(see pp186–7)* and the Mezquita *(see pp140–41)* in Córdoba, and in ruined fortresses and elaborate tilework. Workshops across the region still practice crafts handed down from great Moorish kingdoms. Many of the irrigation networks in use today follow those laid out by the Moors, who built *norias* (waterwheels), *aljibes* (tanks for collecting the rain), *albercas* (cisterns), and *acequias* (irrigation channels).

As these words show, the Moors also left a strong linguistic legacy, not only of agricultural terms, but also of words for foods – *naranja* (orange), for example, and *aceituna* (olive).

Moorish influence may also account for Andalusians' love of poetry and fine language. It is no coincidence that Spain's finest poets, including among them Nobel prize winners, come from this region.

PEOPLE AND CULTURE

Sevillanos work hard to sustain their reputation for flamboyance and hedonism. A 13th-century Moorish commentator noted that they

Moorish-style stuccowork

were "the most frivolous and most given to playing the fool." Living up to that image is a full-time occupation, but the visitor should not be deceived by the exuberant façade. One surprising aspect of both Seville and Andalusia is that although the society may appear open and extroverted, it is, in fact, one that also values privacy.

The Andalusian concept of time can also be perplexing. Progressive business types may try to adjust to the rigorous demands of Europe, but in general, northern Europeans' obsession with time is an object of mirth here. The moment is to be enjoyed and tomorrow will look after itself. A concert will often begin well after the advertised time, and lunch can feasibly take place at any time between 1pm and 4:30pm.

Penitents parading a monstrance, Semana Santa *(see p36)*

Barren, remote countryside, one of the many faces of Andalusia's varied landscape *(see pp18–19)*

Attitudes to women in Andalusia are changing, as elsewhere in western Europe, but southern Spain's tradition for *machismo* means that there is still some way to go. The number of women, for example, who work outside the home is still lower than in other countries of the West. Although many women hold jobs in their twenties, they still give up work when they marry in order to have children and look after the house.

Paradoxically, the mother is an almost sacred figure in Andalusia, where family ties are written in blood. New affluence and a steady movement to the cities is now beginning to erode old values, but Andalusia remains a traditional rural society with a distinct emphasis on personal relationships.

Sevillian lady in the traditional costume of the *feria (see p36)*

Catholicism is Spain's dominant religion, and adoration of the Virgin is a striking feature of Andalusia. Apart from a purely religious devotion, she is also subject to a peculiar admiration from the male population. A man who never attends Mass may be ecstatic about the Virgin at his local church; when she emerges from the church in procession, he feels fiercely possessive of her. If you try to think of the gorgeously robed figure as a pagan earth mother or fertility goddess, the phenomenon is much easier to understand.

As a society, Andalusia is unafraid of its emotions, which are almost always near the surface. There is no shame in the singing of a *saeta*, the "arrow" of praise launched at the Virgin in Semana Santa (Holy Week), nor is there any ambivalence in the matador's desire to kill his antagonist, the bull. The quintessence of this is flamenco; the pain and passion of its songs reflect not just the sufferings and yearnings of gypsies and the poor, but also Andalusia's soul.

Decorative tilework in the Palacio de Viana *(see p139)*

Nun with convent jams

The Landscape of Andalusia

EACH YEAR, several million visitors are drawn to the high-rise resorts along Andalusia's Mediterranean coast. Away from these, however, are empty, windswept Atlantic shores and expansive areas of wet-land wilderness. Inland there are rugged mountain ranges covered with forests of pine, cork, and wild olive. Also

Prickly pear, a native of the Americas

typical of the landscape are the undulating hills awash with vines, grain, and olive trees. Of Andalusia's total land area, some 17 percent has been designated national parks or nature preserves in order to protect the region's unique abundance of animal and plant life.

The fertile plains of the Guadalquivir valley are watered by the river and have been the bread basket of Andalusia since Moorish times. Fields of grains alternate with straight lines of citrus trees.

0 kilometers 50

0 miles 25

SIERRA DE ARACENA

Río Odiel

SIERRA

Córdoba

Río Guadalquivir

Sevilla

Río Genil

Huelva

Embalse del Guadalhorce

Río Guadalete

Río Guadalhorce

Cádiz

SERRANÍA DE RONDA

Má

The Atlantic beaches, where pine trees grow behind the sand dunes, are less developed than the Mediterranean costas. Fishing fleets from Cádiz and Huelva operate offshore.

The Río Guadalquivir runs through the wetlands of Coto Doñana *(see pp126–7)* before finally entering the Atlantic Ocean.

The Costa del Sol and the rest of the Mediterranean coast are mainly characterized by arid cliffs draped in bougainvillea and other subtropical shrubs. The beaches below are either pebbly or of grayish sand.

KEY

▢	Desert
▢	Marshland
▢	Forest
▢	Cultivated land
♠	Olive groves
🍇	Vineyards
🍊	Citrus cultivation

Craggy mountains around Ronda encompass the nature preserve of Sierra de Grazalema. The area is home to a diverse wildlife, including griffon vultures and three species of eagles, and a forest of the rare Spanish fir.

Endless olive groves *give the landscape in the provinces of Córdoba and, in particular, Jaén a distinct, crisscrossed pattern. These long-living trees are of great importance to the local economy, for their oil (see p144) as well as their beautiful wood.*

Vast forests, mainly of Corsican pine, cover the craggy sierras of Cazorla, Segura, and Las Villas *(see p152)* in one of Spain's largest nature preserves.

ANDALUSIAN WILDLIFE

Southern Spain is blessed with some of the richest and most varied flora and fauna in Europe, including some species that are unique to the area. The best time to appreciate this is in spring, when wild flowers bloom and migratory birds stop en route from Africa to northern Europe.

Cork oak *grows mainly in the province of Cádiz. Its prized bark is stripped every ten years.*

The Cazorla violet, *which can only be found in Sierra de Cazorla (see p153), flowers in May.*

A mouflon *is a nimble and agile wild sheep that was introduced to mountainous areas in the 1970s.*

Vegetables and exotic fruits are grown all year in greenhouses covering many acres around El Ejido. The soil of Almería is otherwise unproductive.

The Sierra Nevada, *Spain's highest mountain range, reaches 3,482 m (11,424 ft) at the peak of Mulhacén. Although only 40 km (25 miles) from the Mediterranean beaches, some areas are snowcapped all year. The skiing season starts in December and lasts until spring. In summer the area is perfect for hiking and climbing.*

Flamingos *gather in great flocks in the wetlands of Coto Doñana and the Río Odiel delta in Huelva.*

Moorish Architecture

THE FIRST SIGNIFICANT PERIOD of Moorish architecture arrived with the Cordoban Caliphate. The Mezquita was extended lavishly during this period and possesses all the enduring features of the Moorish style: arches, stuccowork, and ornamental use of calligraphy. Later, the Almohads imported a purer Islamic style, which can be seen at La Giralda *(see p76)*. The Nasrids built the superbly crafted Alhambra in Granada, while the *mudéjares (see p22)* used their skill to create beautiful Moorish-style buildings such as the Palacio Pedro I, part of Seville's Reales Alcázares. *(See also pp44–7.)*

Reflections *in water combined with an overall play of light were central to Moorish architecture.*

Moorish domes *were often unadorned on the outside. Inside, however, an intricate lattice of stone ribs supported the dome's weight. Like this one in the Mezquita (see pp140–41), they were inlaid with multi-colored mosaics featuring flower or animal motifs.*

Defensive walls

Moorish gardens were often arranged around gently rippling pools and channels.

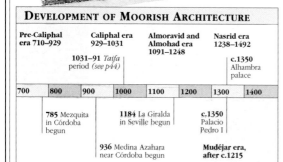

DEVELOPMENT OF MOORISH ARCHITECTURE

Pre-Caliphal era 710–929	Caliphal era 929–1031	Almoravid and Almohad era 1091–1248	Nasrid era 1238–1492
	1031–91 *Taifa period (see p44)*		**c.1350** Alhambra palace

700	800	900	1000	1100	1200	1300	1400
	785 Mezquita in Córdoba begun		**1184** La Giralda in Seville begun		**c.1350** Palacio Pedro I		
		936 Medina Azahara near Córdoba begun		**Mudéjar era, after c.1215**			

Azulejos *(see p74) were used for wall decorations. Patterns became increasingly geometric, as on these tiles in the Palacio Pedro I (p80*

MOORISH ARCHES

The Moorish arch was developed from the horseshoe arch that the Visigoths used in the construction of churches. The Moors modified it and used it as the basis of great architectural endeavors, such as the Mezquita. Subsequent arches show more sophisticated ornamentation and the slow demise of the basic horseshoe shape.

Caliphal arch, Medina Azahara *(see p134)*

Almohad arch, Patio del Yeso *(see p81)*

Mudéjar arch, Salón de Embajadores *(see p81)*

Nasrid arch, the Alhambra *(see p187)*

MOORISH PALACE

The palaces of the Moors were designed with gracious living, culture, and learning in mind. The imagined palace here shows how space, light, water, and ornamentation were combined to harmonious effect.

Arcaded galleries provided shade around courtyards.

Clay tiles

Entrance halls were complex to confuse unwanted visitors.

Moorish baths made use of steam and hot water; like Roman baths, they often had underfloor heating.

Water cooled the Moors' elegant courtyards and served a contemplative purpose. Often, as here in the Patio de los Leones (p187), water had to be pumped from a source far below.

Elaborate stuccowork typifies the Nasrid style of architecture. The Sala de los Abencerrajes (see p187) in the Alhambra was built using only the simplest materials, but it is nevertheless widely regarded as one of the most outstanding monuments of the period of the Moorish occupation.

Post-Moorish Architecture

THE CHRISTIAN RECONQUEST was followed by the building of new churches and palaces, many by *mudéjares (see p46).* Later, prejudice against the Moors grew as Christians began to assert their faith. Gothic styles from northern Europe filtered into Andalusia, though Mudéjar influences survived into the 18th century. In the 16th century, Andalusia was the center of the Spanish Renaissance, and a uniquely Spanish interpretation of the Baroque emerged in the 18th century.

Mudéjar tower, Iglesia de Santa Ana *(see p182)*

THE RECONQUEST (MID-13TH TO LATE 15TH CENTURY)

Moorish craftsmen working on Christian buildings created a hybrid Christian Islamic style known as Mudéjar. Mid-13th-century churches, such as the ones built in Seville and Córdoba, show a varying degree of Moorish influence, but the Palacio Pedro I in the Reales Alcázares *(see pp80–81)* is almost exclusively Moorish in style. By the early 15th century, pure Gothic styles, which are best exemplified by Seville Cathedral *(see pp76–7),* were widespread. After the fall of Granada in 1492 *(see p46),* a late Gothic style, called Isabelline, developed.

Bell towers were often added later; this one is a Baroque addition.

Windows are framed by Islamic-style, marble columns.

The Iglesia de San Marcos (see p88) *is a typical example of a Christian church built at the time of the Reconquest. Mudéjar features include the portal and minaret-like tower.*

Window openings become progressively narrower toward ground level.

Islamic-style decoration on the main entrance is characteristic of many Mudéjar churches.

Mudéjar portal, Nuestra Señora de la O *(see p158)*

Classical arches, a motif of the transitional Isabelline style, look forward to Renaissance architecture.

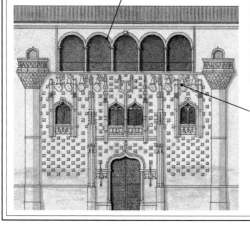

Gothic window, Seville Cathedral

Heavily worked stone reliefs, as decoration on façades of buildings, have their roots in the Gothic style.

The Palacio Jabalquinto (see p148) *has a highly ornate façade. Its coats of arms and heraldic symbols, typical of Isabelline buildings, reveal a strong desire to establish a national style.*

THE RENAISSANCE (16TH CENTURY)

Early Renaissance architecture was termed Plateresque because its fine detailing resembled ornate silverwork. (*Platero* means silversmith.) The façade of the Ayuntamiento *(see p72)* in Seville is the best example of Plateresque in Andalusia. A High Renaissance style is typified by the Palacio Carlos V. The end of the 16th century saw the rise of the austere Herreran style, named after Juan de Herrera, who drafted the initial plans of the Archivo de Indias *(see p78)*.

Plateresque detail on Seville's Ayuntamiento

Courtyard, with Herreran proportions, in the Archivo de Indias

Stone roundels were used as decoration; the central ones would bear the emperor's coat of arms.

Classical pediments adorn the windows.

***The Palacio Carlos V**, begun in 1526, is located in the heart of the Alhambra* (see p187). *Its elegant, grandiose style reflects Carlos V's power as Holy Roman Emperor.*

Rusticated stonework gives the lower level a solid appearance.

BAROQUE (17TH AND 18TH CENTURIES)

Early Spanish Baroque tended to be austere. The 18th century, however, gave rise to the Churrigueresque, named after the Churriguera family of architects. Although the family's own style was fairly restrained, it had many flamboyant imitations. Priego de Córdoba *(see p146)* is a showcase of the Baroque; La Cartuja *(p183)* in Granada contains a Baroque sacristy.

Flamboyant, Baroque sacristy of La Cartuja, Granada

Palacio del Marqués de la Gomera, Osuna (p129)

Baroque pinnacles were carved individually from stone.

Repeated string courses define the church's stories and contribute to the complex decoration of the façade.

Guadix Cathedral (see p190) *comprises a Renaissance building fronted by a Baroque façade. Such a combination of styles is very common in Andalusia.*

The Art of Bullfighting

Poster for a bullfight

BULLFIGHTING is a sacrificial ritual in which men (and also a few women) pit themselves against an animal bred to kill. In this "authentic religious drama," as poet García Lorca described it, the spectator experiences vicariously the fear and exaltation felt by the matador. Some Spaniards oppose it on the grounds of its cruelty, but it remains today as popular as ever in Andalusia.

Maestranza Bullring, Seville
This is regarded, with Las Ventas in Madrid, as one of the top places for bullfighting in Spain.

Bull Breeding
Well treated at the ranch, the toro bravo (fighting bull) is bred specially for aggressiveness and courage.

The matador wears a *traje de luces* (suit of light), a colorful silk outfit embroidered with gold sequins.

The passes are made with a *muleta*, a scarlet cape stiffened along one side.

FIESTA!

Bullfighting is an essential and highly popular part of many *fiestas* in Spain. An enthusiastic and very knowledge-able audience, often in traditional dress, fills the arenas from the start of the season in April until its end in October *(see pp36–7)*.

Fiesta wear

THE BULLFIGHT

The *corrida* (bullfight) has three stages, called *tercios*. In the first one, the *tercio de varas*, the matador is aided by his *peones* (assistants) and *picadores* (horsemen with lances). In the *tercio de banderillas*, *banderilleros* stick pairs of darts in the bull's back. In the *tercio de muleta* the matador makes a series of passes at the bull with a *muleta* (cape). He then executes the kill, the *estocada*, with a sword.

The matador *plays the bull with a* capa *(red cape) in the* tercio de varas *in order to gauge its intelligence and speed.* Peones *then draw it towards the* picadores.

Today, horses are heavily padded

Picadores *goad the bull with steel-pointed lances, testing its bravery as it charges their horses. The lances weaken the animal's shoulder muscles.*

THE BULLRING

The *corrida* audience is seated in the *tendidos* (stalls) or in the *palcos* (balcony), where the *presidencia* (president's box) is situated. Opposite are the *puerta cuadrillas*, through which the matador and team arrive, and the *arrastre toros* (exit for bulls). Before entering the ring, the matadors wait in a corridor *(callejón)* behind the *barreras* and *burladeros* (ringside barriers). Horses are kept in the *patio caballos* and the bulls wait in the *corrales*.

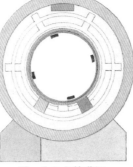

Plan of a typical bullring

KEY

- ☐ Tendidos
- ☐ Palcos
- ☐ Presidencia
- ☐ Puerta cuadrillas
- ☐ Arrastre toros
- ☐ Callejón
- ☐ Barreras
- ☐ Burladeros
- ☐ Patio caballos
- ☐ Corrales

Banderillas, barbed darts, are thrust into the bull's already weakened back muscles.

Manolete
Regarded as one of the greatest matadors ever, Manolete was gored to death by the bull Islero at Linares, Jaén, in 1947.

The bull may go free if it shows courage – spectators wave white handkerchiefs, asking the *corrida* president to let it leave the ring alive.

Joselito
One of Spain's leading matadors, Joselito is famous for his purist approach and for his flair with both the capa *and the* muleta.

Banderilleros *enter to provoke the wounded bull in the* tercio de banderillas, *gauging its reaction to punishment by sticking pairs of* banderillas *in its back.*

The bull weighs about 500 kg (1,100 lb)

The matador *makes passes with the cape in the* tercio de muleta, *then lowers it to make the bull bow its head, and thrusts in the sword for the kill.*

The estocada recibiendo *is a difficult kill, which is rarely seen. The matador awaits the bull's charge rather than moving forward to meet it.*

Flamenco, the Soul of Andalusia

Seville feria poster 1953

MORE THAN JUST A DANCE, flamenco is a forceful expression of the sorrows and joys of life. Although it has interpreters all over Spain and throughout the world, it is a uniquely Andalusian art form, traditionally performed by gypsies. There are many styles of *cante* (song) from different parts of Andalusia, but no strict choreography – dancers improvise from basic movements, following the rhythm of the guitar and their feelings. Flamenco was neglected in the 1960s and 1970s, but serious interest has returned. Recent years have seen a revival of traditional styles and the development of new dance forms.

***Sevillanas**, a folk dance that strongly influenced flamenco, is danced by Andalusians in their bars and homes (see p230).*

At a *tablao* (flamenco club) there will be at least four people on stage, including the hand clapper.

***The origins of flamenco** are hard to trace. Gypsies may have been the main creators of the art, mixing their own Indian-influenced culture with existing Moorish and Andalusian folklore, and with Jewish and Christian music. There were gypsies in Andalusia by the early Middle Ages, but only in the 18th century did flamenco begin to develop into its present form.*

THE SPANISH GUITAR

Classical guitar

The guitar has a major role in flamenco, traditionally accompanying the singer. The flamenco guitar developed from the modern classical guitar, which evolved in Spain in the 19th century. Flamenco guitars have a lighter, shallower construction and a thickened plate below the soundhole, used to tap rhythms. Today, flamenco guitarists often perform solo. One of the greatest, Paco de Lucía, began by accompanying singers and dancers, but made his debut as a soloist in 1968. His slick, inventive style, which combines traditional playing with Latin, jazz, and rock elements, has influenced many musicians outside the realm of flamenco, such as the group Ketama, who play flamenco-blues.

Paco de Lucía playing flamenco guitar

Singing is an integral part of *flamenco, and the singer often performs solo. Camarón de la Isla (1952–92), a gypsy born near Cádiz, is among the most famous contemporary* cantaores *(flamenco singers). He began as a singer of expressive* cante jondo *(literally, "deep songs"), from which he developed his own, rock-influenced style. He has inspired many singers.*

WHERE TO ENJOY FLAMENCO

Flamenco festivals pp32–7, p230
Flamenco guitar pp32–5, p230
Flamenco in Sacromonte p185
Flamenco singing pp32–5, p230
Flamenco tablaos p230
Flamenco dress p225

La Chanca is a baila-ora (female dancer) famous for her fiery and forceful movements. Cristina Hoyos, another dancer known for her personal style, leads her own flamenco dance company which received world-wide acclaim in the 1980s.

The proud yet graceful posture of the *bailaora* seems to suggest a restrained passion.

A harsh, vibrating voice is typical of the singer.

Traditional
polka-dot dress

The bailaor (male dancer) plays a less important role than the bailaora. *However, many have achieved fame, including Antonio Canales. He has introduced a new beat through his original foot movements.*

THE FLAMENCO TABLAO

These days it is rare to come across spontaneous dancing at a *tablao,* but if dancers and singers are inspired, an impressive show usually results. Artists performing with *duende* ("magic spirit") will hear appreciative *olés* from the audience.

FLAMENCO RHYTHM

The unmistakable rhythm of flamenco is created by the guitar. Just as important, however, is the beat created by hand-clapping and by the dancer's feet in high-heeled shoes. The *baila-oras* may also beat a rhythm with castanets; Lucero Tena (born in 1939) became famous for her solos on castanets. Graceful hand movements are used to express the dancer's feelings of the moment – whether pain, sorrow, or happiness. Like the movements of the rest of the body, they are not choreographed, and the styles used vary from person to person.

Castanets made of wood

Flamenco hand movements, always improvised

The Land of Sherry

THE PHOENICIANS INTRODUCED the vine to the Jerez region 3,000 years ago. Later, Greeks, then Romans, exported wine from these gentle hills bordering the Atlantic. However, the foundations of the modern sherry trade were laid by British merchants who settled here after the Reconquest *(see pp46–7)*.

González Byass logo

They discovered that the chalky soil, climate, and local grapes produced fine wines, particularly if fortified with brandy. The connection persists today with companies such as Bodegas John Harvey still in British ownership.

Preparing soil to catch the winter rain

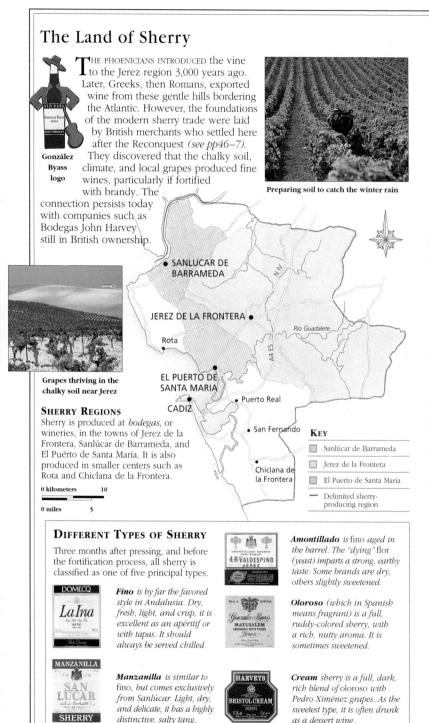

Grapes thriving in the chalky soil near Jerez

SANLÚCAR DE BARRAMEDA

JEREZ DE LA FRONTERA

Río Guadalete

Rota

EL PUERTO DE SANTA MARÍA

CÁDIZ

Puerto Real

San Fernando

Chiclana de la Frontera

SHERRY REGIONS

Sherry is produced at *bodegas*, or wineries, in the towns of Jerez de la Frontera, Sanlúcar de Barrameda, and El Puerto de Santa María. It is also produced in smaller centers such as Rota and Chiclana de la Frontera.

0 kilometers   10

0 miles   5

KEY

⬜ Sanlúcar de Barrameda

⬜ Jerez de la Frontera

⬜ El Puerto de Santa María

— Delimited sherry-producing region

DIFFERENT TYPES OF SHERRY

Three months after pressing, and before the fortification process, all sherry is classified as one of five principal types.

DOMECQ La Ina SHERRY

Fino *is by far the favored style in Andalusia. Dry, fresh, light, and crisp, it is excellent as an apéritif or with tapas. It should always be served chilled.*

MANZANILLA SAN LÚCAR SHERRY

Manzanilla *is similar to fino, but comes exclusively from Sanlúcar. Light, dry, and delicate, it has a highly distinctive, salty tang.*

AR VALDESPINO JEREZ

Amontillado *is fino aged in the barrel. The "dying" flor (yeast) imparts a strong, earthy taste. Some brands are dry, others slightly sweetened.*

MATUSALEM Jerez

Oloroso *(which in Spanish means fragrant) is a full, ruddy-colored sherry, with a rich, nutty aroma. It is sometimes sweetened.*

HARVEYS BRISTOL CREAM SHERRY

Cream *sherry is a full, dark, rich blend of oloroso with Pedro Ximénez grapes. As the sweetest type, it is often drunk as a dessert wine.*

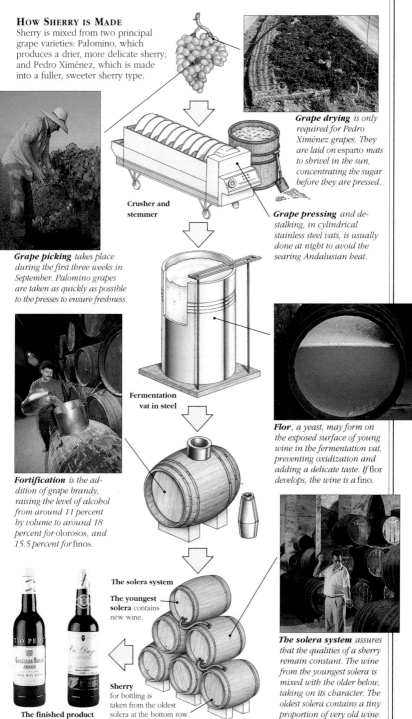

How Sherry is Made

Sherry is mixed from two principal grape varieties: Palomino, which produces a drier, more delicate sherry; and Pedro Ximénez, which is made into a fuller, sweeter sherry type.

Grape drying is only required for Pedro Ximénez grapes. They are laid on esparto mats to shrivel in the sun, concentrating the sugar before they are pressed.

Crusher and stemmer

Grape pressing and destalking, in cylindrical stainless steel vats, is usually done at night to avoid the searing Andalusian heat.

Grape picking takes place during the first three weeks in September. Palomino grapes are taken as quickly as possible to the presses to ensure freshness.

Fermentation vat in steel

Flor, a yeast, may form on the exposed surface of young wine in the fermentation vat, preventing oxidization and adding a delicate taste. If flor develops, the wine is a fino.

Fortification is the addition of grape brandy, raising the level of alcohol from around 11 percent by volume to around 18 percent for olorosos, and 15.5 percent for finos.

The solera system

The youngest solera contains new wine.

Sherry for bottling is taken from the oldest solera at the bottom row.

The finished product

The solera system assures that the qualities of a sherry remain constant. The wine from the youngest solera is mixed with the older below, taking on its character. The oldest solera contains a tiny proportion of very old wine.

Beach Life and Leisure in Andalusia

Painted fishing boat, Costa del Sol

THANKS TO its subtropical climate with an average of 300 days of sunshine a year, the coastline of Andalusia – in particular the Costa del Sol – has become one of the most favored playgrounds for those looking for fun and relaxation. In the 1950s, there was nothing more than a handful of fishing villages *(see p175)*. Now the area attracts several million tourists a year who are well catered to by the vast array of hotels and apartments along the coast. The varied coastline lends itself perfectly to the whole gamut of water sports *(see p232)*, while golf courses have become a major feature of the landscape *(see p232)*. Some of the most popular golf courses are shown on this map, together with a selection of the best beaches.

Sunbathing on one of Marbella's beaches, Costa del Sol

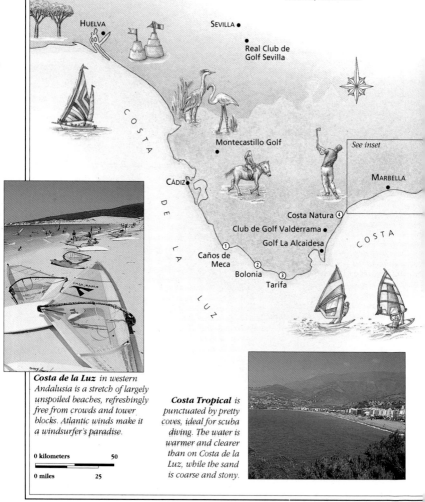

HUELVA

SEVILLA ●

● Real Club de Golf Sevilla

COSTA

Montecastillo Golf ●

CÁDIZ ●

See inset

MARBELLA

Costa Natura ④

Club de Golf Valderrama ●

Golf La Alcaidesa ●

COSTA

DE LA

① Caños de Meca

② Bolonia

③ Tarifa

LUZ

Costa de la Luz in western Andalusia is a stretch of largely unspoiled beaches, refreshingly free from crowds and tower blocks. Atlantic winds make it a windsurfer's paradise.

Costa Tropical is punctuated by pretty coves, ideal for scuba diving. The water is warmer and clearer than on Costa de la Luz, while the sand is coarse and stony.

0 kilometers   50

0 miles   25

ANDALUSIA'S BEST BEACHES

Caños de Meca ①
Charming white, sandy beach sheltered by cliffs and sand dunes.

Bolonia ②
Picturesque beach with Roman ruins close by.

Tarifa ③
Sweeping white sands, and winds and waves perfect for skilled windsurfers.

Costa Natura ④
Popular nudist beach just outside Estepona.

Babaloo Beach ⑤
Trendy spot just off Puerto Banús. Gym and jet skiing.

Victor's Beach ⑥
A classic Marbella beach for stylish barbecue parties.

Don Carlos ⑦
Perhaps Marbella's best beach, shared by the exclusive Don Carlos beach club.

Cabopino/Las Dunas ⑧
Nudist beach and sand dunes beside modern marina. Not too crowded.

Rincón de la Victoria ⑨
Nice unspoiled family beach area just east of Málaga.

La Herradura ⑩
A stony but picturesque bay west of Almuñécar.

Playa de los Genoveses ⑪
One of the unspoiled beaches between Cabo de Gata and San José.

Playa Agua Amarga ⑫
Excellent sand beach in secluded fishing hamlet turned exclusive resort.

Costa de Almería is famous for its picturesque fishing villages and rocky landscapes that come to life in breathtaking sunsets. Most beaches have escaped over-development, in particular those in the nature preserve of Cabo de Gata, such as San José, here.

Agua Amarga ⑫

Playa de los Genoveses ⑪

ALMERÍA

AGA ⑨
Rincón de la Victoria

La Herradura ⑩

COSTA TROPICAL

COSTA DE ALMERÍA

DEL SOL

COSTA DEL SOL

Apart from the crowds of vacationers, half a million foreign residents have chosen to live on the Costa del Sol. Complementing the luxury and high life of Marbella are a number of popular beaches and more than 30 of Europe's finest golf courses, including the prestigious Club de Golf Valderrama, host of the 1997 Ryder Cup tournament.

MÁLAGA

Club de Campo de Málaga

TORREMOLINOS

Golf Torrequebrado

Club Mijas Golf

La Cala Golf

Club de Golf Las Brisas

Golf Río Real
Marbella Golf

Club La Dame de Noche

MARBELLA ⑥
Victor's Beach

Don Carlos ⑦

Guadalmina Golf

Monte Mayor Golf

Babaloo Beach ⑤

Cabopino and Las Dunas ⑧

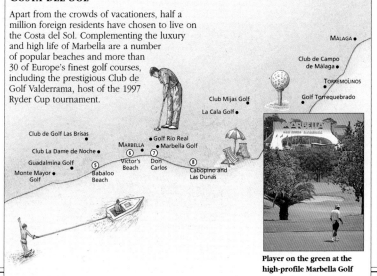

Player on the green at the high-profile Marbella Golf

ANDALUSIA THROUGH THE YEAR

ESTIVALS and cultural events fill Andalusia's calendar. Every town and village has an annual *feria* (fair) featuring parades, dancing, fairs, fireworks, and bullfights. These are held from April to October throughout Andalusia. There are also numerous *fiestas*, all exuberant occasions when religious devotion mixes with *joie de vivre*. Spring is an ideal time to visit; the countryside is at its most beautiful, the climate is mild, and *ferias* and *fiestas*

Poster for 1903 Seville *feria*

celebrate the ending of winter. Summer brings heat to the interior and crowds to the *costas*. Autumn is greeted with more *fiestas* and heralds the opening of music and theater seasons. As autumn leads into winter, jazz, pop, and classical concerts can be enjoyed in the cities. The first snow on the Sierra Nevada marks the start of the skiing season. Note that dates for all events, especially *fiestas*, may change from year to year; check with the tourist board.

Almond trees in bloom on the lush hillsides of Andalusia

SPRING

EW PARTS OF THE WORLD can match the beauty of spring in Andalusia. After winter rains, the hills and plains are green and lush, and water cascades along riverbeds and irrigation channels. Country roads are a riot of wild flowers; almond blossoms cover the hillsides and strawberries are harvested. Popular festivals abound, many of them religious, though often linked with pagan ceremonies marking the end of winter.

MARCH

Cristo de la Expiración *(Friday, nine days before Palm Sunday)*, Orgiva *(see p190)*. One of Andalusia's most ear-splitting *fiestas*, when shotguns, rockets, firecrackers, and gunpowder are set off.
Semana Santa *(Palm Sunday–Good Friday)*. Seville

celebrates this event spectacularly *(see p36)*, and there are processions in every town and village. On Holy Wednesday in Málaga *(see pp172–3)*, a prisoner is freed from jail and in gratitude joins in one of the processions. This tradition began two centuries ago, when prisoners, braving a plague, carried a holy image through the city's streets. In Baena *(see p143)* the streets vibrate to the sound of thousands of drums.

APRIL

Fiesta de San Marcos *(April 25)*, Ohanes, Sierra Nevada. Accompanying the image of San Marcos through the streets are young men leading eight bulls. The bulls are persuaded to kneel before the saint.
Feria de Abril *(two weeks after Easter)*, Seville *(see p36)*.
Romería de Nuestra Señora de la Cabeza *(last Sunday in April)*, Andújar *(see p37)*. Major pilgrimage.

MAY

Día de la Cruz *(first week of May)*, Granada *(see pp182–8)* and Córdoba *(see pp176–8)*.
Feria del Caballo *(first week of May)*, Jerez de la Frontera *(see p158)*. Horse fair.
Festival Internacional de Teatro y Danza *(throughout May)*, Seville. World-class companies perform in Teatro de la Maestranza *(see pp66–7)*.
Festival de los Patios *(second week in May)*, Córdoba *(see p36)*. Patios are on display.
Romería de San Isidro *(May 15)*. *Romerías* are held in many towns, including Nerja *(see p172)*, for San Isidro.
Concurso Nacional de Flamenco *(second week in May; every third year: 1998, 2001)*, Córdoba. National flamenco competition.
Feria de Mayo *(last week of May)*, Córdoba *(see p36)*.
Romería del Rocío *(late May or early June)*, El Rocío *(see p36)*.

Feria del Caballo, held in Jerez de la Frontera in May

Sunshine Chart
Even in winter, few days in Andalusia are entirely without sunshine. In the spring, the sunshine starts to build up progressively, and by midsummer it can be dangerous to go out even for a short time without adequate skin protection.

Bullrunning during the Lunes de Toro *fiesta* **in Grazalema**

SUMMER

DURING THE HOT summer months, the siesta (afternoon nap) comes into its own. Many people finish work at lunchtime, and most of the entertainment takes place in the cool of evening. Foreign tourists flocking to the coasts are joined by thousands of Spaniards. Large rock concerts are held in coastal towns.

JUNE

Corpus Christi *(late May or early June)* is commemorated in Granada *(see p37)*. In Seville the *seises*, young boys dressed in doublet and hose, dance in front of the cathedral altar. At Zahara, near Ronda *(see p166)*, houses and streets are decked out with greenery.
Día de San Juan *(June 23, 24)*. The evening of June 23 sees dancing, drinking, and singing around bonfires on beaches across Andalusia in honor of

John the Baptist. Lanjarón *(see p181)* celebrates with a water battle in its streets in the early hours of June 24.
Romería de los Gitanos *(third Sunday in June)*, Cabra *(see p143)*. A procession made up of thousands of gypsies heads for a hilltop shrine.
Festival Internacional de Música y Danza *(mid-June–early July)*, Granada *(see pp182–8)*. Performers come to Granada from all over the world. Many events are held in the Alhambra *(see pp186–7)*.

JULY

Festival de la Guitarra *(first two weeks of July)*, Córdoba *(see pp136–42)*. Guitar festival presenting all musical styles, from classical to flamenco.
Fiesta de la Virgen del Carmen *(around July 15)*. This Virgin is honored in many coastal communities by regattas and other sports events. In the evening, the Virgin's image is put aboard a fishing boat, which parades

across the sea accompanied by the crackle of fireworks.
Lunes de Toro *(around July 17)*, Grazalema *(see p166)*. Bullrunning daily for a week.

AUGUST

Fiestas Colombinas *(around August 3)*, Huelva *(see p123)*. A Latin American dance and music festival in celebration of Columbus's voyage. It is dedicated to a different Latin American country every year.
Fiestas Patronales de Santa María de la Palma *(August 15)*, Algeciras *(see p162)*. A saint's image is rescued from the sea. It is cleaned, before being carried in a procession of boats to a beach. Afterward it is returned to the sea.
Fiestas de la Exaltación del Río Guadalquivir *(third week in August)*, Sanlúcar de Barrameda *(see p158)*. Horse races are held on the beach.
Feria de Málaga *(last two weeks in August, see p37)*.
Feria de Almería *(last week in August, see p37)*.

The Costa del Sol – popular with tourists and with the Spanish

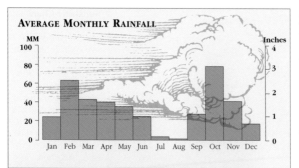

AVERAGE MONTHLY RAINFALL

Rainfall Chart
Rain can be heavy in early spring, but summer is almost dry. Humidity and rainfall increase through September until October, when torrential rains can fall. In recent years, the rains have failed, resulting in severe droughts in the area.

Chirimoya **harvest on the subtropical coast at Almuñécar** *(see p181)*

AUTUMN

THIS IS A most pleasant time to visit Andalusia. The weather is settled, but without the searing summer heat, and the vacation crowds are easing. Grape harvests are in full swing and being celebrated in towns and villages. The theaters start to open for drama and concerts. Along the subtropical coast of the Mediterranean, sweet potatoes and *chirimoyas* (custard apples) are harvested. Inland, mushrooms dishes appear in restaurants.

SEPTEMBER

Feria de Pedro Romero
(first two weeks in September), Ronda *(see pp168–9)*. This *fiesta* celebrates the founder of modern bullfighting *(see p169)*. All participants in the Corrida Goyesca, the highlight, wear costumes designed by Goya, a great bullfighting fan.

Moros y Cristianos
fiesta, **Válor** *(see p191)*

Fiestas Patronales de la Virgen de la Piedad
(September 6), Baza *(see p190)*. A bizarre *fiesta* in which a figure known as Cascamorras comes from neighboring Guadix to try to steal a statue of the Virgin. Youths covered with oil taunt him and chase him out of town. He is sent back to Guadix empty-handed, where he receives further punishment for his failure.

Moros y Cristianos
(September 15), Válor *(see p191)*. This *fiesta* features the recreation of Reconquest battles.

Fiesta de la Vendimia
(second or third week of September), La Palma del Condado *(see p125)*. A lively *fiesta* to bless the first grape juice.

Romería de San Miguel *(last Sunday of September)*, Torremolinos *(see p174)*. One of the largest *romerías* in Andalusia.

Bienal de Arte Flamenco
(last two weeks of September, even-numbered years),

Seville. A fabulous opportunity for enthusiasts to see world-class flamenco artists, such as Cristina Hoyos.

Sevilla en Otoño *(September–November)*, Seville. A variety of cultural events, including dance, theater and exhibitions, and, in addition, sports.

OCTOBER

Fiesta del Vino *(October 5–9)*, Cadiar *(see p191)*. A feature of this *fiesta* in the mountains of the Alpujarras is the construction of a fountain that gushes forth wine.

Festival Iberoamericano de Teatro *(last two weeks of October)*, Cádiz *(see pp160–61)*. Latin American theater festival.

NOVEMBER

Festival Internacional de Jazz *(early November)*, Granada *(see pp182–8)* and Seville.

Festival de Cine Iberoamericano *(last two weeks of November)*, Huelva *(see p123)*. Latin American film festival.

Oil-covered youths chasing Cascamorras in Baza

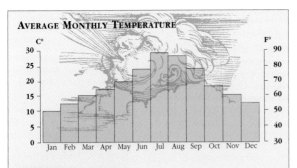

AVERAGE MONTHLY TEMPERATURE

Temperature Chart
Andalusia enjoys a warm Mediterranean climate throughout the year, although it can become cold at night. Temperatures rise from January to the summer months when, in some cities inland, they can far exceed the average for the region.

Medieval music at the Fiesta de los Verdiales in Málaga

WINTER

AT THIS TIME OF YEAR the ripe olives are harvested in abundance. Restaurants serve venison, wild boar, and partridge dishes as this is the hunting season. Skiers flock to the Sierra Nevada. Although winter is the rainy season and it is cold at night, many days are sunny. By February, almond blossoms and strawberries begin to appear again.

DECEMBER

La Inmaculada Concepción *(December 8)*, Seville. The *tuna*, groups of wandering minstrels, take to the streets around the Plaza del Triunfo and Santa Cruz *(see pp70–71)*.
Fiesta de los Verdiales *(December 28)*, Málaga *(see pp172–3)*. To celebrate *El Día de los Santos Inocentes*, thousands of town and country folk gather at the Venta del Túnel, on the outskirts of Málaga. They

come to hear *pandas* (bands) compete in performing *verdiales*, wild, primitive music from Moorish times, played on medieval instruments.

JANUARY

Día de la Toma *(January 2)*, Granada *(see pp182–8)*. This *fiesta* recalls the ousting of the Moors in 1492 *(see p46)*. Queen Isabel's crown and King Fernando's sword are paraded through the streets, and the royal standard flies from the balcony of the Ayuntamiento.
Día de Reyes *(January 6)*. On the evening before this public holiday, the Three Kings arrive, splendidly dressed, to parade through town centers across Andalusia. They ride in small carriages that are drawn by tractors or horses and, during the procession, throw candy to the excited children.
Certamen Internacional de Guitarra Clásica Andrés Segovia *(first week of January)*, Almuñécar *(see p181)*. Classical guitar competition in homage to the master.

FEBRUARY

Los Carnavales *(second or third week in February)*. Carnival is widely celebrated with tremendous enthusiasm, particularly in the western part of Andalusia and, most spectacularly, in Cádiz *(see p37)*. The coastal town of Isla Cristina *(see p122)* is famed for its exuberant festivities.
Festival de Música Antigua *(February and March)*, Seville. Early music is performed on historic instruments.

PUBLIC HOLIDAYS

New Year's Day (Jan 1)
Epiphany (Jan 6)
Día de Andalucía (Feb 28)
Maundy Thursday and Good Friday (variable)
Labor Day (May 1)
Assumption (Aug 15)
National Day (Oct 12)
All Saints' Day (Nov 1)
Constitution Day (Dec 6)
Immaculate Conception (Dec 8)
Christmas Day (Dec 25)

Ski station on the snow-covered slopes of the Sierra Nevada (*see p189*)

Fiestas in Andalusia

THERE IS NOTHING quite like a Spanish *fiesta* or *feria*, and those of Andalusia are among the most colorful. *Fiestas* may commemorate a historic event or a change of season. More often they mark a religious occasion; Semana Santa (Holy Week), for example, is celebrated all over Andalusia. Feasting, dancing, singing, drinking – often all day and night – are all integral to a *fiesta*. At a *feria* there will often be a decorated fairground, revelers dressed in traditional flamenco attire, and processions of horses and carriages. Throughout Andalusia you will also come across *romerías*, in which processions carry holy effigies through the countryside to a shrine.

Costume, Semana Santa, Córdoba

Horsemen and women in their finery at Seville's Feria de Abril

SEVILLE

SEMANA SANTA, or Holy Week (Palm Sunday–Good Friday), is celebrated in flamboyant style in Seville. More than 100 *pasos* (floats bearing religious effigies) are carried through the streets of the city. They are accompanied by *nazarenos*, members of some 50 brother-hoods dating back to the 13th century, wearing long robes and tall pointed hoods. As the processions sway through the streets, singers in the crowd burst into *saetas*, shafts of song in praise of the Virgin. Emotion reaches fever pitch in the early hours of Good Friday, when the Virgen de La Macarena is paraded, accompanied by 2,500 *nazarenos (see p87)*.

During their Feria de Abril, the spring fair held about two weeks after Easter, the *sevillanos* go on a spree for a week.

Daily, from about 1pm, elegant horsemen and women wearing *mantillas* (lace headdresses) show off their finery in a parade known as the *cabalgata*. At night, *casetas* (entertainment booths) throb to *sevillanas*, a popular dance that has a flamenco accent.

(Access to booths sometimes may be limited to private par-ties.) Spain's best matadors feature in bullfights in the Maestranza bullring *(see p66)*.

HUELVA AND SEVILLA

ONE OF SPAIN'S most popular *fiestas*, the Romería del Rocío, is held during Pentecost. More than 70 brotherhoods trek to the shrine of El Rocío *(see p125)* amid Las Marismas, the marshlands at the mouth of the Guadalquivir. They are joined by pilgrims traveling on horseback, on foot, or by car. All pay homage to the Virgen del Rocío, also called the White Dove or the Queen of the Marshes. There is drinking and dancing for several days and nights, until the early hours of Monday morning when the Virgin is brought out of the shrine. Young men from the nearby town of Almonte carry her through the crowds for up to 12 hours, fighting off any-body who tries to get near.

CÓRDOBA AND JAÉN

MAY IS A NONSTOP FIESTA in Córdoba *(see pp136–42)*. The Día de la Cruz – the Day of the Cross – is held on the first three days of the month. Religious brotherhoods and neighborhoods compete with each other to create the most colorful, flower-decorated crosses, which are set up in squares and at street corners. Following this is the Festival de los Patios (May 5–15), when the patios of the city's old quarter are thrown

Pilgrims taking part in the Romería del Rocío in Huelva province

open for visitors to come and admire. Crowds go from patio to patio, at each one launching into flamenco dance or song.

During the last week of May, Córdoba holds its lively *feria*. It is as colorful as the Feria de Abril in Seville, but more accessible to tourists. This festival, with roots in Roman times, welcomes the spring.

The Romería de Nuestra Señora de la Cabeza takes place on the last Sunday in April at the Santuario de la Virgen de la Cabeza *(see p147)*, a remote shrine in the Sierra Morena. Over 250,000 people attend, some making the pilgrimage on foot or on horseback. At the site, flames shoot up day and night from a torch fed by candles lit by the faithful. Then the Virgin, known as La Morenita, is borne through the crowd to cries of *¡Guapa, guapa!* (beautiful, beautiful!).

Penitents at the Romería de Nuestra Señora de la Cabeza in April

CÁDIZ AND MÁLAGA

For TWO WEEKS in February Los Carnavales (Carnival) is celebrated with more flair and abandon in Cádiz *(see p160)* than anywhere else in Andalusia. Some say it rivals the carnival in Río de Janeiro. Groups of singers practice for months in advance, composing outrageous satirical ditties that poke fun at anything from the current fashions to celebrities, especially politicians. Often sumptuously costumed, they perform their songs in the Falla Theater in a competition lasting for several days. Then they take part in a parade. The whole city puts on fancy

Costumed revelers at the February Carnival (Los Carnavales) in Cádiz

clothes, and crowds of revelers throng the narrow streets of the city's old quarter, shouting, singing, dancing, and drinking.

The Feria de Málaga, in the middle of August each year, celebrates the capture of the city from the Moors by the Catholic Monarchs *(see p46)*. Eager to outdo Seville, Málaga *(see pp172–3)* puts on a fine show. The residents, famous for their ability to organize a good party, put on traditional costume and parade, along with decorated carriages and elegant riders, through the city center and the fairground. The entertainment goes on for a week nonstop, and top bullfighters perform at the city's bullring *(see p173)* in La Malagueta.

GRANADA AND ALMERÍA

Corpus Christi, held in late May or early June, is one of the major events in Granada *(see pp182–8)*. On the day before Corpus a procession of bigheads (costumed caricatures with oversized heads) and giants parades through the city, led by the *tarasca*, a woman on a huge dragon. The next day, the *custodia*, or monstrance, is carried from the cathedral all through the streets. For a week afterward there is bullfighting, flamenco, and general revelry.

The *feria* in Almería *(see pp192–3)* is held at the end of August in honor of the Virgen del Mar. There are processions, sports events and bullfights. The Virgin dates back to 1502, when a coast guard on the lookout for Berber pirates found an image of the Virgin on a beach.

Feria de Málaga, celebrating the capture of the city from the Moors

THE HISTORY OF SEVILLE AND ANDALUSIA

**Stone carving of an
Iberian warrior**

ANDALUSIA'S early history is an extraordinary tale of ancient cities – Cádiz *(see pp160–61)*, founded in 1100 BC, is one of the oldest cities in Europe – and waves of settlers, each one contributing new ideas and customs.

Hominids first inhabited the region about one million years ago. *Homo sapiens* had arrived by 25,000 BC, and by the Iron Age a strong Iberian culture had emerged. Later, trade and cultural links developed first with the Phoenicians, then with the Greeks and Carthaginians. These ties, and the abundance of natural raw materials such as iron, gold, and copper ore, made this part of Iberia one of the wealthiest and most sophisticated areas of the Mediterranean.

The Romans were attracted by its riches and made their first forays into southern Spain in 206 BC. They ruled for almost 700 years. Their place was eventually taken by the Visigoths as the Western Roman Empire crumbled in the 5th century AD. The Moors, who followed, flourished first in Córdoba, then in Seville, and, toward the end of their almost 800-year rule, in the Nasrid kingdom of Granada.

After the fall of Granada to the Christians in 1492, Spain entered an era of expansion and prosperity. The conquest of the New World made Seville one of the most affluent cities in Europe, but much of this wealth was squandered on wars by the Hapsburg kings. By the 18th century Spain had fallen into economic decline; in the 19th and early 20th centuries poverty led to political conflict and, ultimately, to the Civil War.

The years following the Civil War saw continuing poverty, though mass tourism in the 1960s and '70s did much to ease this. With Franco's death and Spain's entry into the EU, the Spanish began to enjoy increasing prosperity and democratic freedoms. Andalusia still lagged behind, however, and the Expo '92 was part of government policy to foster its economic growth.

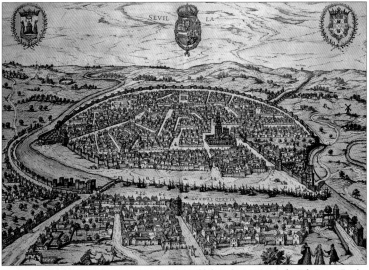

The 16th-century port of Seville, where ships brought wealth from the Americas to the Holy Roman Empire

◁ 18th-century lithograph of the Puerta de la Justicia in the Alhambra *(see pp186–7)*

Early Andalusia

Neanderthal skull

NEANDERTHALS inhabited Gibraltar around 50,000 BC. *Homo sapiens* arrived 25,000 years later, and Neolithic tribespeople from Africa settled in Spain from about 7000 BC on. By the time the Phoenicians arrived to trade in precious metals, they were met by a sophisticated Iberian culture. They later established trading links with the semimythical Iberian kingdom of Tartessus. The Greeks, already settled in northeastern Spain, started to colonize the south from about 600 BC on. Meanwhile, Celts from the north had mixed with Iberians. This culture, influenced by the Greeks, created beautiful works of art. The Carthaginians arrived in about 500 BC and, according to legend, destroyed Tartessus.

AREAS OF INFLUENCE

	Greek
	Phoenician

The short sword and shield denote an Iberian warrior.

Burial Sight at Los Millares
Los Millares (see p193) was the site of an early metal-working civilization in about 2300 BC. Up to 100 corpses were buried on a single site; the huge burial chambers were covered with earth to make a gently sloping mound.

Cave Paintings
From approximately 25,000 BC on, people painted caves in Andalusia. They portrayed fish, land animals, people, weapons, and other subjects with a skillful naturalism.

This figure's arms are outstretched in an attitude of prayer.

IBERIAN BRONZE FIGURES

These bronze figurines from the 5th–4th centuries BC are votive offerings to the gods. They were discovered in a burial ground near Despeñaperros in the province of Jaén. The Romans regarded the Iberians who crafted them as exceptionally noble.

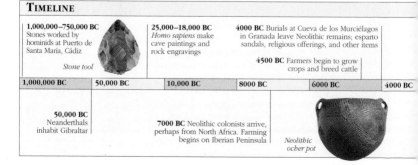

TIMELINE					
1,000,000–750,000 BC Stones worked by hominids at Puerto de Santa María, Cádiz *Stone tool*		**25,000–18,000 BC** *Homo sapiens* make cave paintings and rock engravings	**4000 BC** Burials at Cueva de los Murciélagos in Granada leave Neolithic remains; esparto sandals, religious offerings, and other items **4500 BC** Farmers begin to grow crops and breed cattle		
1,000,000 BC	**50,000 BC**	**10,000 BC**	**8000 BC**	**6000 BC**	**4000 BC**
50,000 BC Neanderthals inhabit Gibraltar		**7000 BC** Neolithic colonists arrive, perhaps from North Africa. Farming begins on Iberian Peninsula		*Neolithic ocher pot*	

Goddess Astarte

The Phoenicians founded Cádiz in about 1100 BC. They brought their own goddess, Astarte, who became popular across Andalusia as the region absorbed eastern influences.

The headdress shows this is a votaress, devoted to her god.

The hand of this priestess is raised in benediction.

Greek Urn

The ancient Greeks imported many artifacts from home; their style of decoration had a strong influence on Iberian art.

WHERE TO SEE EARLY ANDALUSIA

Cave paintings can be seen in the Cueva de la Pileta near Ronda la Vieja (p167) and in the Cuevas de Nerja (p172). At Antequera (p171) there are Bronze Age dolmens dating from 2500 BC; at Los Millares (p193) there are burial chambers. The replicas of the famous Tartessian Carambolo Treasure are in the Museo Arqueológico in Seville (p95), and Iberian stone carvings from Porcuna are exhibited in Jaén (p145).

The Toro de Porcuna *(500–450 BC) was found at Porcuna near Jaén with other sculptures.*

Dama de Baza

This female figure, dating from around 500–400 BC, may represent an Iberian goddess. It is one of several such figures found in southern Spain.

Carambolo Treasure

Phoenician in style, this treasure is from Tartessus. Although many artifacts have been uncovered, the site of this kingdom has yet to be found.

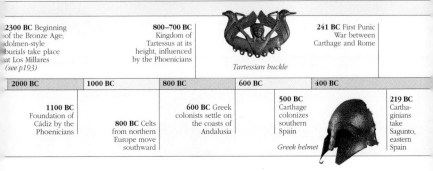

2300 BC Beginning of the Bronze Age; dolmen-style burials take place at Los Millares *(see p193)*

800–700 BC Kingdom of Tartessus at its height, influenced by the Phoenicians

Tartessian buckle

241 BC First Punic War between Carthage and Rome

2000 BC	1000 BC	800 BC	600 BC	400 BC

1100 BC Foundation of Cádiz by the Phoenicians

800 BC Celts from northern Europe move southward

600 BC Greek colonists settle on the coasts of Andalusia

500 BC Carthage colonizes southern Spain

Greek helmet

219 BC Carthaginians take Sagunto, eastern Spain

Romans and Visigoths

Visigothic capital

THE ROMANS came to Spain during a war against Carthage in 206 BC. Attracted by the wealth of the peninsula, they stayed for 700 years; in 200 years they conquered Spain and split it into provinces. Baetica, with Corduba (Córdoba) as its capital, corresponded roughly to what is now Andalusia. Cities were built, while feudal lords created vast estates, exporting olive oil and wheat to Rome. Baetica became one of the wealthiest of Rome's provinces with a rich, Ibero-Roman culture. The Visigoths who followed continued to assert Roman values until the Moors arrived in AD 711.

ROMAN TERRITORY AD 100

  ▢ *Roman Baetica*
  ▢ *Other Roman provinces*

Hadrian
Emperors Hadrian and Trajan were born in Baetica. A great many politicians, writers, and philosophers from the province also moved to Rome, some enjoying great fortune.

Paved streets   Temple
Private villas

Roman Mosaics in Andalusia
Private houses, temples, and public buildings all had mosaic floors. Many themes, from the gods to hunting, were represented.

ITÁLICA RECONSTRUCTED

Scipio Africanus founded Itálica *(see p128)* in 206 BC after his defeat of the Carthaginians. The city reached its height in the 2nd and 3rd centuries AD and was the birthplace of the emperors Hadrian and Trajan. Unlike Córdoba, it was not built over in post-Roman times, and today Itálica is a superbly preserved example of a Roman city.

TIMELINE

206 BC Scipio Africanus gains victory against the Carthaginians at Alcalá del Río; Itálica is founded

55 BC Birth of Seneca the Elder in Córdoba

AD 27 Andalusia is named Baetica

Suicide of Seneca

65 Suicide of Seneca the Younger after plotting against Nero

117 Hadrian is crowned Emperor

200 BC	100 BC	AD 1	100	200

200 BC Romans conquer southern Spain and reach Cádiz

61 BC Julius Caesar is governor of Hispania Ulterior (Spain)

Julius Caesar

98–117 Trajan, from Itálica, is emperor. Spanish senators enjoy influence in Rome

69–79 Emperor Vespasian grants Roman status to all towns in Hispania

Harvesting Olives
Carved on a Roman sarcophagus, this scene shows an olive harvest. Olives were grown extensively in the Guadalquivir valley from Córdoba to Seville. Thousands of amphoras of olive oil were shipped to Rome.

The amphitheater was a standard feature of Roman towns. The one in Itálica is said to have been the third largest in the Roman Empire.

Visigothic Crown
The jeweled pendants on this crown form the name, in Latin, of the Visigothic king, Recceswinth.

WHERE TO SEE ROMAN AND VISIGOTHIC ANDALUSIA

Extensive Roman remains can be seen at the sights of Itálica *(see p128)*, Carmona *(p128)*, and Ronda la Vieja *(p167)*. In Málaga there is a partially excavated Roman amphitheater, and Roman columns can be seen at the Alameda de Hércules in Seville *(p86)*. The Museo Arqueológico in Seville *(p95)*, Córdoba *(p139)*, and Cádiz *(p160)* all have Roman artifacts on display. Visigothic pillars and capitals can be viewed in the Mezquita in Córdoba *(pp140–41)*.

The Roman ruins at Itálica *(see p128) are situated 9 km (5.5 miles) north of Seville.*

San Isidoro and San Leandro
San Isidoro (560–635) of Seville, like his brother, San Leandro, converted Visigoths to Christianity; he also wrote a great scholastic work, Etymologies.

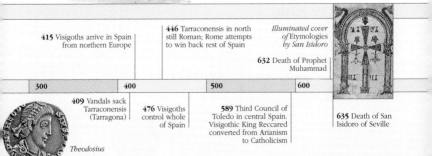

415 Visigoths arrive in Spain from northern Europe

446 Tarraconensis in north still Roman; Rome attempts to win back rest of Spain

Illuminated cover of Etymologies *by San Isidoro*

632 Death of Prophet Muhammad

| 300 | 400 | 500 | 600 |

409 Vandals sack Tarraconensis (Tarragona)

476 Visigoths control whole of Spain

589 Third Council of Toledo in central Spain. Visigothic King Reccared converted from Arianism to Catholicism

635 Death of San Isidoro of Seville

Theodosius

The Moorish Conquest

**10th-century
ivory cask**

CALLED IN TO RESOLVE a quarrel among the Visigoths, the Moors first arrived in 710. They returned in 711 to conquer Spain; within 10 years, the north alone remained under Christian control. The Moors named their newly conquered territories Al Andalus and in 929 they established an independent caliphate. Córdoba, its capital, was the greatest city in Europe, a center for art, science, and literature. In the 11th century the caliphate collapsed into 30 feuding *taifas* (party states). Almoravids, tribesmen from North Africa, invaded the region in 1086, and in the 12th century Almohads from Morocco ousted the Almoravids and designated Seville their capital.

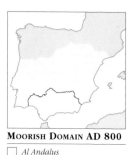

MOORISH DOMAIN AD 800

☐ *Al Andalus*

Abd al Rahman III receives
the Byzantine envoy

Apocalypse
An 11th-century account of an 8th-century text, Commentaries on the Apocalypse *by Beato de Liébana, this illustration shows Christians going to war.*

Bronze Stag
This 10th-century caliphal-style bronze is from Medina Azahara.

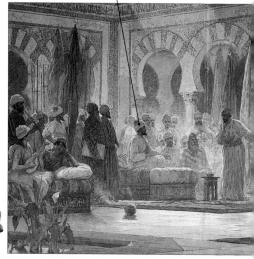

THE COURT OF ABD AL RAHMAN III

Abd al Rahman III began his palace of Medina Azahara *(see p134)* in 936. This 19th-century painting by Dionisio Baixeres shows a Byzantine envoy presenting the caliph with the works of the Greek scientist Dioscorides. The Moors of Córdoba possessed much knowledge of the ancient world, which was later transmitted to Europe. The Medina was sacked by Berber mercenaries in 1010.

TIMELINE

*Visigothic king and
Moorish chief*

756 Abd al Rahman I reaches Spain and asserts himself as ruler, declaring an independent emirate based around Córdoba

936 Medina Azahara begun

929 Abd al Rahman III proclaims caliphate in Córdoba

700	800	900

711 Invasion under Tariq ben Ziyad

710 First Moorish intervention in Spain

785 The Mezquita *(see pp140–41)* begun at Córdoba

Coin from the reign of Abd al Rahman III

822–52 Rule of Abd al Rahman II

912–61 Rule of Abd al Rahman III

961–76 Al Hakam II builds great library at Medina Azahara; expands Mezquita

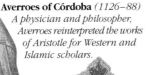

Averroes of Córdoba *(1126–88)*
*A physician and philosopher,
Averroes reinterpreted the works
of Aristotle for Western and
Islamic scholars.*

Horseshoe arches were a major
feature here, as in the Mezquita
(see pp140–41) at Córdoba.

Mozarabic Bible
*Moorish society
integrated Jews and
Mozarabs (Christians
living an Islamic
lifestyle). Illustrations
like this one, from a
10th-century Bible,
are in a Moorish
decorative style.*

Clerics prepare
the manuscript to
be given to Abd
al Rahman III.

WHERE TO SEE MOORISH ANDALUSIA

The Mezquita in Córdoba *(see pp140–41)* and the ruins of the palace at Medina Azahara *(p134)* are the most complete remnants of Spain's Moorish caliphate. Artifacts found at Medina Azahara can be seen in the Museo Arqueológico in Córdoba *(see p139)*. The Alcazaba at Almería *(see p192)* dates from the 10th century, when this city was still part of the caliphate, while the Alcazaba at Málaga *(see p173)* was built during the ensuing Taifa period. The Torre del Oro *(see p67)* and La Giralda *(see p76)* in Seville are both Almohad structures.

The Alcazaba in Almería
*(p192), dating from the 10th
century, overlooks the old town.*

Cufic Script
*Islamic artists,
forbidden to use
representations of
the human figure,
made ample use
of calligraphy
for decoration.*

Irrigation in Al Andalus
*The waterwheel was vital to irrigation,
which the Moors used to grow newly
imported crops such as rice and oranges.*

Al Mansur	**1086** Almoravids invade	**1120** Almoravid power starts to wane
1012 *Taifas* emerge as splinter Moorish states		**1126** Birth of Averroes, Arab philosopher
1031 Caliphate ends		**1147** Almohads arrive in Seville; build Giralda and Torre del Oro

1000	**1100**	**1200**

976–1002 Al Mansur, military dictator, comes to power	**1085** Fall of Toledo in north to Christians decisively loosens Moorish control over central Spain	**1135** Maimonides, Jewish philosopher, born in Córdoba	**1175–1200** Height of Almohad power. Previously lost territory won back from Christians
	1010 Medina Azahara sacked by Berbers	*Maimonides*	

The Reconquest

THE WAR BETWEEN Moors and Christians, which started in northern Spain, arrived in Andalusia with a landmark Christian victory at Las Navas de Tolosa in 1212; Seville and Córdoba fell soon afterwards. By the late 13th century only the Nasrid kingdom of Granada remained under Moorish control. Meanwhile, Christian monarchs such as

Christian horseman

Alfonso X and Pedro I employed Mudéjar *(see p22)* craftsmen to build churches and palaces in the reconquered territories – Mudéjar literally means "those permitted to stay." Granada eventually fell in 1492 to Fernando and Isabel of Aragón and Castilla, otherwise known as the Catholic Monarchs.

MOORISH DOMAIN IN 1350

☐ *Nasrid kingdom*

The Catholic Monarchs enter Granada; Fernando and Isabel were awarded this title for their services to Christendom.

Boabdil

Cantigas of Alfonso X
Alfonso X, who won back much of Andalusia from the Moors, was an enlightened Christian monarch. His illuminated Cantigas *are a vivid account of life in Reconquest Spain.*

THE FALL OF GRANADA
This relief by Felipe de Vigarney (1480–c.1542), in Granada's Capilla Real *(see p182)*, shows Boabdil, the last Moorish ruler, surrendering the city in 1492. Trying to establish a Christian realm, the Catholic Monarchs converted the Moors by force and expelled the Jews. The same year Columbus got funds for his voyage to America *(see p123)*.

Almohad Banner
This richly woven tapestry is widely believed to be the banner captured from the Moors by the Christians at the battle of Las Navas de Tolosa.

TIMELINE

		1252–84 Alfonso X reconquers much of Andalusia. Toledo Translators' School in the north continues to translate important works of Moorish literature			*Pedro I of Castilla*

1226 Fernando III takes Baeza

1236 Fernando III conquers Córdoba

1333 Moors add tower to the 8th-century Keep *(see p164)* on Gibraltar

1220   **1260**   **1300**   **1340**

1212 Almohad *(see p44)* power broken by Christian victory at Las Navas de Tolosa

1248 Fernando III takes Seville

1238 Nasrid dynasty established in Granada. Alhambra *(see p186)* begun

1350–69 Reign of Pedro I of Castilla, who rebuilds Seville Alcázar in Mudéjar style. His lack of Spanish patriotism provokes civil war against Henry II of Trastámara

Alfonso X

Chivalry
*The Moors lived by chivalric codes –
this jousting scene is in the Sala de
los Reyes in the Alhambra (see p186).*

Nasrid warriors

Crown
*This Mudéjar-style
crown, bearing the
coats of arms of Castilla
and León, is made of
silver, ivory, and coral.*

Astrolabe
*As this 15th-century
navigation tool shows,
the Moors had great
technical expertise.*

Boabdil's Demise
*Legend has it that
Boabdil wept as he left
Granada. He moved
to Laujar de Andarax
(see p189) until 1493,
then later to Africa.*

WHERE TO SEE RECONQUEST ANDALUSIA

Many of the Reconquest buildings in Andalusia are Mudéjar in style *(see p22)*. The most notable are the Palacio Pedro I in the Reales Alcázares *(p81)* and parts of the Casa de Pilatos *(p75)*, both in Seville. Christian churches built in Andalusia during the 13th, 14th, and 15th centuries are also either completely Mudéjar in style or have Mudéjar features such as a minaret-like bell tower or portal, as, for example, the Iglesia de San Marcos *(p88)* in Seville. During this period the Nasrids of Granada built the most outstanding example of Moorish architecture in Spain, the Alhambra, and Generalife *(pp186–8)*. Seville Cathedral *(pp76–7)* was constructed in the 15th century as a high Gothic assertion of the Catholic faith.

The Palacio Pedro I *(see p81) in Seville is considered to be the most complete example of Mudéjar architecture in Spain.*

1369 Henry II of Trastámara personally kills Pedro I; lays seeds of monolithic Castilian regime

La Pinta, *one of Columbus's ships*

1492 Fall of Granada to the Catholic Monarchs

1380 **1420** **1460**

1469 Marriage of Fernando of Aragón to Isabel of Castilla

1474 Isabel proclaimed queen in Segovia

1479 Fernando becomes king of Aragón; Castilla and Aragón united

1492 Columbus sails to America

Forced baptism of the Moors

Seville's Golden Age

THE 16TH CENTURY saw the rise of a monolithic Spanish state, led by the Catholic Monarchs. Heretics were persecuted and the remaining Moors treated so unjustly that they often rebelled. In 1503 Seville was granted a monopoly on trade with the New World and Spain entrusted with "converting" the Indians by the pope. In 1516 the Hapsburg Carlos I came to the throne, later to be elected Holy Roman Emperor; Spain became the most powerful nation in Europe. Constant war, however, consumed the wealth that its main port, Seville, generated. By the 1680s the Guadalquivir had silted up, trade had passed to Cádiz, and Seville declined.

Mexican Indian

SPANISH EMPIRE IN 1700
▨ Spanish territories

La Giralda (see p76), once an Almohad minaret, is now the belfry of Seville's cathedral.

Carlos I (1516–56)
Carlos I of Spain was made Holy Roman Emperor Carlos V in 1521. His election enabled the Holy Roman Empire to gain access to the immense wealth that Spain, Seville in particular, generated at this time.

Map of Central America
Within 30 years of Columbus's first voyage, the distant lands and seas of Central America had become familiar territory to Spanish navigators.

SEVILLE IN THE 16TH CENTURY

This painting by Alonso Sánchez Coello (1531–88) shows Seville at its height. With the return of treasure fleets from the New World, astonishing wealth poured into the city, and it became one of the richest ports in Europe. The population grew, religious buildings proliferated, and artistic life found new vigor. Despite the prosperity of the city, poverty, crime, and sickness were endemic.

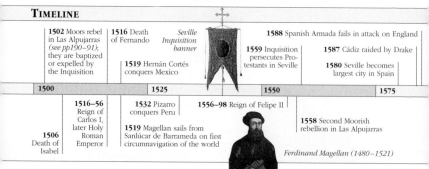

TIMELINE

1502 Moors rebel in Las Alpujarras *(see pp190–91)*; they are baptized or expelled by the Inquisition

1516 Death of Fernando

1519 Hernán Cortés conquers Mexico

Seville Inquisition banner

1559 Inquisition persecutes Protestants in Seville

1588 Spanish Armada fails in attack on England

1587 Cádiz raided by Drake

1580 Seville becomes largest city in Spain

1500 | **1525** | **1550** | **1575**

1506 Death of Isabel

1516–56 Reign of Carlos I, later Holy Roman Emperor

1532 Pizarro conquers Peru

1519 Magellan sails from Sanlúcar de Barrameda on first circumnavigation of the world

1556–98 Reign of Felipe II

1558 Second Moorish rebellion in Las Alpujarras

Ferdinand Magellan (1480–1521)

Inquisition

Fears of heresy laid the ground for the Spanish Inquisition to be set up in the 15th century. In the 16th century autos-da-fé (trials of faith) were held in Seville in the Plaza de San Francisco (see p72).

Unloading and loading took place virtually in the heart of the city.

Velázquez

Born in Seville in 1599, Diego Velázquez painted his earliest works in the city, but later became a court painter in Madrid. This crucifix is a detail of a painting he made at the behest of Felipe IV.

Ships from other parts of Europe brought goods to the city; this merchandise would be traded later in the New World.

The Last Moors

The last Moors were expelled in 1609; this destroyed southern Spain's agriculture, which had taken over 700 years to develop.

WHERE TO SEE THE GOLDEN AGE IN ANDALUSIA

The Isabelline style *(see p22)*, lasting testament to nationalistic fervor of the early 16th century, can be seen in the Capilla Real *(p182)* in Granada and the Palacio de Jabalquinto in Baeza *(pp148–9)*. Baeza and Úbeda *(pp150–51)* both prospered during the Renaissance in Spain and contain some of the best architecture of this period in Andalusia. The Plateresque *(p23)* façade of the Ayuntamiento *(pp72–3)* in Seville is a good example of the style, and the Palacio Carlos V *(p183)* in Granada is the best example of Classical Renaissance architecture in Spain. The Archivo de Indias *(pp78–9)* was built according to the principles of Herreran style *(p23)*. The Hospital de la Caridad *(p67)* is a fine 17th-century Baroque building.

The Capilla Real (see p182) in Granada was built to house the bodies of the Catholic Monarchs, Fernando and Isabel.

1598–1621 Reign of Felipe III

1608 Cervantes, active in Madrid and Seville, publishes *Don Quixote*

1609 Expulsion of Moors by Felipe III

Original edition of Don Quixote

1649 Plague in Seville kills one in three

| 1600 | 1625 | 1650 | 1675 |

1599 Velázquez born in Seville

1596 Sack of Cádiz by the English fleet

1617 Murillo born in Seville

1630 Madrid becomes Spain's largest city. Zurbarán moves to Seville

1665–1700 Carlos II, last of the Spanish Hapsburgs

Young beggar by Murillo (1617–82)

Bourbon Kings

Joseph Bonaparte

THE 13-YEAR War of the Spanish Succession saw Bourbons on the throne in place of the Hapsburgs and, under the Treaty of Utrecht, the loss of Gibraltar to the British *(see pp164–5)*. Later, ties with France dragged Spain into the Napoleonic Wars: following the Battle of Trafalgar, the Spanish king Carlos IV abdicated, and Napoleon Bonaparte placed his brother Joseph on the Spanish throne. The Peninsular War ensued, and, with British help, the French were driven out of Spain. After the Bourbon restoration, Spain, weakened by further strife, began to lose her colonies. Andalusia became one of Spain's poorest regions.

SPAIN IN EUROPE (1812)

▓	*Napoleonic dependencies*
☐	*Napoleonic rule*

Romantic Andalusia
Andalusia's Moorish legacy helped to establish it as a land of beauty and myth, making it popular with travelers of the Romantic era.

The Constitution
is proclaimed to the people of Cádiz.

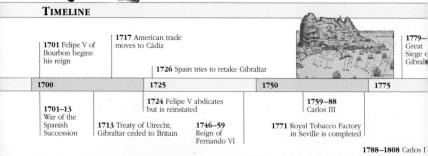

Carlos III
A Bourbon monarch of the Enlightenment and an innovator in matters of society and science, Carlos III tried to establish colonies of farmworkers in the sparsely populated Sierra Morena.

THE 1812 CONSTITUTION

During the Peninsular War, Spain's Parliament met in Cádiz, and in 1812 produced an advanced liberal constitution. However, after the Bourbon restoration in 1814, Fernando VII banned all liberal activity. Ironically, during the First Carlist War, Fernando's daughter, Isabel II, contesting her right to the throne against her uncle Don Carlos, turned to the liberals for support.

TIMELINE

1700	1725	1750	1775
1701 Felipe V of Bourbon begins his reign	**1717** American trade moves to Cádiz		**1779–** Great Siege of Gibraltar
	1726 Spain tries to retake Gibraltar		
1701–13 War of the Spanish Succession	**1724** Felipe V abdicates but is reinstated	**1759–88** Carlos III	
	1713 Treaty of Utrecht; Gibraltar ceded to Britain	**1746–59** Reign of Fernando VI	**1771** Royal Tobacco Factory in Seville is completed
			1788–1808 Carlos I

Battle of Bailén
In 1808, at Bailén, a Spanish army consisting of local militias beat an experienced French army, taking 22,000 prisoners.

Battle of Trafalgar
In 1805, the Spanish, allied at the time to Napoleon, lost their fleet to the British admiral, Nelson.

Support for the constitution came from a wide section of society, including women.

WHERE TO SEE BOURBON ANDALUSIA

Eighteenth-century Baroque architecture can be seen all over Andalusia. The prime examples in Seville are the former Royal Tobacco Factory, now the city's Universidad *(see pp94–5)*, and the Plaza de Toros de la Maestranza *(p66)*. Osuna *(p129)*, Écija *(p129)*, and Priego de Córdoba *(p146)* all have fine examples of the style. The lower levels of Cádiz Cathedral *(p160)* are Spain's most complete example of a Baroque church. The Puente Isabel II *(p101)* is a fine example of 19th-century *arquitectura de hierro* (iron architecture).

The Puente Isabel II *is an example of the architecture of Andalusia's "industrial" age.*

Washington Irving
In Tales of the Alhambra (1832) *the American diplomat Washington Irving perpetuated a highly romanticized view of Andalusia.*

Seville's Tobacco Factory
Carmen *(1845), by Prosper Mérimée* (see p94), *was inspired by the women – over 3,000 of them – who worked in the tobacco factory.*

1808 Joseph Bonaparte made king of Spain. Battle of Bailén	**1812** Liberal constitution drawn up in Cádiz **1814–33** (Bourbon restoration) Reign of Fernando VII	*Isabel II*	**1870–73** Reign of King Amadeo **1868** Isabel II loses her throne in "glorious" revolution	**1873–4** First Republic

1800	1825	1850	1875

805 Battle of Trafalgar	**1814** South American colonies begin struggle for independence **1808–14** Peninsular War	**1843** Isabel II accedes to throne **1833** First Carlist War	**1846–9** Second Carlist War **1874** Second Bourbon restoration: Alfonso XII made king	**1872–6** Third Carlist War

Alfonso XII

The Seeds of Civil War

General Franco

Aᴺᴰᴬᴸᵁˢᴵᴬ ᴄᴼᴺᵀᴵᴺᵁᴱᴰ to decline, remaining so deeply feudal that by the early 20th century social protest was rife. The 1920s brought dictator General Primo de Rivera and short-lived social order. In 1931, a Republican government, consisting of liberals and moderate socialists, came to power. A rigid social order made real reforms slow to arrive, and 1931–36 saw growing conflict between extreme left and right wing (including the Falange) elements. In 1936, the Nationalist General Franco, leading a Moroccan garrison, invaded Spain, declaring war on the Republic.

Aɴᴅᴀʟᴜsɪᴀ ɪɴ 1936

⬛ *Nationalist territory*

⬜ *Republican territory*

Moorish Revival
By the late 19th century, regionalism, andalucismo, *led to a revival of Moorish-style architecture. An example is Seville's Estación de Córdoba.*

Women fought alongside men against the Nationalist army.

Picasso
Pablo Picasso, shown in this self-portrait, was born in Málaga in 1881. His most famous work, Guernica, *depicts the tragic effects of the Civil War.*

Tʜᴇ Rᴇᴘᴜʙʟɪᴄᴀɴ Aʀᴍʏ
In Andalusia, Franco attacked the Republican army at the very start of the war. Cádiz and Seville fell to Nationalists, but other Andalusian towns held out longer. Franco seized Málaga in 1937, executing thousands of Republicans.

Tɪᴍᴇʟɪɴᴇ

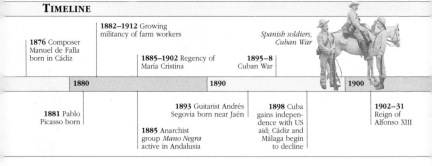

1876 Composer Manuel de Falla born in Cádiz	**1882–1912** Growing militancy of farm workers		*Spanish soldiers, Cuban War*	
	1885–1902 Regency of María Cristina	**1895–8** Cuban War		
1880		**1890**		**1900**
1881 Pablo Picasso born	**1893** Guitarist Andrés Segovia born near Jaén	**1898** Cuba gains independence with US aid; Cádiz and Málaga begin to decline		**1902–31** Reign of Alfonso XIII
	1885 Anarchist group *Mano Negra* active in Andalusia			

Casas Viejas
In 1933, peasants were massacred after an uprising by anarchists at Casas Viejas in the province of Cádiz. The incident further served to undermine the Republican government.

WHERE TO SEE EARLY 20TH-CENTURY ARCHITECTURE IN ANDALUSIA

This period is characterized by architectural revivals. The regionalist style can be seen at the Plaza de España *(see p96)*, the Museo Arqueológico *(p97)*, and the Museo de Artes y Costumbres Populares *(p97)*, all in the Parque María Luisa. The Teatro Lope Vega *(p95)* is in a Neo-Baroque style.

The Pabellón Real (see p97) *in the Parque María Luisa is a pastiche of the late Gothic, Isabelline (see p21) style.*

1929 Exposition
This trade fair was intended to boost Andalusia's economy. Unfortunately, it coincided with the Wall Street Crash.

Arms were supplied to the Republican army by the then Soviet Union.

Federico García Lorca
This poster is for Lorca's play, Yerma. The outspoken poet and playwright was murdered by local Falangists in his home town, Granada, in 1936.

General Queipo de Llano
Queipo de Llano broadcast radio propaganda to Seville as part of the Nationalists' strategy to take the city.

Republican poster

1933 Massacre at Casas Viejas

1936 Civil War starts

1923–30 Dictatorship of General Primo de Rivera

1929 Ibero-American Exposition, Seville

¡ATACAD! SOLDADOS DE LA REPUBLICA

1910 | 1920 | 1930

1917–20 Bolshevik Triennium; communists lead protests in Andalusia

José Antonio Primo de Rivera

1931–39 Second Republic

1933 Falange founded by José Antonio Primo de Rivera; later supports Franco

1936 Franco becomes head of state

1939 Civil War ends

Modern Andalusia

Andalusian flag

Bᵧ 1945 Spain remained the only Nationalist state in Europe. She was denied aid until 1953, when Franco allowed US bases to be built on Spanish soil. The 1960s and 1970s saw economic growth, Andalusia in particular benefiting from tourism. When Franco died in 1975 and Juan Carlos I came to the throne, Spain was more than ready for democracy; the regions clamored for devolution from Franco's centralized government. In 1982 the Sevillian Felipe González came to power, and, in the same year, Andalusia became an autonomous region.

Autonomous Regions

Present-day Andalusia

Feria
Despite the repressive regime that Franco established, the spirit of the Andalusian people remained evident in events such as the feria in Seville.

The Puente de Chapina is distinguished by a geometrically designed canopy running along the top of it.

The Hungry Years
After the Civil War, Spain was isolated from Europe and after World War II received no aid; amid widespread poverty and rationing, many Andalusians left to work abroad.

New Bridges
Despite its recent autonomy, Andalusia still lagged behind much of the rest of Spain economically. Funds were provided by the central government to build the new infrastructure needed to support Expo '92. Five bridges, all of the most innovative, modern design, were built over the Guadalquivir river.

Timeline

1940 Franco refuses to allow Hitler to attack Gibraltar from Spanish territory	**1953** Spain is granted economic aid in return for allowing US bases on Spanish soil	**1962** Development of Costa del Sol begins
1940	**1950**	**1960**
1940–53 The Hungry Years	*Franco meets American President Eisenhower (1953)*	**1966** Palomares incident: two US aircraft collide and four nuclear bombs fall to earth, one in the sea but do not explode. The Duchess of Medina Sidonia, "the red duchess," leads protest march on Madrid

Franco's Funeral *(1975)*
Franco's death was mourned as much as it was welcomed; most people, though, saw the need for democratic change.

Package Vacations
New building for mass tourism transformed Andalusia's coast.

WHERE TO SEE MODERN ANDALUSIA

The most striking buildings of modern Andalusia were built in the early part of the 1990s. Expo '92 left Seville with five new bridges over the Guadalquivir river, and at La Cartuja *(see p102)* Expo's core pavilions still stand, soon to be the site of new attractions. The new Teatro de la Maestranza *(pp66–7)*, in El Arenal, was also built during this period.

The Omnimax theater *(see p102) on the former Expo '92 site was originally built as part of the Pavilion of Discoveries.*

The Puente del Alamillo (Harp) has a single upward arm supporting its weight.

The Puente de la Barqueta, a unique suspension bridge supported by a single overhead beam, spans 168 m (551 ft).

Expo '92
Hosted by Seville, Expo '92 placed Andalusia at the centre of a world stage. In 1996, however, Spain was still recovering the cost.

Felipe González
In 1982, the year after an attempted coup by the Civil Guard colonel Antonio Tejero, Felipe González, leader of the socialist PSOE, claimed a huge electoral victory.

King Juan Carlos I

1975 Franco dies. Third Bourbon restoration; Juan Carlos I accedes to the throne

1981 Colonel Tejero attempts coup and holds Spanish Parliament hostage; Juan Carlos intervenes

1982 Felipe González, head of PSOE, the Spanish Socialist Workers' Party, elected prime minister

1992 Expo '92, Seville

1970 | **1980** | **1990**

1969 Spain closes border with Gibraltar

1976 Adolfo Suárez appointed prime minister by Juan Carlos I; forms center-right government

Colonel Tejero

1986 Spain joins EU

1985 Spain-Gibraltar border opens

1982 Andalusia becomes an autonomous region; returns socialist government in its first regional election

SEVILLE AREA BY AREA

Seville at a Glance

THE CAPITAL OF ANDALUSIA is a compact and relaxing city with a rich cultural heritage. Conveniently, many of its principal sights can be found within or very near the city center, which is set on the east bank of the Río Guadalquivir. Most visitors head straight for the cathedral, La Giralda, Reales Alcázares, and Museo de Bellas Artes. Among other highly popular monuments are the exquisite Renaissance palace of Casa de Pilatos and Seville's bullring, the Plaza de Toros de la Maestranza. There are, however, many other churches, monuments, and neighborhoods to discover in the four central areas described in this section, and more, farther afield, across the river.

Baroque doorway, Parlamento de Andalucía (see p87)

EL ARENAL
Pages 60–67

The splendid ceiling of Museo de Bellas Artes (see pp64–5)

Plaza de Toros de la Maestranza seen from the river (see p66)

The Moorish Torre del Oro, built to defend Seville (see p67)

| 0 meters | 400 |
| 0 yards | 400 |

Patio of Real Fábrica de Tabacos, today the Universidad (see p94)

◁ La Giralda by night over the rooftops of El Arenal

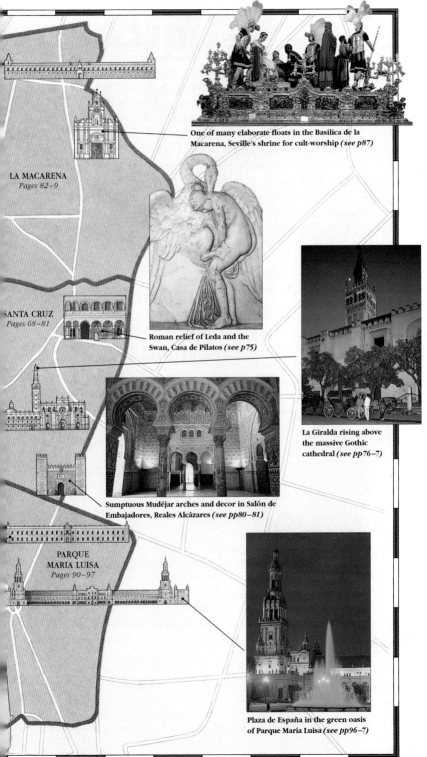

One of many elaborate floats in the Basílica de la Macarena, Seville's shrine for cult-worship *(see p87)*

LA MACARENA
Pages 82–9

SANTA CRUZ
Pages 68–81

Roman relief of Leda and the Swan, Casa de Pilatos *(see p75)*

La Giralda rising above the massive Gothic cathedral *(see pp76–7)*

Sumptuous Mudéjar arches and decor in Salón de Embajadores, Reales Alcázares *(see pp80–81)*

PARQUE MARIA LUISA
Pages 90–97

Plaza de España in the green oasis of Parque María Luisa *(see pp96–7)*

EL ARENAL

BOUNDED BY the Río Guadalquivir and guarded by the mighty 13th-century Torre del Oro, El Arenal used to be a district of munitions stores and shipyards. Today this quarter is dominated by the dazzling white bullring, Plaza de Toros de la Maestranza, where the Sevillians have been staging *corridas* for more than two centuries. The many classic bars and wine cellars in neighboring streets get extra busy during the summer bullfighting season.

Torre del Oro shown on 20th-century tiles

Once central to the city's life, the influence of the Guadalquivir declined as it silted up during the 17th century. By then El Arenal had become a notorious underworld hangout clinging to the city walls. After being converted into a canal in the early 20th century, the river was restored to its former

navigable glory just in time for Expo '92. The east riverfront was transformed into a tree-lined, shady promenade with excellent views of Triana and La Cartuja across the river *(see pp102–3)*. Boat trips and sight-seeing tours depart from the Torre del Oro. Close by is the stylish, new Teatro de la Maestranza, where opera, classical music, and dance take place before well-informed audiences.

The Hospital de la Caridad testifies to the city's continuing love affair with the Baroque. Its church is filled with famous paintings by Murillo, and the story of the Seville School is told with pride in the immaculately restored Museo de Bellas Artes farther north. The city's stunning collection of great works by Zurbarán, Murillo, and Valdés Leal is reason enough to visit Seville.

SIGHTS AT A GLANCE

Historic Buildings
Hospital de la Caridad ⑤
Plaza de Toros de la Maestranza ③
Torre del Oro ⑥

Museums
Museo de Bellas Artes pp64–5 ①

Churches
Iglesia de la Magdalena ②

Theaters
Teatro de la Maestranza ④

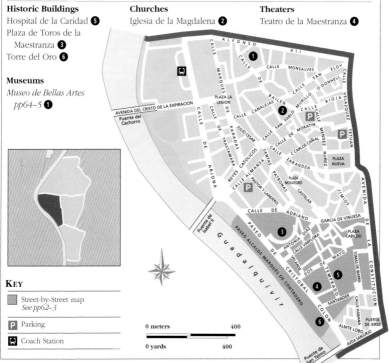

KEY

	Street-by-Street map *See pp62–3*
P	Parking
	Coach Station

0 meters 400
0 yards 400

◁ **Advertisement for a bullfight on the walls of the Plaza de Toros de la Maestranza**

Street-by-Street: El Arenal

Statue of Carmen

ONCE HOME TO THE PORT of Seville, El Arenal also housed the artillery head-quarters and ammunition works. Now its atmosphere is set by Seville's bullring, the majestic Plaza de Toros de la Maestranza, which is located here. During the bull-fighting season *(see pp24–5)* bars and restaurants are packed, but for the rest of the year the backstreets remain quiet. The riverfront is dominated by one of Seville's best-known monuments, the Moorish Torre del Oro, and the long tree-lined promenade beside Paseo de Cristóbal Colón is the perfect setting for a romantic walk along the Guadalquivir.

★ Plaza de Toros de la Maestranza
Seville's 18th-century bullring, one of Spain's oldest, has a Baroque façade in white and ocher ❸

Carmen *(see p94),* sculpted in bronze, stands opposite the bullring.

CALLE DE ADRIANO

CALLE ANTONIA DIAZ

PASEO DE CRISTOBAL COLON

Paseo Alcalde Marqués de Contadero

Teatro de la Maestranza
This showpiece theater and opera house opened in 1991. Home of the Orquesta Sinfónica de Sevilla, it also features inter-national opera and dance companies ❹

STAR SIGHTS

★ **Plaza de Toros de la Maestranza**

★ **Torre del Oro**

★ **Hospital de la Caridad**

The Guadalquivir used to cause catastrophic inundations. Following floods in 1947 a barrage was constructed. Today, tourists enjoy peaceful boat trips, starting from Torre del Oro.

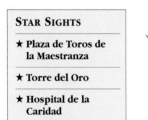

El Buzo (The Diver) is one of many traditional tapas bars and *freidurías* situated on or just off Calle Arfe. Nearby lies Mesón Sevilla Jabugo I, a bar where *jamón ibérico* (*see p223*) is served.

LOCATOR MAP
See Street Finder, maps 3, 5–6.

El Postigo is an arts and crafts market.

GARCIA VINUESA

To Seville Cathedral

On Plaza de Cabildo, a well-hidden square, convent-made sweets are sold in El Torno.

ARFE

AVENIDA DE LA CONSTITUCION

★ Hospital de la Caridad
The Baroque church of this hospital for the elderly is lined with paintings by Bartolomé Esteban Murillo and Juan de Valdés Leal ❺

S. DE MAYO

TOMAS DE IBARRA

TEMPRADO

To Reales Alcázares

Maestranza de Artillería

CALLE SANTANDER

Bodegón Torre del Oro (*see p216*).

| 0 meters | 75 |
| 0 yards | 75 |

KEY

– – – Suggested route

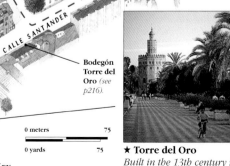

★ Torre del Oro
Built in the 13th century in order to protect the port, this crenellated Moorish tower now houses a small maritime museum ❻

Museo de Bellas Artes ①

Baroque cherubs in Sala 5

T HE FORMER Convento de la Merced Calzada has been restored to create one of the finest art museums in Spain. The convent, which was completed in 1612 by Juan de Oviedo, is built around three patios, which today are adorned with flowers, trees, and *azulejos (see p74)*. The museum's impressive collection of Spanish art and sculpture extends from the medieval to the modern, focusing on the work of Seville School artists such as Bartolomé Esteban Murillo, Juan de Valdés Leal, and Francisco de Zurbarán.

🔼 🏃 **for the disabled**

La Inmaculada
This boisterous In-maculada (1672), by Valdés Leal (1622–90), is in Sala 8, a gallery devoted to the artist's forceful religious paintings.

★ **San Hugo en el Refectorio** (*1655*)
One of several works by Zurbarán for the monastery at La Cartuja (see p103), this scene depicts the Carthusian Order of monks first renouncing the eating of meat.

First floor

The Claustro de los Bojes is enclosed by Tuscan-style arches.

STAR EXHIBITS
★ **San Jerónimo Penitente by Pietro Torrigiano**
★ **La Servilleta by Murillo**
★ **San Hugo en el Refectorio by Zurbarán**
★ **Domed Ceiling**
★ **Claustro Mayor**

★ **San Jerónimo Penitente** (*1528*)
Sculpted by the Florentine Torrigiano, this master-piece in terra-cotta brought the vitality of the Italian Renaissance to Seville.

★ La Servilleta
This lively and attractive Virgin and Child (1665–8), said to be painted on a napkin (servilleta), is one of Murillo's most popular works.

VISITORS' CHECKLIST
Pl del Museo 9. **Map** 1 B5 (5 B2).
(95) 422 07 90. 43, C3.
9am–3pm Tue–Sun (also 4–7pm during temporary exhibitions; phone to check).

★ Domed Ceiling
The magnificent ceiling of the convent church, now restored to its Baroque glory, was painted by Domingo Martínez in the 18th century.

14

12

13

for the disabled

5

Apoteosis de Santo Tomás de Aquino
Zurbarán accomplished this work in 1631, at the age of 33. His sharp characterization of the figures and vivid use of color bring it to life, as can be seen on this detail.

★ Claustro Mayor
The main cloister of the monastery was remodeled by architect Leonardo de Figueroa in 1724.

Entrance

1

Claustro del Aljibe

Ground floor

KEY TO FLOOR PLAN
- Medieval art
- Renaissance art
- Baroque art
- 19th- and 20th-century art
- Nonexhibition space

GALLERY GUIDE
Signs provide a self-guided chronological tour through the museum's 14 galleries, starting by the Claustro del Aljibe. Works downstairs progress from the 14th century through Mannerism; those upstairs from the Baroque to the early 20th century.

Museo de Bellas Artes ❶

See pp64–5.

Madonna and Child in the Baroque Iglesia de la Magdalena

Iglesia de la Magdalena ❷

Calle San Pablo 10. **Map** 3 B1 (5 B2).
█ (95) 422 96 03. ◯ 7:30–11am,
6:30–9pm Mon–Fri; 7:30am–1pm
Sat–Sun. █

THIS IMMENSE BAROQUE church by Leonardo de Figueroa, completed in 1709, is gradually being restored to its former glory. In its southwest corner is the Capilla de la Quinta Angustia, a Mudéjar chapel with three cupolas. This chapel survived from an earlier church where the great Spanish painter Bartolomé Murillo *(see pp64–5)* was baptized in 1618. The font that was used for his baptism today stands in the baptistry of the present building. The sheer west front is surmounted by a belfry painted in vivid colors.

Among the religious works in the church are a painting by Francisco de Zurbarán, *St. Dominic in Soria*, housed in the Capilla Sacramental (to the right of the south door), and frescoes by Lucas Valdés above the sanctuary depicting *The Allegory of the Triumph of Faith*. On the wall of the north transept is a cautionary fresco that depicts a medieval auto-da-fé (trial of faith).

Plaza de Toros de la Maestranza ❸

Paseo de Colón s/n. **Map** 3 B2 (5 B4).
█ (95) 422 45 77. ◯ 10am–
1:30pm Mon–Sat. █ █

SEVILLE'S FAMOUS bullring is arguably the finest in the whole of Spain and is a perfect spot for a first experience of the *corrida*, or bullfight *(see pp24–5)*. Although the art of the matador (bullfighter) is now declining in popularity, the sunlit stage, with its white-washed walls, blood red fences, and merciless circle of sand, remains crucial to the city's psyche. Even if you dis-like the idea of bullfighting, this arcaded arena, dating from 1761 to 1881, is an aesthetic marvel and well worth a visit.

The bullring accommodates as many as 12,500 spectators. Guided tours of this huge building start from the main entrance located on Paseo de Cristóbal Colón. On the west side stands the Puerta del Príncipe (Prince's Gate), through which the very best of the matadors are carried triumphantly on the shoulders of admirers from the crowd.

Passing the *enfermería* (emergency hospital), visitors reach a museum that details the history of the bullfight in Seville. Among its collection of costumes, portraits, and posters are scenes showing early con-tests held in the Plaza de San Francisco and a purple cape painted by Pablo Picasso. The tour continues to the chapel where matadors pray for success, and then on to the

stables where the horses of the *picadores* (lance-carrying horsemen) are kept.

The bullfighting season starts with the April *feria (see p36)* and continues intermittently until October. Most *corridas* are held on Sunday evenings. Tickets can be bought at the *taquilla* (booking office) at the bullring itself.

Entrance with 19th-century iron-work, Teatro de la Maestranza

Teatro de la Maestranza ❹

Paseo de Colón 22. **Map** 3 B2 (5 C5).
█ (95) 422 65 73 (ticket office).
◯ for performances. █ █

NOT FAR FROM the Plaza de Toros, and with echoes of its circular bulk, is Seville's 1,800-seat opera house and theater. It opened in 1991 and many prestigious international opera companies perform there *(see p231)*. Like many of the

Arcaded arena of the Plaza de Toros de la Maestranza, begun in 1761

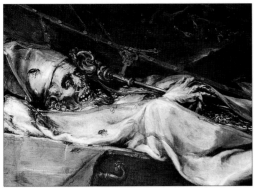

Finis Gloriae Mundi by Juan de Valdés Leal in the Hospital de la Caridad

city's buildings that were built during the prelude to Expo '92 *(see pp54–5)*, it was designed in a rather austere, functionalist style by architects Luis Marín de Terán and Aurelio del Pozo. Ironwork remnants of the 19th-century ammunition works that first occupied the site decorate the river façade. Tickets are sold at the box office situated in the adjacent Jardín de la Caridad.

Hospital de la Caridad ❺

Calle Temprado 3. **Map** 3 B2 (5 C5).
▐ (95) 422 32 32. ⬭ 10am–1pm,
4:30–6:30pm Mon–Sat. ⬤ public
hols. 📷 🚫

THIS CHARITY HOSPITAL was founded in 1674 and it is still used today as a sanctuary for elderly and infirm people. In the gardens opposite the entrance stands a statue of its benefactor, Miguel de Mañara. The complex was designed by Pedro Sánchez Falconete. The façade of the hospital church, with its whitewashed walls, terra-cotta stonework, and framed *azulejos (see p74)*, provides a glorious example of Sevillian Baroque.

Inside are two square patios adorned with plants, 18th-century Dutch *azulejos*, and fountains with Italian statues depicting Charity and Mercy. At their northern end a passage to the right leads to another patio, where a 13th-century arch from the city's shipyards survives. A bust of Mañara stands amid rose bushes.

Inside the church there are many original canvases by some of the leading artists of the 17th century, despite the fact that some of its greatest artworks were looted by Marshal Soult at the time of the Napoleonic occupation of 1810 *(see p51)*. Directly above the entrance is the ghoulish *Finis Gloriae Mundi* (The End of the World's Glory) by Juan de Valdés Leal, and opposite hangs his morbid *In Ictu Oculi* (In the Blink of an Eye). Many of the other works are by Murillo, including *St. John of God Carrying a Sick Man*, portraits of the Child Jesus, *St. John the Baptist as a Boy*, and *St. Isabel of Hungary Curing the Lepers*. Looking south from the Hospital's

entrance you can see the octagonal Torre de Plata (Tower of Silver) rising above Calle Santander. Like the Torre del Oro nearby, it dates from Moorish times and was built as part of the city defenses.

Torre del Oro ❻

Paseo de Colón s/n. **Map** 3 B2 (5 C5).
▐ (95) 422 24 19. ⬭ 10am–2pm
Tue–Fri, 11am–2pm Sat & Sun.
⬤ Aug & public hols. 📷 🚫

IN MOORISH SEVILLE the Tower of Gold formed part of the walled defenses, linking up with the Reales Alcázares *(see. pp80–81)* and the rest of the city. It was constructed as a defensive lookout in 1220, when Seville was under the control of the Almohads *(see pp44–5)*, and had a companion tower on the opposite river bank. A mighty chain would be stretched between the two to prevent ships from sailing upriver. In 1760 the turret was added.

The gold in the tower's name may refer to gilded *azulejos* that once clad its walls, or to New World treasures unloaded here. The tower

The Torre del Oro, built by the Almohads

has been used as a chapel, a prison, a gunpowder store, and port offices. Now it is the Museo Marítimo, exhibiting maritime maps and antiques.

DON JUAN OF SEVILLE

Miguel de Mañara (1626–79), founder and subsequent benefactor of the Hospital de la Caridad, is frequently linked with Don Juan Tenorio. The amorous conquests of the legendary Sevillian seducer were first documented in 1630 in a play by Tirso de Molina. They have since inspired works by Mozart, Molière, Byron, and Shaw. Mañara is thought to have led an equally dissolute life prior to his conversion to philanthropy – apparently this was prompted by a premonition of his own funeral, which he experienced one drunken night.

The legendary Don Juan with two of his conquests

SANTA CRUZ

THE BARRIO DE SANTA CRUZ, Seville's old Jewish quarter, is a warren of white alleys and patios that has long been the most picturesque corner of the city. Many of the best-known sights are grouped here: the cavernous Gothic cathedral with its landmark Giralda; the splendid Reales Alcázares with the royal palaces and lush gardens of Pedro I and Carlos V; and the Archivo de Indias, whose documents tell of Spain's exploration and conquest of the New World.

Spreading northeast from these great monuments is an enchanting maze of whitewashed streets. The artist Bartolomé Esteban Murillo lived here in the 17th century while his contemporary, Juan de Valdés Leal, decorated the Hospital de los Venerables with fine Baroque frescoes.

Farther north, busy Calle de las Sierpes is one of Seville's favorite shopping streets. Its adjacent market squares, such as the charming Plaza del Salvador, provided backdrops for Cervantes's stories. Nearby, the ornate façades and interiors of the Ayuntamiento and the Casa de Pilatos, a gem of Andalusian architecture, testify to the great wealth and artistry that flowed into the city in the 16th century.

Ornate streetlamp, Plaza del Triunfo

SIGHTS AT A GLANCE

Gardens
Jardines de Murillo **13**

Streets and Plazas
Calle de las Sierpes **2**
Plaza del Alfalfa **5**
Plaza del Triunfo **9**
Plaza Virgen de los Reyes **8**

Churches
Seville Cathedral and
La Giralda pp76–7 **7**
Iglesia del Salvador **4**

Historic Buildings
Reales Alcázares pp80–81 **11**
Archivo de Indias **10**
Ayuntamiento **3**

Casa de la Condesa
Lebrija **1**
Casa de Pilatos **6**
Hospital de los Venerables **12**

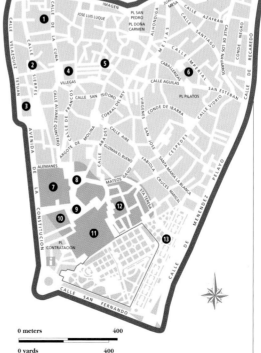

KEY

▨	Street-by-Street map See pp70–71
▌	Tourist information

0 meters 400
0 yards 400

◁ **La Giralda seen from the gardens of the Reales Alcázares**

Street-by-Street: Santa Cruz

THE MAZE of narrow streets to the east of Seville cathedral and the Reales Alcázares represents Seville at its most romantic and compact. As well as the expected souvenir shops, tapas bars, and strolling guitarists, there are plenty of picturesque alleys, hidden plazas, and flower-decked patios to reward the casual wanderer. Once a Jewish ghetto, its restored buildings, with characteristic window grilles, are now a harmonious mix of upscale residences and tourist accommodations. Good bars and restaurants make the area well worth an evening visit.

Window grille, Santa Cruz

Plaza Virgen de los Reyes
Horse carriages line this plaza, which has an early 20th-century fountain by José Lafita **⑧**

Palacio Arzobispal, the 18th-century Archbishop's Palace, is still used by Seville's clergy.

★ **Seville Cathedral and La Giralda**
This huge Gothic cathedral and its Moorish bell tower are Seville's most popular sights **⑦**

Convento de la Encarnación
(See p78)

Archivo de Indias
Built in the 16th century as a merchants' exchange, the Archive of the Indies now houses documents relating to the Spanish colonization of the Americas **⑩**

Museo de Arte Contemporáneo
(See p78)

Plaza del Triunfo
A Baroque column celebrates the city's survival of the grea earthquake of 175 Opposite is a mod statue of the Imma late Conception

Calle Mateos Gago
is filled with souvenir shops and tapas bars. Bar Giralda at No. 2, whose vaults are the remains of a Moorish bath, is particularly popular for its wide variety of tapas *(see pp222–3).*

LOCATOR MAP
See Street Finder, maps 5–6

Plaza Santa Cruz
is adorned by an ornate iron cross from 1692.

MESON DEL MORO

XIMENEZ ENCISO

SANTA TERESA

RODRIGO CARO

JAMERDANA

REINOSO

LOPE DE RUEDA

PLAZA STA CRUZ

GLORIA

JUSTINO DE NEVE

PL DOÑA ELVIRA

SUSONA

PIMIENTA

CALLEJON DEL AGUA

VIDA

★ **Hospital de los Venerables**
This 17th-century home for elderly priests has a splendidly restored Baroque church ⑫

Callejón del Agua,
a whitewashed alley running alongside the Alcázar walls, offers enchanting glimpses into plant-filled patios. Washington Irving *(see p51)* stayed at No. 2.

| 0 meters | 50 |
| 0 yards | 50 |

★ **Reales Alcázares**
Seville's Royal Palaces are a rewarding combination of exquisite Mudéjar (see p22) craftsmanship, regal grandeur, and beautifully landscaped gardens ⑪

KEY
– – – Suggested route

STAR SIGHTS

★ Seville Cathedral and La Giralda

★ Reales Alcázares

★ Hospital de los Venerables

Mosaic, from Itálica (see p128), in the Casa de la Condesa Lebrija

Casa de la Condesa Lebrija ❶

Calle Cuna 8. **Map** 1 C5; 3 C1 (5 C2).
((95) 421 81 83. ◯ 5–7pm Mon & Fri.

This private mansion, the home of the family of the Countess Lebrija, offers a glimpse of palatial life in the heart of Seville. The ground floor only is opened to the public for just a few hours each week. It is masked from the Calle Cuna by imposing wooden doors and by an immense iron grille.

The house dates from the 15th century and has several Mudéjar (see p22) features. Many of its Roman treasures were taken from the ruins at Itálica (see p128), including the mosaic floor in the main patio. The artesonado ceiling above the staircase came from the palace of the Dukes of Arcos in Marchena, near Seville.

Roman glassware and coins, marble from Medina Azahara (see p134), and 18th-century azulejos (see p74) are among countless exhibits displayed in rooms off the main patio.

Calle de las Sierpes ❷

Map 3 C1 (5 C3).

The street of the snakes, running north from Plaza de San Francisco, is Seville's main pedestrianized shopping promenade. Long-established stores selling the Sevillian essentials – hats, fans, and the traditional mantillas (lace headdresses) – stand alongside clothes boutiques, souvenir shops, bargain basements, and lottery kiosks. The best time to stroll along it is when the sevillanos themselves do – during the early evening paseo.

The parallel streets of Cuna and Tetuán on either side also offer some enjoyable window-shopping. Look for the splendid 1924 tiled advert for Studebaker automobiles (see p74) at Calle Tetuán 9.

At the southern end of Calle de las Sierpes, on the wall of the Banco Central Hispano, a plaque marks the site of the Cárcel Real (Royal Prison), where the famous Spanish writer Miguel de Cervantes (1547–1616) (see p49) was incarcerated. Walking north from here, Calle Jovellanos to the left leads to the Capillita de San José. This small, rather atmospheric chapel, built in the 17th century, contrasts

sharply with its commercial surroundings. Farther on, at the junction with Calle Pedro Caravaca, you can take a look back into the anachronistic, upholstered world of the Real Círculo de Labradores, a private men's club founded in 1856. Right at the end of the street, take the opportunity to peruse Seville's best-known pastelería (pastry shop), La Campana.

Ayuntamiento ❸

Plaza Nueva 1. **Map** 3 C1 (5 C3).
((95) 459 01 01. ◯ 5:30–7:30pm Tue & Wed (entry with passport). ⌀

Platoresque doorway, part of the façade of Seville's Ayuntamiento

Seville's city hall stands between the historic Plaza de San Francisco and the modern expanse of Plaza Nueva.

In the 15th–18th centuries, Plaza de San Francisco was the place for autos-da-fé, public trials of heretics held by the Inquisition (see p49). Those found guilty would be taken to the Quemadero and burned alive. (This site is now the Prado de San Sebastián, north of Parque María Luisa, see pp96–7.) These days, Plaza de San Francisco is the focus of activities in Semana Santa and Corpus Christi (see pp32–3).

Plaza Nueva was once the site of the Convento de San Francisco. In its center is an equestrian statue of Fernando III, who liberated Seville from the Moors and was eventually canonized in 1671 (see p46).

The Ayuntamiento, begun in 1527, was finished in 1534. The east side, looking onto

Tables outside La Campana, Seville's most famous pastelería

Plaza de San Francisco, is a fine example of the ornate Plateresque style *(see p23)* favored by the architect Diego de Riaño. The west front is part of a Neo-Classical extension built in 1891. It virtually envelops the original building, but richly sculpted ceilings survive in the vestibule and in the lower Casa Consistorial (Council Meeting Room). This room contains Velázquez's *Imposition of the Chasuble on St. Ildefonso*, one of many artworks in the building. The upper Casa Consistorial has a dazzling gold coffered ceiling and paintings by Zurbarán and Valdés Leal *(see pp64–5)*.

Iglesia del Salvador ❹

Plaza del Salvador. **Map** 3 C1 (6 D3).
[(95) 421 16 79. **◯** 6:30–9pm
daily, 10am–1:30pm Sun.

Baroque façade of the Iglesia del Salvador on the Plaza del Salvador

THIS CHURCH'S cathedral-like proportions result in part from the desire of Seville's Christian conquerors to outdo the architectural splendors of the Moors. The mosque of Ibn Addabas first occupied the site; part of the Moorish patio survives beside Calle Córdoba. It is boxed in by arcades incorporating columns with Roman and Visigothic capitals.

By the 1670s the mosque, long since consecrated for Christian worship, had fallen into disrepair. Work started on a new Baroque structure, designed by Esteban García. The church was completed in 1712 by Leonardo de Figueroa.

Inside, the nave is by José Granados, architect of Granada cathedral *(see p182)*. In the Capilla Sacramental there is a fine statue, *Jesus of the Passion*, made in 1619 by Juan Martínez Montañés (1568–1649). In the northwest corner, a door leads to the ornate Capilla de los Desamparados and a Moorish patio. Over the exit on Calle Córdoba, the bell tower rests on part of the original minaret.

Adjacent to the church is the Plaza del Salvador, which has become a meeting place for Seville's young crowd, with several great tapas bars. The

bronze statue commemorates the sculptor Montañés. On the east side of the church, the Plaza Jesús de la Pasión is given over to shops catering to weddings – the Iglesia del Salvador is a favorite among *sevillanos* for getting married.

Plaza del Alfalfa ❺

Map 3 C1 (6 D3). **◪** *Sun am.*

NAMED AFTER ALFALFA, a cloverlike plant widely cultivated for fodder, this small, tree-shaded square was once used as a hay market. Now, a pet market is held there on Sunday mornings. There are cages of birds and puppies, tanks of exotic fish, and stalls selling tortoises, lizards, mice, and even silkworms.

A short walk east of the plaza, down Calle Jesús de las Tres Caídas, stands the colorfully restored Iglesia de San Isidoro. Dating from the 14th century, it has a neat Gothic portal capped by a Mudéjar star, facing Calle San Isidoro. Inside there stands a dramatic statue of Simón Cirineo that was sculpted by Antonio Francisco Gijón around 1687.

THE SIGN OF SEVILLE

The curious abbreviation "NO8DO" is emblazoned everywhere from the venerable walls of the Ayuntamiento to the sides of the municipal buses. It is traditionally said to stand for "*No me ha dejado*" ("She has not deserted me"). These words were reputedly uttered by Alfonso the Wise, after the city remained loyal to him in the course of a dispute with his son Sancho during the Reconquest *(see pp46–7)*. The double-loop symbol in the middle represents a skein of wool, the Spanish word for which is *madeja*, thus *no (madeja)do*.

The traditional emblem of Seville, here in stone on the Ayuntamiento

The Art of Azulejos

COOL IN SUMMER, durable, and colorful, *azulejos* (glazed ceramic tiles) have been a striking feature of Andalusian façades and interiors for centuries. The techniques for making them were first introduced by the Moors – the word *azulejo* derives from the Arabic *az-zulayj* or "little stone." Moorish *azulejos* are elaborate mosaics

16th-century *azulejos*, Salones de Carlos V *(p80)*

made of monochromatic stones. The craft flourished in the potteries of Triana *(see pp100–101)*. A later process, developed in 16th-century Italy, allowed tiles to be painted in new designs and more colors. The Industrial Revolution enabled *azulejos* to be mass-produced in factories including the famous "Pickman y Cia" at the monastery of La Cartuja *(see p103)*.

MUDÉJAR-STYLE AZULEJOS

The Moors created fantastic mosaics of tiles in sophisticated geometric patterns as decoration for their palace walls. The colors used were blue, green, black, white, and ocher.

16th-century Mudéjar tiles,
Casa de Pilatos

Interlacing motifs, Patio
de las Doncellas

Mudéjar tiles in the Patio de las
Doncellas, Reales Alcázares

Sign for the Royal Tobacco Factory (now part of the Universidad, *see pp94–5*) made in painted glazed tiles in the 18th century

AZULEJOS FOR COMMERCIAL USE

As techniques for making and coloring *azulejos* improved, their use was extended from interior decor to decorative signs and shop façades. Even billboards were produced in multicolored tiles. The eye-catching results can still be seen all over Andalusia.

Contemporary glazed
ceramic beer tap

Azulejo billboard advertising the latest model of Studebaker Motor Cars
(1924), situated on Calle Tetuán, off Calle de las Sierpes *(see p72)*

Genoan fountain and Gothic balustrades in the Mudéjar Patio Principal of the Casa de Pilatos

Casa de Pilatos ❻

Plaza de Pilatos 1. **Map** 4 D1 (6 E3).
((95) 422 52 98. **◯ Ground floor**
9am–8pm. **First floor** 10am–2pm,
4–6pm. 🖼 🚫 ♿ ground floor.

In 1518 the first Marquess of Tarifa departed on a Grand Tour of Europe and the Holy Land. He returned two years later, enraptured by the architectural and decorative wonders of High Renaissance Italy. He spent the rest of his life fashioning a new aesthetic, which was very influential. His palace in Seville, called the House of Pilate because it was thought to resemble Pontius Pilate's home in Jerusalem, became a luxurious showcase for the new style.

Over the centuries, subsequent owners contributed their own embellishments. The Casa de Pilatos is now the residence of the Dukes of Medinaceli and is still one of the finest palaces in Seville.

Visitors enter it through a marble portal, commissioned by the Marquess in 1529 from Genoan craftsmen. Across the arcaded Apeadero (carriage yard) is the Patio Principal. This courtyard is essentially Mudéjar (see p22) in style and decorated with azulejos and intricate

plasterwork. It is surrounded by irregularly spaced arches capped with delicate Gothic balustrades. In its corners are three Roman statues, depicting Minerva, a dancing muse, and Ceres, and a fourth statue, a Greek original of Athena, dating from the 5th century BC. In its center is a fountain that was imported here from Genoa. To the right, through the Salón del Pretorio with its coffered ceiling and marquetry, is the Corredor de Zaquizamí. Among the antiquities in adjacent rooms are a bas-relief of Leda and the Swan and two Roman reliefs commemorating the Battle of Actium of 31 BC. Farther along, in the Jardín Chico, there is a pool with a bronze of Bacchus.

Lantern in the entrance portal

Coming back to the Patio Principal, you turn right into the Salón de Descanso de los Jueces. Beyond this is a rib-vaulted chapel, which has a sculpture dating from the 1st century AD, Christ and the Good Shepherd. Left through the Gabinete de Pilatos, with its small central fountain, is the Jardín Grande. The Italian architect Benvenuto Tortello created the loggias in the 1560s.

Returning once more to the main patio, behind the statue

of Ceres, a tiled staircase leads to the apartments on the upper floor. It is roofed with a wonderful media naranja (half orange) cupola built in 1537. There are Mudéjar ceilings in some rooms, which are filled with family portraits, antiques, and furniture. Plasterwork by Juan de Oviedo and frescoes by Francisco de Pacheco still survive in rooms that bear these artists' names.

West of the Casa de Pilatos, the Plaza de San Ildefonso is bounded by the Convento de San Leandro, famous for the yemas (sweets made from egg yolks) sold from a torno (drum). Opposite the convent is the Neo-Classical Iglesia de San Ildefonso, which has statues of San Hermenegildo and San Fernando by Pedro Roldán.

Escutcheons in the coffered ceiling of the Salón del Pretorio

Seville Cathedral and La Giralda ●

16th-century stained glass

S EVILLE'S CATHEDRAL occupies the site of a great mosque built by the Almohads *(see pp44–5)* in the late 12th century. La Giralda, its bell tower, and the Patio de los Naranjos are a legacy of this Moorish structure. Work on the Christian cathedral, the largest in Europe, began in 1401 and took just over a century to complete. As well as enjoying its Gothic immensity and the works of art in its chapels and Treasury, visitors can climb La Giralda for superb views of the city.

★ La Giralda
The Moorish bell tower is crowned with a 16th-century bronze portraying Faith. This weathervane (giraldillo) *has given La Giralda its name.*

Entrance

★ Patio de los Naranjos
In Moorish times worshipers would wash hands and feet in the fountain under the orange trees before praying.

THE RISE OF LA GIRALDA

The minaret was finished in 1198. In the 14th century the original Muslim bronze spheres at its top were replaced by Christian symbols. In 1568 Hernán Ruiz added the Renaissance belfry, which blends perfectly with the Moorish base.

| 1198 | 1400 | 1557 (plan) | 1568 |

Puerta del Perdón

Roman pillars brought from Itálica *(see p128)* surround the cathedral steps.

Retablo Mayor
*Santa María de la Sede,
the cathedral's patron
saint, sits at the high
altar below a waterfall
of gold. The 44 gilded
relief panels of the
retablo were carved
by Spanish and
Flemish sculptors
between 1482
and 1564.*

VISITORS' CHECKLIST

Plaza Virgen de los Reyes. **Map**
3 C2 (5 C4). ☎ (95) 456 33 21.
🚍 many routes. ◯ **Cathedral**
11am–5pm Mon–Sat; 2–4pm
Sun. **La Giralda** 11am–5pm Mon–
Sat; 10am–4pm Sun. 🚫 📷 ♿
✝ 8:30am, 9am, 10am, noon &
5pm Mon–Sat (Sat also at 1pm &
6pm); 11am, noon & 1pm Sun.

**The Sacristía
Mayor** houses
many works of
art, including
paintings by
Murillo.

★ Capilla Mayor
*The overwhelming, golden
Retablo Mayor in the
main chapel is
enclosed by
monumental iron
grilles forged in
1518–32.*

**The Tomb of
Columbus** dates
from the 1890s. His
coffin is carried by
bearers representing the
kingdoms of Castile, León,
Aragón, and Navarra *(see p46)*.

**Puerta
del Bautismo**

STAR FEATURES

★ La Giralda

★ Capilla Mayor

★ Patio de los
Naranjos

Iglesia del Sagrario,
a large 17th-century
chapel, is now used
as a parish church.

Puerta de la Asunción
*Though Gothic in style, this portal
was not completed until 1833. A
stone relief of the Assumption of the
Virgin decorates the tympanum.*

Upper part of the Baroque doorway of the Palacio Arzobispal

Plaza Virgen de los Reyes ❽

Map 3 C2 (6 D4). **Palacio Arzobispal**
⬤ *to the public.* **Convento de la
Encarnación** ⬤ *to the public.*

THE PERFECT PLACE to pause
for a while and admire the
Giralda *(see pp76–7)*, this plaza
presents an archetypal Sevillian
tableau: horse-drawn carriages,
orange trees, gypsy flower
sellers, and religious buildings.
At its center is an early 20th-
century monumental lamppost
and fountain by José Lafita,
with grotesque heads copied
from Roman originals in the
Casa de Pilatos *(see p75)*.

At the north of the square is
the Palacio Arzobispal (Archbishop's Palace), begun in the
16th century, finished in the
18th, and commandeered by
Marshal Soult during the
Napoleonic occupation of
1810 *(see pp50–51)*.
A fine Baroque
palace, it has a
jasper staircase
and paintings
by Zurbarán and
Murillo. On the
opposite side of

**Giralda relief on the Museo
de Arte Contemporáneo**

the square is the whitewashed
Convento de la Encarnación,
which was founded in 1591.
The convent stands on grounds
that have also been the site of
a mosque and of a hospital.

The Plaza Virgen de los Reyes
was once home to the Corral
de los Olmos, a rogues' inn
that is featured in the writings
of Miguel de Cervantes *(see
p49)* – on one of the convent
walls a plaque bears an inscrip-
tion testifying to this.

Plaza del Triunfo ❾

Map 3 C2 (6 D4). **Museo de Arte
Contemporáneo** Calle Santo Tomás 5.
📞 *(95) 421 58 30.* ⏰ *10am–8pm
Tue–Fri, 10am–2pm Sat & Sun.* ✍

LYING BETWEEN the cathedral
(see pp76–7) and Reales
Alcázares *(see pp80–81)*, the
Plaza del Triunfo was built
to celebrate the triumph of
the city over an
earthquake that
occurred here in
1755. The quake
devastated the
city of Lisbon,
over the border
in Portugal, but

caused comparatively little
damage in Seville – a salvation
attributed to the city's devotion
to the Virgin Mary. She is honored by a Baroque column
beside the Archivo de Indias,
and in the center of the Plaza
del Triunfo there is a modern
monument commemorating
Seville's long-held belief in
the Immaculate Conception.

In Calle Santo Tomás, which
leads off from the southeastern
corner of the Plaza del Triunfo,
the Museo de Arte Contemp-
ráneo has regularly changing
exhibitions of contemporary art.
It was built in 1770 and was
once a barn where tithe
collected by the Church was
stored. Parts of the Moorish city
walls were uncovered during
the renovation of the building.

Archivo de Indias ❿

Avda de la Constitución s/n. **Map** 3 C2
(6 D5). 📞 *(95) 421 12 34.* ⏰ *10am–
1pm Mon–Fri (research 8am–3pm).* ✍

**Façade of the Archivo de Indias
by Juan de Herrera**

THE ARCHIVE of the Indies
punches home Seville's pre-
eminent role in the colonization
and exploitation of the New
World. Built between 1584–98
to designs by Juan de Herrera,
coarchitect of El Escorial near
Madrid, it was originally a *lonja*
(exchange), where merchants
traded. In 1785 Carlos III had
all Spanish documents relating
to the "Indies" collected under
one roof, creating a fascinating
archive. It contains letters from
Columbus, Cortés, Cervantes,
and George Washington, the
first American president, and

the extensive correspondence of Felipe II. The vast collection amounts to some 86 million handwritten pages and 8,000 maps and drawings. Some of the documents are now being stored digitally on CD-ROM.

Visitors to the Archivo de Indias climb marble stairs to library rooms where drawings, maps, and facsimile documents are exhibited in a reverential atmosphere. Displays change on a regular basis; one might include a watercolor map from the days when the city of Acapulco was little more than a castle, drawings recording a royal *corrida* (bullfight) that was held in Panama City in 1748, or designs and plans for a town hall in Guatemala.

Reales Alcázares ⓫

See pp80–81.

Hospital de los Venerables ⓬

Plaza de los Venerables 8. **Map** 3 C2 (6 D4). ☎ *(95) 456 26 96.* ○ *10am–2pm, 4–8pm daily.* 🖾 🖾

LOCATED IN THE HEART of the Barrio de Santa Cruz, the Hospital of the Venerables was founded as a home for elderly priests. It was begun in 1675 and completed around 20 years later by Leonardo de Figueroa. The Hospital has recently been restored as a cultural center by FOCUS (Fundación Fondo de Cultura de Sevilla).

It is built around a central, rose-colored, sunken patio. Stairs lead to the upper floors, which, along with the infirm-ary and the cellar, are used as galleries for exhibitions. A separate guided tour visits the Hospital church, a showcase of Baroque splendors, with frescoes by Juan de Valdés Leal and his son Lucas Valdés.

Other highlights include the sculptures of St. Peter and St. Ferdinand by Pedro Roldán, flanking the east door; and *The Apotheosis of St. Ferdinand* by Lucas Valdés, top center in the *retablo* of the main altar. Its frieze (inscribed in Greek) advises visitors to "Fear God and Honor the Priest."

In the sacristy, the ceiling has an effective *trompe l'oeil* depicting *The Triumph of the Cross* by Juan de Valdés Leal.

Jardines de Murillo ⓭

Map 4 D2 (6 E5).

THESE FORMAL GARDENS at the southern end of the Barrio de Santa Cruz used to be orchards and vegetable plots in the grounds of the Reales Alcázares. They were donated to the city in 1911. Their name commemorates Seville's best-known painter, Bartolomé Murillo (1617–82), who lived in nearby Calle Santa Teresa. A long promenade, Paseo de Catalina de Ribera, pays tribute to the founder of the Hospital de las Cinco Llagas, which is now the seat of the Parlamento de Andalucía *(see p87)*. Rising

Monument to Columbus in the Jardines de Murillo

above the garden's palm trees is a monument to Columbus, incorporating a bronze of the *Santa María*, the caravel that bore him to the New World in the year of 1492 *(see p123)*.

Fresco by Juan de Valdés Leal in the Hospital de los Venerables

Reales Alcázares ⑪

Mudéjar stucco

IN 1364 PEDRO I *(see p46)* ordered the construction of a royal residence within the palaces built by the city's Almohad *(see pp44–5)* rulers. Within two years, craftsmen from Granada and Toledo had created a jewel box of Mudéjar patios and halls, the Palacio Pedro I, which now forms the heart of Seville's Reales Alcázares. Later monarchs added their own distinguishing marks – Isabel I *(see p47)* dispatched navigators to explore the New World from her Casa de la Contratación, while Carlos V *(see p48)* had grandiose, richly decorated apartments built.

Jardín de Troya

Gardens of the Alcázares
Laid out with terraces, fountains, and pavilions, these gardens provide a delightful refuge from the heat and bustle of Seville.

★ **Salones de Carlos V**
Vast tapestries and lively 16th-century azulejos decorate the vaulted halls of the apartments and chapel of Carlos V.

Patio del Crucero lies above the old baths.

PLAN OF THE REALES ALCÁZARES

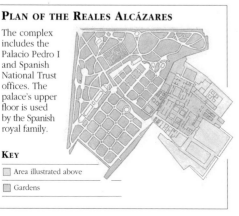

The complex includes the Palacio Pedro I and Spanish National Trust offices. The palace's upper floor is used by the Spanish royal family.

KEY

▢ Area illustrated above

▢ Gardens

★ **Patio de las Doncellas**
The Patio of the Maidens boasts plasterwork by the top craftsmen of Granada.

★ **Salón de Embajadores**
Built in 1427, the dazzling dome of the Ambassadors' Hall is made up of carved and gilded interlaced wood.

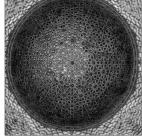

VISITORS' CHECKLIST

Plaza del Triunfo. **Map** 3 C2 (6 D4).
📞 (95) 422 71 63. 🚌 C3, C4, 21, 22, 23, 25, 26, 30, 31, 33, 34, 40, 41, 42. ⬜ 10:30am–5pm Tue–Sat, 10am–1pm Sun. 📷 ♿

Horseshoe Arches
Azulejos and complex plasterwork decorate the Ambassadors' Hall, which has three symmetrically arranged, ornate archways, each with three horseshoe arches.

Casa de la Contratación

The Patio de la Montería was where the court met before hunting expeditions.

Patio de las Muñecas
With its adjacent bedrooms and corridors, the Patio of the Dolls was the domestic heart of the palace. It derives its name from two tiny faces that decorate one of its arches.

The façade of the Palacio Pedro I is a unique example of Mudéjar style.

Puerta del León (entrance)

Patio del Yeso
The Patio of Plaster, a garden with flower beds and a water channel, retains features of the earlier 12th-century Almohad Alcázar.

STAR FEATURES

★ **Patio de las Doncellas**

★ **Salón de Embajadores**

★ **Salones de Carlos V**

LA MACARENA

THE NORTH OF Seville, often overlooked by visitors, presents a characterful mix of decaying Baroque and Mudéjar churches, old-style neighborhood tapas bars and laundry-filled backstreets. Its name is thought to be derived from the Roman goddess, Macaria, the daughter of the hero Hercules. La Macarena is a traditional district, and the power of church and family is still strong there.

The best way to enter this quarter is to walk north up Calle Feria to the Basílica de la Macarena, a cult-worship shrine to Seville's much-venerated Virgen de la Esperanza Macarena. Beside this

Roman column, Alameda de Hércules

modern church stands a restored entrance gate and remnants of defensive walls, which enclosed the city during the Moorish era.

Among many churches and convents in this quarter, the Monasterio de San Clemente and Iglesia de San Pedro retain the spirit of historic Seville, and the Convento de Santa Paula offers a rare opportunity to peep behind the walls of a closed religious community. The 13th-century Torre de Don Fadrique in Convento de Santa Clara is a notable sight to the west of the area. Farther north is the former Hospital de las Cinco Llagas, now restored as the seat of Andalusia's Parliament.

SIGHTS AT A GLANCE

Churches and Convents
Basílica de la Macarena ❹
Convento de Santa Paula ❽
Iglesia de San Marcos ❼
Iglesia de San Pedro ❾
Iglesia de Santa Catalina ❿
Monasterio de San Clemente ❶

Historic Buildings
Parlamento de Andalucía ❺
Torre de Don Fadrique ❷

Monuments
Murallas ❻

Markets
Alameda de Hércules ❸

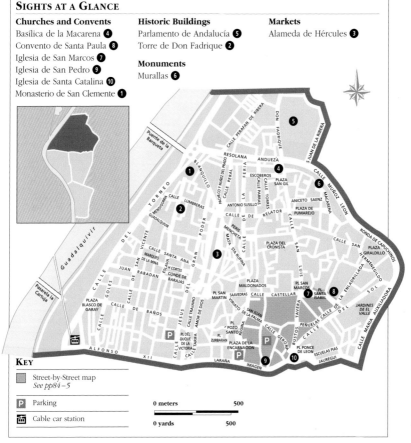

KEY

▨ Street-by-Street map
See pp84–5

🅿 Parking

🚡 Cable car station

0 meters   500

0 yards   500

◁ **Float of Virgen de la Esperanza Macarena during the Semana Santa processions**

Street-by-Street: La Macarena

Tiled image of
Santa Paula

A STROLL IN THIS AREA provides a glimpse of everyday life in a part of Seville that has so far escaped developing the rather tourist-oriented atmosphere of Santa Cruz. Calle de la Feria, the main street for shopping and browsing, is best visited in the morning when there is plenty of activity and its market stalls are filled with fresh fish and vegetables. Early evening, meanwhile, is a good time to discover the area's large number of fine churches, which are open for Mass at that time. It is also the time when local people visit the bars of the district for a drink and tapas.

Palacio de las Dueñas, boxed in by the surrounding streets and houses, is a 15th-century Mudéjar palace with an elegant main patio. It is the private residence of the Dukes of Alba, whose tiled coat of arms can be seen above the palace entrance.

Iglesia San Juan de la Palma is a small Mudéjar church. Its brickwork belfry was added in 1788.

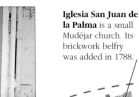

Calle de la Feria is a lively street full of small shops. Thursday morning is the busiest time, when *El Jueves*, Seville's oldest market, takes place.

★ Iglesia de San Pedro
The church where Velázquez was baptized is a mix of styles, from Mudéjar to these modern tiles on its front **9**

In Convento de Santa Inés the nuns make and sell cakes.

KEY

- - - Suggested route

★ Iglesia de San Marcos
This 14th-century church, built on the site of a mosque, has a Mudéjar tower and a beautiful Mudéjar-Gothic portal. The interior preserves unique horseshoe arches **7**

LOCATOR MAP
See Street Finder, maps 2, 5

★ Convento de Santa Paula
The convent church portal is a perfect blend of Gothic, Mudéjar, and Renaissance **8**

San Román is a Mudéjar-Gothic church, popular with the large number of gypsies in Seville.

El Rinconcillo bar is said to be the place where tapas were first invented. Dating back to 1670, it has a suitably old-fashioned atmosphere and a fine selection of food *(see p222).*

| 0 meters | | 75 |
| 0 yards | | 75 |

Iglesia de Santa Catalina
Gothic Santa Catalina has a Mudéjar tower and apse and, inside, a statue of Santa Lucía, patron saint of the blind, by Roldán **10**

STAR SIGHTS

★ **Convento de Santa Paula**

★ **Iglesia de San Marcos**

★ **Iglesia de San Pedro**

Monasterio de San Clemente ❶

Calle Yuste. **Map** 1 C3. 🅲 *(95)* 437 80 40. **Church** ⭕ *for Mass only. For info on temporary art exhibitions call tourist office* 🅲 *(95) 422 14 04.*

Bᴇʜɪɴᴅ ᴛʜᴇ ancient walls of the Monasterio de San Clemente is a tranquil cloister with palms and fruit trees, and an arcade with a side entrance to the monastery's church.

This atmospheric church can also be entered through an arch in Calle Reposo. Its features range from the 13th to 18th centuries, and include a fine Mudéjar *artesonado* ceiling, *azulejos (see p74)* dating from 1588, a Baroque main *retablo* by Felipe de Rivas, and early 18th-century frescoes by Lucas Valdés.

Torre de Don Fadrique ❷

Convento de Santa Clara, Calle Santa Clara 40. **Map** 1 C4. 🅲 *(95)* 437 99 05. ⭕ *11am–5:30pm Mon– Fri.* ⬤ *public hols.*

Oɴᴇ ᴏꜰ ᴛʜᴇ best-preserved historical surprises in Seville, this 13th-century tower stands like a chess-piece castle

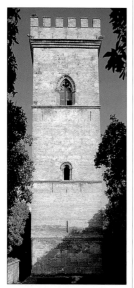

Torre de Don Fadrique in the patio of Convento de Santa Clara

Bric-a-brac in the Sunday morning flea market on Alameda de Hércules

in the Convento de Santa Clara. This is entered from Calle Santa Clara, passing through an arch to a sleepy patio with orange trees and a fountain. To the left is a second courtyard where the tower is situated. The courtyard entrance has a Gothic portal, constructed during the 16th century as part of Seville's first university and transplanted here in the 19th century.

Constructed in 1252, the tower formed part of the defenses for the palace of the Infante Don Fadrique. On the façade Romanesque windows sit below Gothic ones. More than 80 steps lead to the upper floor, from which there are impressive views across the city toward La Giralda and Puente de la Barqueta.

The convent of Santa Clara was founded in 1260, though the present buildings date from the 15th century. The Mannerist entrance portico is by Juan de Oviedo. Inside, the nave has a Mudéjar coffered ceiling and an outstanding main *retablo* sculpted by Juan Martínez Montañés in 1623.

Gargoyle on the Torre de Don Fadrique

Alameda de Hércules ❸

Map 2 D4.

Tʜɪs ᴅᴜsᴛʏ, tree-lined boulevard was originally laid out in 1574. The former marshy area was thus turned into a fashionable promenade for use by *sevillanos* of the Golden Age *(see pp48–9).*

These days the Sunday morning flea market is the main draw. You can buy all sorts of bric-a-brac, from rusty farming tools to brass ornaments, paintings, and old photographs.

At the southern end of the boulevard stand two marble columns. They were brought here from a Roman temple dedicated to Hercules in what is now Calle Mármoles (Marbles Street), where three other columns remain. Time-worn statues of Hercules and Julius Caesar cap the Alameda's columns, standing suitably aloof from what has long been one of Seville's seedier areas.

Basílica de la Macarena ❹

Calle Macarena s/n. **Map** 2 D3.
☎ *(95) 437 01 95.* ○ *9:30am–12:30pm, 5–7pm daily.* **Treasury**
○ *9am–1pm, 5–9pm daily.*

T HE BASÍLICA de la Macarena was built in 1949 in the Neo-Baroque style by Gómez Millán as a new home for the much-loved Virgen de la Esperanza Macarena. It abuts the 13th-century Iglesia de San Gil, where the Virgin was housed until a fire in 1936.

The adored image of the Virgin stands above the principal altar amid waterfalls of gold and silver. It has been attributed to Luisa Roldán (1656–1703), the most talented woman artist of the Seville School. A chapel on the east wall includes a sculpture made by Morales Nieto in 1654, *Christ under Sentence.*

The wall paintings, by Rafael Rodríguez Hernández, were not executed until 1982. The themes focus on the Virgin Mary, such as a scene of the Immaculate Conception.

In a room to the right of the main entrance you can buy mementos associated with the

Float of the Virgen de la Macarena in Semana Santa processions

Virgin, and tickets for the museum entirely devoted to her cult, which is housed in the Treasury. Among a wealth of magnificent processional garments and props are gowns made from *trajes de luces* (suits of lights) donated by famous and no doubt grateful bull-fighters. There is also a display of the Virgin's jewels. The floats used in Semana Santa *(see p36),* among them La Macarena's elaborate silver platform, can also be admired.

VIRGEN DE LA MACARENA

Devotions to the Virgen de la Macarena reach their peak during Semana Santa *(see p36),* when her statue is carried through the streets on a canopied float decorated with white flowers, candles, and ornate silverwork. Accompanied by hooded penitents and cries of *¡guapa!* (beautiful!) from her followers, the procession travels along a route taking it from the Basílica de la Macarena to the cathedral in the early hours of Good Friday.

Renaissance façade and Baroque portal of Parlamento de Andalucía

Parlamento de Andalucía ❺

Plaza de la Macarena. **Map** 2 E3.
Visits by written application or call tourist office ☎ *(95) 422 14 04.*

T HE PARLIAMENT of Andalusia has its seat in an impressive Renaissance building, the Hospital de las Cinco Llagas (five wounds). The hospital, founded in 1500 by Catalina de Ribera, was originally located near Casa de Pilatos.

In 1540 work began on what was to become Europe's largest hospital, with over 1,000 beds. Designed by a succession of architects, its rusticated south front has a Baroque central portal by Asensio de Maeda.

The hospital was completed in 1613 and admitted patients until the 1960s. In 1992 it was restored for the Parliament.

At the heart of the complex, the Mannerist church, built as part of the hospital in 1560 by Hernán Ruiz the Younger, has today been converted into an austere debating chamber.

Virgen de la Macarena – the main reredos in Basílica de la Macarena

Murallas ❻

Map 2 E3.

Asection of the defensive walls that once enclosed Seville survives along calles Andueza and Muñoz León. It runs from the rebuilt Puerta de la Macarena at the Basílica de la Macarena (see p87) to the Puerta de Córdoba some 400 m (1,300 ft) farther east.

Dating from the 12th century, it was constructed as a curtain wall with a patrol path in the middle. The original walls had over 100 towers; the Torre Blanca is one of seven that can be seen here. At the eastern end stands the 17th-century Iglesia de San Hermenegildo, named after the Visigothic king who was allegedly martyred on the site. On the southern corner of this church remains of Moorish arches can be seen.

Iglesia de San Marcos ❼

Plaza de San Marcos 10. **Map** 2 E5 (6E1). ☎ (95) 421 14 25. ◯ 8–9pm Mon–Fri.

This 14th-century church retains several Mudéjar features, notably its Giralda-like tower (based on the minaret of an earlier mosque) and the decoration on the Gothic portal on Plaza de San Marcos. The restoration of the interior, gutted by fire in 1936, has highlighted unique horseshoe arches in the nave. A statue of St. Mark with book and quill pen, attributed to Juan de Mesa, is in the far left corner. In the plaza at the back of the

The Gothic-Mudéjar portal of the 14th-century Iglesia de San Marcos

church is the Convento de Santa Isabel, founded in 1490. It became a women's prison in the 19th century. The church dates from 1609. Its Baroque portal, facing onto Plaza de Santa Isabel, has a bas-relief of *The Visitation* sculpted by Andrés de Ocampo.

Convento de Santa Paula ❽

C/ Santa Paula 11. **Map** 2 E5 (6 F1). ☎ (95) 442 13 07. ◯ 10:30am–1pm, 4:30–6:30pm daily. ☑

Seville has many enclosed religious complexes, but few are accessible. This is one of them, a convent set up in 1475 and still home to 40 nuns. The public is welcome to enter through two different doors in the Calle Santa Paula. Knock on the brown one, marked No. 11, to have a look at the convent museum. Steps lead to two galleries crammed with

religious paintings and artifacts. The windows of the second look onto the nuns' cloister, which echoes with laughter in the afternoon recreation hour. The nuns make a phenomenal range of marmalades and jams, which visitors may purchase in a room near the exit.

Ring the bell by a brick doorway nearby to visit the convent church, reached by crossing a meditative garden. Its portal vividly combines Gothic arches, Mudéjar brickwork, Renaissance medallions, and ceramics by the Italian artist, Niculoso Pisano. Inside, the nave has an elaborate wooden roof carved in 1623. Among its statues are St. John the Evangelist and St. John the Baptist, carved by Juan Martínez Montañés.

St. John the Baptist by Montañés in the Convento de Santa Paula

---

SEVILLIAN BELL TOWERS

Bell towers rise above the rooftops of Seville like bookmarks flagging the passing centuries. The influence of La Giralda (see p76) is seen in the Moorish arches and tracery adorning the 14th-century tower of San Marcos, and the Mudéjar brickwork that forms the base for San Pedro's belfry. The churches of Santa Paula and La Magdalena reflect the ornate confidence of the Baroque period, and the towers of San Ildefonso illustrate the Neo-Classical tastes of the 19th century.

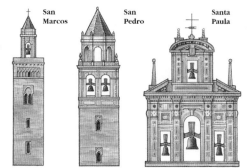

Intricate pattern on a chapel door in the Iglesia de San Pedro

Iglesia de San Pedro ❾

Calle Doña María Coronel 1. **Map** 2 D5 (6 E2). **(** (95) 421 68 58. ☐ 7–10pm Mon–Sat; 9am–noon, 7–8pm Sun.

THE CHURCH where the painter Diego Velázquez was baptized in 1599 presents a typically Sevillian mix of architectural styles. Mudéjar elements survive in the lobed brickwork of its tower, which is surmounted by a Baroque belfry. The principal portal, facing Plaza de San Pedro, is another Baroque adornment added by Diego de Quesada in 1613. A statue of St. Peter looks disdainfully down at the heathen traffic below.

The poorly lit interior has a Mudéjar wooden ceiling and west door. The vault of one of its chapels is decorated with exquisite geometric patterns formed of interlacing bricks. Behind the church, in Calle Doña María Coronel, cakes and cookies are sold from a revolving drum in the wall of the Convento de Santa Inés. An arcaded patio fronts its restored church, with frescoes by Francisco de Herrera and a nun's choir separated from the public by a screen. The preserved body of Doña María Coronel, the convent's 14th-century founder, is honored in the choir every December 2.

Iglesia de Santa Catalina ❿

Calle Santa Catalina s/n. **Map** 2 D5 (6 E2). **(** (95) 421 74 41. ☐ 7pm–8pm Mon–Fri.

BUILT ON THE FORMER site of a mosque, this 14th-century church has a Mudéjar tower modeled on La Giralda *(see p76)* (best viewed from Plaza Ponce de Léon) that has been spared the customary Baroque hat. On the west side, by Calle Alhóndiga, the Gothic portal is originally from the Iglesia de Santa Lucía, which was knocked down in 1930. Within its entrance is a surprisingly placed horseshoe arch. At the far left end of the nave, the Capilla Sacramental is by Leonardo de Figueroa. On the right, the Capilla de la Exaltación has a decorative ceiling from about 1400 and a figure of Christ, the work of Pedro Roldán.

Detail of horseshoe arch in the Iglesia de Santa Catalina

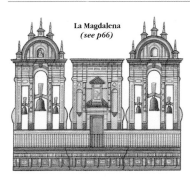
La Magdalena *(see p66)*

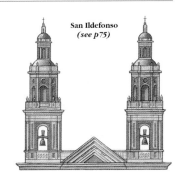
San Ildefonso *(see p75)*

PARQUE MARÍA LUISA

THE AREA SOUTH of the city center is dominated by the extensive, leafy Parque María Luisa, Seville's principal green area. A great part of it originally formed the grounds of the Baroque Palacio de San Telmo, dating from 1682. Today the park is devoted to recreation; with its fountains, flower gardens, and mature trees it provides a welcome place to relax during the long, hot summer months. Just north of the park lies Prado de San Sebastián, the former site of the *quemadero*, the platform

Ceramic urn in the Parque María Luisa

where many victims of the Inquisition (*see p49*) were burned do death. The last execution took place here in 1781.

Many of the historic buildings situated within the park were erected for the Ibero-American Exposition of 1929. This international jamboree sought to reinstate Spain and Andalusia on the world map. Exhibitions from Spain, Portugal and Latin America were displayed in attractive, custom-built pavilions that are today used as museums, embassies, military headquarters, and also cultural and educational institutions. The grand five-star Hotel Alfonso XIII and the crescent-shaped Plaza de España are the most striking legacies from this surge of Andalusian pride. Nearby is the Royal Tobacco Factory, forever associated with the fictional gypsy heroine, Carmen, who toiled in its sultry halls. Today it is part of the Universidad, Seville's university.

SIGHTS AT A GLANCE

Museums
Museo Arqueológico ⑦
Museo de Artes y Costumbres Populares ⑥

Theaters
Teatro Lope de Vega ④

Gardens
Parque María Luisa pp96–7 ⑤

Historic Buildings
Hotel Alfonso XIII ①
Palacio de San Telmo ②
Universidad ③

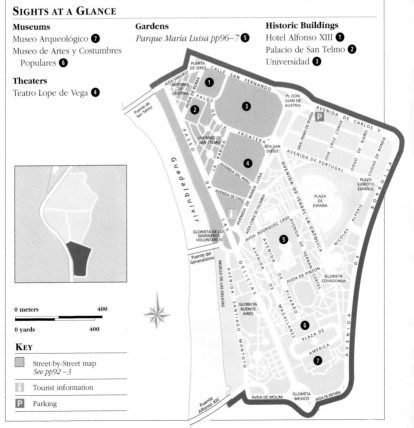

0 meters 400
0 yards 400

KEY

	Street-by-Street map See pp92–3
i	Tourist information
P	Parking

◁ **Horse-drawn carriage on Calle San Fernando**

Street-by-Street: Around the Universidad

Statue of El Cid by Anna Huntington

SOUTH OF the Puerta de Jerez, a cluster of stately buildings stands between the river and Parque María Luisa. The oldest ones owe their existence to the Guadalquivir itself – the 17th-century Palacio de San Telmo was built as a training school for mariners – and the arrival of tobacco from the New World prompted the construction of the monumental Royal Tobacco Factory, today the Universidad de Sevilla. The 1929 Ibero-American Exposition added pavilions in various national and historic styles and also the opulent Hotel Alfonso XIII, creating an area of proud and pleasing architecture that will entertain visitors as they walk toward the Parque María Luisa.

To Triana

Paseo de las Delicias, a riverside walk flanking the Jardines de San Telmo, is a busy road despite its name, the "walk of delights."

Pabellón de Chile is now the Escuela de Artes Aplicadas (School of Applied Arts).

Pabellón de Perú, which is modeled on the Archbishop's Palace in Lima, has a vividly carved façade. It is typical of the nationalistic designs used for the Exposition buildings.

Pabellón de Uruguay

PASEO DE LAS DELICIAS

LA RABIDA

GUADALQUIVIR

Costurero de la Reina, the "Queen's sewing box," used to be a garden lodge that Princess María Luisa enjoyed visiting. Today it houses the municipal tourist office.

AVENIDA DE MARIA LUISA

Monument to El Cano, who completed the first world circumnavigation in 1522 after Magellan was killed on route.

0 meters   75
0 yards   75

KEY

- - -   Suggested route

★ Palacio de San Telmo

Originally a mariners' college, this palace now houses the Junta de Andalucía. Presiding over its Churrigueresque doorway is a statue of St. Telmo ❷

LOCATOR MAP
See Street Finder, maps 2, 5

To Santa Cruz

AVENIDA DE ROMA

PALOS DE LA FRONTERA

LA RABIDA

Hotel Alfonso XIII
Seville's premier hotel, with a sumptuous Neo-Mudéjar interior, welcomes non-guests to have a drink in its elegant bar ❶

AVENIDA DEL CID

To Parque María Luisa

★ Universidad

The vast 18th-century former Royal Tobacco Factory has many fine features, including this Baroque fountain ❸

Teatro Lope de Vega
This grandiose theater and casino, the 1929 Pabellón de Sevilla, is now a major spot for staging the arts and exhibitions ❹

STAR SIGHTS

★ Palacio de San Telmo

★ Universidad

Hotel Alfonso XIII ❶

Calle San Fernando 2. **Map** 3 C3
(6 D5). **[** *(95) 422 28 58.* **&** *except toilets.*

A T THE SOUTHEAST corner of Puerta de Jerez is Seville's best-known luxury hotel. This is named in honor of King Alfonso XIII *(see p52)*, who reigned from 1902 until 1931, when Spain became a republic. It was built between 1916–28 for visitors to the 1929 Ibero-American Exposition *(see p53)*. The building is in Regionalista style, decorated with *azulejos (see p74)*, wrought iron, and ornate brickwork. Its center-piece is a grand patio with a fountain and orange trees. Nonresidents are welcome to visit the bar or to dine in the hotel's Itálica restaurant.

Churrigueresque adornments of the portal of Palacio de San Telmo

Palacio de San Telmo ❷

Avenida de Roma s/n. **Map** 3 C3.
[*(95) 459 75 05. Visits by pre-arranged appointment only.* **✗**

T HIS IMPOSING PALACE was built in 1682 to serve as a marine university, training ships' pilots, navigators, and high-ranking officers. It is named after St. Telmo, the patron saint of navi-gators. In 1849 the palace became the private residence of the Dukes of Montpensier – until 1893 its vast grounds included what is now the Parque María Luisa *(pp96 – 7)*.

Central patio with fountain in the elegant Hotel Alfonso XIII

The building became a semi-nary in 1901, and today it is the presidential headquarters of the Junta de Andalucía (the regional government).

The palace's star feature is the exuberant Churrigueresque portal overlooking Avenida de Roma by Antonio Matías de Figueroa, completed in 1734. Surrounding the Ionic columns are allegorical figures of the Arts and Sciences. St. Telmo can be seen holding a ship and charts, flanked by the sword-bearing St. Ferdinand and St. Hermenegildo with a cross. The north façade, which is on Avenida de Palos de la Frontera, is crowned by a row of Sevillian celebrities. These sculptures were added in 1895 by Susillo. Among them are representations of several notable artists such as Murillo, Velázquez, and Montañés.

Façade detail of the Universidad

Universidad ❸

Calle San Fernando 4. **Map** 3 C3.
[*(95) 455 10 00.* **◻** *8am–8:30pm Mon–Fri.* **●** *public hols.*

T HE FORMER Real Fábrica de Tabacos (Royal Tobacco Factory) is now part of Seville University. It was a popular attraction for 19th-century travelers in search of Romantic Spain. Three-quarters of Europe's cigars were then manufactured here. They were rolled on the thighs of over 3,000 *cigar-reras* (female cigar makers), who were "reputed to be more impertinent than chaste," as the writer Richard Ford observed in his 1845 *Handbook for Spain*. The factory complex is the largest building in Spain after El Escorial in Madrid and was built between 1728–71. The

CARMEN

The hot-blooded *cigarreras* working in Seville's Royal Tobacco Factory inspired the French author Prosper Mérimée to create his famous gypsy heroine, *Carmen*. The short story he wrote in 1845 tells the tragic tale of a sensual and wild woman who turns her affections from a soldier to a bullfighter and is then murdered by her spurned lover. Bizet based his famous opera of 1875 on this impassioned drama, which established Carmen as an in-carnation of Spanish romance.

Carmen and Don José

moat and watchtowers are evidence of the importance given to protecting the king's lucrative tobacco monopoly. To the right of the main entrance, on Calle San Fernando, is the former prison where workers caught smuggling tobacco were kept. To the left is the chapel, which is now used by university students.

The discovery of tobacco in the New World is celebrated in the principal portal, which has busts of Columbus *(see p123)* and Cortés. This part of the factory was once used as residential quarters – to either side of the vestibule lie small patios with plants and green ironwork. Ahead, the Clock Patio and Fountain Patio lead to the former working areas. The tobacco leaves were first dried on the roof, then shredded by donkey-powered mills below. Production now takes place in a modern factory situated on the other side of the river, by the Puente del Generalísimo.

Baroque fountain in one of the patios in the Universidad

Teatro Lope de Vega ➍

Avenida María Luisa s/n. **Map** 3 C3.
(95) 423 45 46 (ticket office with answer phone).

L OPE DE VEGA (1562–1635), often called "the Spanish Shakespeare," was a brilliant and prolific playwright who wrote more than 1,500 plays. This Neo-Baroque theater, which honors his name, was opened in 1929 as a casino and theater for the Ibero-American Exposition *(see p53)*. Its colon-

Dome of the Neo-Baroque Teatro Lope de Vega, opened in 1929

naded and domed buildings are still used to stage performances and exhibitions *(see pp230–31)*. Visitors to the Café del Casino have an opportunity to relax and to enjoy a coffee amid its faded opulence.

Parque María Luisa ➎

See pp96–7.

Museo de Artes y Costumbres Populares ➏

Pabellón Mudéjar, Parque María Luisa.
Map 4 D5. *(95) 423 25 76.*
9am–2:30pm Tue–Sun.

H OUSED IN the Mudéjar Pavilion of the 1929 Ibero-American Exposition *(see p53)*, this museum is devoted to the popular arts and traditions of Andalusia. Exhibits in the basement include a series of workshop scenes detailing

crafts such as leatherwork, ceramics, and cooperage. There is also an informative account of the history of the *azulejo*. Upstairs is a display of 19th-century costumes, accessories, furniture, musical instruments, and rural machinery. Romantic images of flamenco, bull-fighting, and the Semana Santa and Feria de Abril *(see p36)* amount to a compendium of the Sevillian cliché.

Museo Arqueológico ➐

Parque María Luisa. **Map** 4 D5.
(95) 423 24 01. 9am–2pm Tue–Sun.

T HE RENAISSANCE PAVILION of the 1929 Ibero-American Exposition is now Andalusia's museum of provincial archae-ology. The basement houses finds from Paleolithic to early Roman times, such as copies of the remarkable Tartessian Carambolo treasures *(see p41)*. This hoard of 6th-century BC gold jewelry was discovered near Seville in 1958.

Upstairs, the main galleries are devoted to the Roman era, with statues and fragments from Itálica *(see p128)*. Highlights include a 3rd-century BC mosaic from Écija *(see p129)* and sculptures of local-born emperors Trajan and Hadrian. The rooms continue to Moorish Spain via Palaeo-Christian sarcophagi, Visigothic relics, and artifacts discovered at Medina Azahara *(see p134)*.

Museo de Artes y Costumbres Populares, the former Mudéjar Pavilion

Parque María Luisa ⑤

Statue of María Luisa (1929)

Tʜɪs ᴠᴀsᴛ ᴘᴀʀᴋ takes its name from Princess María Luisa de Orleans, who donated part of the grounds from the Palacio de San Telmo *(see p94)* to the city in 1893. The area was landscaped by Jean-Claude Forestier, director of the Bois de Boulogne in Paris, who created a leafy setting for the pastiche pavilions of the 1929 Ibero-American Exposition *(see p53)*. The most dazzling souvenirs from this extravaganza are the Plaza de España and Plaza de América, both the work of Aníbal González, which set the park's theatrical mood. Sprinkling fountains, flowers, and cool, tree-shaded avenues all go to make this park a refreshing retreat from the heat and dust of the city.

★ Plaza de España
Tiled benches line this semicircular plaza, centerpiece of the 1929 Exposition.

Glorieta de la Infanta
has a bronze statue honoring the park's benefactor, the Princess María Luisa de Orleans.

Starting point for horse-and-carriage rides

Glorieta de Bécquer
Allegorical figures, depicting the phases of love, add charm to this tribute to Gustavo Adolfo Bécquer (1836–70), the Romantic Sevillian poet. It was sculpted by Lorenzo Coullaut Valera in 1911.

Isleta de los Patos
In the center of the park is a lake graced by ducks and swans. A gazebo situated on an island provides a peaceful resting place.

Fuente de los Leones
Ceramic lions guard this octagonal fountain, which is surrounded by myrtle hedges. Its design was inspired by the fountain in the Patio de los Leones at the Alhambra (see p187).

★ **Museo de Artes y Costumbres Populares**
The pavilions of Plaza de América evoke the triumph of the Mudéjar, Gothic, and Renaissance styles. The Pabellón Mudéjar houses a museum of Andalusian folk arts ❻

Pabellón Real

The Monte Gurugú is a minimountain with a tumbling waterfall.

★ **Museo Arqueológico**
The Neo-Renaissance Pabellón de las Bellas Artes today houses a regional archaeological museum. Many finds from nearby Roman Itálica (see p128) are among the exhibits ❼

Ceramics
Brightly painted Sevillian ceramics from Triana decorate the park in the form of floral urns, tiled benches, and playful frogs and ducks placed around the fountains.

STAR FEATURES

★ **Plaza de España**

★ **Museo Arqueológico**

★ **Museo de Artes y Costumbres Populares**

ACROSS THE RIVER

O N THE WEST BANK of the Guadalquivir, old Seville meets the new. Since Roman times, pottery has been made in Triana, which was named after the emperor Trajan. It has traditionally been a working-class district, famous for the bullfighters and flamenco artists that came from its predominantly gypsy community. With cobbled streets and shops selling ceramics, it still has an authentic, lived-in feel. Iglesia de Santa Ana is a fine Mudéjar-Gothic church. From the riverside restaurants and bars along Calle Betis there are views of Seville's towers and belfries.

Tile from Triana, a manufacturing center for *azulejos* and ceramics

In the 15th century, a Carthusian monastery was built in what was then a quiet, isolated area north of Triana – hence the name that the district acquired: Isla de la Cartuja. Later Columbus resided here, planning his future exploits. Mainly due to this connection, La Cartuja was the site for Expo '92 *(see pp102–03)*. The monastery buildings were restored and several pavilions of strikingly modern design built at considerable cost. The Expo site has been redeveloped into different theme parks. Some of the pavilions are still in use, such as Omnimax, a hi-tech movie theater.

SIGHTS AT A GLANCE

Theme Parks
Espacio Cultural Puerta
   Triana ❸
Parque Científico y
   Tecnológico ❷
Parque Temático ❶

Traditional Areas
Triana pp100–101 ❺

Churches and Monasteries
Iglesia de Nuestra Señora
   de la O ❻
Iglesia de Santa Ana ❼
Monasterio de Santa María de
   las Cuevas ❹

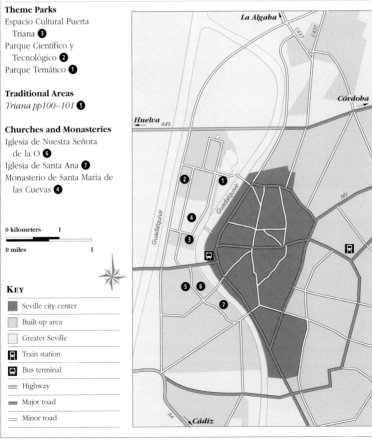

0 kilometers   1

0 miles   1

KEY

▓	Seville city center
▢	Built-up area
▢	Greater Seville
🚆	Train station
🚌	Bus terminal
═	Highway
▬	Major road
─	Minor road

◁ **Pabellón de Andalucía, built for the Expo '92 on Isla de la Cartuja**

Triana ❺

NAMED AFTER the Roman emperor Trajan, this quarter has, since early times, been famous for its potteries. Plenty of workshops still produce and sell tiles and ceramics. Once Seville's gypsy quarter, this *barrio* also has a reputation for producing great bull-fighters, sailors, and flamenco artists. It remains a traditional working-class district, with compact, flower-filled streets and a tangibly independent atmosphere. Visitors to Triana can buy tiles and wander through its narrow streets during the day, and enjoy the lively bars and romantic views across the Río Guadalquivir at night.

Statue, Plaza del Altozano

To Nuestra Señora de la O
(see p103)

Callejón de la Inquisición

CASTILLA

ANTILLANO CAMPOS

SAN JORGE

PLAZA ALTOZ

SAN JACINTO

COVADONGA

RODRIGO

DE TRIANA

Cerámica Santa Ana
Founded in 1870, this is the best known of Triana's tile shops. It sells anything from replicas of 16th-century tiles to ashtrays.

Plaza del Altozano
At the west end of Puente de Isabel II, this plaza features glass-fronted, wrought-iron balconies called miradores.

SANTA JUSTA AND SANTA RUFINA

Two Christians working in the Triana potteries in the 3rd century have become Seville's patron saints. The city's Roman rulers are said to have thrown the young women to the lions after they refused to join a procession venerating Venus. This martyrdom has inspired many works by Sevillian artists, including Murillo and Zurbarán *(see pp64–5)*. The saints are often shown with the Giralda, which, apparently, they protected from an earthquake in 1755.

Santa Justa and Santa Rufina as represented by Murillo (c.1665)

Calle Rodrigo de Triana
This street in white and ocher is named after the Andalusian sailor who first caught sight of the New World on Columbus's epic voyage of 1492 (see p49).

Puente de Isabel II, also known as Puente de Triana, leads to El Arenal.

Capillita del Carmen
A chapel, built by Aníbal González in 1926, stands at the west end of Puente de Isabel II, an iron bridge designed by Gustavo Steinacher and Fernando Bernadet in 1845.

LOCATOR MAP
See Street Finder, map 3

Kiosko de las Flores
Ideally located by the river, this freiduría is famous for its fried fish, a Seville specialty.

Capilla de los Marineros, a sailors' chapel, was built between 1759 and 1815.

Calle Pelay y Correa
With flowers and, often, hanging laundry, these narrow streets evoke the close-knit flavor of old Triana.

Iglesia de Santa Ana
Founded in the 13th century by Alfonso X, this is the oldest parish church in Seville. Triana's most popular place of worship, it has been splendidly restored ⓐ

0 meters		75
0 yards		75

KEY

– – – Suggested route

The Pabellón de Andalucía, built on Isla de la Cartuja for Expo '92

Parque Temático ❶

Camino de los Descubrimientos. **Map 1 B2.** 🚻 *(95) 446 14 93.* ⏰ *daily (site); check with individual attractions for specific opening times.* 🏛 ♿

THE MAIN PART of the Expo '92 *(see pp54–5)* site on Isla de la Cartuja is now the focus of a new theme park. The attractions occupy the core pavilions of Expo '92, including the dramatically leaning Pabellón de Andalucía.

The pavilions are reopening one by one, with exhibits and multimedia shows in which visitors can participate rather than just watch. One of the first, the Pabellón de España, has a mass-capacity Movimas Cinema, a 3-D laser show, and multimedia journey into Spain's history and literature.

Lago de España, the lake, is transformed into a mock ocean with exotic islands and a reproduction of Seville's port in the 16th century. State-of-the-art entertainment technology will recreate exciting naval battles, and desert islands with simulated movements, temperature changes, sounds, and smells.

Theme park attractions will be open during the day, but the Cartuja riverside will be a nightspot, its medley of bars, shops, restaurants, movies, and nightclubs open into the early hours all year.

Phone first for up-to-date information on new openings, their times, and prices.

Parque Científico y Tecnológico ❷

Paseo del Oeste (renamed Calle Leonardo da Vinci). **Map 1 A3.**

THE NEW Science and Technology Park occupies the western side of the Expo '92 site. Visitors can walk along Calle Leonardo da Vinci and the service roads for close-up views of some of Expo '92's most spectacular pavilions. These buildings, however, now part of the Andalusian World Trade Center, belong to private companies and are closed to visitors. Groups of buildings south and east of the Parque Alamillo are part of Seville University, which has links with the new Parque Científico y Tecnológico. To its south are the gardens surrounding the ancient Monasterio de Santa María de las Cuevas.

Espacio Cultural Puerta Triana ❸

Camino de los Descubrimientos, near Pasarela de la Cartuja. **Map 1 B5.** 🚻 *(95) 448 19 92.* ⏰ *daily (site); check with individual attractions for specific opening times.* 🏛 ♿

ISLA DE LA CARTUJA, south of the old monastery, is rapidly emerging as a cultural theme park of museums and educational exhibits. The site has since been redeveloped and has been reopening one exhibit at a time since late 1995.

The first attraction to reopen in October 1995 was the high-tech Omnimax theater, whose specially created films about the Earth, the adventurers of the past who explored it, and space travel today were among the most popular of the Expo '92 exhibits. Films are projected on a huge, semicircular screen, 24 m (80ft) in diameter.

Next door is the Pabellón de los Descubrimientos. The original pavilion burned down before the opening of Expo '92, but is now being rebuilt. When ready it will host a museum of popular science.

Exterior of the spherical Omnimax theater, built in 1992

Down by the river lies the Pabellón de la Navegación with exhibitions focusing on the sea and seafarers. Nearby is the *Nao Victoria*, a faithful replica of 16th-century sailing ship. She used to be moored by the riverside but can now be visited in a drydock.

From the large terrace of the original 1992 Torre Mirador, there are magnificent views of the area's striking modern architecture as well as of old Seville across the river.

***Nao Victoria*, replica of Magellan's 16th-century ship**

Main entrance of the Carthusian Monasterio de Santa María de las Cuevas, founded in 1400

New theaters, movies, and attractions for children are also planned, and the site will soon have its full complement of cafés, bars and restaurants.

Call the information number, or check with the tourist office *(see p237)* for up-to-date site maps, news of openings, plus information about events, and charges and opening times for museums and attractions.

Monasterio de Santa María de las Cuevas ❹

Camino de los Descubrimientos, near Pasarela de la Cartuja. **Map** 1 A4. ☎ *(95) 448 06 11.* ⏰ *Oct–Mar; 11am–7pm (last adm 6:15pm) Tue–Sun; Apr–Sep 11am–9pm (last adm 8:15pm) Tue–Sun.* 🅿 ♿

T HIS HUGE monastic complex, built by the Carthusians in the 15th century, is closely associated with the evolution of Seville. Columbus stayed and worked here, and even lay buried in the crypt of the monastery church, the Capilla Santa Ana, from 1507 to 1542. Carthusian monks lived in the monastery until 1836. They commissioned some of the finest works of the Seville School, among them masterpieces by Zurbarán and Montañés, now housed in the Museo de Bellas Artes *(see pp64–5)*.

In 1841 Charles Pickman, a British industrialist, built a ceramics factory on the site. After decades of successful business, production ceased in 1980, and the monastery then began to be meticulously restored as a central exhibit for Expo '92.

Of interest are the Capilla de Afuera by the main gate, and the Casa Prioral, which has an exhibition of the restoration. There is a Mudéjar cloister of marble and brick. The nearby chapter house has a ghostly dormitory – the marble tombstones of some wealthy former patrons of the monastery.

Triana ❺

See pp100–101.

The colorful belfry of Nuestra Señora de la O in Triana

Iglesia de Nuestra Señora de la O ❻

C/ de Castilla. **Map** 3 A1. ☎ *(95) 433 75 39.* ⏰ *9–11am, 7–9pm daily.*

T HE CHURCH OF Our Lady of O, built in the late 17th century, has a brightly painted belfry decorated with *azulejos* made locally. Inside, Baroque sculptures include a Virgin

and Child with silver haloes, attributed to Duque Cornejo, in the far chapel to the left as you enter. On the other side of the high altar is a fine group by Pedro Roldán depicting St. Anne, St. Joachim and Mary, the Virgin; a Jesus of Nazareth bearing his cross is in the main chapel on the far wall, also by the same sculptor.

The church is in Calle de Castilla, whose name comes from the notorious castle in Triana where the Inquisition had its headquarters from the 16th century on. The Callejón de la Inquisición, a nearby alley, leads down to the river.

Iglesia de Santa Ana ❼

C/ de la Pureza. **Map** 3 B2. ☎ *(95) 927 13 82.* ⏰ *9–11am, 7–9pm daily.*

O NE OF THE FIRST churches built in Seville after the Reconquest *(see pp46–7)*, Santa Ana was founded in 1276 but has been remodeled over the centuries. Today it is a focal point for the residents and *cofradias* (the religious brotherhoods) of Triana.

The vaulting of the nave is similar to Burgos cathedral's vaulting, suggesting that the same architect worked on the two churches. The west end of the nave has a 16th-century *retablo*, richly carved by Alejo Fernández. The sacramental chapel in the north wall has a Plateresque entrance.

In the baptistery is the *Pila de los Gitanos*, or Gypsy Font, which is believed to pass on the gift of flamenco song to the children of the faithful.

Street Finder Index

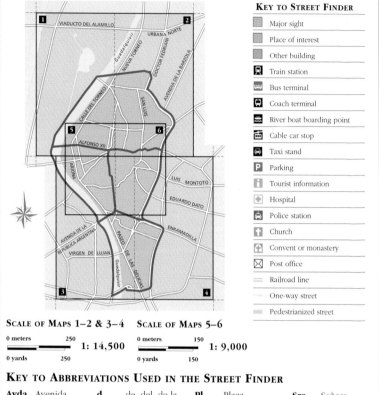

KEY TO STREET FINDER

	Major sight
	Place of interest
	Other building
	Train station
	Bus terminal
	Coach terminal
	River boat boarding point
	Cable car stop
	Taxi stand
P	Parking
	Tourist information
	Hospital
	Police station
	Church
	Convent or monastery
⊠	Post office
=	Railroad line
—	One-way street
	Pedestrianized street

SCALE OF MAPS 1–2 & 3–4   **SCALE OF MAPS 5–6**

0 meters 250		0 meters 150	
	1: 14,500		**1: 9,000**
0 yards 250		0 yards 150	

KEY TO ABBREVIATIONS USED IN THE STREET FINDER

Avda	Avenida	**d**	de, del, de la,	**Pl**	Plaza	**Sra**	Señora
C	Calle		de las, de los	**Po**	Paseo	**Sta**	Santa

A

Abad Gordillo, C d	**2 C5 (5 B2)**
Abades, C de los	**3 C1 (6 D4)**
Abogado R Medina, C	**2 E2**
Abril, Calle	**2 F2**
Abuyacub, Calle	2 F3
Acetres, Calle	**3 C1 (6 D2)**
Adelantado, Calle	**2 D3**
Adolfo R Jurado, C	**5 C5**
Adriano, Calle de	**3 B2 (5 B4)**
Agata, Calle	**2 E1**
Aguamarina, Calle	**2 E2**
Aguiar, Calle	**1 B5 (5 A2)**
Aguilas, Calle	**4 D1 (6 E3)**
Aire, Calle del	**3 C1 (6 D4)**
Alameda de Hércules	**2 D4**
Alamillo, Viaducto del	**1 A1**
Alamillo, Puente del	**2 D1**
Albacara, Calle	**2 F3**
Albaida, Calle de la	**2 F3**
Albareda, Calle de	**3 B1 (5 C3)**
Alberto Lista, C d	**6 D1**
Albuera, Calle	**3 A1 (5 A3)**
Alcaicería d Loza, C	**3 C1 (6 D3)**
Alcalde Isacio Contreras, C	**4 D2 (6 F4)**
Alcalde Marqués d Contadero, Po	**3 B2 (5 B4)**
Alcázares, C de	**2 D5 (6 D2)**
Alcores, Pasaje los	**4 D1 (6 E4)**
Alcoy, Calle de	**1 C4**
Alejo Fernández	**4 D2 (6 F4)**
Alemanes, Calle	**3 C2 (6 D4)**

Alerce, Calle	**4 E1**
Alfalfa, Calle	**3 C1 (6 D3)**
Alfalfa, Plaza del	**3 C1 (6 D3)**
Alfaqueque, Calle	**1 B5 (5 B1)**
Alfarería, Calle de	**3 A1**
Alfaro, Plaza	**4 D2 (6 E5)**
Alfonso de Cossio, C	**4 E4**
Alfonso de Orleans y Borbón, C de	**3 A5**
Alfonso XII, C de	**1 B5 (5 B2)**
Alfonso XIII, Puente de	**3 C5**
Algamitas, Calle	**2 F3**
Alhelí, Calle	**2 E2**
Alhóndiga, C d	**2 D5 (6 E2)**
Almadén d Plata, C	**2 F4**
Almansa, Calle	**3 B1 (5 B4)**
Almensilla, Calle	**2 F3**
Almirante Lobo, C	**3 B2 (5 C5)**
Almirante Tenorio, Calle	**2 E5 (6 F2)**
Almirante Topete, C d	**4 F5**
Almirante Ulloa, C d	**5 B2**
Almonacid, Calle	**4 E3**
Alonso Tello, Calle	**4 E2**
Altozano, Pl del	**3 A2 (5 A4)**
Alvarez Quintero, C	**3 C1 (6 D3)**
Amadeo Jannone, Pl	**3 A3**
Amador de los Ríos, Calle	**4 E1 (6 F2)**
Amante Laffon, C	**2 F3**
Amapola, Calle	**2 D4 (6 E1)**
Amargura, Calle	**2 D4**
Amatista, Calle	**2 E2**
América, Plaza de	**1 B2**

América, Plaza de	**4 D5**
Amistad, Calle	**4 D1 (6 E3)**
Amor de Dios, C d	**1 C5 (5 C1)**
Amores, Pasaje de	**2 D4**
Amparo, Calle del	**6 D1**
Andreu, Pasaje	**6 D4**
Andueza, Calle de	**2 D3**
Angel María Camacho, C	**3 C1 (6 D3)**
Angeles, Calle	**3 C2 (6 D4)**
Aniceto Saenz, C d	**2 E4**
Animas, Calle	**3 A4**
Antilla, Playa de la	**2 E2**
Antillano, Calle	**3 A2**
Antolinez, Calle	**1 C5 (5 B1)**
Antonia Díaz, C d	**3 B2 (5 B4)**
Antonia Saenz, C d	**2 E4**
Antonio Bienvenida, C	**3 B5**
Antonio Martelo, Plaza	**2 F5**
Antonio M Montaner, C	**4 E5**
Antonio Pantión, C	**2 E3**
Antonio Salado, C	**1 B5 (5 B2)**
Antonio Susillo, C	**2 D4**
Aponte, C	**1 C5 (5 C2)**
Aposentadores, C	**2 D5 (6 D1)**
Arapiles, Calle	**2 E5 (6 F2)**
Archeros, Calle	**4 D2 (6 E4)**
Arcos, Calle	**3 B3**
Ardilla, C de la	**3 A3**
Arenal, Calle	**3 B1 (5 B4)**
Arenal, Calle	**4 F5**
Arfe, Calle	**3 B2 (5 C4)**
Argote de Molina, Calle	**3 C1 (6 D4)**

Arguijo, Calle	**2 D5 (6 D2)**
Arjona, Calle de	**3 A1 (5 A3)**
Armas, Plaza de	**1 B5 (5 A2)**
Armenta, Calle	**6 E3**
Arqueros, Calle	**3 A4**
Arrayán, Calle	**2 D4**
Arroyo, Calle de	**2 F5**
Arte de la Seda, C	**1 C3**
Artemisa, Calle	**2 E5 (6 F1)**
Asunción, C d	**3 B3**
Atanasio Barrón, C	**4 D1 (6 F4)**
Ateneo, Pasaje	**3 C1 (5 C3)**
Atienza, C	**2 D5 (6 D1)**
Augusto Peyre, C	**4 D5**
A Plasencia, C	**3 C1 (6 D3)**
Aurora, Calle	**3 B2 (5 C4)**
Autonomía, Plaza	**2 F3**
Ave María, Calle	**6 E2**
Avellana, Calle	**2 E3**
Averroes, Calle	**4 E1**
Azafrán, Calle del	**2 E5 (6 E2)**
Aznalcazar, Calle	**4 F3**
Aznalcollar, Calle	**4 F3**
Aznalfarache, Calle	**2 E3**
Azoaifo, Calle	**5 C2**

B

Badajoz	**3 B1 (5 C3)**
Bailén, Calle de	**1 B5 (5 B2)**
Bajeles, Calle	**1 B5 (5 A1)**
Bamberg, Calle	**3 C1 (6 D3)**
Baños, Calle de	**1 B5 (5 B1)**
Barcelona, Calle	**3 B1 (5 C3)**
Barco, Calle	**2 D4**

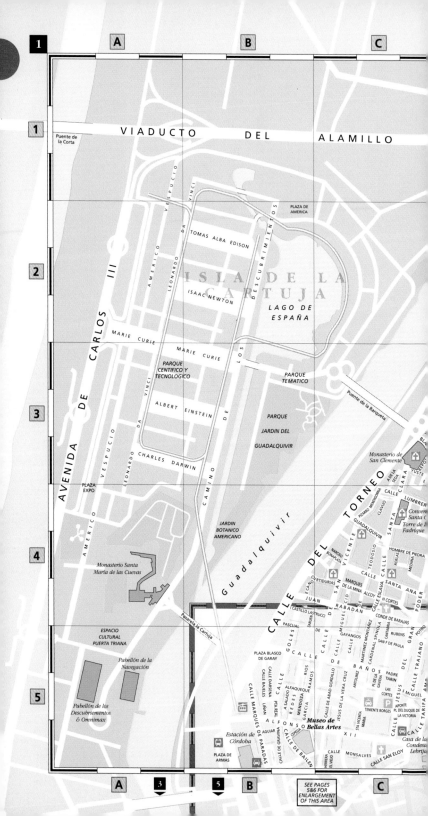

1

| **A** | **B** | **C** |

1 Puente de la Corta

VIADUCTO DEL ALAMILLO

VESPUCIO

DA VINCI

DESCUBRIMIENTOS

PLAZA DE AMERICA

AMERICO

LEONARDO

TOMAS ALBA EDISON

2

CARLOS III

ISLA DE LA CARTUJA

ISAAC NEWTON

LAGO DE ESPAÑA

MARIE CURIE

MARIE CURIE

AVENIDA DE

DA VINCI

VESPUCIO

Parque CENTIFICO Y TECNOLOGICO

CAMINO DE LOS

PARQUE TEMATICO

3 PLAZA EXPO

ALBERT EINSTEIN

PARQUE JARDIN DEL GUADALQUIVIR

Puente de la Barqueta

Monasterio de San Clemente

BLA

YUSTE

LEONARDO

CHARLES DARWIN

Convento Santa C Torre de Fadrique

CALLE CLARA

AGUJA SEDA

LUMBRER

4

AMERICO

JARDIN BOTANICO AMERICANO

Guadalquivir

CALLE DEL TORNEO

PIZARRO MENDOSOBRA

CLAVIJO

GUADALQUIVIR

SAN VICENTE

SANTA ANA

TEODOSIO

HOMBRE DE PIEDRA

MEDINA

ROBLES

Monasterio Santa María de las Cuevas

Pasarela la Cartuja

CURTIDURIAS

CAÑO

MARQUES DE LA MINA

ALCOY

H. CORTES

SAN MIGUEL

JUAN RABADAN

CASTILLO LASTRUCCI

CONDE DE BARAJAS

PODER

5

ESPACIO CULTURAL PUERTA TRIANA

Pabellón de la Navegación

Pabellón de los Descubrimientos & Omnimax

PASCUAL

ZABERA

CALLE GOLES

DE

GAYANGOS

MARTINEZ MONTAÑEZ

CARDENAL SPINOLA

RUBENS

GRAN

POTRO

PLAZA BLASCO DE GARAY

DARSENA

RIOS

MENDOZA RAMOS

ANTOLINEZ

PJE. DE LA GAVIDIA

GARCIA

SAN F DE PAULA

JESUS DE LA VERA CRUZ

LAS CORTES

PADRE TARIN

CALLE TRAJANO

CALLE MIGUEL

CALLE BAJELES

CALLE MARQUES DE

LIMAN

A SADAO

ALFAQUEQUE

REDES

PTA REAL

APONTE

TENIENTE BORGES

PL. DEL DUQUE DE LA VICTORIA

CALLE TARIFA

Estación de Córdoba

PLAZA DE ARMAS

CALLE DE BAILEN

STA VICENTA

MARIA

GRAVINA

JESUS DEL G EY

ALFONSO XII

CEPEDA

Museo de Bellas Artes

MONSALVES

Casa de la Condesa Lebrija

HERRERA EL VIEJO

CALLE SAN ELOY

| **A** | ▼3 ▼5 | **B** | **C** |

SEE PAGES 586 FOR ENLARGEMENT OF THIS AREA

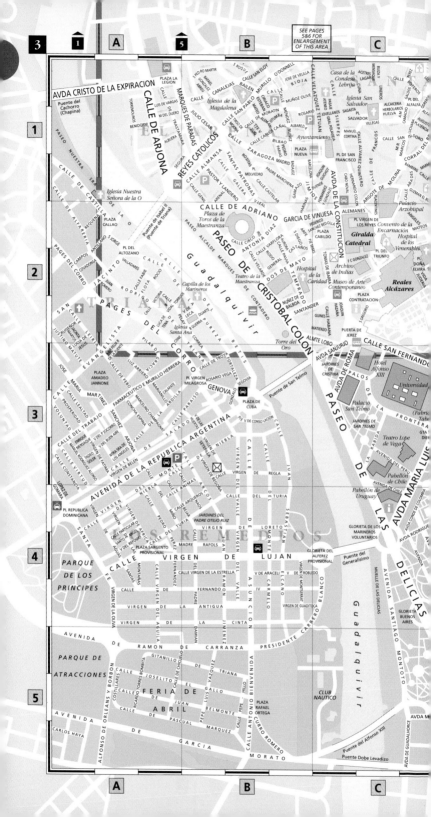

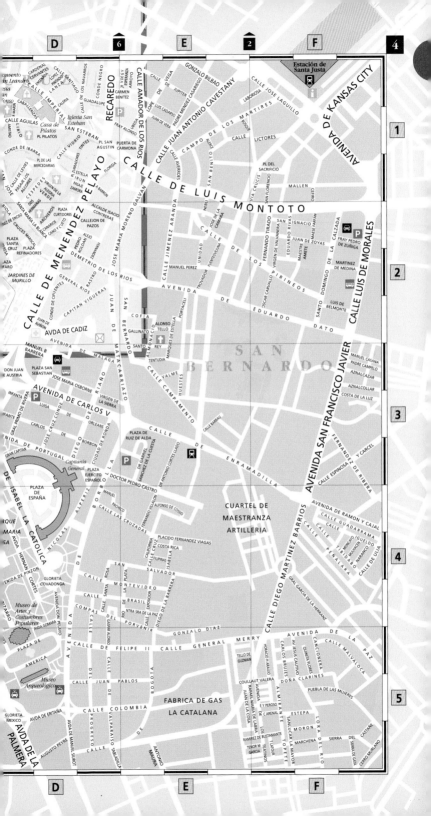

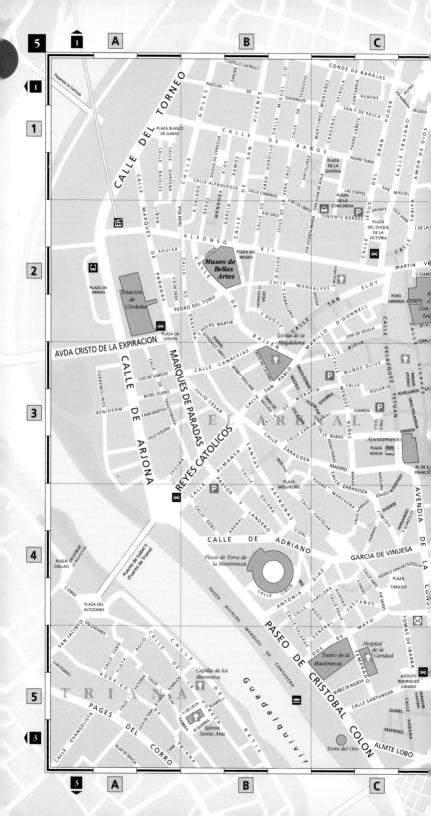

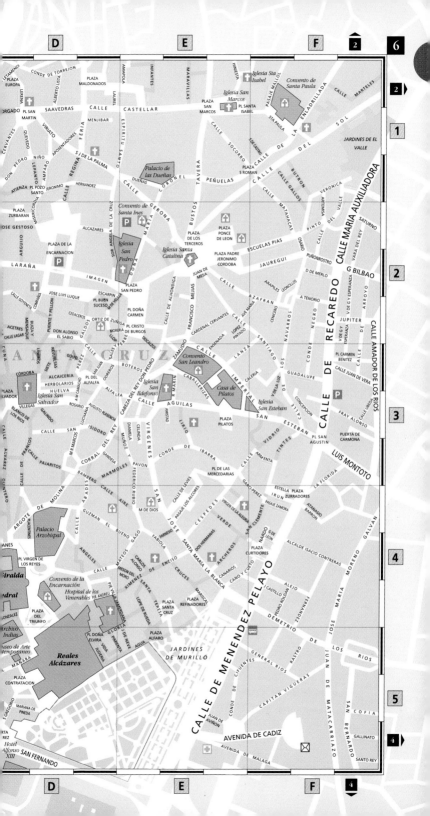

ANDALUSIA
AREA BY AREA

Andalusia at a Glance

ANDALUSIA IS A REGION OF CONTRASTS where snowcapped mountains rise above deserts and Mediterranean beaches, and Moorish palaces can be found standing next to Christian cathedrals. Its eight provinces, which in this guide are divided into four areas, offer busy towns such as Granada and Córdoba with their astonishing architectural treasures, in addition to sleepy villages, endless olive groves, and nature preserves of great beauty.

Roof of the Mihrab in the Mezquita, Córdoba's top sight *(see pp140–41)*

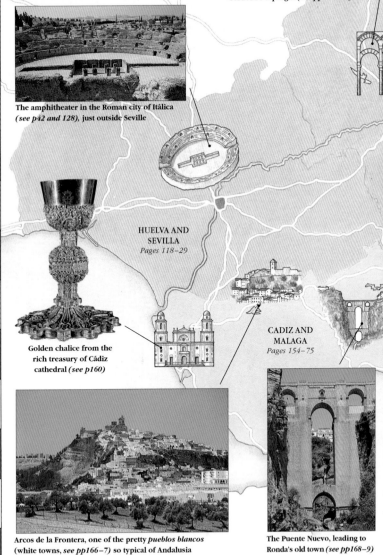

The amphitheater in the Roman city of Itálica *(see p42 and 128)*, **just outside Seville**

HUELVA AND SEVILLA
Pages 118–29

CADIZ AND MALAGA
Pages 154–75

Golden chalice from the rich treasury of Cádiz cathedral *(see p160)*

Arcos de la Frontera, one of the pretty *pueblos blancos* **(white towns, see pp166–7) so typical of Andalusia**

The Puente Nuevo, leading to Ronda's old town *(see pp168–9)*

◁ **Dawn at Montefrío in Granada province**

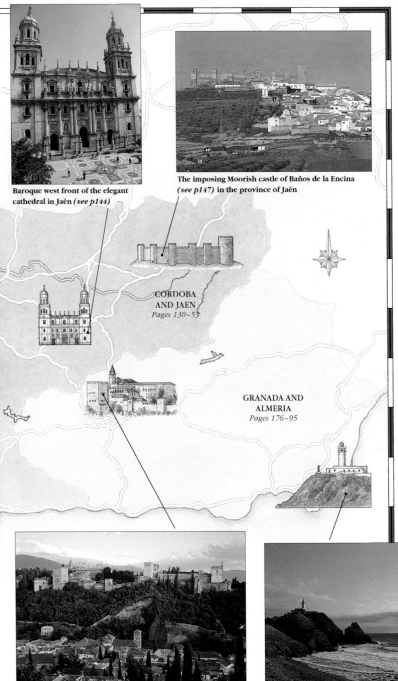

Baroque west front of the elegant
cathedral in Jaén *(see p144)*

The imposing Moorish castle of Baños de la Encina
(see p147) in the province of Jaén

CORDOBA
AND JAEN
Pages 130–53

GRANADA AND
ALMERIA
Pages 176–95

Magical Alhambra overlooking the Albaicín, Granada *(see pp182–8)*

0 kilometers   50

0 miles   25

Cabo de Gata, a nature preserve
with excellent beaches *(see p194)*

HUELVA AND SEVILLA

NDALUSIA'S WESTERN EXTREMITIES *and the plains surrounding Seville are rarely explored by travelers in southern Spain. There are isolated beaches along Huelva province's Atlantic coast and good walking country in the northern sierras. The Coto Doñana on the Guadalquivir delta is Europe's largest nature preserve; inland, orange groves straddle the river's broad valley.*

As Roman legions under Scipio Africanus crossed southern Spain on their westward trek in the 3rd century BC, they founded a formidable city, Itálica. Its ruins can still be seen north of Seville. Later, the Moors held the region as part of the Emirate of al Andalus. They peppered it with their whitewashed, fortified towns, of which Carmona, in Sevilla province, is a fine example.

After the Christian Reconquest *(see pp46–7)*, Moorish traditions persisted through Mudéjar architecture *(see pp22–3)*, blending with Baroque and Renaissance in cities such as Osuna, which flourished in the 16th century.

Huelva province is inextricably bound up with another chapter in the history of world conquest – in 1492 Columbus set out on his epic voyage from Palos de la Frontera, which at the time was an important port. He stayed nearby, at the Franciscan Monasterio de la Rábida, built earlier that century. Running along Huelva's northern border is a ridge of mountains, of which the forested Sierra de Aracena forms part. This ridge continues into Sevilla province as the Sierra Norte de Sevilla. Here, goats forage, birds of prey fly overhead, and streams gush through chasms. The landscape erupts in a riot of wildflowers in spring, turning brown as the searing summer sets in.

The Parque Nacional de Coto Doñana preserves the dunes and marshlands near the mouth of the Guadalquivir to the south. Here, teeming bird life and wetland fauna thrive on the mudflats and shallow, saline waters.

Iglesia de Nuestra Señora del Rocío, El Rocío, where many pilgrims converge each Pentecost Sunday

◁ The famed *jamón ibérico* (cured ham) hanging in a bar in Jabugo, Sierra de Aracena

Exploring Huelva and Sevilla

C OSMOPOLITAN SEVILLE *(see pp56–113)* is the natural
base from which to explore the far-flung corners
of Huelva and Sevilla provinces, such as the little-
visited and awesomely beautiful Sierra de Aracena
and the rugged Sierra Norte. The Atlantic coast
offers a virtually unbroken stretch of beaches, and
the Parque Nacional de Coto Doñana features a
fascinating marsh landscape abundant in wildlife.
Between the coast and the mountains are rolling
agricultural plains, interrupted by vineyards in fertile El Condado. Among the
region's historic towns are Écija and
Osuna, with fine Baroque features,
and the history of Columbus
can be traced in the towns
around Huelva.

The mines of Ríotinto, Sierra de Aracena

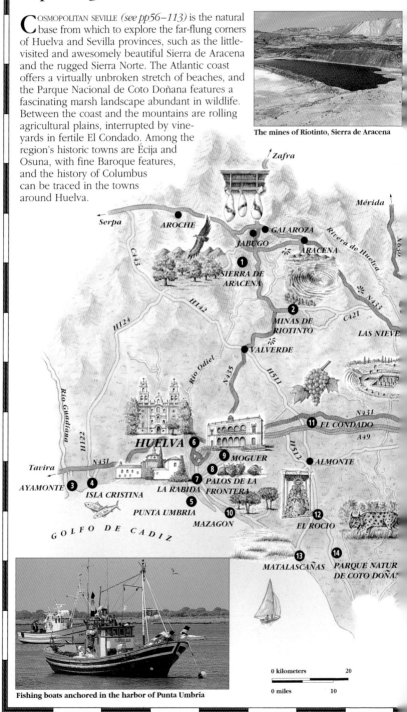

Zafra

Serpa

Mérida

AROCHE

GALAROZA

JABUGO

ARACENA

Rivera de Huelva

C443

①

**SIERRA DE
ARACENA**

H142

N433

H124

②

**MINAS DE
RIOTINTO**

CA21

LAS NIEVE

Río Odiel

VALVERDE

N435

H511

Río Guadiana

HUELVA ⑥

⑪ EL CONDADO

N431

A49

H122

Tavira

N431

⑨ MOGUER

H512

⑧

⑦ **PALOS DE LA
FRONTERA**

ALMONTE

AYAMONTE ③ ④

ISLA CRISTINA

LA RABIDA

⑤

PUNTA UMBRIA

⑩

MAZAGON

⑫

EL ROCIO

G O L F O   D E   C A D I Z

⑬

MATALASCAÑAS

⑭

**PARQUE NATUR
DE COTO DOÑA**

Fishing boats anchored in the harbor of Punta Umbría

| 0 kilometers | 20 |
| 0 miles | 10 |

GETTING AROUND

The busy NIV E5 linking Córdoba with Seville slices
through the eastern half of the region, bypassing Écija
and Carmona, then streaks down to Jerez de la
Frontera and Cádiz. Another main highway, the N334,
connects Málaga and Granada. All join a periphery
road at Seville, with the A49 (E1) continuing to Huelva.
All these cities are connected by rail. A complex and
inexpensive bus network run by different companies
links most towns. To explore the more remote parts
of the region, particularly the beautiful mountain roads,
it is essential to have private transportation.

**A well-known *bodega* advertisement in
the rolling hills of the Sierra de Aracena**

ALANIS

CAZALLA DE
LA SIERRA

SIERRA NORTE ⑰

CONSTANTINA

EL PEDROSO

Córdoba

Río Guadalquivir

ÉCIJA ⑲

ITALICA

SEVILLA

CARMONA ⑱

Río Corbones

Río Blanco

ESTEPA ㉑

OSUNA ⑳

Málaga

LEBRIJA

Jerez de la
Frontera

SIGHTS AT A GLANCE

KEY

▨	Highway
▨	Major road
▨	Minor road
▨	Scenic route
≈	River
☆	Viewpoint

A ham shop in Jabugo, Sierra de Aracena

Sierra de Aracena ❶

Huelva. **Road map** A3. 🚉 *El Repilado.* 🚌 *Aracena.* ℹ️ *Plaza San Pedro s/n, Aracena. (959) 12 83 55.*

THIS WILD MOUNTAIN RANGE in northern Huelva province is one of the most remote and least visited corners of Andalusia. Its slopes, covered with cork, oak, chestnut, and wild olive trees, are cut by rushing streams and extremely tortuous mountain roads.

The main town of the region, Aracena, squats at the foot of a ruined Moorish fortress on a hillside pitted with caverns. One of these, the **Gruta de las Maravillas**, can be entered to see its underground lake in a chamber with stalactites. Near the fortress, the fine **Iglesia del Castillo**, which was built in the 13th century by the Knights Templar, has a Mudéjar tower and foundations.

The village of **Jabugo** also nestles amid these mountains. It is known across Spain as the home of the country's tastiest cured ham, *jamón ibérico,* or *pata negra (see p223).*

🏛 Gruta de las Maravillas
Calle San Jose s/n. ☎ *(959) 12 83 55.* ◯ *daily.* 📷

Minas de Ríotinto ❷

Huelva. **Road map** B3. 🚉 *Riotinto.* ☎ *(959) 59 00 25.* ◯ *Tue–Sun (and public hols).* 📷 ♿

A FASCINATING DETOUR off the beautiful N435 between Huelva city and the Sierra de Aracena leads off to the giant opencast mines at Ríotinto. These have been excavated since Phoenician times; the Greeks, Romans, and Visigoths in turn exploited their bountiful reserves of iron, copper, silver, and mineral ores.

The lip of the crater above the mines overlooks walls of rock that are streaked with green and dark red fissures. Below, the trucks at work in the mines appear toy-sized. The **Museo Minero,** sited in the village itself, explains the history both of the mines and of the Rio Tinto Company.

🏛 Museo Minero
Plaza del Museo s/n. ☎ *(959) 59 00 25.* ◯ *Tue–Sun.* 📷

Ayamonte ❸

Huelva. **Road map** A4. 🚶 *15,000.* 🚌 ℹ️ *Avenida Ramón y Cajal s/n. (959) 47 09 88.* 🛒 *Sat.*

BEFORE THE ROAD BRIDGE over the lower Guadiana River was completed in 1992, anyone crossing between southern Andalusia and the Algarve coast of Portugal had to pass through Ayamonte. The small, flat-bottomed car ferry across the jellyfish-infested mouth of the Guadiana River still operates and is an interesting alternative for those making the journey between the two countries. Visitors can watch the ferry from above by climbing the tower of Ayamonte's **Iglesia San Francisco**, which has a fine Mudéjar ceiling.

Isla Cristina ❹

Huelva. **Road map** A4. 🚶 *18,000.* 🚌 ℹ️ *Ayuntamiento, Gran Via 43. (959) 33 19 12.* 🛒 *Thu.*

ONCE A DISTINCT ISLAND, Isla Cristina is now surrounded by marshes. Situated near the mouth of the Guadiana River, it is an important fishing port, home to a fleet of tuna and sardine trawlers. With a fine sandy beach, it has, in recent years, also become a summer resort popular especially with Spanish families. There is an excellent choice of restaurants situated on the main seafront that serve delicious, freshly landed fish and seafood.

Tuna and sardine trawlers moored for the night in the port of Isla Cristina

Frescoes depicting the life of Columbus at Monasterio de la Rábida

Punta Umbría ❺

Huelva. **Road map** A4. 🚶 *12,000.*
🚌 ℹ️ *Avenida Huelva s/n. (959) 31
46 19.* 🎪 *Mon.*

Punta Umbría is one of the main beach resorts in Huelva province. It sits at the end of a long promontory, with the Marismas del Odiel wetlands to one side and an outstanding sandy beach bordering the Gulf of Cádiz to the other. The Rio Tinto Company first developed the resort in the late 19th century for its British employees. These days, however, it is mainly Spanish vacationers who stay in the beachside villas.

A long bridge crosses the marshes, giving road access from Huelva. It is more fun to follow a trail blazed by Rio Tinto expatriates seeking the sun and to take the ferry across the bird-rich wetlands.

Huelva ❻

Huelva. **Road map** A3. 🚶 *142,000.*
🚆 🚌 ℹ️ *Avenida Alemania 12.
(959) 25 74 03.* 🎪 *Fri.*

Founded as onuba by the Phoenicians, the town had its grandest days as a Roman port. It prospered again in the early days of trade with the Americas, but Seville soon took over. Its decline culminated in 1755, when Huelva was almost wiped out by the great Lisbon earthquake. Today, industrial suburbs sprawl around the

Bronze jug, Museo Provincial, Huelva

Odiel quayside, from which the Rio Tinto Company once exported its products all over the commercial world.

That Columbus set sail from Palos de la Frontera, across the estuary, is Huelva's main claim to international renown. This fact is celebrated in the excellent **Museo Provincial**, which also has several exhibitions charting the history of the mines at Ríotinto. Some archaeological finds from the very early days of mining are cleverly presented. To the east of the center the Barrio Reina Victoria is a bizarre example of English suburbia in the very heart of Andalusia. It is a district of bungalows in mock-Tudor style, built by the Rio Tinto Company for its staff in the early 20th century.

South of the town, at Punta del Sebo, the Monumento a Colón, a rather bleak statue of Columbus created by Gertrude Vanderbilt Whitney in 1929, dominates the Odiel estuary.

🏛️ **Museo Provincial**
Alameda Sundheim 13. 📞 *(959) 25
93 00.* ⏰ *Tue –Sat.* ♿

Monasterio de la Rábida ❼

Huelva. **Road map** A4. 🚌 *from
Palos de la Frontera.* 📞 *(959) 35 04
11.* ⏰ *Tue –Sun.* ♿

In 1491 a dejected Genoese explorer found refuge in the Franciscan friary at La Rábida, across the Odiel estuary from Huelva. King Fernando and Queen Isabel had refused to back his plan to sail west to the East Indies. The prior, Juan Pérez, who as the confessor of the queen had great influence, eventually succeeded in getting this decision reversed. The following year, this sailor, by name Columbus, became the first European to reach the Americas since the Vikings.

La Rábida friary, which was built on Moorish ruins in the 15th century, is now a shrine to Columbus's exploits. Inside, frescoes painted by Daniel Vásquez Díaz in 1930 glorify the explorer's life and discoveries. The Sala de las Banderas contains a small casket of soil from each of the Latin American countries. Also worth seeing on your visit are the Mudéjar cloisters, the lush gardens, and the beamed chapter house.

COLUMBUS IN ANDALUSIA

Cristóbal Colón – Christopher Columbus to the English-speaking world – was born in Genoa in Italy, trained as a navigator in Portugal, and conceived the idea of reaching the Indies by sailing westward. In 1492 he sailed from Palos de la Frontera and later the same year landed on Watling Island in the Bahamas, believing that he had fulfilled his ambition.

Columbus made three further voyages from bases in Andalusia, reaching mainland South America and other islands in what are still termed the West Indies in deference to his mistake. He died at Valladolid in 1506.

Columbus takes his leave before setting sail

Historic map, Casa Museo de Martín Alonso Pinzón, Palos de la Frontera

Palos de la Frontera ⑧

Huelva. **Road map** A4. 🏠 *7,000.*
🚌 🚹 *Ayuntamiento, Calle Rábida 3.*
(959) 35 08 51. 🚌 *Sat.*

PALOS IS AN unprepossessing agricultural town on the eastern side of the Río Odiel's marshy delta. Yet, as a major attraction on the Columbus heritage trail, it draws its fair share of visitors.

On August 3, 1492, Columbus set sea from Palos in his caravel, the *Santa María*, with the *Pinta* and the *Niña*, whose captains were Martín and Vicente Pinzón, brothers from Palos. A statue of Martín Pinzón stands in the town's main square, and his former home has been turned into a small museum of exploration, named the **Casa Museo de Martín Alonso Pinzón**.

The Gothic-Mudéjar **Iglesia San Jorge** dates from the 15th century. It has a fine portal, through which Columbus left after hearing Mass before his famous voyage. Afterward, he boarded the *Santa María* at a pier, which is now forlornly silted up.

These days, Palos's prosperity comes from the thousands of acres of strawberry beds in the surrounding fields, which soak up the sun.

🏛 **Casa Museo de Martín Alonso Pinzón**
Calle Colón 28. 📞 *(959) 35 01 99.*
🕐 *Tue –Sun.*

Moguer ⑨

Huelva. **Road map** A3. 🏠 *12,000.*
🚌 🚹 *Calle Andalucia 5. (959) 37 23 77.* 🚌 *Thu.*

A BEAUTIFUL, whitewashed town, Moguer is a network of discreet shaded courtyards and narrow streets lined with flower boxes. It is a delight to wander around, exploring treasures such as the 16th-century hermitage of **Nuestra Señora de Montemayor** and the Neo-Classical **Ayuntamiento**. Moguer is also the birthplace of the poet and 1956 Nobel laureate, Juan Ramón Jiménez. His former home, now the **Museo de Zenobia y**

Juan Ramón Jiménez, charts his life and his work.

The town's other two main sights are its convent and its monastery. The crenellated walls of **Convento de Santa Clara**, dating from the 14th century, enclose some splendid, stone-carved Mudéjar cloisters. The nuns' dormitory, kitchen, and refectory capture some of the atmosphere of their life inside the enclosure.

The **Monasterio de San Francisco** is worth seeing for its cloisters and for its church, which has a superb white tower and Baroque portals.

🏛 **Museo de Zenobia y Juan Ramón Jiménez**
Calle Juan Ramón Jiménez 10.
📞 *(959) 37 21 48.* 🕐 *daily.* 🎫
🚹 **Convento de Santa Clara**
Plaza de las Monjas. 📞 *(959) 37 01 07.* 🕐 *Tue –Sat.* 🌑 *public hols.* 🎫

Mazagón's sandy beach on the Costa de la Luz

Mazagón ⑩

Huelva. **Road map** A4. 🏠 *3,000.* 🚌
🚹 *Edificio Mancomunidad, Avda Descubridores s/n. (959) 37 60 44.* 🚌 *Fri.*

ONE OF THE MORE remote beach resorts of the Costa de la Luz, Magazón is sheltered by pine woods 23 km (14 miles) southeast of Huelva. Virtually deserted in winter, it comes to life in the summer when a hardy group of regular, mainly Spanish, vacationers arrives to fish, sail, and enjoy the enormous, and often windswept, beach. Visitors to the resort may still take pleasure in the solitude, however, while walking for miles along the endless Atlantic shoreline and among the sand dunes.

The 16th-century Nuestra Señora de Montemayor in Moguer

Moorish walls surrounding Niebla in El Condado

El Condado ⓫

Huelva. **Road map** B3. 🚐 🚌 *Palma del Condado.* 🛈 *Avda Alemania 14, Huelva. (959) 25 74 03.*

THE ROLLING, fecund hills to the east of Huelva produce several of Andalusia's finest wines. El Condado, a fertile area defined roughly by Niebla, Palma del Condado, Bollullos del Condado, and Rociana del Condado, is the heart of this wine-growing district.

Niebla is of ancient origin. Its bridge is Roman, but its solid walls are Moorish, as is the now ruined 12th-century **Castillo de los Guzmanes**.

Around Niebla, vineyards spread out over the gently undulating landscape, which is dotted with the villages that have grown up close to the main *bodegas*. These include Bollullos del Condado, which has the largest cooperative winery in Andalusia and also the **Casa del Vino**. Here you can learn about wine-growing techniques and taste a wide selection of their wines before making your purchase.

Bollullos and Palma del Condado are good examples of the popular young white wines produced in the region.

Palma del Condado is the place to visit in September, when you can watch as the inhabitants celebrate the year's *vendimia* (grape harvest).

♙ **Castillo de los Guzmanes**
C/ Castillo, Niebla. 🎧 *(959) 36 22 70.* 🕐 *Mon–Sat. Phone to arrange visit.*
🍸 **Casa del Vino**
Avenida 28 de Febrero s/n, Bollullos del Condado. 🎧 *(959) 41 08 00.* 🕐 *Mon–Fri. Phone to arrange visit.*

El Rocío ⓬

Huelva. **Road map** B4. 🚶 *1,200.* 🚌 🛈 *Centro Ecoturístico, Avda de la Canaliega s/n. (959) 44 26 84.* 🚐 *Tue.*

BORDERING the wetlands of the Coto Doñana region *(see pp126–7)*, the village of El Rocío is for most of the year a tranquil, rural backwater that attracts few visitors.

At the Romería del Rocío *(see pp36–7)* in May, however, nearly a million people converge on the village. Many are pilgrims who travel from all over Spain by bus, car, horse, or even on gaudily decorated oxcarts, or on foot. They come to **Ermita de Nuestra Señora del Rocío**, which has a statue reputed to have been behind miraculous apparitions since 1280. Pilgrims are joined by revelers, who are enticed by the promise of plentiful wine, music, and a great party.

Matalascañas ⓭

Huelva. **Road map** B4. 🚶 *1,500.* 🚌 🛈 *Avenida de las Adelfas s/n. (959) 43 00 86.* 🚐 *Thu.*

MATALASCAÑAS is the largest Andalusian beach resort west of the Guadalquivir River. Thousands vacation here in its hotels and apartment blocks, lying in the sun, riding, sailing, or waterskiing by day and dancing to the latest disco beat at night. At the Romería del Rocío, the resort overflows with pilgrims and revelers.

Matalascañas is totally self-contained. To one side there are dunes and forests stretching as far as Mazagón, to the other the wild peace of the Coto Doñana *(see pp126–7)*.

Iglesia de Nuestra Señora del Rocío in the village of El Rocío

Parque Nacional de Coto Doñana ⓴

THE NATIONAL PARK of Coto Doñana is ranked among Europe's greatest wetlands. Together with its adjoining protected areas, the park covers over 75,000 hectares (185,000 acres) of marshes and sand dunes. The area used to be hunting grounds *(coto)* belonging to the Dukes of Medina Sidonia and was never a suitable land for human settlers. The wild-

Bird-spotting from boat on the Guadalquivir

life flourished and, in 1969, the area became officially protected. In addition to a wealth of endemic species, thousands of migratory birds stop over in winter when the marshes become flooded again, after months of draught.

Shrub Vegetation
Backing the sand dunes is a thick carpet of lavender, rock rose, and other low shrubs.

Umbrella Pine
This species of pine tree (Pinus pinea) *thrives in the wide dune belt, putting roots deep into the sand. The trees may get buried beneath the dunes.*

Coastal Dunes
Softly rounded, white dunes, up to 30 m (98 ft) high, fringe the park's coastal edge. The dunes, ribbed by prevailing winds off the Atlantic, shift constantly.

Monte de Doñana, the wooded area behind the sand dunes, provide shelter for lynx, deer, and boar.

Official Tour
Numbers of visitors are controlled very strictly. On official day tours along rough tracks, the knowledgable guides point out elusive animals while ensuring minimal environmental impact.

Map labels: La Rocina · El Acebrón · El Rocío · H312 · El Acebuche · Matalascañas · Palacio de Doñana · Laguna de Santa Olay

KEY

▦	Marshes
▦	Dunes
•••	National park boundary
•••	Protected area
▬	Road
☀	Viewpoint
ℹ	Tourist information
P	Parking
⛟	Coach station

Deer

Fallow deer (Dama dama) *and larger Red deer* (Cervus elaphas) *roam the park. Stags engage in fierce contests in late summer as they prepare for breeding.*

Wild cattle use the marshes as water holes.

Imperial Eagle

The very rare Imperial eagle (Aquila heliaca adalberti) *preys on small mammals.*

Greater Flamingo

During the winter months, the salty lakes and marshes provide the beautiful, pink Greater flamingo (Phoenicopterus ruber) *with crustaceans, its main diet.*

Río Guadiamar

Marisma de Iznalcázar

Marisma Gallega

Río Guadalquivir

Sanlúcar de Barrameda

THE LYNX'S LAST REFUGE

The lynx is one of Europe's rarest mammals. In Coto Doñana about 60 pairs of Spanish lynx *(Lynx pardinus)* have found a refuge. They have yellow-brown fur with dark brown spots and pointed ears with black tufts. A research program is under way to study this shy animal, which tends to stay hidden in scrub. It feeds mainly on rabbits and ducks, but might catch an unguarded deer faun.

The elusive lynx, seen very rarely

0 kilometers 5

0 miles 5

Scenic view over the rooftops of Lebrija with their distinctive red tiles

Lebrija ⓯

Sevilla. **Road map** B4. 👤 *24,000.*
🚉 🚌 🛈 *Casa de Cultura, Calle
Tetuán 15. (95) 597 40 68.* 🛂 *Tue.*

THE PRETTY, WALLED town of
Lebrija enjoys panoramic
views over the neighboring
sherry-growing vineyards of
the Jerez region *(see p214).*
   Narrow cobbled streets lead
to **Iglesia de Santa María de
la Oliva**. This is a 12th-century
Almohad mosque, which was
consecrated as a church by
Alfonso X *(see p46)*. Many original Islamic features survive,
including the domed roof and
internal horseshoe arches.

Itálica ⓰

Sevilla. **Road map** B3. 🚌 *from Plaza
de Armas, Seville.* 📞 *(95) 599 73 76.*
🌙 *Tue–Sun* 🎫

SCIPIO AFRICANUS established
Itálica in 206 BC, as one of
the first cities founded by the
Romans in Hispania. Later, it
burgeoned, both as a military
headquarters and as a cultural
center, at one time supporting
a population of several thousands. Emperors Trajan and
Hadrian were
both born
in Itálica.
The latter
bestowed imperial
largesse on the city
during his reign in
the 2nd century AD,
adding marble temples
and other fine buildings.
   Archaeologists have
speculated that the changing
course of the Guadalquivir

**Roman mosaic
from Itálica**

may have led to the demise
of Itálica. Certainly, the city
declined steadily after the fall
of the Roman Empire, unlike
Seville, which flourished.
   At the heart of the site you
may explore the crumbling
remains of a vast amphitheater,
which once seated 25,000.
Next to it is a display of finds
from the site, although many
of the treasures are displayed
in the Museo Arqueológico in
Seville *(see p195)*. Visitors can
wander among the traces of
streets and the mosaic floors
of villas. Little remains of the
city's temples or of its baths,
as most stone and marble was
plundered by builders over
the subsequent centuries.
   The village of **Santiponce**
lies just outside the site. Here,
some better-preserved Roman
remains, including baths and a
theater, have been unearthed.

Sierra Norte ⓱

Sevilla. **Road map** B3. 🚉 *Estación de
Cazalla y Constantina.* 🚌 *Constantina;
Cazalla.* 🛈 *El Robledo. (95) 588 15 97.*

AN AUSTERE mountain range
flanks the northern border
of Sevilla province. Known as
the Sierra Norte de Sevilla, it
is a part of the greater Sierra
Morena, which forms a
natural frontier be-
tween Andalusia
and the plains
of La Mancha
and Extrema-
dura. The region,
gashed by rushing
streams, is sparsely
populated, and, as it is
relatively cool in summer, it

can offer a much needed
escape from the relentless heat
of Seville. In winter, you may
meet the occasional hunter
carrying a partridge or hare.
   Cazalla de la Sierra, the
main town of the area, seems
surprisingly cosmopolitan and
is highly popular with young
sevillanos on weekends. It has
made a unique contribution
to the world of drink, namely
Liquor de Guindas. This is a
concoction of cherry liqueur
and anise, whose taste is
acquired slowly, if at all.
   Constantina, to the east, is
more peaceful and has superb
views across the countryside.
A romantic aura surrounds the
ruined castle, which is situated
high above the town.

Grazing cow in the empty expanses
of the Sierra Norte de Sevilla

Carmona ⓲

Sevilla. **Road map** B3. 👤 *25,000.*
🚉 🚌 🛈 *Plaza de San Fernando 14.
(95) 419 09 55.* 🛂 *Mon & Thu.*

TRAVELING EAST from Seville
on the NIV E5, Carmona is
the first major town you come
to. It rises above expansive
agricultural plains. Sprawling
suburbs spill out beyond the
Moorish city walls, which can
be entered through the old,
imperious **Puerta de Sevilla**.
Inside them, there is a dense
concentration of mansions,
Mudéjar churches, squares,
and winding, cobbled streets.
   The grandeur of Plaza de San
Fernando is characterized by
the strict Renaissance façade
of the old **Ayuntamiento**. The
present town hall, located just
off the square, dates from the

Tomb of Servilia, Necrópolis Romana, Carmona

18th century; in its courtyard are some fine Roman mosaics. Close by lies **Iglesia de Santa María la Mayor**. Built in the 15th century over a mosque, whose patio still survives, this is the finest of the churches. Dominating the town, however, are the imposing ruins of the **Alcázar del Rey Pedro**, once a palace of Pedro I, also known as Pedro el Cruel (the Cruel) *(see p46)*. Parts of it now form a parador *(see p202)*.

Just outside Carmona is the **Necrópolis Romana**, the extensive remains of a Roman burial ground. A site museum displays some of the worldly goods buried with the bodies. These include statues, glass, and jewelry, as well as urns.

🏛 **Ayuntamiento**
Calle Salvador 2. ((95) 414 00 11.
◻ Mon–Sat. ● public hols.
🏛 **Necrópolis Romana**
Avenida Jorge Bonsor 9. ((95) 414
08 11. ◻ Tue–Sun. ● public hols.

Écija ⓳

Sevilla. **Road map** C3. 🏃 38,000.
🚌 🛈 Ayuntamiento, Plaza de
España 1. (95) 590 02 40. 🛒 Thu.

É̲CIJA IS NICKNAMED "the frying pan of Andalusia" owing to its famously torrid climate. In the searing heat, the palm trees that stand on the Plaza de España provide some blissful shade. This is an ideal place to sit and observe daily life. It is also the focus of evening strolls and coffee drinking.

Écija has 11 Baroque church steeples. Most are adorned with gleaming *azulejos (see p74)* and together they make an impressive sight. The most florid of these is the **Iglesia de Santa María** overlooking

Plaza de España. **Iglesia de San Juan**, adorned with an exquisite bell tower, is a very close rival.

The façade of the **Palacio de Peñaflor** is also in the Baroque style. Its pink marble doorway is topped by twisted columns, and a pretty wrought-iron balcony runs along the whole front façade of the building.

🏛 **Palacio de Peñaflor**
C/ Caballeros s/n. ((95) 483 02 73.
◻ daily (courtyard only).

Osuna ⓴

Sevilla. **Road map** C4.
🏃 17,500. 🚌 🚌 🛈 Casa
de Cultura, Calle Sevilla 22.
(95) 481 22 58. 🛒 Mon.

O̲SUNA WAS ONCE a key Roman garrison town before being eclipsed during the Moorish era. The Dukes of Osuna, who wielded immense power, restored the town to prominence in the 16th century. During the 1530s they founded the grand collegiate church, **Colegiata de Santa**

María. Inside is a Baroque *retablo*, and paintings by José de Ribera. The dukes were also the founders of the town's **Universidad**, a rather severe building with a beautiful patio.

Some fine mansions, among them the Baroque **Palacio del Marqués de la Gomera**, are also a testament to the former glory of this town.

Estepa ㉑

Sevilla. **Road map** C4. 🏃 12,000. 🚌
🛈 Casa de Cultura, Calle Saladillo 12.
(95) 591 27 71. 🛒 Mon, Wed & Fri.

L̲EGEND HAS IT that when the invading Roman army closed in on Estepa in 207 BC, the townsfolk committed mass suicide rather than surrender. These days, life in this small town in the far southeast of Sevilla province is far less dramatic. Its fame today derives from the production of its renowned biscuits – *mantecados* and *polvorones (see p213)*. Wander among the narrow streets of iron-grilled mansions, and sit on the main square. From here you can contemplate the beautiful black and white façade of the Baroque church, **Iglesia del Carmen**, which overlooks the square.

Iglesia del Carmen statuary

Wall painting on the ornate Baroque façade of Palacio de Peñaflor, Écija

CÓRDOBA AND JAÉN

CÓRDOBA, WITH ITS MAGNIFICENT MOSQUE *and pretty Moorish patios, is northern Andalusia's star attraction. Córdoba province encompasses the Montilla and Moriles wine towns and also Baroque treasures such as Priego de Córdoba. Jaén's mountain passes are gateways to the province's beautiful Renaissance towns of Úbeda and Baeza, and to the great wildlife preserves of the mountain ranges.*

Córdoba, on Andalusia's great river, Guadalquivir, was a Roman provincial capital 2,000 years ago, but its golden age came with the Moors. In the 10th century it was the western capital of the Islamic empire, rivaling Baghdad in wealth, power, and sophistication. Today it is an atmospheric city, its ancient quarters and great buildings reflecting a long and glorious history.

Córdoba's surrounding countryside is dotted with monuments to its Moorish past – like the Caliph's palace of Medina Azahara. To the south lies the Campiña, an undulating landscape covered in regiments of olives and vines, and green and gold expanses of sunflowers and grain. Here and there are whitewashed villages and hilltop castles with crumbling walls.

Running across the north of Córdoba and Jaén provinces is the Sierra Morena. Deer and boars shelter in the forest and scrub of this broad mountain range. The sierras dominate Jaén province. The great Río Guadalquivir springs to life as a sparkling stream in the Sierra de Cazorla, the craggy wilderness along its eastern border. Through the ages, mule trains, highwaymen, and armies have used the cleft in Sierra Morena, known as Desfiladero de Despeñaperros, to cross from La Mancha and Castilla to Andalusia.

Ancient castles perched on heights, once strategic outposts on the Muslim/Christian frontier, now overlook the peaceful olive groves punctuated by historic towns preserving gems of post-Reconquest architecture.

The city of Jaén with its cathedral in the foreground, as viewed from Castillo de Santa Catalina

◁ Elaborate stonework and Islamic inscriptions surrounding a doorway into Córdoba's Mezquita

Exploring Córdoba and Jaén

THIS REGION OF ROLLING FIELDS and craggy heights is divided by the fertile Guadalquivir valley. On the northern banks of the river is Córdoba with its famous Mezquita. The wild, uninhabited Sierra Morena lies to the north, and southward is a prosperous farming area dotted with historic towns, such as Priego de Córdoba. Farther east, amid the olive groves of Jaén, are the Renaissance jewels, Baeza and Úbeda. From these towns it is an easy excursion to the nature preserve of Cazorla, which offers dramatic scenery and a glimpse of deer and wild boar.

Main street of Cabra during siesta

BELALCAZAR

HINOJOSA DEL DUQUE

① SIERRA MORENA

C420

ANORA

PEDROCHE

C421

POZOBLANO

N502

CO121

Puertollano

PENARROYO

FUENTE OBEJUNA

BELMEZ

N432

VILLANUEVA DE CORDOBA

C420

SANTUA VIRGE LA CA

Embalse de Puente Nuevo

N432

Embalse de Yeguas

ANDUJAR

Embalse del Guadalmellato

MONTORO **⑥**

N420

N IV

MEDINA AZAHARA **④**

Río Guadalquivir

⑤ CORDOBA

N324

CO142

C329

C431

③ CASTILLO DEL ALMODOVAR DEL RIO

② PALMA DEL RIO

N IV

Sevilla

MONTILLA **⑦**

N432

⑪ BAENA

ALCAUDE

AGUILAR **⑧**

⑩ CABRA

CO241

PRIEGO D CORDOBA

⑫

⑨ LUCENA

C336

N321

N331

C334

Embalse de Iznájar

Málaga

Olive groves stretching across the countryside

Sights at a Glance

The town of Cazorla on the border of
the nature preserve

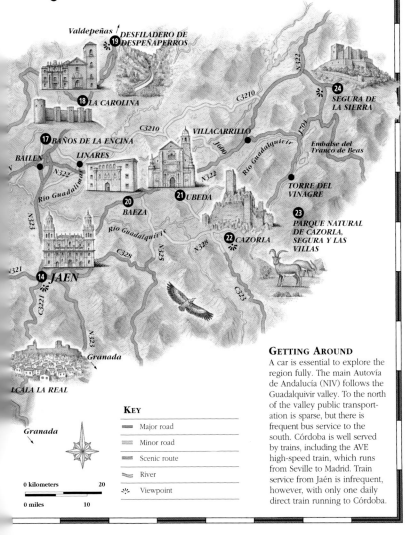

Getting Around

A car is essential to explore the
region fully. The main Autovía
de Andalucía (NIV) follows the
Guadalquivir valley. To the north
of the valley public transportation is sparse, but there is
frequent bus service to the
south. Córdoba is well served
by trains, including the AVE
high-speed train, which runs
from Seville to Madrid. Train
service from Jaén is infrequent,
however, with only one daily
direct train running to Córdoba.

Key

- ▬ Major road
- ▭ Minor road
- ▬ Scenic route
- ⪥ River
- ☀ Viewpoint

```
0 kilometers        20
0 miles        10
```

Palma del Río ❷

Córdoba. **Road map** C3. 🏛 *19,000.*
🚉 🚌 ℹ️ *Casa de Cultura, Calle
Gracia 15. (957) 71 02 45.* 🎭 *Tue.*

REMAINS OF THE WALLS built by
the Almohads in the 12th
century are a reminder of the
frontier days of this farming
town. The Romans established
a settlement here, on the main
route from Córdoba to
Itálica *(see p128)*, al-
most 2,000 years ago.
The Baroque **Iglesia
de la Asunción**
dates from the
18th century. The
monastery of San
Francisco is now
a delightful hotel
(see p207), and
guests dine in
the 15th-century
refectory of
the Franciscan
monks. Palma is
the home town
of El Cordobés,

**Bell tower,
La Asunción**

one of Spain's most famous
matadors. As a youth he would
creep out into the fields around
the town to practice with the
bulls. His biography, *Or I'll
Dress You in Mourning*, gives
a vivid view of Palma and of
the days of desperate hard-
ship that followed the end
of the Civil War.

Castillo del Almodóvar del Río ❸

Córdoba. **Road map** C3.
📞 *(957) 63 51 16.* ⏰ *daily for
guided tours only.*

ONE OF ANDALUSIA'S most
dramatic silhouettes breaks
the skyline as the traveler
approaches Almodóvar del
Río. The Moorish castle, with
parts dating back to the 8th
century, looks down on the
straggling whitewashed town
and on the surrounding fields
of cotton and grain.

**Detail of wood carving in the
main hall of Medina Azahara**

Medina Azahara ❹

Córdoba. **Road map** C3. 📞 *(957) 32
91 30.* ⏰ *Tue–Sun.* 📷 ♿

THIS ONCE-GLORIOUS palace was
built in the 10th century for
Caliph Abd al Rahman III, who
named it after his favorite
wife. He spared no expense
in its construction, em-
ploying more than 15,000

Sierra Morena Tour ❶

THE AUSTERE SIERRA MORENA runs across northern
Andalusia. This route through Córdoba province
takes in a region of oak- and pine-covered hills,
where hunters stalk deer and boar. It also
includes the open plain of Valle de los Pedroches,
where storks make their nests on church towers.
The area, little visited by tourists, is sparsely
populated. Its individual character is more sober
than the usual image of Andalusia, and it makes
a delightful day-trip from Córdoba.

Hinojosa del Duque ④
"Catedral de la Sierra," the vast, 15th-
century pile of the Gothic-Renaissance
Iglesia San Juan Bautista, dominates the
town. It has a Churrigueresque *retablo*.

RISING AT FUENTE OBEJUNA

**Lope de Vega
(1562–1635)**

On April 23, 1476, townsfolk
stormed the palace of the
hated lord, Don Fernando
Gómez de Guzmán. He
was hurled from a palace
window, then hacked to
pieces in the main plaza.
When questioned by a
judge who committed
the crime, the men
and women replied
as one, "Fuente Obe-
juna, señor!" Nobody was punished, at
least according to Lope de Vega's best-
known play, named after the village.

Peñarroya-Pueblonuevo ②
This was once an important
copper- and iron-
mining center.

Fuente Obejuna ③
The Plaza Lope de Vega
is often the site for
Lope de Vega's famous
play. The parish church,
Nuestra Señora del
Castillo, was built in
the 15th century.

Bélmez ①
Remains of a 13th-century
castle crown a hill, from
which there are fine views.

mules, 4,000 camels, and 10,000 workers to bring building materials from Andalusia and North Africa to the site.

The palace is built on three levels and includes a mosque, the caliph's residence, and fine gardens. Alabaster, ebony, jasper, and marble decorations adorned its many halls, and, it is said, shimmering pools of mercury added luster.

Unfortunately, the glory was short-lived. The palace was sacked by Berber invaders in 1010. Then, over centuries, it was ransacked for its building materials. Now, the ruins give only glimpses of its former splendor – a Moorish main hall, for instance, decorated with marble carvings, still with its fine ceiling of carved wood. The palace is being restored, but progress is slow.

Córdoba ❺

See pp136–42.

Montoro ❻

Córdoba. **Road map** D3. 🏘 *10,000.* 🚌 ℹ *Plaza de España 7. (957) 16 00 89.* 🛒 *Tue.*

SPREAD OVER FIVE HILLS that span a bend in the Guadalquivir River, Montoro dates from the times of the Greeks and Phoenicians. Today the economy of this rather lethargic town depends on its olive groves. The solid bridge, designed by Enrique de Egas of Brussels, was started in the time of the Catholic Monarchs

(*see pp46–7*) and took more than 50 years to finish. The townswomen sold their jewelry to raise funds for building the bridge, hence its name: **Puente de las Donadas** (Bridge of the Donors).

Steep, tortuous streets give the town charm. In Plaza de España are two imposing buildings, the **Ayuntamiento**, former seat of the ducal rulers, with a Plateresque façade, and the Gothic-Mudéjar **Iglesia de San Bartolomé**.

Leather goods are among several enduring crafts that are still produced in Montoro.

The 16th-century bridge spanning the Guadalquivir at Montoro

Belalcázar ⑤
An immense tower, part of a ruined castle built in 1466, dominates the skyline. Around 1480, Sebastián de Belalcázar, conqueror of Nicaragua, was born here.

Añora ⑥
This town is famous for preserving old customs, such as *Cruces de Mayo* (May Crosses) (*see p36*).

Pozoblanco ⑧
Pozoblanco entered Spanish folklore on September 26, 1984, when matador Paquirri was fatally gored by a bull.

TIPS FOR DRIVERS

Length: 190 km (118 miles).
Stopping-off points: There are many shady places to stop along the way to have a picnic. Some of the villages along this route, such as Fuente Obejuna, have restaurants and bars.

Pedroche ⑦
A 56-m (184-ft) high granite church tower, with an alarming crack in it, rises above this village.

KEY

▨▨	Tour route
⹀	Other roads
▲	Mountain peak

0 kilometers   10

0 miles   5

CO424 El Viso

C420

Villaralto

Fuente la Lancha

Alcaracejos

▲ PELAYO

N502

N432

CORDOBA

Street-by-Street: Córdoba ⑤

Statue of Maimónides

THE HEART OF CORDOBA is the old Jewish quarter near the Mezquita, known as the Judería. A walk around this area gives the visitor the sensation that little has changed since this was one of the greatest cities in the Western world. Narrow, cobbled streets where cars cannot penetrate, secluded niches, wrought iron gates, and tiny workshops where silversmiths create fine jewelry – all appears very much as it was 1,000 years ago. Traffic roars along the riverfront, past the replica of a Moorish waterwheel and the towering walls of the Great Mosque. Most of the sights are in this area, while modern city life takes place some blocks north, around the Plaza de las Tendillas.

Sinagoga
Hebrew script covers the interior walls of this medieval synagogue, the only one remaining in Andalusia.

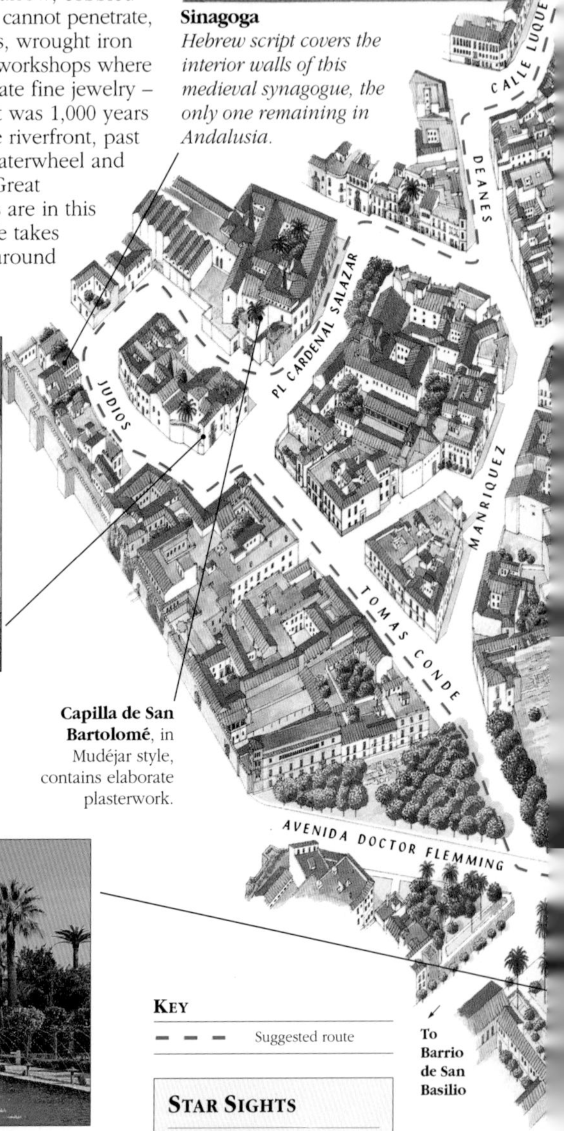

Museo Taurino
A replica of the tomb of the famous torero, Manolete, and the hide of the bull that killed him (see p25) are in this museum of bullfighting.

Capilla de San Bartolomé, in Mudéjar style, contains elaborate plasterwork.

★ Alcázar de los Reyes Cristianos
Water terraces and fountains add to the tranquil atmosphere of the gardens belonging to the palace-fortress of the Catholic Monarchs, constructed in the 14th century.

KEY

– – – Suggested route

To Barrio de San Basilio

STAR SIGHTS

★ **Mezquita**

★ **Alcázar de los Reyes Cristianos**

Callejón de las Flores
Colorful geraniums stand out vividly against this whitewashed narrow alley leading to a tiny square.

VISITORS' CHECKLIST

Córdoba. **Road map** C3. 🌟
305,000. 🚉 Avda de America.
(957) 49 02 02. 🚌 Avenida
Medina Azahara 29. (957) 23 64
74. 🛈 Palacio de Congresos y
Exposiciones, Calle Torrijos 10.
(957) 47 12 35. 🗓 daily.
🎭 Carnaval (Feb); Semana Santa
(Easter); Cruces de Mayo, Festival
de los Patios, Feria (May).

★ Mezquita
The mighty walls of the Great Mosque hide a forest of delicate arches, pillars and a dazzling mihrab.

Puerta del Puente

Triunfo de San Rafael
St. Raphael, the city's patron saint, is honored by this 18th-century statue. Puerta del Puente, nearby, was once part of the city walls.

Palacio Episcopal, today the Palacio de Congresos y Exposiciones, houses the tourist office.

Puente Romano
The Romans were the first to build a bridge over the Río Guadalquivir. Rebuilt many times, the bridge still rests on its original Roman foundations, hence its name.

| 0 meters | 75 |
| 0 yards | 75 |

Exploring Córdoba

Sculpture by Mateo Inurria

CÓRDOBA'S CORE is the old city around the Mezquita on the banks of the Guadalquivir. Its origins are probably Carthaginian; the name may be derived from Kartuba, Phoenician for "rich and precious city." Under the Romans it was a provincial capital and birthplace of philosopher Seneca. However, Córdoba's golden age was in the 10th century when Abd al Rahman III created an independent caliphate with Córdoba as its capital. Its influence spread to North Africa and the Balearic Islands. Córdoba was a center of trade, industry, and learning, where Jews and Christians lived alongside Muslims. Civil war *(see pp44–5)* ended the caliphate and the city was pillaged. It declined after falling to Fernando III in 1236, although a number of fine buildings have since been erected.

Naranjas y Limones in Museo Julio Romero de Torres

🔒 Mezquita

See pp140–41.

♣ Alcázar de los Reyes Cristianos

C/ Caballerizas Reales s/n. 📞 *(957) 42 01 51.* ⏰ *Tue–Sun.* 🎫
This palace-fortress was built in 1328 on the orders of Alfonso XI. Fernando II and Isabel stayed here when they visited Córdoba during their campaign to conquer Granada from the Moors *(see p46)*. Later it was used by the Inquisition *(see p49)*, and then as a prison.

The beautiful gardens with fish ponds and fountains, restored in the 1950s, make for a pleasant stroll. From the battlements there are good views of the river. Behind the palace's thick walls are striking Roman mosaics and a Roman sarcophagus dating from the 3rd century AD.

✡ Sinagoga

Calle Judíos 10. 📞 *(957) 20 29 28.* ⏰ *Tue–Sun.* 🎫
Constructed around 1315, the small Mudéjar-style synagogue is one of three in Spain preserved from that era. The other two are both in Toledo, just south of Madrid. The women's gallery and decorative plasterwork with Hebrew script are of particular interest.

The synagogue lies in the Judería, the Jewish quarter, which has hardly changed since Moorish times. It is a labyrinth of narrow streets and alleys, with whitewashed houses and private patios.

In a plaza nearby is a statue of Maimonides, Jewish sage and physician. He was born in Córdoba in the 12th century.

🏛 Museo Taurino

Plaza Maimónides s/n. 📞 *(957) 20 10 56.* ⏰ *Tue–Sun.* 🎫
This museum displays old posters, the stuffed heads of famous bulls, and other relics of the *corrida (see pp24–5)*. Rooms are dedicated to the local idols, matadors Lagartijo, Manolete, and Machaquito. Manolete, a legendary fighter, was gored to death by the bull Islero in Linares in 1947.

🏛 Museo Julio Romero de Torres

Plaza del Potro 1. 📞 *(957) 49 19 09.* ⏰ *Tue–Sun.* 🎫
Julio Romero de Torres (1874–1930), who was born in this house, captured the soul of Córdoba in his paintings. Many depict well-proportioned nudes in stilted poses; others are painfully mawkish, including the deathbed scene *Look How Lovely She Was* (1895). Perhaps his most macabre work is *Cante Hondo* (1930). His humor emerges in a nude study, *Naranjas y Limones* (Oranges and Lemons) (1928).

🏛 Museo Provincial de Bellas Artes

Plaza del Potro 1. 📞 *(957) 47 33 45.* ⏰ *Tue–Sun.*
Located in a former charity hospital, this museum lies just across the patio from Museo Julio Romero de Torres. Exhibits include sculptures by local artist Mateo Inurria (1867–1924) as well as works by Murillo, Valdés Leal, and Zurbarán of the Seville School *(see p64)*.

♟ Plaza de la Corredera

Built in the 17th century in Castilian style, this handsome arcaded square has been the scene of bullfights and other

Daily market in the arcaded Plaza de la Corredera

public events. The buildings
are gradually being restored,
but the cafés under the arches
still retain an air of the past.
A market is held here.

⛩ Palacio de Viana

Plaza Don Gome 2. **(** *(957) 48 01
34.* ⬜ *Thu–Tue.* ⬤ *June 1–15
(except patios).* 🈶
A wealth of tapestries, furniture, paintings, and porcelain
is displayed in this 17th-
century mansion. Purchased

**Central fountain in the garden of
the 17th-century Palacio de Viana**

by a savings bank in 1981,
the former home of the Viana
family is kept much as they
left it. There are 14 beautiful
patios and a delightful garden
of citrus trees, date palms,
and rose bushes, with a
fountain in the center.

🏛 Museo Arqueológico

Plaza Jerónimo Páez 7. **(** *(957) 47
40 11.* ⬜ *Tue–Sun.* 🈶
Roman remains, including
mosaics, pottery, and relief
carvings, are on display in this
Renaissance mansion. Other
exhibits include impressive
finds from the Moorish era,
such as a bronze stag dating
from the 10th century, found
at Medina Azahara *(see p134)*.

⛩ Puente Romano

This arched bridge has Roman
foundations, but was rebuilt
by the Moors. Nearby, south
of the Mezquita, stands the
Puerta del Puente, designed by
Hernán Ruiz in 1571.

**Moorish bronze stag in the Museo
Arqueológico**

⛩ Torre de la Calahorra

An impressive end to the
Puente Romano, this tower was
built for defense during the
14th century. It houses an
intriguing little museum which
explains the life, culture, and
philosophy of 10th-century
Córdoba through models and
audiovisual shows.

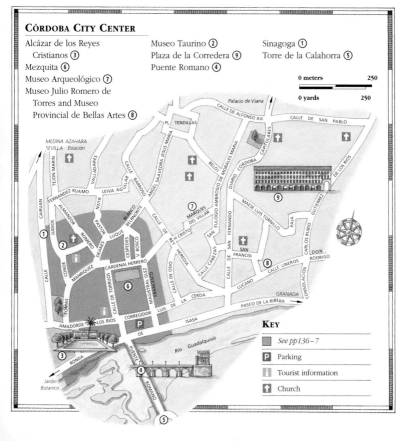

CÓRDOBA CITY CENTER

Alcázar de los Reyes
    Cristianos ③
Mezquita ⑥
Museo Arqueológico ⑦
Museo Julio Romero de
    Torres and Museo
    Provincial de Bellas Artes ⑧

Museo Taurino ②
Plaza de la Corredera ⑨
Puente Romano ④

Sinagoga ①
Torre de la Calahorra ⑤

0 meters 250
0 yards 250

KEY

	See pp136–7
P	Parking
i	Tourist information
✝	Church

Córdoba: the Mezquita

CÓRDOBA'S GREAT MOSQUE, dating back
12 centuries, embodied the power of
Islam on the Iberian peninsula. Abd al
Rahman I *(see p44)* built the original
mosque between 785 and 787. The
building evolved over the centuries,
blending many architectural forms.
In the 10th century al Hakam II
(see p44) made some of the most
lavish additions, including the
elaborate *mihrab* (prayer niche)
and the *maqsura* (caliph's
enclosure). In the 16th century a
cathedral was built in the heart
of the reconsecrated mosque,
part of which was destroyed.

Patio de los Naranjos
*Orange trees grow in the courtyard
where the faithful washed
before prayer.*

Torre del Alminar
*This bell tower, 93 m (305
ft) high, is built on the site
of the original minaret.
Steep steps lead to the top
for a fine view of the city.*

**The Puerta del
Perdón** is a Mudéjar-
style entrance gate, built
during Christian rule in
1377. Penitents were
pardoned here.

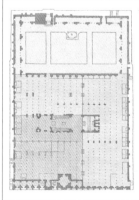

EXPANSION OF THE MEZQUITA

Abd al Rahman I built the
original mosque. Extensions
were added by Abd al Rahman
II, al Hakam II, and al Mansur.

**Puerta de San
Esteban** is set in
a section of wall
from an earlier
Visigothic church.

KEY TO ADDITIONS

☐ Mosque of Abd al Rahman I

☐ Extension by Abd al Rahman II

☐ Extension by al Hakam II

☐ Extension by al Mansur

☐ Patio de los Naranjos

STAR FEATURES

★ **Mihrab**

★ **Capilla de
Villaviciosa**

★ **Arches and Pillars**

Cathedral
Part of the mosque was destroyed to accommodate the cathedral, started in 1523. Featuring an Italianate dome, it was chiefly designed by members of the Hernán Ruiz family.

VISITORS' CHECKLIST

Calle Torrijos 10. ☎ (957) 47 05 12. ◑ 10am–6pm Mon–Sat; 3:30–5:30pm Sun (Apr–Sep: until 7pm daily). ✎ ✝ 8am & 9am Mon–Fri; 8pm & 9pm Sat; 9am, 10:30am, 11:30am, noon, 12:30pm & 1pm Sun.

The cathedral choir has Churrigueresque stalls, carved by Pedro Duque Cornejo in 1758.

Capilla Mayor

Capilla Real

★ Arches and Pillars
More than 850 columns of granite, jasper, and marble support the roof, creating a dazzling visual effect. Many were taken from Roman and Visigothic buildings.

★ Mihrab
This prayer niche, richly ornamented, held a gilt copy of the Koran. The worn flagstones indicate where pilgrims circled it seven times on their knees.

★ Capilla de Villaviciosa
The first Christian chapel to be built in the mosque, in 1371, the Capilla de Villaviciosa has stunning multilobed arches.

The Patios of Córdoba

Since early times, family and social life in Andalusia have revolved around the courtyard or patio, which is at the heart of the classic Mediterranean house. The sleeping accommodations and living rooms are built around this space, which introduces air and light into the house. Brick arches, colorful tiles, ironwork, orange and lemon trees, and pots full of flowers add to the charm of these cool and tranquil retreats. Córdoba takes pride in all its patio gardens, be they palatial spaces in the grandest residences or tiny courtyards in humble homes, shared by many. There are traditional patios in the San Lorenzo and Judería quarters and in Barrio San Basilio, west of the Mezquita.

Regional pottery as patio decoration

Whitewashed walls   **Tiled portrait of saint**   **Orange trees**

Festival de los Patios, when scores of patios are thrown open to the public, takes place in early May (see pp36–7). The most beautifully decorated patio wins a prestigious prize.

ANDALUSIAN PATIO

This scene, painted by García Rodríguez (1863–1925), evokes a style of patio that is still common in Andalusia. The patio walls are usually immaculately whitewashed, contrasting with the colorful display of geraniums and carnations in terra-cotta pots. Fragrant blooms of jasmine add to the atmosphere.

Moorish-style lamps, *which now have electric bulbs, light the patio in the late evening.*

Azulejos, *a reminder of the region's Moorish past, decorate many patios, adding to their colorful display.*

Cancelas *are attractively designed iron gates that screen the private patio from the street outside.*

A central fountain *or well traditionally provided water and remains a feature of many patios today.*

Montilla **7**

Córdoba. **Road map** C3. ⚐ 24,000.
🚉 🚌 ℹ️ *Calle Padre Miguel Molina 1.
(957) 65 41 94.* 🅿️ *Fri.*

MONTILLA IS THE CENTER of an important wine-making
region, but one that finds it
difficult to emerge from the
shadow of a more famous rival.
The excellent white wine is
made in the same way as sherry
(*see pp28–9*) and tastes rather
like it but, unlike sherry, does
not need fortifying with alcohol.
Some *bodegas*, including
Alvear and **Pérez Barquero**,
are happy to welcome visitors
by prior arrangement.

The Mudéjar **Convento de
Santa Clara** dates from 1512.
The town library is in the **Casa
del Inca**, so named because
Garcilaso de la Vega, who
wrote about the Incas, lived
there in the 16th century.

**The historic crest of the Bodega
Pérez Barquero**

🍷 **Bodega Alvear**
Avenida María Auxiliadora 1.
📞 *(957) 65 28 00.* 🕐 *Mon–Fri (call
first to arrange visit).* ⬤ *public hols.*

🍷 **Bodega Pérez Barquero**
Avenida de Andalucía. 📞 *(957) 65
05 00.* 🕐 *Mon–Fri (call first to
arrange visit).* ⬤ *public hols.*

Aguilar **8**

Córdoba. **Road map** C3. ⚐ 13,000.
🚉 🚌 ℹ️ *Ayuntamiento, Plaza San
José 1. (957) 66 00 00.* 🅿️ *Fri.*

CERAMICS, WINE, and olive oil
are important local pro-
ducts in Aguilar, which was a
settlement in Roman times.
There are several seigneurial
houses, but of more interest is
the unusual, eight-sided **Plaza
de San José**. Built in 1810, it
houses the town hall. Nearby
is a Baroque clock tower.

Lucena **9**

Córdoba. **Road map** D3. ⚐ 35,000.
🚉 ℹ️ *Ayuntamiento, Plaza Nueva 1.
(957) 50 05 42.* 🅿️ *Wed.*

LUCENA PROSPERS from furniture
making and brass and
copper manufacturing, and
produces interesting ceramics.
Under the caliphs of Córdoba
(*see p44*) it was an important
trading and intellectual center,
with a dynamic, independent
Jewish community.

Iglesia de Santiago, with a
Baroque turret, was built on the
site of a synagogue in 1503. The
Torre del Moral is the only
remaining part of a Moorish
castle. Granada's last sultan,
Boabdil, was captured in battle
in 1483 and was imprisoned
here. Nearby, the 15th-century
Iglesia de San Mateo has a
flamboyant Baroque sacristy
and three naves, separated by
delicate arches.

On the first Sunday in May
Lucena stages an elaborate
ceremony that honors the
Virgen de Araceli.

Cabra **10**

Córdoba. **Road map** D3. ⚐ 21,000.
🚉 ℹ️ *Calle Martín Belda 31. (957)
52 01 10.* 🅿️ *Mon.*

SET AMID FERTILE fields and
vast olive groves, Cabra
was an episcopal seat in the
3rd century. On a rise stands
the former castle, which is

**Statue of Santo Domingo, Iglesia
Santo Domingo in Cabra**

now a school. There are also
some noble mansions and the
Iglesia Santo Domingo with
a Baroque façade.

Just outside the town, the
Fuente del Río, source of the
Río Cabra, is a pleasantly leafy
spot in which to picnic.

Baena **11**

Córdoba. **Road map** D3. ⚐ 21,000.
🚉 ℹ️ *Ayuntamiento, Pl de la Constitución 1. (957) 67 00 00.* 🅿️ *Thu.*

BAENA'S OLIVE OIL has been
famed since Roman times.
At the top of the whitewashed
town is **Iglesia Santa María
la Mayor**. On the Plaza de la
Constitución stands the handsome, modern town hall. The
Casa del Monte, an arcaded
mansion dating from the 18th
century, flanks it on one side.

Easter week is spectacular,
when thousands of drummers
take to the streets (*see p32*).

Decoration on façade of the 18th-century Casa del Monte, Baena

Jaén ⓮

THE MOORS KNEW JAEN as *geen*, meaning "way station of caravans." Their lofty fortress, later rebuilt as the Castillo de Santa Catalina, symbolizes Jaén's strategic importance on the route to Andalusia from the more austere Castile. For centuries this area was a battleground between Moors and Christians *(see pp46–7)*. The older, upper part of the city holds most interest. Around the cathedral and toward the Barrio San Juan are numerous seigneurial buildings, long winding streets, and steep alleys. The city center is filled with fancy shops, and in the evenings the narrow streets near Plaza de la Constitución are filled with people enjoying the *tapeo* in the many bars.

Bamboo crucifix at Santa Clara

Mighty ramparts of Castillo de Santa Catalina

♟ Castillo de Santa Catalina
Carretera al Castillo. 【 *(953) 23 00 00* (parador). ○ *daily.*
Hannibal is believed to have erected a tower on this rocky pinnacle, high above the city. Later the Moors established a fortress, only to lose it to the crusading King Fernando III in 1246. A larger castle was then built with huge ramparts. This has been restored and a medieval-style *parador* (inn) built next door *(see pp22–3)*.

It is worthwhile taking the sinuous road up to the Torre del Homenaje and the castle chapel. Even more rewarding are the fantastic views to be had of the city, the surrounding mountains, and the landscape, thick with olive trees.

🔒 Catedral
Andrés de Vandelvira, responsible for many of Ubeda's fine buildings *(see pp150–51)*, designed the cathedral in the 16th century. Later additions include the two handsome 17th-century towers that flank the west front. Inside are beautifully carved choir stalls. There is also a museum that contains valuable works of art.

Every Friday, between 11:30am and 12:45pm, worshipers can view the Lienzo del Santo Rostro. St. Veronica is said to have used this piece of cloth to wipe Christ's face, which left a permanent impression on it.

Statuary on the cathedral façade

♨ Baños Arabes
Palacio Villardompardo, Plaza Santa Luisa de Marillac. 【 *(953) 23 62 92.* ○ *Tue–Sun.* ● *public hols.* 🔲
These 11th-century baths are known as the baths of Ali, a Moorish chieftain. They were restored during the 1980s. The interior of the baths features horseshoe arches, ceilings decorated with tiny star-shaped windows, a hemispherical dome, and two earthenware vats in which bathers once immersed themselves. The baths are entered through the Palacio Villardompardo, which also houses a museum of local arts and crafts.

OLIVE OIL

Olive oil is the lifeblood of Jaén and its province. Since the Phoenicians, or possibly the Greeks, brought the olive tree to Spain it has flourished in Andalusia, particularly in Jaén, which today has an annual production of more than 200,000 tons of oil. Harvesting, mostly by hand, takes place from December onward. Quality is controlled by a system known as *Denominación de Origen Controlada*. The best product, virgin olive oil, is made from the first cold-pressing, so that the full flavor, vitamins, and nutrients of the oil are preserved.

Harvest time in one of the many olive groves in Andalusia

Horseshoe arches supporting the dome at the Baños Arabes

Shrine of Virgen de la Capilla in Iglesia San Ildefonso

🛈 Capilla de San Andrés

Tucked away in a narrow alley next to a college lies this Mudéjar chapel. It was founded in the 16th century, possibly on the site of a synagogue, by Gutiérrez González, who was treasurer to Pope Leo X and endowed with extensive privileges. A magnificent gilded iron screen by Maestro Bartolomé de Jaén is the highlight of the chapel.

🛈 Iglesia San Ildefonso

This mainly Gothic church has façades in three different styles. One is Gothic, with a mosaic of the Virgin descending on Jaén during a Moorish siege in 1430. A second is partly Plateresque *(see p23)* and the third, by Ventura Rodríguez in the late 18th century, is Neo-Classical. Inside, the high altar is by Pedro and José Roldán. There is also a chapel that enshrines the Virgen de la Capilla, Jaén's patron saint. The museum next door is devoted to the Virgin.

🛈 Real Monasterio de Santa Clara

Founded in the 13th century, just after the reconquest of the city by Christian forces, this is one of the most ancient monasteries in Jaén. It has a lovely cloister, which dates from about 1581. The church has an *artesonado* ceiling and shelters a curious 16th-century bamboo image of Christ made in Ecuador. Sweet cakes are offered for sale by the nuns from the convent.

VISITORS' CHECKLIST

Jaén. **Road map** D3. 🚗 110,000. 🚉 *Paseo de la Estación. (953) 25 17 56.* 🚌 *Plaza Coca de la Piñera. (953) 25 01 06.* 🛈 *Calle Arquitecto Berges 1. (953) 22 27 37.* 🗓 *Thu.* 🎉 *Semana Santa (Easter); Festividad de Nuestra Señora de la Capilla (Jun 11); Feria de San Lucas (Oct); Romería de Santa Catalina (Nov 25).*

🏛 Museo Provincial

Paseo de la Estación 27. ☎ *(953) 25 03 20.* 🗓 *Tue–Sun.* ● *public hols.* 🎫
This building incorporates part of the remains of the Iglesia de San Miguel and the façade of a 16th-century granary. A Palaeo-Christian sarcophagus, Roman mosaics and sculptures, and ceramics from the Iberian, Greek, and Roman periods are among the articles on display.

A short walk along Paseo de la Estación is the Plaza de las Batallas, where there stands a memorial to the defeat of the Moors at Las Navas de Tolosa *(see p46)* and of Napoleon's army at Bailén *(see p51).*

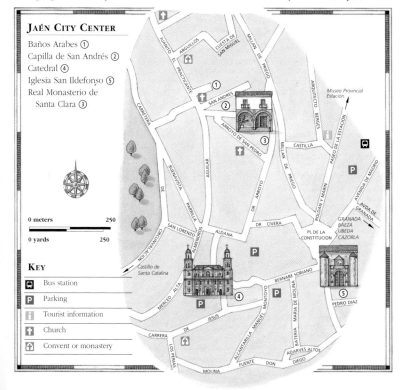

JAÉN CITY CENTER

Baños Arabes ①
Capilla de San Andrés ②
Catedral ④
Iglesia San Ildefonso ⑤
Real Monasterio de Santa Clara ③

0 meters   250
0 yards   250

KEY

🚌	Bus station
🅿	Parking
🛈	Tourist information
🛐	Church
🏛	Convent or monastery

The Moorish Castillo de la Mota and the ruined church crowning the hill above Alcalá la Real

Priego de Córdoba ⑫

Córdoba. **Road map** D3. 🏘 22,000. 🚌 🚉 *Calle del Río 33. (957) 70 06 25.* 🛒 *Sat.*

PRIEGO DE CORDOBA lies on a fertile plain at the foot of La Tiñosa, the highest mountain in Córdoba province. It is a pleasant small town with an unassuming air, well away from the main routes, and it claims to be the capital of Córdoba Baroque. The title is easy to accept in view of the dazzling work of local carvers, gilders, and ironworkers.

The town's labyrinthine old quarter was the site of the original Arab settlement. But the 18th century, when silk manufacturing prospered, was Priego's golden age. During this time elegant houses were built, and money was lavished on fine Baroque architecture, particularly churches.

A recently restored Moorish fortress, standing on Roman foundations, introduces visitors to the fine medieval quarter, which is called **Barrio de la Villa**. Impeccably whitewashed buildings line its narrow streets and flower-decked squares. Paseo Colombia leads to the Adarve, a long promenade with excellent views of the surrounding countryside.

The nearby **Iglesia de la Asunción** is an outstanding structure. Originally Gothic in style, it was converted to a Baroque church by Jerónimo Sánchez de Rueda in the 18th century. Its *pièce de résistance* is the sacristy chapel, created in 1784 by local artist Francisco Javier Pedrajas. Its sumptuous ornamentation in the form of sculpted figures and plaster scrolls and cornices can be overwhelming. The main altar is in Plateresque style *(see p23)*.

The **Iglesia de la Aurora** is another fine Baroque building. At midnight every Saturday the cloaked brotherhood, Nuestra Señora de la Aurora, parades the streets singing songs to the Virgin and collecting alms.

Silk merchants built many of the imposing mansions that follow the curve around the Calle del Río. Niceto Alcalá Zamora was born at No. 33 in 1877. A brilliant orator, he became Spain's president in 1931, but was forced into exile during the Civil War. Today this building is the tourist office.

At the end of the street is the **Fuente del Rey**, or King's Fountain. This is a Baroque extravaganza, with three pools, 139 spouts gushing water, and Neptune among its exuberant statuary.

May is one of the liveliest months to visit Priego. Every Sunday a procession celebrates the town's deliverance from a plague that devastated the population centuries ago.

Fine statuary ornaments the 16th-century Fuente del Rey at Priego de Córdoba

Alcalá la Real ⑬

Jaén. **Road map** D3. 🏘 23,000. 🚌 🛈 *Ayuntamiento, Plaza Arcipreste de Hita 1. (953) 58 00 00 ext 119.* 🛒 *Tue.*

ALCALÁ WAS A STRATEGIC point held by the military Order of Calatrava during Spain's Reconquest *(see pp46–7)*. On the hilltop of La Mota are the ruins of the Moorish **Castillo de la Mota**, built by the rulers of Granada in the 14th century, with later additions. Nearby are ruins of the town's main church. There are splendid views over the countryside and the historic town, with its air of past glories. The Renaissance **Palacio Abacial** and **Fuente de Carlos V** are the chief attractions found around the plaza in the center of the town.

Jaén ⓮

See pp144–5.

Andújar ⓯

Jaén. **Road map** D3. 🏘 *35,000.* 🚉
🚌 🛈 *Ayuntamiento, Plaza de
España 1. (953) 50 12 50.* 🛑 *Tue.*

THIS STRATEGICALLY situated
town was once the site of
Iliturgi, an Iberian town that
was destroyed by Scipio's army
in the Punic Wars *(see p42)*. A
15-arched bridge built by the
Roman conquerors still spans
the Guadalquivir River.

In the central plaza is the
Gothic **Iglesia San Miguel**,
with paintings by Alonso Cano.
The **Iglesia Santa María la
Mayor** features a Renaissance
façade and a splendid Mudéjar
tower. Inside is the painting
Christ in the Garden of Olives
(c.1605) by El Greco.

The town is also renowned
for its potters who still turn
out ceramics in traditional style.
Olive oil *(see p144)*, which is
produced in Andújar, figures
strongly in the local cuisine.

Santuario Virgen de la Cabeza ⓰

Jaén. **Road map** D2. 📞 *(953) 50 34
15.* ⏰ *8am–8:30pm daily.* 🅿 ♿

NORTH OF Andújar, amid the
oak trees and bull ranches
of the Sierra Morena, stands
the Santuario Virgen de la
Cabeza. Within this grim stone
temple, founded in the 13th

Roman bridge spanning the Guadalquivir at Andújar

century, is a much-venerated
Virgin. According to tradition
her original image was sent to
Spain by St. Peter.

Much of the building and
the original statue of the Virgin
were destroyed in 1937 in the
Civil War *(see pp52–3)*. For
nine months 230 civil guards
held out against Republican
forces. Some 20,000
men attacked the
sanctuary before
it burned down.
Captain Santiago
Cortés, the
commander of
the civil guard,
died from his
battle wounds.

On the last
Sunday in April
every year, many
thousands make
a pilgrimage to the
sanctuary to pay
homage to the Virgin *(see p37)*.

**Façade of the palace of
Pablo de Olavide**

Baños de la Encina ⓱

Jaén. **Road map** D2. 🚉 *from Linares
& Bailén.* 📞 *Ayuntamiento. (953) 61
30 04.* ⏰ *daily.*

CALIPH AL-HAKAM II *(see p44)*
ordered the construction
of this mighty fortress in the
foothills of the Sierra Morena
in AD 967. Rising above the
village, it is a daunting sight
with its 15 towers and soaring
ramparts. Its heights give fine
views across the surrounding
pastures and olive groves.

During the spring fair there
is a *romería (see p36)* to the
town's shrine of the Virgen de
la Encina. According to local
tradition, the Virgin made a
miraculous appearance on an
encina (holm oak tree).

La Carolina ⓲

Jaén. **Road map** E2. 🏘 *15,000.* 🚌
🛈 *Ayuntamiento. (953) 66 00 34.*
🛑 *Tue & Fri.*

FOUNDED in 1767, La Carolina
was populated by settlers
from Germany and Flanders.
This was an ill-fated plan
to develop the area
and to make it safer
for travelers.
The person in
charge, Carlos III's
minister, Pablo
de Olavide, had
a palace built on
the main square.
Just outside town
is a monument to
a battle that took
place at Las Navas
de Tolosa in 1212.
Alfonso VIII, king
of Castile, was led
by a shepherd over the hills to
Las Navas, where he crushed
the forces of the Moors. His
victory began the reconquest
of Andalusia *(see pp46–7)*.

Desfiladero de Despeñaperros ⓳

Jaén. **Road map** E2. 🛈 *La Carolina.
(953) 66 00 34.*

THIS SPECTACULAR PASS in the
Sierra Morena is the main
gateway to Andalusia. In the
past, armies, stagecoaches,
mule trains, and brigands all
used the pass, so robberies
and ambushes were common.

The four-lane Autovía de
Andalucía and a railroad line
thread their way through the
chasm, which offers views of
rock formations – *Los Organos*
(the organ pipes) and the *Salto
del Fraile* (monk's leap).

**Replica of the statue of the Virgin
Mary, Santuario de la Cabeza**

Street-by-Street: Baeza ⑳

**Coat of arms,
Casa del Pópulo**

Nestling amid the olive groves that characterize much of Jaén province, beautiful Baeza is a small town, unusually rich in Renaissance architecture. Called Beatia by the Romans and later the capital of a Moorish fiefdom, Baeza is portrayed as a "royal nest of hawks" on its coat of arms. It was conquered by Fernando III in 1226 – the first town in Andalusia to be definitively won back from the Moors – and was then settled by Castilian knights. An era of medieval splendor followed, reaching a climax in the 16th century, when Andrés de Vandelvira's splendid buildings were erected. In the early 20th century, Antonio Machado, one of his generation's greatest poets, lived here for some years.

★ Palacio de Jabalquinto
An Isabelline (see p22) style façade, flanked by elaborate, rounded buttresses, fronts this splendid Gothic palace.

Antigua Universidad
From 1542 until 1825, this Renaissance and Baroque building was the site of one of Spain's first universities.

Torre de los Aliatares is a 1,000-year-old tower built by the Moors.

To Úbeda

PLAZA DE ESPAÑA

Ayuntamiento
Formerly a jail and a courthouse, the town hall is a dignified Plateresque structure (see p23). The coats of arms of Felipe II, Juan de Borja, and of the town of Baeza adorn its upper façade.

La Alhóndiga, the old corn exchange, has impressive triple-tier arches running along its front.

Casas Consistoriales Bajas

Map street labels: SAN FELIPE · PLAZA SANTA CRUZ · BEATO AVILA · COMPAÑIA · ROMANO · BARBACANA · MERCADERIAS · PASEO DE LA CONSTITUCION · PASEO DE TUNDIDORES · O. NARVAEZ · BECERRA · GASPAR

VISITORS' CHECKLIST

Jaén. **Road map** E3. 🏛 *19,000.*
🚇 *Linares-Baeza 13 km (8 miles).
(953) 65 02 02.* 🚌 *Avda Alcalde
Puche Pardo. (953) 74 04 68.*
ℹ️ *Plaza del Pópulo s/n. (953) 74
04 44.* 🛒 *Tue.* 🎭 *Semana
Santa (Easter); Feria (mid-Aug);
Romería de la Yedra (early Sep).*

★ Catedral
*The impressive
cathedral was rebuilt
in 1567 by Andrés de
Vandelvira. The
Capilla Sagrario
has a beautiful
choir screen by
Bartolomé
de Jaén.*

PLAZA
SANTA
MARIA

OBISPO MENGIBAR

Fuente de Santa María
*Architect-sculptor Ginés
Martínez of Baeza designed
this fountain in the form of
a triumphal arch. It was
completed in 1564.*

**Antigua
Carnicería** is the
16th-century former
slaughterhouse.

SAN GIL

**Puerta de Jaén y
Arco de Villalar**
*This gateway in the city
ramparts is adjoined by
an arch erected in 1521
to appease Carlos I (see
p48) after a rebellion.*

| 0 meters | | 75 |
| 0 yards | | 75 |

KEY

ℹ️ Tourist information

– – – Suggested route

To
Jaén

★ Plaza del Pópulo
*The Casa del Pópulo, a fine Plateresque palace,
now the tourist office, overlooks this square. In
its center is the Fuente de los Leones, a fountain
with an Ibero-Roman statue flanked by lions.*

STAR SIGHTS

★ **Palacio de
Jabalquinto**

★ **Catedral**

★ **Plaza del Pópulo**

Úbeda ㉑

Hospital de Santiago, detail

Perched on the crest of a ridge, Úbeda is a showcase of Renaissance magnificence. Thanks to the patronage of some of Spain's most influential men of the 16th century, such as Francisco de los Cobos, secretary of state, and his great nephew, Juan Vázquez de Molina, a number of noble buildings are dotted around the town. The Plaza de Vázquez de Molina, which is surrounded by elegant palaces and churches, is undoubtedly the jewel in the crown. The narrow streets of the old quarter contrast sharply with modern Úbeda, which expands north of the Plaza de Andalucía and around the Avenida de la Libertad.

Maestro Bartolomé's choir screen at Capilla del Salvador

🏛 Capilla del Salvador

Three architects, Andrés de Vandelvira (credited with refining the Renaissance style), Diego de Siloé, and Esteban Jamete contributed to the design of this 16th-century landmark. It was built as the personal chapel of Francisco de los Cobos, whose tomb is to be found in the crypt.

Although the church was pillaged during the Civil War *(see pp52–3)*, it retains a number of treasures. These include a carving of Christ, which is all that remains of an altarpiece by Alonso de Berruguete, Maestro Bartolomé de Jaén's choir screen, and a sacristy by Vandelvira.

Behind the church are two other buildings dating from the 16th century – Cobos's palace, which is graced by a Renaissance façade, and the Hospital de los Honrados Viejos (Honored Elders). At the end of Baja del Salvador is the Plaza de Santa Lucía. A promenade leads from this point along the Redonda de Miradores, following the line of the old walls and offering views of the countryside.

🏛 Palacio de las Cadenas

Pl de Vázquez de Molina. 📞 *(953) 75 04 40.* ⬛ *Mon–Sat.* ⬤ *public hols.*
Two stone lions guard Úbeda's town hall, which occupies this palace built for Vázquez de Molina by Vandelvira during the mid-16th century. The building gets its name from the iron chains *(cadenas)* once attached to the columns supporting the main doorway.

Crowning the corners of the Classical façade are carved stone lanterns. There is a museum of local pottery in the basement and a fine patio. Part of the building houses the tourist information office.

🏛 Parador de Úbeda

Plaza de Vázquez de Molina s/n. 📞 *(953) 75 03 45.* **Patio** ⬜ *to nonguests daily. See also p203.*
Built in the 16th century but considerably altered in the 17th century, this was the residence of Fernando Ortega Salido, Dean of Málaga and chaplain of El Salvador. The austere palace has been turned into a hotel, which is also known as the Parador del Condestable Dávalos in honor of a warrior famed during the Reconquest *(see pp46–7)*. Its patio is an ideal place to have a drink.

🏛 Santa María de los Reales Alcázares

Built on the site of an original mosque, this church, mainly dating from the 13th century, is now undergoing restoration. Inside there is fine ironwork by Maestro Bartolomé. The Gothic cloister, with pointed arches and ribbed vaults, and a Romanesque doorway, are particularly noteworthy.

Near the church is the Cárcel del Obispo (Bishop's Jail), so called because nuns punished by the bishop were confined there. Today the building contains the town's courthouse.

Stone lions guarding the Palacio de las Cadenas

Statuary on the main entrance of Iglesia de San Pablo

Iglesia de San Pablo

The three doors of this church all date from different periods. The main entrance is in late Gothic style while the others are in transitional Romanesque and Isabelline. Inside is an apse which dates from the 13th century and a beautiful 16th-century chapel by Vandelvira. The church is surmounted by a Plateresque tower (1537).

Nearby on Plaza de Vázquez de Molina is a monument to the poet and mystic San Juan de la Cruz (1549–91).

🏛 Museo Arqueológico

Casa Mudéjar, C/ Cervantes s/n. 🔲 *(953) 75 37 02.* ⭕ *Tue–Sun.* 🔲🔲

This archaeological museum exhibits artifacts from Neolithic times to the Moorish era. The display includes tombstones from the 1st century AD and Moorish and Mudéjar works in wood and plaster. It is located in the 15th-century Casa Mudéjar, among the many palaces, churches, and convents gracing the sinuous streets of the old quarter.

🏨 Hospital de Santiago

Calle Obispo Cobos 28. 🔲 *(953) 75 08 42.* ⭕ *daily.*

Created on the orders of the Bishop of Jaén around 1562, this colossal former hospital was designed by Vandelvira. The façade is flanked by square towers, one topped with a distinctive blue-and-white tiled steeple. Santiago (St. James) is depicted above the entrance. Marble columns grace the patio with its central fountain. A broad staircase leads up to the gallery roofed by a lofty, frescoed ceiling.

Today the building houses the Palacio de Congresos y Exposiciones. At the entrance

VISITORS' CHECKLIST

Jaén. **Road map** D3. 🏘 *34,000.*
🚌 *to Linares-Baeza (953) 65 02 02, then bus.* 🚌 *Calle San José s/n. (953) 75 21 57.*
ℹ *Plaza de los Caidos s/n (953) 75 08 97.* 🔲 *Fri.* 🎭 *Semana Santa (Easter); Fiestas de San Miguel (Sep 28–Oct 4).*

is an information office, and in a corner of the patio there is a stone-vaulted café.

Nearby, on Avenida de la Constitución, is Úbeda's bullring, open during the *fiesta*.

Distinctive steeple above the Hospital de Santiago

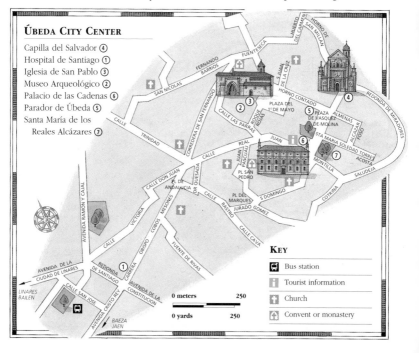

ÚBEDA CITY CENTER

Capilla del Salvador ④
Hospital de Santiago ①
Iglesia de San Pablo ③
Museo Arqueológico ②
Palacio de las Cadenas ⑥
Parador de Úbeda ⑤
Santa María de los
  Reales Alcázares ⑦

KEY

🚌 Bus station

ℹ Tourist information

🔲 Church

🔲 Convent or monastery

0 meters   250
0 yards   250

Ruins of La Iruela, spectacularly situated above the road outside Cazorla

Cazorla ②

Jaén. **Road map** E3. 🚶 10,000. 🚌
ℹ️ Paseo del Santo Cristo 17 (953) 71 01 02. 🛒 Mon & Sat.

CAZORLA WAS WEALTHY in ancient times when the Romans mined the surrounding mountains for silver. Today it is better known as the starting point for those who wish to visit the Parque Natural de Cazorla, Segura y Las Villas.

Modern buildings have proliferated, but it is pleasant to stroll along the crooked streets between the Plaza de la Corredera and the charming Plaza Santa María. The ruined Iglesia de Santa María forms a picturesque backdrop to this popular meeting place. Above stands the imposing Moorish **Castillo de la Yedra**, which houses a folklore museum.

On the road leading to the park are the remains of **La Iruela**, a much-photographed fortress atop a rocky spur.

On May 14 the locals pay homage to a former resident of Cazorla, San Isicio, one of seven apostles who preached Christianity in Spain before the arrival of the Moors.

🏛 **Castillo de la Yedra**
📞 (953) 71 00 39. 🕐 Tue–Sat.
● public hols. 🎫

Parque Natural de Cazorla, Segura y Las Villas ②

Jaén. **Road map** E3. 🚌 Cazorla.
ℹ️ Quercus Sociedad Cooperativa Andaluza, Calle Juan Domingo 2, Cazorla. (953) 72 01 15.

FIRST-TIME VISITORS are amazed by the spectacular scenery of this 214,336-ha (529,409-acre) nature preserve with its thick woodland, tumbling streams, and abundant wildlife. Bristling mountains rise over 2,000 m (6,560 ft) above the source of the Guadalquivir.

The river flows north through a delightful valley before reaching the Tranco de Beas dam, where it turns to run down toward the Atlantic.

Cars are allowed only on the main road, not on the forest trails. Many visitors choose to explore the area on foot, but horses and mountain bikes can be rented from the **Centro de Recepción e Interpretación**, in the preserve. The Center also provides information on flora and fauna, and guide services. There are also opportunities for hunting and fishing.

🏛 **Centro de Recepción e Interpretación**
Carretera del Tranco km 17, Torre del Vinagre. 📞 (953) 72 01 15. 🕐 daily.

Segura de la Sierra ②

Jaén. **Road map** E2. 🚶 2,300. 🚌
ℹ️ Ayuntamiento, Calle Regidor Juan de Isla 1. (953) 48 02 80.

THIS TINY VILLAGE at 1,200 m (4,000 ft) above sea level is dominated by its restored Moorish **castillo** (ask for keys in the village). From the ramparts there are splendid views of the harsh mountain ranges. Below is an unusual bullring, partly chipped out of rock. It sees most action at the *fiesta* in the first week of October.

Olive oil in the Segura de la Sierra area is one of four which bear Spain's prestigious *Denominación de Origen Controlada* label *(see p144)*.

Moorish castillo at Segura de la Sierra, surrounded by olive groves

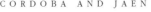

Wildlife in Cazorla, Segura, and Las Villas

Mouflon
(Ovis musimon)

THE NATURE PRESERVE of Sierra de Cazorla, Segura, and Las Villas protects a profusion of wildlife. Most is native to the region, but some species have recently been introduced or reintroduced for hunting. More than 100 species of birds live in Cazorla, some very rare. It is the only habitat in Spain, apart from the Pyrenees, where the lammergeier can be seen. The extensive forests are home to a range of plant life, such as the indigenous *Viola cazorlensis (see p19)*, which grows among rocks.

The golden eagle (Aquila chrysaetus), *king of the air, preys on small mammals living in the preserve.*

Griffon vultures (Gyps fulvus) *circle high above the preserve, descending rapidly when they catch sight of their prey.*

The lammergeier (Gypaetus barbatus) *drops bones from a height onto rocks to smash them and eat the marrow.*

LANDSCAPE
The area's craggy limestone heights and riverside meadows are part of its attraction. Water trickles down the mountains, filling the lakes and brooks of the valley. This lush landscape provides ideal habitats for a diversity of wildlife.

Red deer (Cervus elaphus), *reintroduced to the area in 1952, are most commonly seen in the autumn months.*

The Spanish ibex (Capra pyrenaica) *is amazingly sure-footed on the rocky terrain. Today, the few that remain only emerge at dusk in order to feed.*

Otters (Lutra lutra) *live around lakes and streams and are active at dawn and dusk.*

Wild boars (Sus scrofa) *hide in woodland by day and forage at night for anything from acorns to roots, eggs of ground-nesting birds, and small mammals.*

CÁDIZ AND MÁLAGA

NDALUSIA'S SOUTHERN PROVINCES *offer striking contrasts. Behind Málaga's suburbs are forested mountains with awesome natural wonders such as the Garganta del Chorro. Behind the tourist resorts of the Costa del Sol is the Serranía de Ronda, habitat of elusive wildlife. Here, white Moorish towns command strategic hilltop locations. East of Gibraltar are the sherry towns of Cádiz province and the raw coastal strands of the Costa de la Luz.*

In Málaga province the mountains fall steeply to the Mediterranean. The ancient port of Málaga town was a wintering place for English travelers in the 19th century; then in the 1960s, the narrow strip of coast to its east and west was claimed by the nascent tourist industry as the "Costa del Sol."

A rash of high-rise development around the beaches of gray sand at its eastern end soon made the name "Torremolinos" synonymous with the excesses of cheap package vacations for the mass market. Meanwhile, at Marbella, farther east, an exclusive playground for international film stars and Arab royalty was taking shape.

Gibraltar, a geographical and a historical oddity, is a decisive full stop at the end of the Costa del Sol.

The mountains of North Africa loom across the Strait of Gibraltar, and the spirit of the Moors can be felt very clearly in Tarifa and Cádiz – author Laurie Lee's city "sparkling with African light."

Between these two towns is the Cádiz section of the Costa de la Luz ("Coast of Light") *(see p30)*, which continues along the shores of Huelva province. Very little developed, it is characterized by long stretches of windswept sand, popular with locals.

North of Cádiz is sherry country, with its hills and large vineyards. To taste sherry visit Jerez de la Frontera – a link in a chain of towns on the frontier of the Christian war to reconquer Andalusia from its Muslim rulers.

Ronda with its 18th-century bridge spanning the Guadalevín River

◁ Beach life at Nerja, east of Málaga, one of the Costa del Sol's busy resorts

Exploring Cádiz and Málaga

W ITH A NEW NETWORK of excellent roads across
the region, the mountains of Málaga province's
interior are easily accessible to vacationers who are
staying on the Costa del Sol. Day trips can be
made from either Marbella or Torremolinos to the
glorious Montes de Málaga and Grazalema nature
preserves, or to the Serranía de Ronda, with lunch
stops at classic *pueblos blancos*. In the heart of this
characteristic Andalusian landscape lies the capti-
vating town of Ronda, ensouled by clear, stark light
and the lingering aura of Moorish times.

Farther west, on the Atlantic coast beyond Tarifa,
where mass-market developers fear to tread, the
same spirit lingers. The once great city of Cádiz
and the small ports of El Puerto de Santa María,
Chipiona, and Sanlúcar de Barrameda all make
excellent bases for exploring sherry country.

**Outside dining at a restaurant close
to the cathedral in Málaga**

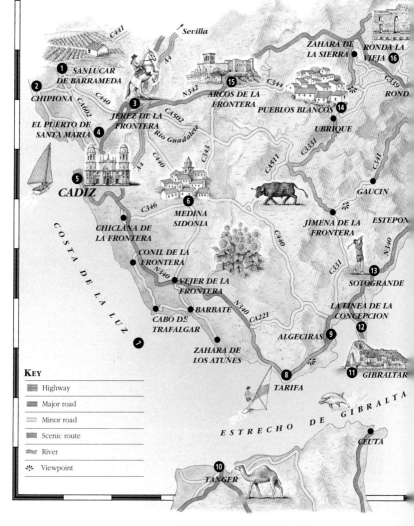

C441

Sevilla

A4

ZAHARA DE
LA SIERRA

RONDA LA
VIEJA ⑯

① SANLÚCAR
DE BARRAMEDA

② N342

C344

RONDA

CHIPIONA

CA440

C602

③ ⑮ ARCOS DE LA
FRONTERA

CA502

PUEBLOS BLANCOS ⑭

C339

JEREZ DE LA
FRONTERA

EL PUERTO DE
SANTA MARÍA ④

Río Guadalete

UBRIQUE

C333J

A4

C440

C343

C451I

C341

CADIZ ⑤

C346

⑥

MEDINA
SIDONIA

GAUCÍN

CHICLANA DE
LA FRONTERA

C331I

JIMENA DE LA
FRONTERA

ESTEPON

C
O
S
T
A
D
E
L
A
L
U
Z

C340

N340

CONIL DE LA
FRONTERA

N340

VEJER DE LA
FRONTERA

C331

⑬

SOTOGRANDE

CABO DE
TRAFALGAR

BARBATE

N340

LA LÍNEA DE LA
CONCEPCIÓN

CA221

ALGECIRAS ⑨

⑫

⑦

ZAHARA DE
LOS ATUNES

⑪ GIBRALTAR

⑧

TARIFA

KEY

▬	Highway
▬	Major road
▬	Minor road
▬	Scenic route
▬	River
❂	Viewpoint

E S T R E C H O D E G I B R A L T A

CEUTA

⑩

TANGER

SIGHTS AT A GLANCE

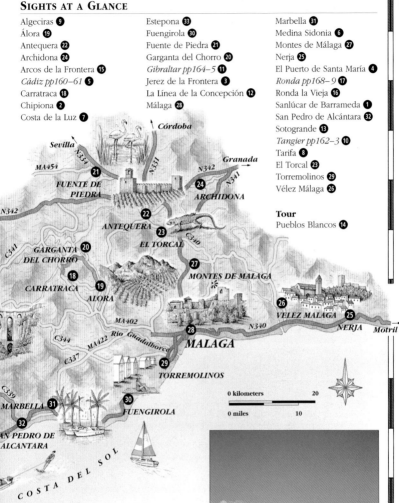

GETTING AROUND

Málaga's international airport *(see p246)* is the busiest airport in Andalusia. From here, the fast, new N340 highway traces the coastline as far as Algeciras, but bypasses Torremolinos, Fuengirola, and Marbella. After Algeciras, the road narrows and continues to Cádiz. The new C339 from San Pedro de Alcántara northward to Ronda is a sensationally beautiful route. The N342 cuts across the north of both provinces from Jerez to Antequera, where it continues as the A92 to Granada. A railroad running along the Costa del Sol links Málaga, Torremolinos, and Fuengirola. Another heads north from Málaga, stopping at Álora, El Chorro, and Fuente de Piedra. Although it is possible to explore remote corners of Cádiz and Málaga provinces by using the complex bus network, it requires some patience.

The beach of Nerja, situated at the foot of Sierra de Almijara on the Costa del Sol

Entrance to the Barbadillo *bodega* in Sanlúcar de Barrameda

Sanlúcar de Barrameda ●

Cádiz. **Road map** B4. 🚶 55,000.
🚏 ℹ️ *Calzada del Ejército s/n. (956) 36 61 10.* 🗓️ *Wed.*

A FISHING PORT at the mouth of the Guadalquivir River, Sanlúcar is overlooked by the Moorish **Castillo de Santiago**. The Parque Nacional de Coto Doñana *(see pp126–7)*, over the river, can be reached by boat from the riverside quay. From here Columbus set off on his third trip to the Americas, in 1498, and in 1519 Ferdinand Magellan left the port intending to circumnavigate the globe.

However, Sanlúcar is now best known for its *manzanilla (see p28)*, a light, dry sherry from, among other producers, **Bodegas Barbadillo**.

Tourists and wine enthusiasts come from all over the world to watch the sun set over the river, sip a *copita* (little glass) of *manzanilla*, and feast on the local shellfish, *langostinos*.

Sights in the town include the **Iglesia de Nuestra Señora de la O** *(see p22)*, which has superb Mudéjar portals.

❢ Bodegas Barbadillo
C/ Luis de Eguílaz 11. ℹ️ *(956) 36 08 94.* ◯ *Thu (by appointment).* ♿

Chipiona ●

Cádiz. **Road map** B4. 🚶 15,600.
🚏 ℹ️ *Ayuntamiento, Plaza Juan Carlos I. (956) 37 01 00.* 🗓️ *Mon.*

A LIVELY LITTLE resort town, Chipiona is approached through sherry vineyards. It has an excellent beach and in the summer, when the Spanish flock here, a vacation atmosphere. Days on the beach are followed by a *paseo* along the quay or the main street of the Moorish old town, where many cafés and ice-cream parlors *(heladerías)* stay open well past midnight. There are also street entertainers and horse-drawn carriages. The **Iglesia de Nuestra Señora de Regla**, the main church, has a natural spring feeding a fountain and an adjoining cloister decorated with 17th-century *azulejos*.

Jerez de la Frontera ●

Cádiz. **Road map** B4. 🚶 190,000.
🚉 🚏 ℹ️ *Alameda Cristina 7. (956) 33 11 50.* 🗓️ *Mon.*

J EREZ, THE CAPITAL of sherry production, is surrounded by chalky countryside blanketed with vines in long, neat rows. British merchants have been involved for centuries in producing and shipping sherry, and they have created Anglo-Andaluz dynasties with names such as Sandeman and John Harvey, which can be seen emblazoned over the *bodega* entrances. A tour of a *bodega*, through darkened cellars piled high with *soleras (see p29)*, will enable interested visitors to learn how to distinguish a *fino* from an *amontillado* and an *oloroso* sherry *(see 28)*.

Jerez has a second claim to world fame, the **Real Escuela Andaluza de Arte Ecuestre** – the school of equestrian art. On Thursdays, in a display of exquisite dressage, teams of horses dance to music amid colorful pageantry. On other days, visitors can sometimes watch horses being trained.

Nearby is the **Museo de Relojes**, where you can see one of the largest collections of timepieces in Europe – some will claim in the world.

The old city walls flank the Barrio de Santiago. On Plaza de San Juan is the 18th-century **Palacio de Pemartín**, the home of the Centro Andaluz de Flamenco, which, through a combination of exhibitions and audio-visual shows, gives a stimulating introduction to this music and dance tradition *(see pp26–7)*. The 16th-century Gothic **Iglesia de San Mateo** is just one of several interesting churches nearby.

The partially restored, 11th-century **Alcázar** encompasses a well-preserved mosque, now a church. Just to the north of the Alcázar is the **Catedral del Salvador**, whose most interesting sight, *The Sleeping Girl* by Zurbarán, is in the sacristy.

♞ Real Escuela Andaluza de Arte Ecuestre
Avenida de Abrantes s/n. ℹ️ *(956) 31 11 11.* ◯ *Mon–Fri.* ● *public hols.* 🈲 ♿
♠ Alcázar
Alameda Vieja s/n. ℹ️ *(956) 33 11 50 (tourist office).* ◯ *Mon–Sat.* ● *public hols.* ♿
🏛 Museo de Relojes
Calle Cervantes s/n. ℹ️ *(956) 18 21 00.* ◯ *Mon–Sat.* ● *public hols.* 🈲 ♿
♞ Palacio de Pemartín
Centro Andaluz de Flamenco, Plaza de San Juan 1. ℹ️ *(956) 34 92 65.* ◯ *Mon–Fri.* ● *public hols.*

Antique clock in the Museo de Relojes, Jerez de la Frontera

El Puerto de Santa María ❹

Cádiz. **Road map** B4. 🏛 60,000.
🚶 🚏 �e 🛈 *Calle Guadalete 1.*
(956) 54 24 13. 🕭 *Tue.*

SHELTERED from the Atlantic wind and waves of the Bay of Cádiz, El Puerto de Santa María is a tranquil town that has burgeoned as one of the main ports for the exportation of sherry in Andalusia. A number of sherry companies, such as **Terry** and **Osborne**, have *bodegas* here, which can be visited for tours and tasting.

Among the town's sites are the 13th-century **Castillo San Marcos** and a **Plaza de Toros** – one of the largest and most famous bullrings in Spain. The town's main square, the Plaza Mayor, is presided over by the 13th-century Gothic **Iglesia Mayor Prioral**, which is worth a look for its unusual choir.

Scattered around the town are several fine old *palacios*, or stately houses, adorned with the coats of arms of wealthy families who prospered in the port during colonial times.

The waterfront is lined with quite a few first-rate seafood restaurants, among them La Resaca (the Hangover), where, when it is dark, gypsies perform fiery flamenco.

♠ **Castillo San Marcos**
Plaza del Castillo. ◯ *Sat.* &

🎪 **Plaza de Toros**
Plaza de Toros s/n. 📞 *(956) 54 24 13
(tourist office).* ◯ *Tue–Sun.*
◑ *public hols, and to nonticket
holders on bullfight days.* &

🍷 **Bodegas Osborne**
Calle de los Moros. 📞 *(956) 85 52
11.* ◯ *Mon–Fri.* ◑ *Aug, public
hols.*

🍷 **Bodegas Terry**
Calle Santísima Trinidad. 📞 *(956) 48
30 00.* ◯ *Mon–Fri.* ◑ *Aug, public
hols.* &

El Puerto de Santa María's 13th-century Castillo San Marcos

BODEGAS OF JEREZ

Touring *bodegas* and tasting sherry is the principal reason for visiting Jerez. The tourist office here will supply a list of *bodegas* offering tours, and a tour time-table. The most comprehensive tours are those that are offered by González Byass, Pedro Domecq, and Sandeman.

0 meters   500

0 yards   500

KEY

	Bodega
P	Parking
🛈	Tourist information

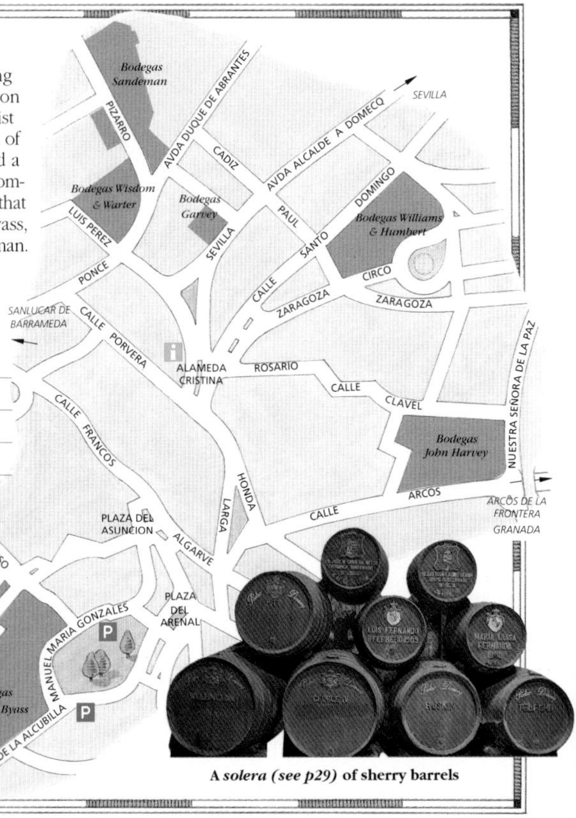

A *solera* (see p29) of sherry barrels

Cádiz ❺

Egyptian mask, the Museo de Cádiz

Jᴜᴛᴛɪɴɢ ɪɴᴛᴏ the Bay of Cádiz, and almost entirely surrounded by water, Cádiz can lay claim to being Europe's oldest city. Legend names Hercules as its founder, although history credits the Phoenicians with establishing the town of Gadir in 1100 BC. Occupied by the Carthaginians, Romans, and Moors in turn, the city also prospered after the Reconquest *(see pp46–7)* on wealth taken from the New World. In 1587 Sir Francis Drake raided the port in the first of many British attacks in the war for world trade. In 1812 Cádiz briefly became Spain's capital when the nation's first constitution was declared here *(see p50)*.

Saint Bruno in Ecstasy by Zurbarán in the Museo de Cádiz

Exploring Cádiz

Writers have waxed lyrical over Cádiz for centuries: " . . . the most beautiful town I ever beheld . . . and full of the finest women in Spain," gushed Lord Byron in 1809. Modern Cádiz is a busy port, with a few ugly suburbs to get through before arriving at the historic center. This is situated on a peninsula that juts sharply into the sea, and consists of haphazardly heaped, Moorish-style houses.

The joy of visiting Cádiz is to wander the harbor quayside, with its well-tended gardens and open squares, then plunging into the center.

The old town is full of narrow, dilapidated alleys, where flowers sprout from rusting cans mounted on walls beside religious tile paintings. Markets pack into tiny squares, alive with the bartering of fish and vegetables, and street vendors selling pink boiled shrimp in newspaper.

The pride of Cádiz is Los Carnavales *(see p37)*, an explosion of festivities. Under the dictator Franco *(see pp54–5)*, Cádiz was the only city where the authorities failed to suppress the anarchy of carnival.

🄰 Catedral
Known as the Catedral Nueva (New Cathedral) because it was built over the site of an older one, this huge Baroque and Neo-Classical church is one of Spain's largest. It has a dome of yellow tiles, which, from a distance, look like gilt glinting in the sun. The interior, with its twin aisles and side chapels,

is light and cool in summer. Its carved stalls came from a Carthusian monastery. In the crypt is the tomb of the composer Manuel de Falla (1876–1946), a native of Cádiz.

The cathedral's treasures are stored in the adjacent museum. The collection includes jewel-studded monstrances of silver and gold, painted wood panels and notable paintings.

CÁDIZ CATHEDRAL

🏛 Museo de Cádiz
Plaza de Mina s/n. 🄲 *(956) 21 22 81.* ⬭ *Tue–Sun.* ⬤ *public hols.* ♿
On the ground floor of this spacious museum there are archaeological exhibits charting the history of Cádiz, including statues of Roman leaders, such as emperor Trajan, and Phoenician stone sarcophagi. Upstairs is one of Andalusia's largest art galleries, displaying

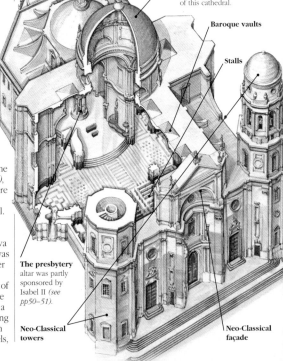

The cupola was built between 1812 and 1838 by Juan Daura, the last in a long line of architects of this cathedral.

Baroque vaults

Stalls

The presbytery altar was partly sponsored by Isabel II *(see pp50–51).*

Neo-Classical towers

Neo-Classical façade

works by Rubens, Murillo, and
Zurbarán, as well as paintings
by recognized contemporary
Spanish artists. On the third
floor is a collection of puppets
made for village *fiestas* around
Andalusia. There are also some
more recent ones satirizing
current political figures.

**Commemorative plaques on the
Oratorio de San Felipe Neri**

⛪ Oratorio de San Felipe Neri
Calle Santa Inés s/n. ☎ (956) 21 16
12. ◯ daily. ⚙
People visit this 18th-century
church to pay homage to an
event of 1812. As Napoleon
tightened his grip on Spain, a
provisional government, which
had been set up in Cádiz, proclaimed a liberal constitution
(*see p50*). The site has been a
shrine to liberalism ever since.

🏛 Museo Municipal
Calle Santa Inés s/n. ☎ (956) 22 17 88.
◯ Tue–Sun. ◐ public hols. ⚙
This museum is devoted to the
declaration of the constitution
in 1812. The exhibits include
a mural of the declaration and
the original documents. There
is also an 18th-century wood
and ivory model of Cádiz.

🏛 Plaza de España
On this square is another monument to the events of 1812,
the Monumento a la Constitución, erected in 1912.

Medina Sidonia ❻

Cádiz. **Road map** B5. 🏛 12,000.
🚉 🛈 Plaza Iglesia Mayor s/n. (956)
41 24 04. 🚇 Mon.

AS YOU DRIVE along the N440,
between Algeciras and
Jerez, Medina Sidonia appears
startlingly white atop a conical
hill. The town was taken from
the Moors in 1264 by Alfonso
X, and during the 15th century
the Guzmán family were established as the Dukes of Medina
Sidonia to defend the territory
between here and the Bay of
Cádiz. After the Reconquest
(*see pp46–7*), the family grew
rich from investments in the
Americas, and Medina Sidonia
became one of the most important ducal seats in Spain.

Much of the town's medieval
walls still stand and cobbled
alleys nestle beneath them.

The **Iglesia Santa María la
Coronada** is the town's most
important building. Begun on
the foundations of a castle in
the 15th century, after the Reconquest, it is a fine example
of Andalusian Gothic. Inside,
there is a collection of religious
works of art dating from the
Renaissance, including paintings and a charming *retablo*
with beautifully carved panels.

Costa de la Luz ❼

Málaga. **Road map** B5. 🚉 Cádiz.
🚌 Cádiz, Tarifa. 🛈 Cádiz (956)
24 01 61.

THE COSTA DE LA LUZ between
Cádiz and Tarifa is a raw,
wind-harassed stretch of coast.
Strong, pure light characterizes

**Carved *retablo*, Iglesia de Santa
María la Coronada, Medina Sidonia**

this unspoiled region and is the
source of its name. From the
Sierra del Cabrito, just to the
west of Algeciras (*see p162*),
are views across the Strait of
Gibraltar. On clear days you
can just make out the outline
of Tangier (*see pp162–3*) and
the parched Moroccan landscape – not unlike the Costa
de la Luz – visible below the
purple-tinged Rif mountains.

Off the N340, at the end of a
long, narrow road that strikes
out across a wilderness of
cacti, sunflowers, and lone-
some cork trees, is **Zahara de
los Atunes**, a modest vacation resort with a few hotels.

Conil de la Frontera to the
west, divided from Zahara by
a large area reserved for the
military, is busier. It specializes
in the cheaper end of the market for domestic tourism.

Other fine beaches on this
coast include Caños de Meca
and Bolonia (*see pp30–31*).

Fishing boats at the resort of Zahara de los Atunes on the Costa de la Luz

Tarifa ❽

Cádiz. **Road map** B5. 🏠 15,000.
🚉 ℹ️ *Paseo de la Alameda s/n.*
(956) 68 09 93. 🚌 *Tue.*

Tarifa, Europe's windsurfing capital *(see p30),* takes its name from Tarif ben Maluk, an 8th-century commander who landed there during the Moorish Conquest *(see pp44–5).*

The 10th-century **Castillo de Guzmán el Bueno** is the site of a well-known heroic legend. In 1292 Guzmán, who was defending Tarifa during a siege by the Moors, was told his hostage son would die if he did not surrender; rather than give in, Guzmán threw down his dagger for the captors to use.

♟ Castillo de Guzmán el Bueno

Pl Santa Maria s/n. 📞 *(956) 68 41 86*
(ayuntamiento). ⬤ *for*
restoration.

Castillo de Guzmán el Bueno

Algeciras ❾

Cádiz. **Road map** C5. 🏠 150,000.
🚉 🚉 ℹ️ *Calle Juan de Cierva s/n.*
(956) 57 26 36. 🚌 *Tue.*

The town of Algeciras was central to General Franco's attempts to regain Spanish control over Gibraltar by economic rather than military means. In 1969 the frontier was closed and massive investment made to develop Algeciras as an industrial base to absorb surplus labor and end the dependence of the area on Gibraltar. The resulting urban sprawl of factories and refineries is given a wide berth by most travelers except those on their way to or from North Africa.

Tangier ❿

Tangier is only a couple of hours by ferry from Algeciras or Gibraltar, making it a perfect day trip. Despite its proximity, this ancient port, founded by the Berbers before 1000 BC, will be a sharp culture shock for those used to life in Europe. Tangier is vibrant with eastern color, and the vast, labyrinthine Medina, the market quarter, pulsates with noise.

Water seller, Grand Socco

From their workshops in back alleys, craftsmen make traditional goods for busy shops and stalls in the crowded streets. Yet behind wrought-iron railings the traveler will see tranquil courts decorated with mosaics, cool fountains, and mosques.

🏛 Dar El Makhzen

Place de la Kasbah. 📞 *(09) 93*
20 97. ⬤ *Wed–Mon.* 📷
Sultan Moulay Ismail, who unified Morocco in the 17th century, had the Dar El Makhzen built within the Kasbah. The sultans lived here with their wives, harems, and entourages until 1912. It is now a museum exhibiting traditional crafts such as carpets, ceramics, embroidery, and wrought ironwork. The exhibits are arranged around a central courtyard, decorated with beautifully carved stone-work, and in cool rooms with carved ceilings that are decorated with painted tiles. There are illuminated Korans in the Fez room and a courtyard in the style of Andalusian Moorish gardens.

🏯 Kasbah

The Kasbah or citadel, built in Roman times and where the Sultans once held court, is at the Medina's highest point. It is separated from its alleys by sturdy fortress walls and four massive stone gateways. From the battlements there are views over the Medina, the port, and the Strait of Gibraltar.

The Kasbah encloses the Dar El Makhzen and other palaces, the treasury house, the old prison, and the law courts around the Mechour square. Villas that were once owned by American and European celebrities, such as Paul Bowles, the author of *The Sheltering Sky,* who came here during the early part of the 20th century, are also situated within the Kasbah walls.

Façade of the Dar El Makhzen, the museum of Moroccan arts

**View into the labyrinthine
Medina from the Grand Socco**

🕌 American Legation
Rue du Portugal. 📞 *(09) 93 53 17.*
⬤ *Mon, Wed & Thu or by appt.*
This former palace, a gift from
Sultan Moulay Slimane in 1821,
was the United States' first dip-
lomatic mission and remained
the American Embassy until
1961. It is now an art museum
and holds regular exhibitions.

🕌 Hôtel Continental
Rue Dar El Baroud. 📞 *(09) 93 10 24.*
⬤ *daily.* ♿
Numerous intrigues have been
played out in this hotel overlooking the port. Today it is a
fine place to sit and drink tea.

🕌 Rue es Siaghin
The Medina's main artery
offers a staggering array
of merchandise; shop
owners along the street
will offer you
mint tea in a
bid to get you
to buy.

VISITORS' CHECKLIST

Morocco. **Road map** B5.
👥 *315,000.* ⛴ *from Algeciras
by Transmediterránea (956) 66 52
00 (ferry and hydrofoil); from
Gibraltar by TourAfrica (350) 77
666.* ℹ *29 boulevard Pasteur.
(09) 94 80 50.* **Languages:**
Arabic; French. **Currency:**
dirhams. **Visas:** *holders of a full
passport from the UK, Ireland,
New Zealand, Australia, the US,
or Canada require no visa for a
visit of up to 90 days.*

The carved façade of Tangier's Grand Mosque

0 meters   100

0 yards   100

KEY

▨	Old city walls
✝	Church
🕌	Mosque

SIGHTS AT A GLANCE

☾ Grand Mosque
Green and white minarets rise
above this massive edifice built
in the 17th century by Sultan
Moulay Ismail. An exquisitely
carved gateway suggests more
treasures within – non-Muslims,
however, are forbidden to
enter this mosque.

🕌 Grand Socco
Traders from the Rif mountains
come to barter their goods at
this busy main square at the
heart of Tangier. The square's
official name, Place du 9 Avril
1947, commemorates a visit by
Sultan Muhammad V.

THE INTERNATIONAL ERA

From 1932 until its incorporation into Morocco in 1956,
Tangier was an international
zone, tax free and under the
control of a committee of 30
nations. This was an era characterized by financial fraud,
espionage, outrageous sexual
license, large-scale smuggling,
and profligacy by wealthy tax
exiles such as heiress Barbara
Hutton. Celebrities such as
Henri Matisse, Jack Kerouac,
and Orson Welles added
color to the scene.

**Orson Welles, once a familiar
sight on the streets of Tangier**

Gibraltar

NATIVE GIBRALTARIANS are descendents of British, Genoese Jews, Portuguese, and Spanish who remained after the Great Siege *(see p50)*. Britain seized Gibraltar during the War of the Spanish Succession in 1704 and was granted it "in perpetuity" by the Treaty of Utrecht *(see p50)* nine years later. As the gateway to the Mediterranean, the Rock was essential to Britain in colonial times, and the treaty is still invoked in response to Spanish claims to Gibraltar. Each year around 4 million people stream across the frontier at La Línea to visit this speck of England bolted on to Andalusia. Pubs, pints of ale, fish and chips, British pounds, and bobbies on the beat all contrast with Spain. Most visitors are Spaniards, seduced by duty-free shopping.

Gibraltarian barbary ape

The Keep
The lower part of this Moorish castle, built in the 8th century, is still used to house Gibraltar's prison population.

Siege Tunnels
Soldiers' barracks and storerooms fill 80 km (50 miles) of tunnels.

Spanish border and customs

Cable Car
A cable car runs from the center of the town to the Top of the Rock, Gibraltar's summit, which, at 450 m (1,475 ft) high, is often shrouded in mist.

The airport runway crosses over the main road from La Línea to Gibraltar.

St. Michael's Cave
During World War II these caves served as a bomb-proof military hospital. These days classical concerts are performed here.

VISITORS' CHECKLIST

United Kingdom. **Road Map** C5.
🏠 *29,000.* ✈ *Gibraltar.*
🚌 *Waterport bus station.*
ℹ *John Macintosh Hall. (350) 74 289.* 🕐 *Wed, Sat.* 📷 *National Day (Sep 10).* **Gibraltar Museum** ⭕ *Mon–Sat.* ● *public holidays.* 🎫 **The Keep, Siege Tunnels, St. Michael's Cave, Apes' Den** ⭕ *daily.* ● *Christmas Day, New Year's Day.* 🎫 ♿
Currency: *Gibraltar pound, British pound.* **Visas:** *not required for citizens of the US, EU, Canada, or Australia.*

The Apes' Den is home to Gibraltar's tailless apes; legend has it that the British will keep the Rock only as long as the apes remain.

Europa Point, on the southernmost tip, looks across the Strait of Gibraltar to North Africa.

The 100-Ton Gun was put here in 1884; it took two hours to load and it could fire shells weighing 910 kg (2,000 lb).

Cable car station

Gibraltar Museum
This museum, built on the foundations of Moorish baths, houses an exhibition of Gibraltar's history under British rule.

La Línea de la Concepción, with Gibraltar in the distance

La Línea de la Concepción ⓬

Cádiz. **Road map** C5. 🏠 *70,000.*
🚌 ℹ *Avenida de 20 Abril s/n. (956) 76 99 50.* 🕐 *Wed.*

LA LÍNEA is a town on the Spanish side of the border with Gibraltar. Its name, "The Line," refers to the old walls that once formed the frontier but which were demolished during the Napoleonic wars to prevent the French using them for defense. Now it is a lively trading town, with several hotels patronized by people who want to avoid the higher prices of Gibraltar hotels.

The elegant marina at Sotogrande

Sotogrande ⓭

Cádiz. **Road map** C5. 🏠 *2,600.* 🚌 *San Roque.* ℹ *Ayuntamiento, Plaza de Armas 13, San Roque. (956) 78 01 06.* 🕐 *Sun.*

JUST ABOVE Gibraltar, on the Costa del Sol, Sotogrande is an exclusive residential seaside town where wealthy Gibraltarians, who commute daily to the Rock, reside in exclusive villas. The marina is filled with expensive yachts and lined with excellent seafood restaurants. Nearby there are several immaculately manicured golf courses *(see p30)*.

A Tour Around the Pueblos Blancos ⓮

INSTEAD OF SETTLING on Andalusia's plains, where they would have fallen prey to bandits, some Andalusians chose to live in fortified hilltop towns and villages. The way of life in these *pueblos blancos* – so called because they are whitewashed in the Moorish tradition – has barely changed for centuries. Touring the *pueblos blancos,* which crown the mountains rising sharply from the coast, will show visitors a world full of references to the past. Yet today they are working agricultural towns, not just tourist sights.

Zahara de la Sierra ③ This fine *pueblo blanco*, a tightly huddled hillside village below a castle ruin, has been declared a national monument.

Ubrique ② This town, nestling at the foot of the Sierra de Ubrique, has become a flourishing producer of leather goods.

Grazalema ④ At the heart of the Parque Natural de la Sierra de Grazalema, this village has the highest rainfall in Spain. Lush vegetation fills the park.

Arcos de la Frontera ① This strategically positioned town has been fortified for centuries. From the commanding heights of this stronghold there are views over the Guadalete valley.

Jimena de la Frontera ⑧ An expanse of cork and olive trees blankets the hills leading up to this village. A ruined Moorish castle, which is open to visitors, overlooks the surroundings where wild bulls graze peacefully.

SEVILLA

CADIZ, JEREZ

El Bosque Benamahoma

C344 C524 C339

Embalse de los Hurones

Charco de los Hurones

Benaocaz C3331

SIERRA UBRIQUE

Cortes de la Frontera

Rio Majaceite C521 C503

MA504

Rio Hozgarganta *Rio Guadiaro*

RESERVA NACIONAL DE CORTES DE LA FRONTERA

C3331

La Sauceda

C3331

Embalse de Zar C34

Gaucín ⑦ From here there are unsurpassed vistas over the Mediterranean, the Atlantic, the great hump of Gibraltar, and across the strait to the Rif mountains of North Africa.

0 kilometers 1

0 miles 5

Setenil ⑤
The streets of this white town are formed from the ledge of a gorge, carved from tufa rock by the river Trejo.

Ronda ⑥
With the Tajo gorge as an efficient moat, Ronda was one of the last towns recaptured from the Moors. It later became the cradle of modern bullfighting *(see pp168–9).*

KEY

━━ Tour route

══ Other roads

Arcos de la Frontera ⑮

Cádiz. **Road map** B4. 🏛 *30,000.*
🚌 🛈 *Calle Cuesta de Belén s/n.*
(956) 70 22 64. 🚃 *Fri.*

Aᴿᴄᴏs ʜᴀs ʙᴇᴇɴ inhabited since prehistoric times. Its strategic position encouraged settlement, first as the Roman town of Arcobriga, and later as the stronghold of Medina Arkosh under the Caliphate of Córdoba *(see p44).* It was captured by Alfonso X's *(see p46)* Christian forces in 1264.

An archetypal white town, it has a labyrinthine Moorish quarter that twists up to its ruined castle. At its center is the Plaza de España, one side of which gives views across sunbaked plains. Fronting the square are the superb **Parador de Arcos de la Frontera** *(see p207)* and the **Iglesia de Santa María de la Asunción**, a late Gothic-Mudéjar building worth seeing for its extravagant choir stalls and altarpiece. A small museum displays the church treasures. More striking is the massive, Gothic **Parroquia de San Pedro** built at the very edge of the gorge. Its thick-set tower provides a view over the sheer drop down to the Guadalete river. Nearby is the **Palacio del Mayorazgo** with an ornate, Renaissance façade. The **Ayuntamiento** is also worth seeing, particularly to view its beautiful Mudéjar ceiling.

🏛 **Palacio del Mayorazgo**
Calle San Pedro 2. 🛈 *(956) 70 30 13 (Casa de Cultura).* ◯ *Mon–Fri.* ● *public hols.* ♿
🏛 **Ayuntamiento**
Plaza Cavildo s/n. 🛈 *(956) 70 00 02.* ◯ *on request.* ● *public hols.*

Roman theater set amid the ruins of Acinipo (Ronda la Vieja)

Ronda la Vieja ⑯

Málaga. **Road map** C4. 🚌 🚍
Ronda. 🛈 *(95) 287 12 72 (Ronda tourist info).* ◯ *Tue–Sun.*

Rᴏɴᴅᴀ ʟᴀ ᴠɪᴇᴊᴀ is the modern name for the remains of the Roman city of Acinipo, 12 km (7 miles) northwest of Ronda *(see pp168–9).* An important town in the 1st century AD, it later declined, probably because its position made it difficult to defend, unlike the growing town of Ronda, which was called Arunda by the Romans.

The ruins are beautifully sited on a hillside and scattered over a wide area, only a small fraction of which has yet been excavated. The town's most important sight is the theater, but visitors are free to wander among the lines of stones that mark foundations of houses, and of the forum and other public buildings.

Along the C339, 22 km (14 miles) from Ronda la Vieja, are the Cuevas de la Pileta, the site of prehistoric cave paintings dating from about 25,000 BC *(see p41).*

The Gothic-Mudéjar Iglesia de Santa María de la Asunción

Street-by-Street: Ronda ⑰

Plate hand-painted in Ronda

O NE OF THE MOST spectacularly located cities in Spain, Ronda sits on a massive rocky outcrop, straddling a precipitous limestone cleft. Because of its impregnable position this town was one of the last Moorish bastions, finally falling to the Christians in 1485. On the south side perches a classic Moorish *pueblo blanco* (*see p166*) of cobbled alleys, window grilles and dazzling whitewash – most historic sights are in this old town. Across the gorge in El Mercadillo, the newer town, is one of Spain's oldest bullrings.

★ **Puente Nuevo**
Building the "New Bridge" over the nearly 100 m (328 ft) deep Tajo gorge was a feat of civil engineering in the late 18th century.

Convento de Santo Domingo was the local headquarters of the Inquisition.

To El Mercadillo, Plaza de Toros, and Parador de Ronda (*see p208*)

SANTA DOMINGO

CALLE ARMIÑAN

TENORIO

PLAZA DEL CAMPILLO

Casa del Rey Moro
From this 18th-century mansion, built on the foundations of a Moorish palace, 365 steps lead down to the river.

Mirador El Campillo

0 meters   75
0 yards   75

★ **Palacio Mondragón**
Much of this palace was rebuilt after the Reconquest (see pp46–7), but its arcaded patio is adorned with original Moorish mosaics and plasterwork.

STAR SIGHTS

★ **Palacio Mondragón**

★ **Puente Nuevo**

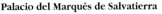

Palacio del Marqués de Salvatierra
Bizarre images of biblical scenes and South American Indians embellish the façade of this palace, built in Renaissance style in the 18th century.

VISITORS' CHECKLIST

Málaga. **Road map** C4. 🏠 40,000. 🚌 Avda Andalucía s/n. (95) 287 16 73. 🚉 Pl Concepción García Redondo s/n. (95) 287 22 62. 🛈 Plaza de España 1. (95) 287 12 72. 🖸 Sun. 🎉 Virgen de la Paz (Jan 24), Semana Santa (Easter), Feria de la Primavera (May 21), Feria de Pedro Romero (Sep). **Casa del Rey Moro** 🚫 to the public. **Palacio del Marqués de Salvatierra** 🖸 Mon–Wed, Fri, Sat. 🚫 Jul 25 – Sep 15. 📷 ♿ **Palacio Mondragón** 🖸 daily. 📷 ♿ **Plaza de Toros and Museo Taurino** 🖸 daily. 📷 ♿

Santa María la Mayor
A minaret and a Muslim prayer niche survive from the 13th-century mosque that once stood on the site of this church.

Minarete San Sebastián is all that remains of a 14th-century mosque.

To Puente Viejo, Baños Arabes

MARQUES DE SALVATIERRA

CARMEN

ESCALERA

ARMIÑAN

PLAZA DUQUESA DE PARCENT

Ayuntamiento
The town hall was remodeled in the 20th century and incorporates parts of older buildings. It has a two-tier arcaded façade and Mudéjar ceiling.

KEY

– – – Suggested route

BULLFIGHTING AT RONDA

Ronda's Plaza de Toros is the spiritual home of bullfighting. Inaugurated in 1785, it is one of the oldest, most important bullrings in Spain. Aficionados travel from all over the country for the singular atmosphere of the Corrida Goyesca *(see p34)*; millions watch the spectacle on television. It is the dream of every aspiring matador to fight at Ronda. The classic Ronda style (more severe than the exuberant School of Seville) was developed by Pedro Romero. Born in 1754, he is known as the father of modern bullfighting.

Romero, who killed around 6,000 bulls

Carratraca ⑱

Málaga. **Road map** C4. 🎟 *900.*
🚻 🛈 *Glorieta 1. (95) 245 80 16.*
🚌 *Sat.*

Aᵀᴱᴱᴾ, ᵀᵂᴵˢᵀᴵᴺᴳ mountain road leads up to this small village, which in the 19th and early 20th centuries attracted Europe's highest society and members of royalty. They came here for the healing powers of the village's natural sulfurous spring. Lord Byron, Alexandre Dumas, and Empress Eugénie of France are on the town's list of illustrious past visitors.

These days Carratraca retains a faded glory, and there is a forlorn atmosphere amid the long-closed casinos and in the Hostal el Príncipe, where the famous and the sick used to stay. Water still gushes out of the mountainside – at a rate of 700 liters (185 gal) per minute – and the outdoor baths remain open, although they are little used these days. A pungent smell of sulfur in the air ensures that the existence of the springs is not forgotten.

Outdoor hot baths in the village of Carratraca

Álora ⑲

Málaga. **Road map** C4. 🎟 *14,000.*
🚉 🚌 🛈 *Avda de la Constitución s/n. (95) 249 83 80.* 🚌 *Mon.*

Sᴵᵀᵁᴬᵀᴱᴰ in the Guadalhorce river valley, Álora is an important agricultural center. It is a classic white town *(pueblo blanco, see pp166–7)*, perched on a hillside overlooking an expanse of wheat fields, citrus orchards, and olive groves.

The town's cobbled streets radiate from the 18th-century **Iglesia de la Encarnación**. At the weekly market, stalls of farm produce and clothing fill nearby streets. On the higher of Álora's twin hills stands the **Castillo,** with a cemetery of niche tombs set in neat blocks.

♣ **Castillo**
Calle Ancha. 📞 *(95) 249 61 00 (Ayuntamiento).* ⬜ *daily.*

Garganta del Chorro ⑳

Málaga. **Road map** C4. 🚉 *El Chorro.*
🚍 *Parque Ardales.* 🛈 *Avda de la Constitución, Álora. (95) 249 83 80.*

Uᴾ ᴛʜᴇ ꜰᴇʀᴛɪʟᴇ Guadalhorce valley, 12 km (7 miles) on from Álora, is one of the geographical wonders of Spain. The Garganta del Chorro is an immense gaping chasm 180 m (590 ft) high, slashing through a limestone mountain. In some places, where the Guadalhorce river hurtles through, waters foaming white, it is only 10 m (33 ft) wide. Below the gorge is a hydroelectric plant, which detracts slightly from the wildness of the place.

For the truest sense of the gorge's dizzying dimensions, take a walk along the **Camino del Rey**. This precipitous catwalk takes its name from King Alfonso XIII, who opened it in 1921. Clinging to the rock face, it crosses from one side of the gorge to the other via a precarious bridge. Access is via the village of **El Chorro**, which offers the visitor a wide range of outdoor activities.

Fuente de Piedra ㉑

Málaga. **Road map** C4. 🚉 🚌
🛈 *Antequera. (95) 284 21 80.*

Tʜᴇ ʟᴀʀɢᴇꜱᴛ of several lakes in an expanse of wetlands north of Antequera, the Laguna de la Fuente de Piedra teems with bird life, including huge flocks of flamingos. In March, every year, up to 25,000 of them arrive to breed before

The Garganta del Chorro, rising high above the Guadalhorce River

migrating back to West Africa for the winter. Visitors should note that if there is a drought in the region, the birds are likely to be discouraged from breeding. Apart from flamingos, there are also cranes, herons, bee-eaters, and snow-white egrets, as well as different species of ducks and geese. Their numbers have increased encouragingly since new conservation and antihunting laws were introduced and the area declared a sanctuary.

A road off the N334 leads to the lakeside, from where visitors can watch the birds. It is forbidden to join the waders in the lake and its wildlife is available from a visitors' center near the village of Fuente de Piedra.

Limestone formations in the Parque Natural del Torcal

The triumphal 16th-century Arco de los Gigantes, Antequera

Antequera ❷

Málaga. **Road map** D4. 🏘 *40,000.* 🚍 🚌 🛈 *Plaza San Sebastián 7. (95) 270 25 05.* 🔄 *Sun.*

A BUSY MARKET TOWN and commercial center in the Guadalhorce river valley, the town of Antequera has long been strategically important; first as Roman Anticaria and later as a Moorish border fortress defending Granada.

Of Antequera's large number of churches, one in particular, the **Iglesia de Nuestra Señora del Carmen**, with its vast, exuberant, Baroque altarpiece, is not to be missed. To the west of here, at the opposite end of the town, is the 19th-century **Plaza de Toros**, where there is a museum of bullfighting.

High on a hill overlooking the town is the **Castillo Arabe**, a Moorish castle built in the 13th century on the site of a Roman fort. Visitors cannot go inside but can walk around the castle walls – the approach is through the 16th-century **Arco de los Gigantes**. There are fine views from the **Torre del Papabellotas**, on the best-preserved part of the wall. In the town below, the 18th-century **Palacio de Nájera** is the setting for the Municipal Museum; the star exhibit here is a 2,000-year-old statue, in bronze, of a Roman boy.

Just outside of town, to the northeast, there are massive prehistoric dolmens. They are thought to be between 4,000 and 4,500 years old, the burial chambers of some of the region's early tribal leaders.

🐃 Plaza de Toros
Crta de Sevilla s/n. [(95) 270 26 76. ☐ *Tue–Sun.* **Museo Taurino** ☐ *Sat, Sun, public hols.*

🏛 Palacio de Nájera
Coso Viejo s/n. [(95) 270 40 51. ☐ *Tue–Sun.* ⬤ *public hols.* 🎦 🛗

El Torcal ❸

Málaga. **Road map** D4. 🚍 🚌 *Antequera.* 🛈 *Antequera. (95) 270 25 05.*

A HUGE EXPOSED HUMP of limestone upland that has been battered into bizarre formations by wind and rain, the **Parque Natural del Torcal** is very popular with hikers. Most follow a network of footpaths leading from a visitors' center in the middle, on which short walks of up to two hours are marked by yellow arrows; the longer walks are marked in red. There are canyons, caves, mushroom-shaped rocks, and other geological curiosities to see. The park is also a joy for natural historians, with fox and weasel populations and colonies of eagles, hawks, and vultures. It also protects rare plants and flowers, among them species of wild orchid.

Archidona ❷

Málaga. **Road map** D4. 🏘 *11,000.* 🚍 🚌 🛈 *Calle Carreras 10. (95) 271 63 21.* 🔄 *Mon.*

T HIS SMALL TOWN is worth a stop to see its extraordinary **Plaza Ochavada**. This is an octagonal square built in the 18th century in a French style, but which also incorporates traditional Andalusian features.

From the **Ermita Virgen de Gracia** on a hillside above the town, there are commanding views over rolling countryside.

The 18th-century, octagonal Plaza Ochavada in Archidona

Nerja

Málaga. **Road map** D4. 15,000.
🚌 ℹ *Calle Puerta del Mar 2. (95)*
252 15 31. 🚃 *Tue.*

THIS FASHIONABLE resort at
the eastern extremity of the
Costa del Sol lies at the foot
of the beautiful mountains of
the Sierra de Almijara and is
perched on a cliff above a succession of sandy coves. The
main area for tourist activity
in the resort centers around
the promenade, running along
a rocky promontory known
as **El Balcón de Europa** (the
Balcony of Europe). Spread
along its length are cafés and
restaurants with outdoor tables,
and there are sweeping views
up and down the coast. On the
edges of town, vacation villas,
many of which have private
swimming pools and verdant
lawns, proliferate, as do newly
built apartment blocks.

The town of Nerja overlooking the sea from El Balcón de Europa

Due east of the town are the
Cuevas de Nerja, a series of
vast caverns of considerable
archaeological interest, which
were discovered in 1959. Wall
paintings *(see p40)* found in
them are believed to be about
20,000 years old. Only a few
of the many cathedral-sized
chambers are open to public

view. One of these has been
turned into an impressive underground auditorium large
enough to hold audiences of
several hundred. Concerts are
held there in the summer.

🏛 **Cuevas de Nerja**
Carretera de las Cuevas de Nerja.
📞 *(95) 252 95 20.* ⭕ *daily.* 📷

Málaga

Málaga. **Road map** D4. 600,000.
✈ 🚌 🚃 ℹ *Pasaje de Chinitas 4.*
(95) 221 34 45. 🚃 *Sun.*

A THRIVING PORT, Málaga is
Andalusia's second
largest city. Initial im-
pressions tend to be of
ugly suburbs, shabby
high-rise blocks, and
lines of rusting cranes,
but this belies a city
that is rich with his-
tory, and is filled with
splendid monuments
and the soulful vib-
rancy of Andalusia.

Malaca, the Phoenician *(see
pp40–41)* city, was an important trading port on the Iberian
peninsula. After Rome's victory
against Carthage in 206 BC
(see p42), it became a major
port for Roman trade with
Byzantium. Málaga's heyday
came in the years after 711,
when it fell to the Moors and
became their main port serving
Granada. It was recaptured by
the Christians in 1487 after a
bloody siege. The Moors who
stayed behind were expelled
(see pp48–9) after a rebellion.

Following a long decline,
the city flourished once again
during the 19th century, when

Málaga wine became one of
Europe's most popular drinks.
Unfortunately, phylloxera, the
grape disease that ravaged the
vineyards of Europe, reached
Málaga, ending the prosperity
of its vineyards. This, however,
was when tourists –
the British especially
– began to spend
their winters here.

The old town at
the heart of Málaga
radiates from the
catedral. It was
begun in 1528 by
Diego de Siloé,
but it is a bizarre
mix of styles.
Its construction was
interrupted by an
earthquake in
1680. The
half-built
second
tower,

**Façade detail,
Málaga Cathedral**

abandoned in 1765 when the
funds ran out, is the reason for
the cathedral's nickname: La
Manquita (the one-armed one).

Málaga's **Museo de Bellas
Artes** has several fine paintings
by Murillo, Ribera, Zurbarán,
and Morales, and a number
of childhood sketches by
Pablo Picasso *(see p52),*
who was born in Málaga.
The **Casa Natal de
Picasso**, where the

Amphitheater

**Puerta
Principal**

Entrance

**Puerta de
las Columnas**

Plaza de Armas

Vélez Málaga ㉖

Málaga. **Road map** D4. 👥 55,000.
🚉 🚌 ℹ️ *Casa Larios, Carretera de Almería, Torre del Mar. (95) 284 21 80.* 🚌 *Sun.*

O N THE COSTA DEL SOL, just 5 kilometers (3 miles) inland from Torre del Mar, is the market town of Vélez-Málaga, in the fertile Vélez River valley. The modern district is sprawling and industrial, while the old Moorish town is dominated by the **Fortaleza de Belén**, a fortress with a restored tower that juts out dramatically from a rocky outcrop against the sky.

Immediately below the fortress is the medieval **Barrio de San Sebastián**, with its dark cobbled alleys, whitewashed walls, and iron window-grilles. Here, two churches stand out: the **Iglesia de Santa María la Mayor**, which still retains an original Moorish minaret; and

the **Iglesia de Nuestra Señora de la Encarnación**, which was once a Visigothic church and then, later, a mosque.

🏰 **Fortaleza de Belén**
Vélez Málaga Alta. ⭘ *daily.*

Narrow street in the Barrio de San Sebastián, Vélez Málaga

Montes de Málaga ㉗

Málaga. **Road map** D4. 🚌 *to Colmenar.* ℹ️ *Agencia de Medio Ambiente, Málaga (95) 222 58 00.*

T O THE NORTH and east of Málaga are the beautiful hills of Montes de Málaga. A wide area is undergoing reforestation and forms the **Parque Natural de Montes de Málaga**. Wildlife thrives in the strongly scented undergrowth of lavender and wild herbs. Occasionally there are glimpses of wild cats, stone martens, wild boars, eagles, and other birds of prey.

Walkers can follow marked trails. A farmhouse has been restored and converted into an ethnological museum. Along the C345 road between Málaga and the park, there are sensational views down to the sea.

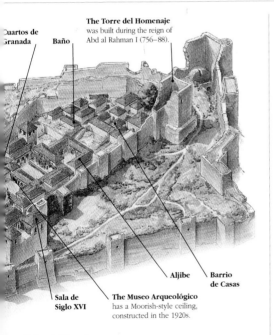

Cuartos de Granada   **Baño**

The Torre del Homenaje was built during the reign of Abd al Rahman I (756–88).

Sala de Siglo XVI

The Museo Arqueológico has a Moorish-style ceiling, constructed in the 1920s.

Aljibe   **Barrio de Casas**

Malaga's Alcazaba
Málaga's vast Alcazaba was built between the 8th and 11th centuries on the site of a Roman town. The two are curiously juxtaposed, with the Roman amphitheater, discovered in 1951 and only partially excavated, just outside the entrance. The remains of Moorish walls can be seen, but the real attraction is the Museo Arqueológico, housing collections of Phoenician, Roman, and Moorish artifacts, including fine ceramics.

painter spent his early years, is now the headquarters of the Picasso Foundation.

On the hill directly behind the Alcazaba are the ruins of the **Castillo de Gibralfaro**, a 14th-century Moorish castle. Connected to the fortress by a pair of parallel ramparts, it can be reached through some beautiful gardens. There are views over the old town, the port, and the Málaga bullring, immediately below. The road to the Parador de Málaga also leads to the top of this hill; there are commanding views over the city from both.

East of Málaga on the road to Vélez Málaga is the unspoiled family beach of Rincón de la Victoria *(see p31).*

🏛 **Museo de Bellas Artes**
Calle San Agustín 8. 📞 *(95) 221 83 82.* ⭘ *Tue–Sun.* 🎫
🏛 **Casa Natal de Picasso**
Plaza de la Merced 15. 📞 *(95) 221 50 05.* ⭘ *Mon–Fri.* ● *public hols.*
🏰 **Castillo de Gibralfaro**
● *for restoration.*
🏰 **Alcazaba**
Calle Alcazabilla s/n. 📞 *(95) 221 60 05.* ⭘ *Tue–Sun.* 🎫 *(also covers Museo Arqueológico).*
🏛 **Museo Arqueológico**
Calle Alcazabilla. 📞 *(95) 221 60 05.* ⭘ *Tue–Sun.*

Torremolinos, the brash capital of the Costa del Sol's tourist industry

Torremolinos 🟠

Málaga. **Road map** D4. 🏛 *30,000.*
🚉 🚌 ℹ *Ayuntamiento, Avda Rafael Quintana s/n. (95) 237 95 51.* 🕐 *Thu.*

TORREMOLINOS was a pioneer in the development of mass tourism in Spain and, until the mid-1970s, an archetype of the successful sun-and-beach resort. Later, a victim of its own success, Torremolinos became a byword for all that is wrong with unchecked development.

"Torrie" or "T-Town" to its friends, this high-rise vacation metropolis rounds a headland dividing two beaches. It grew from a village in the 1950s to one of the busiest and most boisterous resorts on the Costa del Sol, where British, and to a lesser extent, German and Scandinavian vacationers enjoyed their inexpensive package trips. It also developed its red-light district and a raffish nightlife to provide "R and R" for sailors of the US Navy in port at Málaga.

Recently the town has been cleaned up as part of a project that has seen huge sums spent on new squares, a promenade, green spaces, and enlarging the beach with millions of tons of fine golden sand.

Although Torremolinos still has dozens of English bars run by expatriates, the atmosphere is now decidedly less brash, especially at Carihuela Beach toward the adjoining resort of Benalmádena. Bajondillo Beach is nearer the busy town center. As elsewhere on the Costa del Sol, Torremolinos has a thriving scene in winter, as well as in the summer.

Fuengirola 🟠

Málaga. **Road map** C4. 🏛 *45,000.*
🚉 🚌 ℹ *Avda Jesús Santos Rein 6. (95) 246 74 57.* 🕐 *Tue.*

SPRAWLING ALONG THE FOOT OF southern Andalusia's gray and ocher Serranía de Ronda, which drops steeply down to

the edge of the Mediterranean, Fuengirola is another cheap, mass-market package-vacation resort. In recent years, some of the wilder elements of its mostly British clientele have moved on to newer pastures elsewhere. Nowadays it is predominantly families who take their sun-and-sea summer vacations here. During the mild winter months, planeloads of retired people arrive from the UK; they stroll along the seaside promenade, go to English bars, and waltz the afternoons away at hotel dances.

Boxes of fresh fish, Fuengirola

Marbella 🟠

Málaga. **Road map** C4. 🏛 *80,000.*
🚉 ℹ *Glorieta de la Fontanilla s/n. (95) 277 14 42.* 🕐 *Mon.*

IN GLITTERING CONTRAST with Torremolinos and Fuengirola, Marbella is one of Europe's most exclusive resorts. Royalty, movie stars, and other members of an international jet set spend their summers here in fancy villas or stay at one of Marbella's five-star, luxury hotels. In winter the

Yachts and motorboats in the exclusive marina of Marbella – the summer home of the international jet set

LIFE IN THE SUN

The idealized image of the Costa del Sol before tourism is of idyllic fishing villages where life was always at an easy pace. It is true that local economies have turned away from fishing and agriculture, and that the natural beauty of this coast has been marred by development. Any measured view, however, should consider the situation described by Laurie Lee, the writer who in 1936 wrote of ". . . salt-fish villages, thin-ribbed, sea-hating, cursing their place in the sun." Today few Andalusians curse their new-found prosperity.

19th-century lithograph of the harbor at Málaga

major attraction is the golf *(see pp30–31)*. A short walk from many of the fanciest hotels is an old town of clean alleys, squares, courtyards, and fashionable restaurants. One of the delights of Marbella is eating outside in **Plaza de los Naranjos**, the main square, shaded by orange trees. The **Ayuntamiento**, overlooking the square, has an exquisite, paneled Mudéjar ceiling. The **Iglesia de Nuestra Señora de la Encarnación**, just off the Plaza de los Naranjos, is a cool, peaceful refuge. Devotees of Picasso might want to see some of his least-known work in the **Museo de Grabado Contemporáneo**.

Anybody interested in the nightlife should come with a full wallet; luckily the beaches – Victor's, Cabopino, Don Carlos, Babaloo, and Las Dunas *(see pp30–31)* – are free.

🏛 **Museo de Grabado Contemporáneo**
C/ Hospital Bazan s/n. ▌ *(95) 282 50 35.* ◯ *Mon–Fri.* ⬤ *public hols.* 🈺
🏛 **Ayuntamiento**
Plaza de los Naranjos 1. ▌ *(95) 276 11 00.* ◯ *by appointment only.*
🈺 ♿

San Pedro de Alcántara ㉜

Málaga. **Road map** D4. 🏘 *25,000.*
🚉 🛈 *Conjunto San Luis bloque.*
(95) 278 13 60. 🔺 *Thu.*

SAN PEDRO IS A SMALL, rather exclusive, resort, which lies within Marbella's sphere of influence. It is quiet, with a

sleepy atmosphere, especially in the Plaza de la Iglesia, the town square, set back from the modern marina. Most of the stylish vacation developments are on the town's fringes, set amid a number of golf courses *(see pp30–31)*, on the lower slopes of the Sierra Blanca.

Estepona ㉝

Málaga. **Road map** C5. 🏘 *37,000.*
🚉 🛈 *Paseo Maritimo s/n. (95) 280 09 13.* 🔺 *Wed & Sun.*

THIS FISHING VILLAGE, situated midway between Marbella and Gibraltar, has been altered, but not totally overwhelmed, by tourist developments. It is not particularly attractive at first sight, with big hotels and apartment blocks fronting the

The leafy Plaza de las Flores hidden in Estepona's backstreets

town's busy main tourist area. Behind, however, if you take the trouble to look, you find endearing pockets of all that is quintessentially Spanish – orange trees lining the streets, and the lovely **Plaza Arce** and **Plaza de las Flores**, peaceful squares where old men sit reading newspapers while around them children kick soccer balls. There are also a few good, relatively inexpensive fish restaurants and tapas bars. The beach is pleasant enough, and evenings in the town tend to be quiet, making the resort popular for families with young children.

Not far away from Estepona, however, is a popular nudist beach called the Costa Natura *(see pp30–31)*.

Relaxing in sleepy San Pedro de Alcántara

GRANADA AND ALMERÍA

EASTERN ANDALUSIA *is dominated by the Sierra Nevada, Iberia's highest range and one of Spain's premier winter-sports areas. At its foot is Granada, once a Moorish kingdom, with a royal palace, the Alhambra, straight out of* One Thousand and One Nights. *Ruined fortresses, relics of a warring past, dominate the towns of Granada province. In Almería's arid interior, film directors have put to use atmospheric landscapes reminiscent of Arabia and the Wild West.*

At the point where the mountains of the Sierra Nevada meet the plain, 670 m (2,200 ft) above sea level, nestles the ancient city of Granada, founded by the Iberians. For 250 years it was the capital of a Moorish kingdom whose borders enclosed both Almería and Málaga provinces. On a ridge overlooking the city rises the royal citadel of the Alhambra, a complex of spacious palaces and water gardens.

The mountainous terrain of Granada province is starkly impressive. Amid the ravines, crags, and terraced fields of Las Alpujarras on the southern flank of the Sierra Nevada, the villages seem to cling to the sheer slopes.

Along the coastal strip of Granada province, avocados and custard apples flourish in the subtropical climate.

Hotels, villas, and vacation apartment blocks are also much in evidence here.

East of Granada the landscape becomes more arid. Around the town of Guadix, founded in Phoenician and Roman times, thousands of people live in cave houses. A statue of an Iberian goddess from pre-Roman times was found at Baza, and at Los Millares, near Almería, there are traces of a 4,000-year-old settlement.

Almería, a flourishing port in the Moorish era, has been revitalized by a new form of agriculture. Plastic greenhouses now cover hectares of its surrounding province, producing fruit and vegetables all year.

Along the sparsely populated coast of Cabo de Gata, little-visited villages and bays doze in year-round sunshine.

The Renaissance castle of Lacalahorra at the foot of the Sierra Nevada

◁ Patio de los Leones, Alhambra, Granada; a fountain resting on the backs of 12 lions

Exploring Granada and Almería

G RANADA AND THE ALHAMBRA are the obvious
highlights of this region, but are only a
part of its appeal. Improved roads make it
easy to reach most places within a few hours,
and from Granada it is possible to explore the
Sierra Nevada, plunge into the clear waters of
the Costa Tropical, or wander through beautiful, spectacularly situated old towns, such as
Montefrío and Alhama de Granada. From
Almería it is a short hop to the Arizona-like
country around Tabernas, where spaghetti
westerns were made, or to the secluded
beaches of the Parque Natural de Cabo de
Gata. Each town and whitewashed village
that lies in between has its own charm.

**The Alhambra, with the snow-covered Sierra
Nevada mountain range in the background**

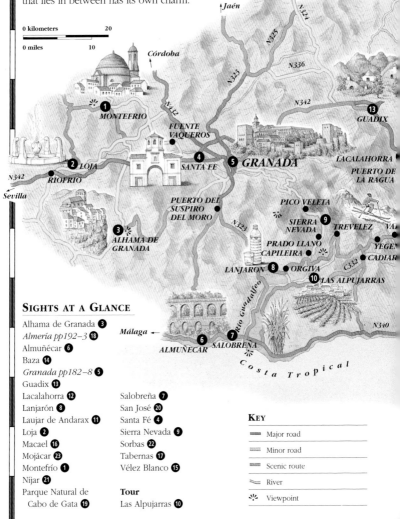

SIGHTS AT A GLANCE

Alhama de Granada **3**
Almería pp192–3 **18**
Almuñécar **6**
Baza **14**
Granada pp182–8 **5**
Guadix **13**
Lacalahorra **12**
Lanjarón **8**
Laujar de Andarax **11**
Loja **2**
Macael **16**
Mojácar **23**
Montefrío **1**
Níjar **21**
Parque Natural de
    Cabo de Gata **19**
Salobreña **7**
San José **20**
Santa Fé **4**
Sierra Nevada **9**
Sorbas **22**
Tabernas **17**
Vélez Blanco **15**

Tour
Las Alpujarras **10**

KEY

━━ Major road

▨▨▨ Minor road

▨▨▨ Scenic route

≈ River

☼ Viewpoint

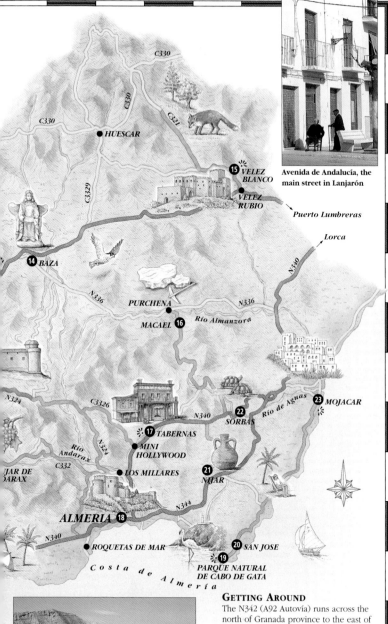

Avenida de Andalucía, the
main street in Lanjarón

Arizona-like landscape near Tabernas

GETTING AROUND

The N342 (A92 Autovía) runs across the
north of Granada province to the east of
Almería province, via Granada. The N340
follows the coast via Almería and the Costa
Tropical. The N323 links Granada's coast
with the provincial capital; and the C332
connects the villages of the Alpujarras.

There are three trains a day between
Granada and Almería, but no coastal
service. Buses run frequently from both
cities to towns on main routes, but only
once or twice a day to more remote towns.

Whitewashed houses on the edge of the gorge at Alhama de Granada, surrounded by olive groves

Montefrío ❶

Granada. **Road map** D3. 🏯 *8,500.*
🚌 ℹ️ *Ayuntamiento, Plaza España 7.*
(958) 33 61 36. 🕮 *Mon.*

MONTEFRÍO IS the archetypal
Andalusian town, which,
approached by road from the
south, offers wonderful views
of tiled rooftops and whitewashed houses running up to
a steep crag. The village is
surmounted by remains of
Moorish fortifications and
the 16th-century Gothic
Iglesia de la Villa, which
is attributed to Diego
de Siloé. Located in
the center of town
stands the **Iglesia de
la Encarnación,** in
Neo-Classical design;
the architect Ventura
Rodríguez (1717–85)
is credited with its
design. Montefrío
is also famed for
the high quality of
its pork products.   **Belfry of Templo de San
Gabriel at Loja**

Loja ❷

Granada. **Road map** D4. 🏯 *21,000.*
🚌 🚃 ℹ️ *Duque de Valencia 1.*
(958) 32 39 49. 🕮 *Mon.*

A RUINED MOORISH fort rises
above the crooked streets
of the old town of Loja, which
was built at a strategic point on
the Río Genil. The Renaissance
Templo de San Gabriel
(1566) has a striking façade,
designed by Diego de Siloé.
Known as "the city of water,"
Loja also has some beautiful
fountains. East of the town,

the fast-flowing Río Genil cuts
through **Los Infiernos** gorge.
To the west is **Riofrío,** where
the local trout is served in a
number of restaurants.

Alhama de Granada ❸

Granada. **Road map** D4. 🏯 *6,000.*
🚌 ℹ️ *Calle Vendederas s/n. (958)
36 06 86.* 🕮 *Fri.*

A LHAMA IS a charming
little town balanced
above a gorge. It was
known as al Hamma
(hot springs) to the
Arabs. Their baths
can still be seen in
Hotel Balneario
on the edge of the
town. Alhama's fall
to the Christians in
1482 was a major
Moorish defeat. It
led to the final
humiliation of the
Nasrid kingdom at
Granada in 1492
(see p46).
The 16th-century **Iglesia
de Carmen** has a number
of very fine paintings on
its dome, which had
to be restored after
damage incurred
during the Spanish
Civil War *(see pp52–3).*
Narrow, immaculately whitewashed streets lead to the
Iglesia de la Encarnación,
which was founded by the
Catholic Monarchs *(see
pp46–7)* in the 16th
century. Some of the
vestments worn by the
present-day priests are   **Spire tip of the
church, Santa Fé**

said to have been embroidered
by Queen Isabel herself. The
church also has a striking Renaissance bell tower designed
by Diego de Siloé. Nearby is
the 16th-century **Hospital de
la Reina,** which is now used
as a library and also houses a
fine *artesonado* ceiling.

🏨 **Hotel Balneario**
Carretera de Granada. 🕿 *(958) 36
02 71.* 🕒 *Jun 10–Oct 10.*
🏨 **Hospital de la Reina**
Calle Vendederas s/n. 🕿 *(958) 36 06
86 (tourist office).* 🕒 *Mon–Sat.* ♿

Santa Fé ❹

Granada. **Road map** D4. 🏯 *14,000.*
🚌 🚃 ℹ️ *Plaza España 6. (958) 44
00 00.* 🕮 *Thu.*

T HE ARMY of the Catholic
Monarchs camped in this
small town as it lay siege to
Granada *(see p46).* The camp
burned down, it is said, after a
maid placed a candle too close
to a curtain in Isabel's tent, and
Fernando ordered a model
town to be built. Its name,
"holy faith," was chosen
by the devout Isabel.
In November 1492
the Moors made a
formal surrender at
Santa Fé and here,
in the same year, the
two monarchs backed
Columbus's voyage of
exploration *(see p123).*
An earthquake destroyed
some of the town in
1806. A Moor's severed
head, carved in stone,
decorates the spire of
the parish church.

Granada **5**

See pp182–8.

Almuñécar **6**

Granada. **Road map** D4. 20,500.
Avenida Europa s/n. (958) 63 11 25. *Fri.*

ALMUÑÉCAR LIES on southern Spain's most spectacular coast, the **Costa Tropical** *(see p30)*, where mountains rise to over 2,000 m (6,560 ft) from the shores of the Mediterranean Sea. The Phoenicians founded the first settlement, called Sexi, at Almuñécar, and the Romans built an aqueduct here, which is still in use today. When the English writer Laurie Lee made his long trek across Spain in 1936, he described Almuñécar as "a tumbling little village . . . fronted by a strip of grey sand which some hoped would be an attraction for tourists." On returning in the 1950s, Lee found a village still coming to terms with the Spanish Civil War *(see pp52–3)*, which he recounts in his novel titled *A Rose for Winter.*

Almuñécar is now a vacation resort, and apartment blocks fringe its beaches. Above the old town is the **Castillo de San Miguel**. In its shadow are botanic gardens, the **Parque**

Castillo de San Miguel, overlooking the village of Almuñécar

Ornitológico, and a Roman fish-salting factory. There are Phoenician artifacts on display in the **Museo Arqueológico**.

⛪ Castillo de San Miguel
for restoration.

🦜 Parque Ornitológico
Plaza de Abderraman s/n. *(958) 63 54 75.* *daily.*

🏛 Museo Arqueológico
Cueva 7 Palacios. *Mon–Sat.*

Salobreña **7**

Granada. **Road map** E4. 10,000.
Plaza de Goya s/n. (958) 61 03 14. *Tue & Fri.*

FROM ACROSS the coastal plain Salobreña looks like a white liner sailing above a sea of waving sugar cane.

Narrow streets wend their way up a hill first fortified by the Phoenicians. The hill later became the site of the restored **Castillo Arabe**, which gives fine views of the peaks of the Sierra Nevada *(see p189)*. Modern developments, bars, and restaurants line part of this resort's lengthy beach.

⛪ Castillo Arabe
Calle Castillo. *(958) 61 03 14 (tourist office).* *daily.*

Lanjarón **8**

Granada. **Road map** E4. 24,000.
Ayuntamiento, Plaza de la Constitución. (958) 77 00 02. *Tue & Fri.*

SCORES OF SNOW-FED springs bubble from the slopes below the Sierra Nevada, and Lanjarón, on the threshold of Las Alpujarras *(see pp190–91)*, has a long history as a spa. From June to October tourists flock to the town to take the waters and, under medical supervision, enjoy various water treatments for arthritis, obesity, nervous tension, and other ailments. Lanjarón bottled water is sold all over Spain.

The town occupies a lovely site, but it sometimes seems somewhat melancholic. The exception to this is during the early hours of the festival of San Juan *(see p33)* when an uproarious water battle takes place. Anybody who dares venture into the streets ends up being liberally doused.

♨ Balneario
Balneario de Lanjarón. *(958) 77 10 77.* *May–Oct: daily.*

The village of Salobreña viewed across fields of sugar cane

Granada

T<small>HE GUITARIST ANDRES SEGOVIA</small> (1893–1987) described Granada as a "place of dreams, where the Lord put the seed of music in my soul." It was ruled by the Nasrid dynasty *(see pp46–7)* from 1238 until 1492 when it fell to the Catholic Monarchs. Before the Moors were expelled, artisans, merchants, scholars, and scientists all contributed to the city's reputation as a center for culture. Under Christian rule the city became a focus for the Renaissance. After a period of decline in the 19th century, Granada has recently been the subject of renewed interest and efforts are being made to restore parts of it to their past glory.

Relief at the Museo Arqueológico

🏛 Alhambra and Generalife
See pp186–188.

Façade of Granada cathedral

🏛 Catedral
On the orders of the Catholic Monarchs, work on the cathedral began in 1523 to Gothic-style plans by Enrique de Egas. It continued under the Renaissance maestro Diego de Siloé, who also designed the façade. Corinthian pillars support his magnificent, circular Capilla Mayor. Under its dome, windows of 16th-century glass depict Juan del Campo's *The Passion.* The west front was designed by the Baroque artist Alonso Cano, who was born in Granada. His grave and many of his works are housed in the cathedral. Near the entrance arch are wooden statues of the Catholic Monarchs, carved by Pedro de Mena in 1677.

🏛 Capilla Real
The Royal Chapel was built for the Catholic Monarchs between 1505 and 1507 by Enrique de Egas. A magnificent *reja* (grille) by Maestro Bartolomé de Jaén

encloses the mausoleums and high altar. The *retablo* by the sculptor Felipe de Vigarney has reliefs depicting the fall of Granada *(see pp46–7).* Carrara marble figures of Fernando and Isabel, designed by Domenico Fancelli in 1517, repose next to those of their daughter Juana la Loca (the Mad) and her husband Felipe el Hermoso (the Handsome), both by the sculptor Bartolomé Ordóñez.

Steps lead down to the crypt where their bodies are stored in lead coffins. In the sacristy there are yet more statues of the two monarchs and many art treasures, including paintings by Van der Weyden and Botticelli from Isabel's collection. Glass cases house Isabel's crown, Fernando's sword, and their army's banners.

🏛 Palacio de la Madraza
Calle Oficios 14. 📞 (958) 22 34 47. 🕐 Sep–Jul: Mon–Fri. 🚻
Originally an Arab university, this building later became the city hall. The façade dates from the 18th-century. Inside there is a Moorish hall with a finely decorated mihrab.

Entrance to the Moorish mihrab in the Palacio de la Madraza

🏛 Corral del Carbón
Calle Mariana Pineda s/n. 📞 (958) 22 59 90. 🕐 Mon–Sat. 🚻
This galleried courtyard is a unique relic of the Moorish era. Originally it was a storehouse and inn for merchants. In Christian times it was a place for theatrical performances; it later became a coal exchange. These days it houses local craft vendors and the main tourist office.

🏛 Casa de los Tiros
C/ Cementerio Santa Escolástica 19. 📞 (958) 22 10 72. ⬤ to the public.
This curious, fortresslike palace was built in Renaissance style in the 16th century. It was once the property of a family that was awarded the Generalife after the fall of Granada *(see pp46–7);* among their possessions was a sword belonging to Boabdil *(see p47).* The sword is represented on the façade together with five statues of Hercules, Mercury, Theseus, Hector, and Jason. The building owes its name to the muskets in its battlements, *tiros* being the Spanish word for shot.

Reja by Maestro Bartolomé de Jaén enclosing the altar of the Capilla Real

🏛 Mirador de San Nicolás

From this square visitors can enjoy splendid sunset views. Tiled rooftops drop away to the Darro River, on the far side of which stands the Alhambra; the Sierra Nevada provides a suitably dramatic backdrop.

🏛 El Bañuelo

Carrera del Darro 31. 📞 *(958) 22 23 39.* ◯ *Tue–Sat.* ● *public hols.*
These brick-vaulted Arab baths, located near the Darro River, were built in the 11th century. Roman, Visigothic, and Arab capitals were all incorporated into the baths' columns.

🏛 Museo Arqueológico

Carrera del Darro 41. 📞 *(958) 22 56 40.* ◯ *Tue–Sun.* ● *public hols.*
The Casa de Castril, a fine Renaissance mansion with a Plateresque portal, houses the Museo Arqueológico. Iberian, Phoenician, and Roman antiquities, found in the province of Granada, are exhibited here.

Cupola in the sanctuary of the Monasterio de la Cartuja

🏛 Palacio Carlos V

Alhambra. 📞 *(958) 22 91 05.* ◯ *Tue–Sun.* ● *public hols.* 🎟 ♿
This palace in the Alhambra houses the Museo Hispano-Musulmán and the Museo de Bellas Artes (at present closed for renovation). The highlight of the Muslim art collection is an exquisite 15th-century vase from the Alhambra, which has blue and gold designs.

🏛 Monasterio de la Cartuja

A Christian warrior, El Gran Capitán, donated the land on which the monastery was built in 1516, in thanks for surviving a skirmish with the Moors. A dazzling cupola by Antonio Palomino tops the sanctuary. The extravagant Churriguer-esque sacristy *(see p23)* is by the mason Luis de Arévalo and the sculptor Luis Cabello.

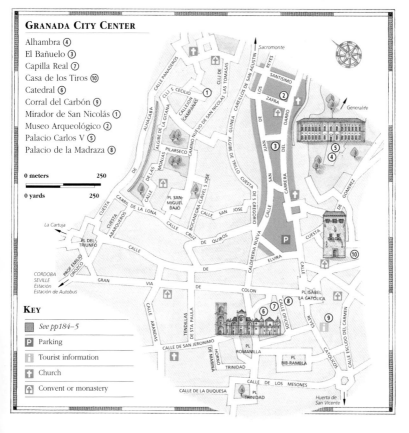

GRANADA CITY CENTER

0 meters   250
0 yards   250

KEY

▨	*See pp184–5*
P	Parking
ℹ	Tourist information
✚	Church
⌘	Convent or monastery

Street-by-Street: the Albaicín

Ornate plaque for house in the Albaicín

THIS CORNER OF THE CITY, clinging to the hillside opposite the Alhambra, is where one feels closest to the city's Moorish ancestry. A fortress was first built here in the 13th century, and there were once over 30 mosques, some of which can still be traced. Along narrow, cobbled alleys stand *cármenes*, villas with Moorish decoration and gardens, secluded from the world by their high walls. In the evening, when the scent of jasmine lingers in the air, take a walk up to the Mirador de San Nicolás. From here the view over a maze of rooftops and the Alhambra glowing in the sunset is magic.

Albaicín Street
Steep and sinuous, the Albaicín streets form a virtual labyrinth. Many street names start with Cuesta, *meaning slope.*

Real Chancillería
Commissioned by the Catholic Monarchs, the Royal Chancery dates from 1530. Its patio is attributed to de Siloé.

0 meters   50
0 yards   50

Casa de los Pisa displays works of art belonging to the Spanish Knights Hospitalers, founded by Juan de Dios in the 16th century.

STAR SIGHTS

★ El Bañuelo

★ Museo Arqueológico

★ Iglesia de Santa Ana

★ **Iglesia de Santa Ana**
At the end of the Plaza Nueva stands this 16th-century brick church in Mudéjar style. It has an elegant Plateresque portal and, inside, a coffered ceiling.

Carrera del Darro
The road along the Río Darro leads past fine façades and crumbling bridges. At the top end, a café-terrace offers views of the Alhambra.

VISITORS' CHECKLIST

Granada. **Road map** D4. 🏘 262,000. ✈ 17 km (10.5 miles) SE of city. 🚌 Avenida de los Andaluces s/n. (958) 27 12 72. 🚉 Camino de Ronda, (958) 25 13 58. 🛈 Corral de Carbón. C/ Mariana Pineda s/n. (958) 22 59 90. 🚐 Sun. 🎭 Semana Santa (Easter), Día de la Cruz (May 3), Corpus Christi (May/Jun).

★ **Museo Arqueológico**
The ornate façade of this museum has Plateresque carvings, including reliefs of mythological figures.

KEY

– – – Suggested route

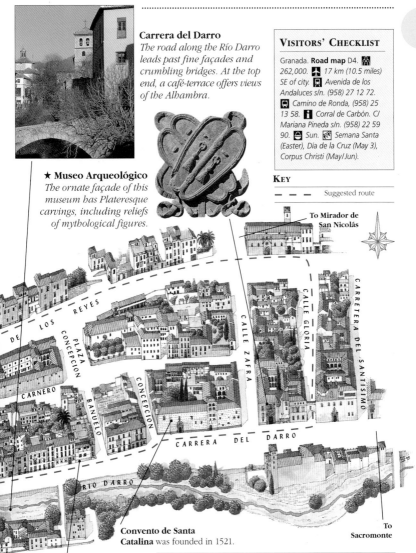

To Mirador de San Nicolás

Convento de Santa Catalina was founded in 1521.

To Sacromonte

★ **El Bañuelo**
Star-shaped openings in the vaults let light into these well-preserved Moorish baths, which were built in the 11th century.

SACROMONTE

Granada's gypsies formerly lived in the caves honeycombing this hillside. Travelers such as Washington Irving *(see p51)* would go there to enjoy spontaneous outbursts of flamenco. Today, virtually all the gypsies have moved away, but touristy flamenco shows of variable quality are still performed here in the evenings *(see p230)*. A Benedictine monastery, the Abadía del Sacromonte, sits at the very top of the hill. Inside, the ashes of San Cecilio, Granada's patron saint, are stored.

Gypsies dancing flamenco, 19th century

Granada: Alhambra

A MAGICAL USE of space, light, water, and decoration characterizes this most sensual piece of architecture. It was built under Ismail I, Yusuf I, and Muhammad V, caliphs when the Nasrid dynasty *(see p46)* ruled Granada. Seeking to belie an image of waning power, they constructed their idea of paradise on Earth. Modest materials were used (tiles, plaster, and wood), but they were superbly worked. Although the Alhambra suffered from decay and pillage, including an attempt by Napoleon's troops to blow it up, in recent times it has undergone extensive restoration and its delicate craftsmanship still dazzles the eye.

Sala de la Barca

★ Salón de Embajadores
The ceiling of this sumptuous throne room, built between 1334 and 1354, represents the seven heavens of the Muslim cosmos.

★ Patio de Arrayanes
This pool, set amid myrtle hedges and graceful arcades, reflects light into the surrounding halls.

Patio de Machuca

Entrance

Patio del Mexuar
This council chamber, completed in 1365, was where the reigning sultan listened to the petitions of his subjects and held meetings with his ministers.

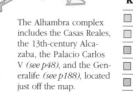

PLAN OF THE ALHAMBRA

To the Generalife

The Alhambra complex includes the Casas Reales, the 13th-century Alcazaba, the Palacio Carlos V *(see p48)*, and the Generalife *(see p188)*, located just off the map.

KEY

- ☐ Casas Reales (shown above)
- ☐ Palacio Carlos V
- ☐ Alcazaba
- ☐ Park
- ☐ Other buildings

Palacio del Partal

A tower and its pavilion, with a five-arched portico, are all that remain of the Palacio del Partal, the Alhambra's oldest palace.

VISITORS' CHECKLIST

For the Alhambra and Generalife.
((958) 22 75 27. **Group reservations (** (958) 22 09 12.
━ 2. **○** summer: 9am–8pm Mon–Sat, 9am–6pm Sun; winter: 9am–6pm Mon–Sun. **Last adm:** 15 minutes before closing time. **Night visits:** summer: 10pm–midnight Tue, Thu & Sat; winter: 8–10pm Sat.

Washington Irving's apartments

Baños Reales

Jardín de Lindaraja

The Sala de las Dos Hermanas, with its honeycomb dome, is regarded as the finest example of Spanish Islamic architecture.

Sala de los Reyes

This great banqueting hall was used to hold extravagant parties and feasts. Beautiful ceiling paintings on leather, from the 14th century, depict tales of hunting and chivalry.

Puerta de la Rawda

★ Sala de los Abencerrajes

This hall takes its name from a noble family who were rivals of Boabdil (see pp46–7). According to legend, he had them massacred while they attended a banquet here. The pattern of the stalactited ceiling was inspired by Pythagoras' theorem.

The Palacio Carlos V *(see p48)*, a fine Renaissance building, was added to the Alhambra in 1526.

★ Patio de los Leones

Built by Muhammad V, this patio is lined with arcades supported by 124 slender marble columns. At its center a fountain rests on 12 marble lions.

STAR FEATURES

★ **Salón de Embajadores**

★ **Patio de Arrayanes**

★ **Patio de los Leones**

★ **Sala de los Abencerrajes**

Granada: Generalife

Located north of the Alhambra, the Generalife was the country estate of the Nasrid kings. Here, they could escape the intrigues of the palace and enjoy tranquillity high above the city, a little closer to heaven. The name Generalife, or Yannat al Arif, has various interpretations, perhaps the most pleasing being "the garden of lofty paradise." The gardens, begun in the 13th century, have been modified over the years. They originally contained orchards and pastures for animals. The Generalife provides a magical setting for Granada's yearly International Music and Dance Festival *(see p33).*

Patio de la Acequia
This enclosed oriental garden is built around a long central pool. Rows of water jets make graceful arches above it.

Sala Regia

Jardines Altos (Upper Gardens)

The Escalera de Agua is a staircase with water flowing gently down it

The Patio de los Cipreses, otherwise known as the Patio de la Sultana, was the secret meeting place for Zoraya, wife of the Sultan Abu l Hasan, and her lover, the chief of the Abencerrajes.

Entrance

The Patio de Polo was the courtyard where palace visitors, arriving on horseback, would leave their horses.

Patio del Generalife
Leading up from the Alhambra to the Generalife are the Jardines Bajos (lower gardens). Above them, just before the main compound, is the Patio del Generalife.

The majestic peaks of the Sierra Nevada towering, in places, over 3,000 m (9,800 ft) above sea level

Sierra Nevada 🌑

Granada. **Road map** E4. 🚌 *from Granada*. 🚶 *Plaza Andalucia s/n, Cetursa Sierra Nevada. (958) 24 91 95.*

FOURTEEN PEAKS more than 3,000 m (9,800 ft) high crown the heights of the Sierra Nevada. The snow lingers until July and begins falling again in late autumn. One of Europe's highest roads runs past the ski resort of Solynieve, at 2,100 m (6,890 ft), and skirts the two highest peaks, **Pico Veleta** at 3,398 m (11,145 ft) and **Mulhacén** at 3,482 m (11,420 ft). Its altitude and closeness to the Mediterranean account for the great diversity of fauna and flora native to this glaciated mountain range. It is a habitat for golden eagles, rare butterflies, and many wildflowers.

Visitors to the Sierra Nevada should take some precautions to ensure their safety. There are several mountain refuges, but hikers and climbers should let someone know their route and take tents, food, and the right equipment in case they get lost or meet bad weather and cannot find a refuge.

Las Alpujarras 🌑

See pp190–91.

Painting, la Encarnación

Laujar de Andarax 🌑

Almeria. **Road map** E4. 🏔 *1,900.* 🚌 🚶 *Carretera de Laujar, Orgiva. (950) 51 31 03.* 🔔 *3 & 17 of each month.*

LAUJAR, IN THE ARID foothills of the Sierra Nevada, looks across the Andarax valley toward the Sierra de Gador. In this area the grapes are grown to eat but in the town a hearty red wine is produced. A legend says that the village was founded by Noah's grandson. In the 16th century, Abén Humeya, leader of a rebellion by the Moors *(see p48)*, made his base at Laujar. Christian troops crushed the rebellion cruelly, and Abén Humeya was then murdered by his treacherous followers. The Moors were eventually expelled.

The 17th-century **Iglesia de la Encarnación** has a statue of the Virgin by the Granada sculptor Alonso Cano. Next to the 18th-century Baroque **Ayuntamiento** is a fountain bearing a plaque with lines by the poet and dramatist Francisco Villespesa, born in the village in 1877:

*"Six fountains has my pueblo
And he who drinks their waters
Will never forget them,
So heavenly is their taste."*

A pleasant park and picnic spot has been created east of the town, at El Nacimiento.

Lacalahorra 🌑

Granada. **Road map** E4. 🚌 *Guadix.* 🚻 *(958) 67 70 98.* ⭕ *Wed.*

GRIM, IMMENSELY THICK walls with cylindrical towers circle Lacalahorra, a castle perched on a hillock above the village. Rodrigo de Mendoza, son of Cardinal Mendoza, ordered the castle to be built for his bride between 1509 and 1512, employing architects and craftsmen from Italy. Inside is an ornate, two-story, Renaissance courtyard with a staircase and pillars carved from Carrara marble.

The castle of Lacalahorra above the village of the same name

Whitewashed cave dwellings in the troglodyte quarter of Guadix

Guadix ⓭

Granada. **Road map** E4. 🏘 20,000.
🚍 🚉 ▮ *Carretera de Granada s/n.*
(958) 66 26 65. 🚌 *Sat.*

THE TROGLODYTE QUARTER, with 2,000 caves that have been inhabited for centuries, is the town's most remarkable sight. The cave dwellers say they prefer living in caves because the temperature remains constant all year. The **Cueva-Museo** (cave museum) shows how they live underground.

Approximately 2,000 years ago Guadix had iron, copper, and silver mines. The town thrived under the Moors and continued to do so after the Reconquest (*see pp46–7*), but declined in the 18th century.

Relics of San Torcuato, who established the first Christian bishopric in Spain, are kept in the Cathedral museum. The **Catedral**, begun in 1594 by Diego de Siloé, was later finished between 1701 and 1796 by Gaspar Cayón and Vicente de Acero. Near the 9th-century **Alcazaba**, the town's Mudéjar **Iglesia de Santiago** has a fine coffered ceiling. **Palacio de Peñaflor**, dating from the 16th century, is under restoration.

🏛 **Cueva-Museo**
Plaza de la Ermita Nueva s/n.
◯ daily. 🔲

Baza ⓮

Granada. **Road map** E3. 🏘 16,000.
🚍 ▮ *Casa de Cultura, Arco de la Magdalena s/n. (958) 70 06 91.*
🚌 *Wed.*

IMPRESSIVE EVIDENCE of ancient cultures based around Baza came to light in 1971, when a large, seated, female figure was

Trevélez ④
Trevélez, in the shadow of Mulhacén, is built in typical Alpujarran style and is famous for its cured hams.

A Tour of Las Alpujarras ❿

LAS ALPUJARRAS lie on the southern slopes of the Sierra Nevada. The villages in this area cling to valley sides clothed with oak and walnut trees. Their flat-roofed houses are distinctive and seen nowhere else in Andalusia. Local food is rustic. A specialty is *plato alpujarreño*: pork loin, ham, sausage, and blood sausage, accompanied by a blush wine from the Contraviesa mountains. Local crafts include handwoven rugs (*see p228*) and curtains with Moorish-influenced designs.

Orgiva ①
This is the largest town of the region, with a Baroque church in the main street and a lively Thursday market.

Poqueira Valley ②
Three villages typical of Las Alpujarras in this picturesque river valley are Capileira, Bubión, and Pampaneira.

Fuente Agria ③
People come here from far and wide to drink the iron-rich, naturally carbonated waters.

SIERRA
▲ MULHACÉN
3,482 m
11,420 ft
GR421
Pórtugos
Pitres
Juvile
C333
LANJARÓN
GRANADA
GR421
C332
SIERRA DE LA

found in a necropolis. She is the Dama de Baza *(see p41)*, believed to represent an Iberian goddess and estimated to be 2,400 years old. Subsequently, she was removed to the Museo Arqueológico in Madrid but a replica can be still seen in the **Museo Arqueológico** in Baza.

The Renaissance **Colegiata de Santa María**, nearby, has a Plateresque entrance and a fine 18th-century tower.

During the first few days of September a riotous fiesta takes place *(see p34)*. An emissary, El Cascamorras, is dispatched from the neighboring town of Guadix to try to bring back a coveted image of the Virgin from Baza's **Convento de la Merced**. He is covered in oil and chased back to Guadix by youths, also covered in oil. There, he is taunted again for returning empty-handed.

🏛 Museo Arqueológico
Plaza Mayor s/n. ◯ *by appointment with Casa de Cultura (958) 70 06 91.*

Vélez Blanco ⓯

Almería. **Road map** F3. 🏘 *2,400.*
🚌 *Vélez Rubio.* 🈯 *Ayuntamiento, Calle Corredera 38. (950) 41 50 01.*
🈶 *Wed.*

DOMINATING THIS pleasant little village is the mighty **Castillo de Vélez Blanco**. It was built from 1506 to 1513 by the first Marquis de Los Vélez, and its interior richly

The village of Vélez Blanco, overlooked by a 16th-century castle

adorned by Italian craftsmen. Unfortunately for the visitor, its Renaissance splendor has since been removed and sent to the Metropolitan Museum of Art in New York. There is, however, a reconstruction of one of the original patios.

A blend of Gothic, Renaissance, and Mudéjar styles *(see pp22–3)* can be seen in the **Iglesia de Santiago**, located in the village's main street.

Just outside Vélez Blanco is the **Cueva de los Letreros**, which contains paintings from around 4000 BC. One image depicts a horned man holding sickles; another the Indalo, a figure believed to be a deity with magical powers, still used as a symbol of Almería.

⛫ Castillo de Vélez Blanco
📞 *(950) 41 50 01 (Ayuntamiento).*
◯ *Sat–Sun.* ⌨
⛏ Cueva de los Letreros
Camino de la Cueva de los Letreros.
📞 *(950) 41 50 01 (Ayuntamiento).*
◯ *Sat–Sun.*

Yegen ⑥
A plaque marks the house where Gerald Brenan, the author of *South from Granada*, lived in the 1920s.

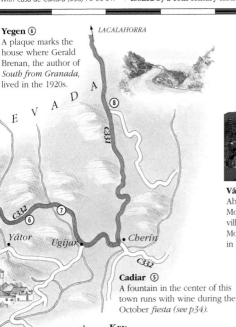

LACALAHORRA

Puerto de la Ragua ⑧
This pass, which leads across the mountains to Guadix, is nearly 2,000 m (6,560 ft) high and often snowbound in winter.

Válor ⑦
Aben Humeya, leader of a rebellion by Moriscos *(see p48)*, was born in this village. A commemorative battle between Moors and Christians is staged each year in mid-September *(see p34)*.

Cadiar ⑤
A fountain in the center of this town runs with wine during the October *fiesta (see p34).*

KEY

━━━ Tour route
--- Other roads
▲ Mountain peak

0 kilometers 10
0 miles 5

TIPS FOR DRIVERS

Tour length: 85 km (56 miles).
Stopping-off points: Orgiva and Trevélez have bars, restaurants, and hotels (see p209). Bubión has hotels and one good restaurant (see p221). Capileira has bars and restaurants. Orgiva is the last gas stop before Cadiar.

Almería ⑱

A COLOSSAL FORTRESS bears witness to Almería's golden age, when it was an important port for the Caliphate of Córdoba. Known as al Mariyat (the Mirror of the Sea), the city was a center for trade and textile industries, with silk, cotton, and brocade among its chief exports. After the city fell to the Catholic Monarchs *(see pp46–7)* in

Taking a break in the Plaza Vieja

Detail of the Renaissance portal of Almería cathedral

1489, it went into decline for the next 300 years. During the 19th and early 20th centuries, mining and a new port revived the city's fortunes, but this period ended abruptly with the start of the Civil War *(see pp52–3)*. Today a North African air still pervades the city, with its flat-roofed houses, desertlike environs, and palm trees. North African faces are common since ferries link the city with Morocco.

The 10th-century Alcazaba overlooking the old town of Almería

♣ Alcazaba
C/ Almanzor s/n. ☎ (950) 27 16 17. ◯ daily. ● Dec 25, Jan 1. ⚙

Fine views over the city are offered by this 1,000-year-old Moorish fortress. It has recently been undergoing restoration and within its walls are pleasant gardens and a Mudéjar chapel. It was the largest fortress built by the Moors and covered an area of more than 25,000 sq m (269,000 sq ft). The walls extend for 430 m (1,410 ft). Abd al Rahman III started construction in AD 955, but there were considerable additions later. The fort withstood two major sieges but fell to the Catholic Monarchs *(see pp46–7)* in 1489. Their coat of arms can be seen on the Torre del Homenaje, which was built during the monarchs' reign.

In the past, a bell in the Alcazaba was rung to advise the farmers in the surrounding countryside when irrigation was allowed. Bells were also rung to warn the citizens of Almería when pirates had been sighted off the coast.

It is inadvisable for visitors to wander around the Alcazaba district alone or after dark.

♠ Catedral
From North Africa, Berber pirates would often raid Almería. Consequently, the cathedral looks more like a fortress than a place of worship, with four towers, thick walls, and small windows. A mosque once stood on the site. It was later converted to a Christian temple but destroyed by an earthquake in 1522. Work began on the present building in 1524 under the direction of Diego de Siloé. Juan de Orea designed the Renaissance façade. He also created the beautifully carved walnut choir stalls. The naves and high altar are Gothic.

♠ Templo San Juan
Traces of Almería's most important mosque can still be seen here – one wall of the present church is Moorish. Inside is a 12th-century mihrab, a prayer niche with cupola. The church, built over the mosque, was damaged in the Spanish Civil War and abandoned until 1979. It has since been restored.

♛ Plaza Vieja
Also known as the Plaza de la Constitución, this is a 17th-century arcaded square. On one side of the square is the Ayuntamiento, a flamboyant building with a cream and pink façade dating from 1899.

The pedestrianized 17th-century Plaza Vieja, surrounded by elegant arcades

⊞ Puerta de Purchena

Located at the heart of the city, the Puerta de Purchena was once one of the main gateways in the city walls. From it runs a number of shopping streets, including the wide Paseo de Almería. A tree-lined thoroughfare, this is the focus of city life, with its cafés, Teatro Cervantes, and nearby food market.

✕ Centro Rescate de la Fauna Sahariana

C/ General Segura 1. ☎ (950) 27 64 00 (call to arrange visit).

At the rear of the Alcazaba, this rescue center shelters endangered species from the Sahara, particularly different kinds of gazelle. Having flourished in Almería's arid climate, some animals have been shipped to restock African nature preserves.

⊞ La Chanca

This gypsy and fishermen's quarter is near the Alcazaba. A number of families live in caves decorated with

Brightly colored entrance to a gypsy cave in La Chanca district

flowers and brightly painted façades (though the interiors are modern). On Mondays a lively street market is held.

Although this area is picturesque, it is also desperately poor; it is unwise to walk around with valuables or at night.

Saharan gazelle

ENVIRONS: One of the most important examples of a Copper Age settlement in Europe, **Los Millares** lies

VISITORS' CHECKLIST

Almería. **Road map** 4F.
🏠 170,000. 🚉 Plaza de la Estación. (950) 25 11 35.
🚌 Plaza Barcelona. (950) 21 00 29. 🛈 Parque Nicolás Salmerón. (950) 27 43 55. 🖰 Fri & Sat.
🎉 Fiestas de Invierno (Dec–early Jan), Semana Santa (Easter), Feria de Almería (last week Aug).

17 km (10.5 miles) north of Almería. As many as 2,000 people occupied the site from around 2700 to 1800 BC (see pp40–41). Discovered in 1891, remains of houses, defensive ramparts, and a necropolis that contains more than 100 tombs have since been uncovered.

The community here lived from agriculture but also had the capability to forge tools, arms, and jewelry from copper, which was mined in the nearby of Sierra de Gador.

⋔ Los Millares

Carretera Santa Fé de Mondújar.
☎ (950) 23 50 10. ◯ Tue–Sun.

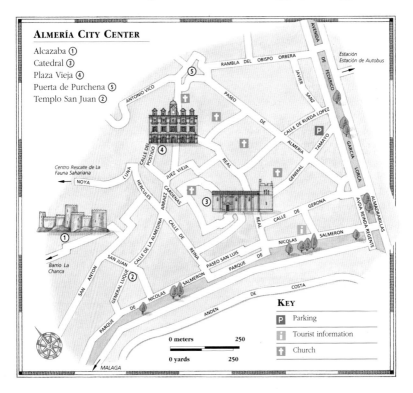

ALMERÍA CITY CENTER

Alcazaba ①
Catedral ③
Plaza Vieja ④
Puerta de Purchena ⑤
Templo San Juan ②

KEY

🅿 Parking
🛈 Tourist information
✝ Church

0 meters 250
0 yards 250

SPAGHETTI WESTERNS

Two Wild West towns lie off the N340 highway west of Tabernas. Here, visitors can reenact classic film scenes or watch stuntmen performing bank holdups and saloon brawls. The Poblados del Oeste were built during the 1960s and early 1970s when low costs and eternal sunshine made Almería the ideal location for spaghetti westerns. Sergio Leone, director of *The Good, the Bad and the Ugly*, built a ranch here and filmsets sprang up in the desert. Local gypsies played Indians and Mexicans. The deserts and Arizona-style badlands are still used occasionally for television commercials and series, and by film directors such as Steven Spielberg.

Still from *For a Few Dollars More* by Sergio Leone

Macael **⑯**

Almería. **Road map** F3. 🏠 *6,500*.
🚌 ℹ️ *Ayuntamiento, Plaza de la Constitución 1. (950) 12 83 16.* 🅿️ *Fri.*

MACAEL IS THE CENTER of an important marble industry. Dozens of local companies carve and polish the marble, which comes in white, veined gray, and green. The finished product has been used in many fine buildings, including the Alhambra in Granada *(see pp186–7).* To the east is Purchena, where there are the remains of a strategic Moorish castle. One notable local dish is the *fritada de Purchena,* a mixture of fried tomatoes and peppers, which makes a great partner for meat dishes.

Tabernas **⑰**

Almería. **Road map** F4. 🏠 *3,100*.
🚌 ℹ️ *Ayuntamiento, Plaza del Pueblo 1. (950) 36 50 02.* 🅿️ *Wed.*

A MOORISH HILLTOP fortress presides over the town of Tabernas and the surrounding dusty, cactus-dotted scenery of eroded hills and dried-out riverbeds. The harsh, rugged scenery has figured in many so-called spaghetti westerns.
  Not far from Tabernas is a solar energy research center, where hundreds of heliostats follow the course of southern Andalusia's powerful sun.

Almería **⑱**

See pp192–3.

Parque Natural de Cabo de Gata **⑲**

Almería. **Road map** F4. 🚌 *to San José.* ℹ️ *Centro Visitante Amoladeras, Carretera Cabo de Gata km 6. (950) 16 04 35.*

TOWERING CLIFFS of volcanic rock, sand dunes, salt flats, small secluded coves, and a few lonely fishing settlements can be found in the 29,000-ha (71,700-acre) Parque Natural de Cabo de Gata. The end of the cape, near the Arrecife de las Sirenas (Sirens' Reef), is marked by a lighthouse. The park includes a stretch of seabed about 2 km (1.2 miles) wide, which allows protection of the marine flora and fauna; the clear waters attract scuba divers and snorkelers.
  The area of dunes and saltpans between the cape and the Playa de San Miguel is a habitat for thorny jujube trees. Thousands of migrating birds stop here en route to and

from Africa. Among the 170 or so bird species recorded in the park are flamingos, avocets, Dupont's larks, and griffon vultures. Attempts are also being made to reintroduce the monk seal, which died out in the 1970s. At the northern end of the park, where there is a cormorants' fishing area, is Punta de los Muertos ("dead man's point"); this takes its name from the bodies of shipwrecked sailors said to have washed ashore there.

San José **⑳**

Almería. **Road map** F4. 🏠 *200*. 🚌
ℹ️ *Calle Correos s/n. (950) 38 02 99.*
🅿️ *Sun (Easter & summer).*

LOCATED ON a fine, sandy bay, San José is a small but fast-growing sea resort within the Parque Natural de Cabo de Gata. Rising behind it is the arid **Sierra de Cabo de Gata**, a range of bleak grandeur.

Lighthouse overlooking the cliffs of the Parque Natural de Cabo de Gata

The harbor at the traditional fishing village of La Isleta

Nearby are fine beaches, including Playa de los Genoveses *(see p31)*. Along the coast are **Rodalquilar**, a town once important for gold mining, and **La Isleta**, a fishing hamlet.

Níjar ㉑

Almería. **Road map** F4. 🏘 14,000. 🚌 🛈 *Calle Correos s/n, San José. (950) 38 02 99.* 🛒 *Wed.*

SET AMID a lush oasis of citrus trees on the edge of the severe Sierra Alhamilla, Níjar's fame stems from the colorful pottery and the *jarapas*, the handwoven rugs and blankets, that are made here. The town's historic quarter is typical of Andalusia, with its narrow streets and wrought-iron balconies garlanded with flowers.

The **Iglesia de Nuestra Señora de la Anunciación**, dating from the 16th century, has a coffered Mudéjar ceiling, delicately inlaid. The barren plain between Níjar and the sea has begun to blossom recently, thanks to irrigation.

In Spanish minds, the name of Níjar is closely associated with a poignant and violent incident that occurred here in the 1920s, and which later became the subject of a play by Federico García Lorca.

Sorbas ㉒

Almería. **Road map** F4. 🏘 3,000. 🚌 🛈 *Ayuntamiento, Calle Terraplen 19. (950) 36 44 81.* 🛒 *Thu.*

BALANCED ON THE edge of a deep chasm, Sorbas overlooks the Río de Aguas, which flows far below. There are two buildings in this village worth a look: the 16th-century **Iglesia de Santa María** and a 17th-century mansion said to have once been a summer retreat for the Duke of Alba.

Another point of interest for visitors is the traditional, rustic earthenware produced and sold by Sorbas's local potters.

Located near Sorbas is the peculiar **Yesos de Sorbas** nature preserve. This is an unusual region of karst, where water action has carved out hundreds of subterranean galleries and chambers in the limestone and gypsum strata. Speleologists are allowed to explore the caves, but only if they are granted permission by Andalusia's environmental department. On the surface, the green, fertile valley of the Río de Aguas cuts through dry, eroded hills. Local wildlife in this area includes tortoises and peregrine falcons.

Mojácar ㉓

Almería. **Road map** F4. 🏘 3,800. 🚌 🛈 *Plaza de Castillo. (950) 47 51 62.* 🛒 *Wed & Sun.*

FROM A DISTANCE, the village of Mojácar shimmers like the mirage of a Moorish citadel, its white houses cascading over a lofty ridge near to the sea. The village was taken by the Christians in 1488 and the Moors were later expelled. In the years after the Spanish Civil War *(see pp52–3)* the village fell into ruin, as much of its population emigrated. In the 1960s Mojácar was discovered by tourists, giving rise to a new era of prosperity. The old gateway in the walls is still here, but otherwise the village has been completely rebuilt.

***Pensión* façade in the picturesque, recently rebuilt village of Mojácar**

BLOOD WEDDING AT NÍJAR

Bodas de Sangre (Blood Wedding), a play by Federico García Lorca *(see p53)*, is based on a tragic event that occurred in 1928 near the town of Níjar. A woman called Paquita la Coja agreed, under pressure from her sister, to marry a suitor, Casimiro. A few hours before the ceremony, however, she fled with her cousin. Casimiro felt humiliated and Paquita's sister, who had hoped to benefit from the dowry, was furious. The cousin was found shot dead and Paquita half-strangled. Paquita's sister and her husband, Casimiro's brother, were found guilty of the crime. Shamed by this horrific scenario, Paquita hid from the world until her death in 1987. Lorca never visited Níjar, but based his play on newspaper reports.

The dramatist Federico García Lorca (1899 – 1936)

TRAVELERS'
NEEDS

WHERE TO STAY

SOME OF THE MOST charming places to stay in Spain are in Andalusia. They range from restored castles to family guest houses, and from one of the most luxurious hotels in Europe to an organic farm deep in the countryside. For budget travel there are pensions and youth hostels, and for hikers there are mountain refuges. A night or two in a bed-and-breakfast is becoming

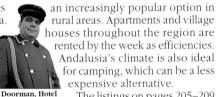

Doorman, Hotel Alfonso XIII

an increasingly popular option in rural areas. Apartments and village houses throughout the region are rented by the week as efficiencies. Andalusia's climate is also ideal for camping, which can be a less expensive alternative.

The listings on pages 205–209 describe some of the region's best hotels in every style and all price ranges, from basic to luxurious.

The Hospedería de San Francisco in Palma del Río *(see p207)*

WHERE TO LOOK

IN SEVILLE THE MOST appealing places to stay are mainly in the center of town, especially around the Santa Cruz district *(see pp68–81)*, where there is a broad range of hotels. As in most cities, the least expensive hotels tend to be found around the train station. Parking can be a problem in the town center, so if you want a hotel with a garage or a private lot, you

may have to look around the city's outer suburbs. A reasonable alternative is to stay in a town close to Seville, such as Carmona *(see pp128–9).*

Granada has two main hotel districts: around the Alhambra *(see pp186–7)*, which is quiet, and around the center, which is livelier, noisier, and usually less expensive. Central hotels make the best base for going out on the town at night.

In Córdoba the Judería *(see pp136–7)* is the most convenient place to stay if you plan to get around on foot. If you have a car, you may prefer a hotel on the outskirts of the city.

Hotels in Andalusia's coastal resorts are mainly the modern chains that cater to package vacationers or jet-setters. If you want somewhere more relaxing, there are good small hotels a short way inland; the countryside here is dotted with them. Look for them in the white towns between Arcos de la Frontera *(see p167)* and Ronda *(see pp168–9)*, and around Cazorla *(see p152)*.

HOTEL GRADING AND FACILITIES

HOTELS IN ANDALUSIA are awarded categories and stars by the regional tourist authorities. Hotels (H is the abbreviation) are awarded between one and five stars and pensions (P) between one and two stars. The star-rating system assesses the quantity of facilities a hotel has (such as whether there is an elevator or air-conditioning) rather than the quality of service to expect. Most hotels have restaurants that can be used by non-residents. Hotel-Residencias (HR), however, do not have dining rooms, although they may serve breakfast.

PARADORS

PARADORS are government-run hotels that fall into the three- to five-star classifications. The best ones occupy historic monuments, such as castles, monasteries, palaces, and old hunting lodges, but a number

The hillside terrace of the Alhambra Palace hotel *(see p209)*, with views across Granada

◁ Bar on Calle Gerona, Seville

of them have been custom-built in attractive settings. Though a parador will not always be the best hotel in town, they can be counted on to deliver a predictable level of comfort: regional dishes will always be on the menu, and rooms are generally comfortable and often spacious. The bedroom furniture varies little from parador to parador.

If you are traveling around during tourist season, or intending to stay in smaller paradors, it is wise to book ahead through agents for the paradors *(see p201)*.

PRICES

HOTELS ARE REQUIRED by law to display their range of prices behind the reception area and in every room. As a rule the more stars a hotel has the more you pay. Rates for a double room start from 1,500 ptas per night in the least expensive one-star pension and can go as high as 30,000 ptas in a five-star hotel.

Prices vary according to the room, and the region and season. The rural hotels are generally cheaper than the city ones. All the prices quoted on pages 205–9 are based on the rates for mid-season or tourist season, usually July and August or from April to October. City hotels charge higher rates during major *fiestas*, such as Semana Santa *(see p36)* in Seville.

Five-star hotel restaurant logo

Note that the majority of hotels will quote prices per room and meal prices per person without *IVA* (VAT).

BOOKING AND CHECKING IN

YOU DO NOT NEED to book ahead if you are traveling off-season in rural Andalusia, unless you want to stay in a particular hotel. On the other hand, it is essential to reserve rooms by phone or through a travel agent if you travel in tourist season. You will also need to reserve if you want a specific room or one on the

Swimming pool in a courtyard of the Hotel Alfaros, Córdoba *(see p207)*

ground floor, with a good view, with a double bed (twin beds are the norm), or away from a noisy road. Hotels in many coastal resorts close between autumn and spring, so check before you travel that any hotels you want to stay in are sure to be open.

Some hotels will request a deposit of 20–25 percent for booking during peak times, or for a long stay. Send it by a giro in Spain and by wire transfer from abroad. Try to make cancellations at least a week in advance, or you may lose all or some of your deposit. A reserved room will be held only until 8pm unless you inform the hotel that you are going to arrive late.

When you check in you will be asked for your passport or identity card, to comply with police regulations. It will be returned to you when your details have been copied.

You are expected to check out of your room by noon, or to pay for another night.

PAYING

HOTELS THAT TAKE credit cards are indicated in the listings *(see pp205–9)*. In some large and busy hotels you may be asked to sign a blank credit card pay slip on arrival. Under Spanish law it is fraudulent to ask you to do this and you are advised to refuse to sign.

Although some hotels will accept a Eurocheque, no hotel in Andalusia will take an ordinary check, even when it is backed by a guarantee card or drawn on a Spanish bank.

In Spain it is customary to tip the porter and the maid in a hotel. Leave 200 to 300 ptas. The usual tip to leave in hotel restaurants is 5–10 percent of the check although some restaurants will have already included a service charge.

Seville's beautiful Hotel San Gil *(see p205)*, in a former mansion

Interior of Hostal de San José, Aguilar

EFFICIENCIES

VILLAS AND VACATION apartments let by the week are plentiful along the Costa del Sol and the coasts of Granada and Almería. Inland, an increasing number of village and farm houses are now also being let all over the region. In the US, a number of private companies, including **Hometours International, Inc.**, act as agents for owners of apartments and houses. Many agents belong to an organization called the **RAAR** (Red Andaluza de Alojamientos Rurales or Andalusian Rural Accommodations Network), through which it is possible to make direct bookings.

Prices charged for efficiency accommodations sometimes vary considerably: prices are determined by location, the season, and type of property. A four-person villa with a pool costs as little as 40,000 pesetas for a week if it is inland and up to and over 160,000 pesetas per week if it is in a prime coastal location.

Another possibility is the *villa turística* (vacation village), which is part hotel, part efficiencies.

BED-AND-BREAKFAST

ANDALUSIA'S 20 OR MORE *casas rurales* offering bed-and-breakfast range from a stately *cortijo* (manor house) to a small organic farm. Do not expect usual hotel service or a long list of facilities. However, you may be met with a friendly welcome and be spoiled with good home cooking.

A stay at a bed-and-breakfast can be booked through **RAAR**, the owners' association, or directly. If you are booking from abroad you may be asked to send a 10 percent deposit and to stay for at least two nights.

YOUTH HOSTELS AND MOUNTAIN REFUGES

TO USE ANDALUSIA'S extensive network of *albergues juveniles* (youth hostels) you have to buy an international YHA card from a hostel or show a card from your country. Bed and breakfast costs between 1,100 and 1,500 pesetas per person. You can book a bed or room in a hostel directly or through the central booking office of Inturjoven – **Central de Reservas de Inturjoven**.

If you backpack in remote mountain areas, you can stay in *refugios*, which are shelters with basic kitchens and dormitories. The *refugios* are marked on all good large-scale maps of the mountains and national parks. They are administered by the **Federación Andaluza de Montañismo**.

The rustic-style youth hostel, Cazorla, on the edge of the nature preserve

CAMPSITES

THERE ARE MORE THAN 110 campsites scattered across the region of Andalusia, many of them along the coasts but also some outside the major cities and in the popular countryside areas. Most have electricity and running water; some also have launderettes, restaurants, shops, play areas for children, and pools.

It is wise to take with you an international camping *carnet* (card). It can be used to check in at sites, and it also gives you third-party insurance. *Carnets* are issued by the National Campers and Hikers Association.

A map of all the region's campsites, entitled *Campings en Andalucía*, is published by the regional tourist authority, the **Dirección General de Turismo, Junta de Andalucía**.

Logo for a five-star hotel

DISABLED TRAVELERS

HOTEL MANAGERS will advise on wheelchair access, and staff will always assist, but few hotels are equipped for disabled people. However, some of the youth hostels are.

The **SATH** (Society for the Advancement of Travel for the Handicapped, Inc. – *see p239*) publishes a magazine, *Access to Travel*, which provides useful information on traveling at home and abroad.

In Spain, the Confederación Coordinadora Estatal de Minusválidos Fisicos de España, also known as **Servi-COCEMFE** *(see p239),* and **Viajes 2000**

have details of hotels with special facilities in Andalusia.

IHD (International Help for the Disabled) arranges accessible accommodations, nurses, transportation, and other help for visitors to the Costa del Sol who have special needs.

FURTHER INFORMATION

EVERY YEAR the **Dirección General de Turismo** in Andalusia publishes its *Guía de Hoteles, Pensiones, Apartamentos, Campings y Agencias de Viajes*. This gives the star ratings and a summary of facilities available of all hotels, pensions, campsites, and youth hostels in the area.

Having chosen the type of accommodations you want and where you want to stay, it is wise to fax or phone directly to obtain the most up-to-date information on prices

and facilities. In the hotel listings *(pp204–209)*, the hotels and pensions have been listed at their highest rates. This means that prices for specific rooms on certain nights, or out of season, may turn out to be cheaper.

El Nacimiento bed-and-breakfast hotel, Almería *(see p209)*

Andalusia's Best: Paradors

PARADOR IS AN OLD SPANISH WORD for a lodging place for travelers of respectable rank. In the late 1920s a national network of state-run hotels called Paradors was established. Many of them are converted castles, palaces, or monasteries, although some have been custom-built in strategic tourist locations. The paradors are generally well marked, making them easy to find. All offer a high degree of comfort and service and have restaurants in which regional cuisine is served.

Parador de Ronda
This parador sits on the edge of the Tajo gorge, opposite Ronda's old town. Some rooms have incomparable views. (See p208.)

Parador de Carmona
Carmona's Moorish-style parador, in the palace of Pedro the Cruel, makes a relaxing base from which to explore nearby Seville. (See p206.)

HUELVA AND
SEVILLA

SEVILLE

CADIZ AND
MALAGA

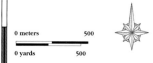

Parador de Mazagón
This custom-built parador, in a peaceful and scenic spot near a long sandy beach, makes a convenient base for exploring the Coto Doñana. (See p206.)

| 0 meters | 500 |
| 0 yards | 500 |

**Parador de Arcos
de la Frontera**
Situated in one of the archetypal pueblos blancos *(white towns) this parador has a wide terrace with panoramic views over the Guadalete River.* (See p207.)

Parador de Cazorla
A secluded mountain lodge, Cazorla's parador is set amid the dense forests of one of the principal nature preserves in Andalusia, close to the source of the Guadalquivir river. (See p206.)

Parador de Jaén
A re-created fortress, complete with small arched windows and vaulted chambers, this parador stands on top of a hill above the city. (See p207.)

Parador de Úbeda
This is one of many fine Renaissance buildings in Úbeda. It has a delightful patio bordered with slender columns. (See p207.)

CORDOBA
AND JAEN

GRANADA
AND ALMERIA

Parador de Granada
Advance booking is essential if you want to stay in this atmospheric 15th-century convent, built in the gardens of the Alhambra at the instruction of the Catholic Monarchs. (See p209.)

Parador de Mojácar
A modern white building, imitating the Cubist style of Mojácar's architecture, this parador stands by a beach and has a spacious sun terrace. (See p209.)

Choosing a Hotel

THIS CHART is a quick reference guide to hotels in Seville, Córdoba, and Granada, and to Andalusia's best paradors. These and a selection of other hotels in Andalusia are described in detail on the following pages. Between them they offer a wide range of prices and facilities to suit all needs and budgets. For information on other types of accommodations see pages 198–201.

Hotel	Price	Number of Rooms	Family Rooms	Hotel Parking	Restaurant	Swimming Pool	Attractive Views	Quiet Location
SEVILLE CITY CENTER (see p205)								
Hostal Goya	₱	20	●					●
Hotel Simón	₱₱	31	●		●			
Las Casas de la Judería	₱₱₱	29	●	●				●
Hostería del Laurel	₱₱₱	21	●		●			●
Hotel Baco	₱₱₱	25	●					
Hotel San Gil	₱₱₱	39	●	●		●		
Hotel Doña María	₱₱₱₱	60	●	●		●	●	●
Taberna del Alabardero	₱₱₱₱	7	●	●	●		●	●
Alfonso XIII	₱₱₱₱₱	149	●	●	●	●		
Ciudad de Sevilla	₱₱₱₱	93	●	●	●	●		●
CÓRDOBA (see p206–7)								
Hotel Maestre	₱	26		●				●
Occidental	₱₱₱	154	●	●	●	●		●
Alfaros	₱₱₱₱	133	●	●	●	●		
GRANADA (see p209)								
Hotel América	₱₱	13	●		●			●
Reina Cristina	₱₱	42	●	●	●			
Alhambra Palace	₱₱₱₱₱	140	●		●		●	●
PARADORS								
Parador de Arcos de la Frontera (see p207)	₱₱₱₱	24	●		●		●	
Parador de Carmona (see p206)	₱₱₱₱	63	●	●	●	●	●	●
Parador de Cazorla (see p206)	₱₱₱₱	33	●	●	●	●	●	●
Parador de Jaén (see p207)	₱₱₱₱	45	●	●	●	●	●	●
Parador de Mazagón (see p206)	₱₱₱₱	43	●	●	●	●	●	●
Parador de Mojácar (see p209)	₱₱₱₱	98	●	●	●	●		
Parador de Ronda (see p208)	₱₱₱₱	79	●	●	●	●	●	●
Parador de Úbeda (see p207)	₱₱₱₱	31	●	●	●			
Parador de Granada (see p209)	₱₱₱₱₱	35	●	●	●		●	●

Price categories for a double room per night, including breakfast and tax:
₱ under 8,000 ptas
₱₱ 8,000–12,000 ptas
₱₱₱ 12,000–16,000 ptas
₱₱₱₱ 16,000–20,000 ptas
₱₱₱₱₱ over 20,000 ptas

RESTAURANT
The hotel has a restaurant on the premises serving breakfast, lunch, and dinner. Nonresidents are usually welcome to use the restaurant, but priority may be given to guests staying at the hotel. Breakfast is served in most of the hotels listed, but it is advisable to check before booking.

SWIMMING POOLS
Hotel pools are, with few exceptions, outdoors, and so may only be open during the summer months.

FAMILY ROOMS
Rooms for more than two people are available, or an extra bed may be put into a double room.

SEVILLE

CITY CENTER

Hostal Goya

C/ Mateos Gago 31, 41004. **Map** 3 C2 (6 E4). **[** (95) 421 11 70. **FAX** 456 29 88. **Rooms**: 20. ⬛ 1 ⊞

The popular Hostal Goya is located in the most visited part of the city. It offers only basic comfort, but it is an inexpensive base for sightseeing, even during Semana Santa and the April *feria (see p36)*.

Hotel Simón

Calle García de Vinuesa 19, 41001. **Map** 3 B2 (5 C4). **[** (95) 422 66 60. **FAX** 456 22 41. **Rooms**: 31. ⬛ ⊞ 🗐 ♿ 🔃 🇪 AE, DC, MC, V. ⓇⓇ

The centrally located Hotel Simón is an 18th-century mansion built around a pleasant patio filled with ferns. The rooms vary in size and quality, and some have balconies overlooking the street.

Las Casas de la Judería

Callejón de Dos Hermanas 7, 41004. **Map** 4 D2 (6 E4). **[** (95) 441 51 50. **FAX** 442 21 70. **Rooms**: 29. ⬛ 1 ⊞ 🗐 ♿ 🔃 P 🇪 AE, DC, MC, V. ⓇⓇⓇ

Less a hotel, more a labyrinth of suites, some with a private terrace, this is a peaceful place to get away from the rush of the city. The hotel is popular with business travelers.

Hostería del Laurel

Plaza de los Venerables 5, 41004. **Map** 3 C2 (6 D4). **[** (95) 422 02 95. **FAX** 421 04 50. **Rooms**: 21. ⬛ 1 ⊞ 🗐 🗐 ♿ 🔃 🍽 🇪 AE, DC, MC, V. ⓇⓇⓇ

A hotel in a small square near the Hospital de los Venerables *(see p79)*. The reception area is in a little covered courtyard, reached through an inn with cured hams and strings of garlic hanging. Rooms are quite simply furnished but spacious.

Hotel Baco

Plaza Ponce de León 15, 41003. **Map** 2 E5 (6 E2). **[** (95) 456 50 50. **FAX** 456 36 54. **Rooms**: 25. ⬛ 1 ⊞ 🗐 🔃 🇪 AE, MC, V. ⓇⓇⓇ

What was once just an old house has now been transformed into a modern hotel in typical Sevillian style. From the reception area, a spiral staircase leads to the upper floors. The quieter bedrooms, located away from the street, look over small courtyards decorated with tiles and potted plants.

Hotel San Gil

Calle Parras 28, 41002. **Map** 2 D3. **[** (95) 490 68 11. **FAX** 490 69 39. **Rooms**: 39. ⬛ 1 ⊞ 🗐 🔃 P 🇪 AE, DC, MC, V. ⓇⓇⓇ

The Hotel San Gil is in a beautiful, early 20th-century mansion, which is classified as one of Seville's 100 most important buildings. In its tranquil garden are palm trees and an old cyprus tree. Inside there are magnificent ornate tiles. Rooms are spacious and beautifully furnished.

Hotel Doña María

Calle Don Remondo 19, 41004. **Map** 3 C2 (6 D4). **[** (95) 422 49 90. **FAX** 421 95 46. **Rooms**: 60. ⬛ 1 ⊞ 🗐 🗐 ♿ 🔃 P 🇪 AE, DC, MC, V. ⓇⓇⓇ

This hotel is on a street which runs alongside the Palacio Arzobispal, and its terrace and swimming pool overlook the nearby Giralda. The lobby lounge is decorated with exotic plants. Guests can choose from bedrooms in a variety of styles.

Taberna del Alabardero

C/ Zaragoza 20, 41001. **Map** 3 B1 (5 B3). **[** (95) 456 06 37. **FAX** 456 36 66. **Rooms**: 7. ⬛ 1 ⊞ 🗐 🗐 ♿ 🔃 P 🍽 🇪 AE, DC, MC, V. ⓇⓇⓇ

An exquisite restaurant-with-rooms occupying a 19th-century mansion. The house is built around a central courtyard illuminated by a stained-glass roof. There are cozy rooms on the top floor and five elegant private dining rooms downstairs, often frequented by politicians.

Alfonso XIII

Calle San Fernando 2, 41004. **Map** 3 C3 (6 D5). **[** (95) 422 28 50. **FAX** 421 60 33. **Rooms**: 149. ⬛ 1 ⊞ 🗐 🗐 ♿ 🔃 P 🍽 🇪 AE, DC, MC, V. ⓇⓇⓇⓇ

Seville's classic grand hotel *(see p94)*, built in a Neo-Moorish style and set among palm trees, hosts some of the city's most prestigious social events. Its interior preserves crystal chandeliers, oil paintings, statues, and inlaid marble floors. Elegance is assured and the service is appropriately formal.

Ciudad de Sevilla

Avenida Manuel Siurot 25, 41013. **Road map** B3. **[** (95) 423 05 05. **FAX** 423 85 39. **Rooms**: 93. ⬛ 1 ⊞ 🗐 🗐 ♿ 🔃 P 🍽 🇪 AE, DC, MC, V. ⓇⓇⓇⓇ

Behind its solid façade, this hotel, at some distance from the city center, is wholly modern. The rooms are large and light, and there is a quaint rooftop swimming pool.

HUELVA AND SEVILLA

ALCALÁ DE GUADAIRA

Hotel Oromana

Sevilla. **Road map** 3B. Avda de Portugal s/n, 41500. **[** (95) 568 64 00. **FAX** 568 64 00. **Rooms**: 30. ⬛ 1 ⊞ 🗐 P 🍽 🇪 AE, DC, MC, V. ⓇⓇ

The Oromana occupies a cool and shady place among pine trees on the edge of this town, within easy reach of Seville. The hotel is managed by a team of women, who go out of their way to cater to families with children, and for the disabled. Ballroom dances are held in the hotel on weekends.

ARACENA

Sierra de Aracena

Huelva. **Road map** A3. Gran Via 21, 21200. **[** (959) 12 61 75. **FAX** 12 62 18. **Rooms**: 43. ⬛ 1 ⊞ 🗐 ♿ 🔃 P 🇪 DC, MC, V. ⓇⓇ

This quiet hotel in the center of the attractive town of Aracena, is a convenient overnight stop for a visit to the nearby Gruta de las Maravillas *(see p122)*. Rooms at the back overlook the town's castle.

Finca Buen Vino

Huelva. **Road map** A3. Los Marines, 21293. **[** (959) 12 40 34. **FAX** 12 40 34. **Rooms**: 4. ⬛ 1 ⊞ P 🍽 🇪 DC, MC, V. ⓇⓇⓇ

This stylish modern villa, a private home open to guests, stands on the top of a hill in the heart of a wooded nature preserve. All rooms are individually furnished, and there are magnificent views from the windows. The atmosphere is informal. Fine cuisine is served in the evenings by candlelight.

AYAMONTE

Riu Canela

Huelva. **Road map** A4. Paseo de los Gavilanes s/n, Playa de Isla Canela, 21470. **[** (959) 47 71 24. **FAX** 47 71 70. **Rooms**: 350. ⬛ 1 ⊞ 🗐 🗐 🍽 🇪 AE, DC, MC, V. ⓇⓇⓇ

The Riu Canela is more a summer vacation center than a hotel. It has three swimming pools, one for children only. It is beside a beach on Isla Canela close to the Portuguese border and to the Algarve.

CARMONA

Casa de Carmona

Sevilla. **Road map** B3. Plaza de Lasso 1, 41410. **(** (95) 414 33 00. **FAX** 414 37 52. **Rooms:** 30. ⛺ 1 🎚 TV 🔲 🕴 P 🍴 🅎 AE, DC, MC, V. Ⓟ Ⓟ Ⓟ Ⓟ

This 16th-century converted palace, decorated in a well-blended mixture of modern and period styles, has been featured in design magazines. It has a two-story, porticoed patio and a delightful interior garden.

Parador de Carmona

Sevilla. **Road map** B3. Calle Alcázar s/n, 41410. **(** (95) 414 10 10. **FAX** 414 17 12. **Rooms:** 63. ⛺ 1 🎚 TV 🔲 🕴 P 🍴 🅎 AE, DC, MC, V. Ⓟ Ⓟ Ⓟ Ⓟ

Originally a Moorish fortress, later the palace of the Christian King Pedro the Cruel (*see pp46–7*), this historic cliff-top parador has great views over the plains below. The ancient town of Carmona makes a good base from which to explore the nearby city of Seville.

CASTILLEJA DE LA CUESTA

Hacienda de San Ygnacio

Sevilla. **Road map** B3. Calle Real 194, 41950. **(** (95) 416 04 30. **FAX** 416 14 37. **Rooms:** 18. ⛺ 1 🎚 TV 🔲 P 🍴 🅎 AE, DC, MC, V. Ⓟ Ⓟ Ⓟ

This 17th-century Andalusian farmhouse, complete with original beams and iron grilles, is built around a large patio dominated by tall palm trees. The dining room was once an olive oil mill. Close to Seville, the town of Castilleja de la Cuesta makes a relaxing base for sightseeing, away from the city.

CAZALLA DE LA SIERRA

Las Navazuelas

Sevilla. **Road map** B3. Apartado 14, 41370. **(** (95) 488 47 64. **FAX** 488 47 64. **Rooms:** 8. ⛺ 1 🎚 🔲 P 🍴 🅎 V. Ⓟ

Rooms in this charming, family-run farmhouse are furnished with handmade fabrics, which gives them a homey feel. Staying here will give visitors a rare opportunity to experience living in an authentic Andalusian *cortijo* (farmstead).

Hospedería La Cartuja

Sevilla. **Road map** B3. Carretera Cazalla-Constantina km 55.2, 41370. **(** (95) 488 45 16. **FAX** 488 45 16. **Rooms:** 11. ⛺ 1 🎚 🔲 P 🍴 🅎 MC, V. Ⓟ Ⓟ

Art lovers will feel right at home in this old monastery, which has been eccentrically rehabilitated by its crusading owner as a refuge for artists. The walls are decorated with paintings on display and for sale. Organic produce straight from the farm is served at dinner.

ÉCIJA

Platería

Sevilla. **Road map** C3. C/ Garcilópez 1-A, 41400. **(** (95) 483 50 10. **FAX** 483 50 10. **Rooms:** 18. ⛺ 1 🎚 TV 🔲 🕴 🔼 🅎 AE, DC, MC, V. Ⓟ

In a town famous for its searing heat, this hotel was opened to handle business generated by Expo '92 (*see pp54–5*). It is named after the former silversmiths' quarter in which it stands. Its ample rooms are cool and relaxing. It is a good place to break a journey between Córdoba and Seville.

MAZAGÓN

Parador de Mazagón

Huelva. **Road map** A4. Carretera Huelva-Matalascañas km 24, 21130. **(** (959) 53 63 00. **FAX** 53 62 28. **Rooms:** 43. ⛺ 1 🎚 TV 🔲 🕴 🔼 P 🍴 🅎 AE, DC, MC, V. Ⓟ Ⓟ Ⓟ

A modern parador on the Huelva coast, sited between a large sandy beach and a pine forest. This hotel is in a good location for visiting the nearby Parque Natural de Coto Doñana (*see pp126–7*).

SANLÚCAR LA MAYOR

Hacienda de Benazuza

Sevilla. **Road map** B3. Virgen de las Nieves s/n, 41800. **(** (95) 570 33 44. **FAX** 570 34 10. **Rooms:** 44. ⛺ 1 🎚 TV 🔲 🕴 🔼 P 🍴 🅎 AE, DC, MC, V. Ⓟ Ⓟ Ⓟ Ⓟ Ⓟ

Plenty of sumptuous Moorish and Andalusian furnishings fill this 10th-century country house on a hilltop, now a luxury hotel. Many of the rooms are suites. There are three restaurants and, should you need them, a chapel, a private game preserve, and a heliport.

CORDOBA AND JAEN

BAENA

Hotel El Zambudio

Córdoba. **Road map** D3. Carretera Baena-Zuheros km 2.5, 14850. **(** (957) 67 08 37. **FAX** 67 08 37. **Rooms:** 14. ⛺ 1 🎚 TV 🔲 🔼 P 🍴 🅎 AE, V. Ⓟ

This hotel-cum-restaurant on a hillside near Baena has views over the Sierra Subbética and is close to the village of Zuheros. It is comfortable, quiet, and a good value.

CAZORLA

Molino de la Farraga

Jaén. **Road map** E3. Apartado de Correos 55, 23470. **(** (953) 72 12 49. **Rooms:** 5. 1 🔼 Ⓟ

This recently renovated 200-year-old mill near Plaza Santa María is a relaxing home away from home for travelers. An annex can be rented as an efficiency apartment.

Parador de Cazorla

Jaén. **Road map** E3. Cazorla 23470. **(** (953) 72 70 75. **FAX** 72 70 75. **Rooms:** 33. ⛺ 1 🎚 TV 🔲 🔼 🍴 🅎 AE, DC, MC, V. Ⓟ Ⓟ Ⓟ Ⓟ

The forests and mountains of the Sierra de Cazorla make a wonderful setting for this modern parador, built deep in one of Andalusia's major nature preserves (*see p152*).

CÓRDOBA

Hotel Maestre

Córdoba. **Road map** C3. C/ Romero Barros 4–6, 14003. **(** (957) 47 24 10. **FAX** 47 53 95. **Rooms:** 26. ⛺ 1 🔲 🕴 🔼 P 🅎 AE, MC, V. Ⓟ

Near the Mezquita (*see pp140–41*) in Córdoba's town center, this is a simple, very economically priced hotel with basic modern amenities.

Occidental

Córdoba. **Road map** C3. Calle Poeta Alonso Bonilla 7, 14012. **(** (957) 40 04 40. **FAX** 40 04 39. **Rooms:** 154. ⛺ 1 🎚 TV 🔲 🕴 🔼 P 🅎 AE, DC, MC, V. Ⓟ Ⓟ Ⓟ

This modern hotel in a residential suburb in the north of the city is decorated with coffered ceilings, tinted mirrors, plush fabrics, brass lamps, and polished hardwoods.

Alfaros

Córdoba. **Road map** C3. Calle Alfaros 18, 14001. ▮ *(957) 49 19 20.* ▮ *49 22 10. Rooms: 133.* ▮ ▮
▮ ▮ ▮ ▮ ▮ ▮ ▮ ▮
▮ *AE, DC, MC, V.* ⓟⓟⓟⓟ

Although this hotel is located on a busy street, its interior is sound-proofed against the outside noise. The Neo-Mudéjar style building has three attractive courtyards, one with a swimming pool.

JAÉN

Parador de Jaén

Jaén. **Road map** D3. Carretera del Castillo, 23001. ▮ *(953) 23 00 00.* ▮ *22 09 30. Rooms: 45.* ▮ ▮
▮ ▮ ▮ ▮ ▮ ▮ ▮ *AE, DC, MC, V.* ⓟⓟⓟⓟ

From this castle-parador above Jaén there are spectacular views of the city and of the Sierra Morena. The interior decor re-creates the feel of a castle, with dimly lit corridors, small arched windows, and huge doors with heavy bolts. Suits of armor and tapestries add to the atmosphere. The parador is next to a Moorish fortress, which in 1246 was conquered by Fernando III and was later modified by him.

MONTILLA

Don Gonzalo

Córdoba. **Road map** C3. Carretera Córdoba-Málaga km 47, 14550. ▮ *(957) 65 06 58.* ▮ *65 06 66. Rooms: 29.* ▮ ▮ ▮ ▮ ▮ ▮
▮ ▮ ▮ *AE, DC, MC, V.* ⓟⓟ

This is a comfortable and well-run roadside hotel outside a town famous for its producers of *fino* wine. The hotel is useful as a stopover for drivers en route from Córdoba to the coast. Among the facilities it offers is its own discotheque.

PALMA DEL RÍO

Hospedería de San Francisco

Córdoba. **Road map** C3. Avenida Pío XII 35, 14700. ▮ *(957) 71 01 83.* ▮ *71 01 83. Rooms: 17* ▮ ▮ ▮
▮ ▮ ▮ ▮ ▮ *MC, V.* ⓟⓟ

Some of the rooms in this former Franciscan monastery, built in the 15th century, were once monks' cells *(see p134)*. They are basic, but they have great character, with bed-covers woven by local nuns and beautiful, hand-painted basins. Meals are served in the cloister.

ÚBEDA

Palacio de la Rambla

Jaén. **Road map** E3. Pl del Marqués 1, 23400. ▮ *(953) 75 01 96.* ▮ *75 02 67. Rooms: 8.* ▮ ▮ ▮ ▮ ▮ ▮
▮ *AE, V.* ⓟⓟⓟ

This 17th-century urban mansion is run by its aristocratic owner as a small, exclusive, central hotel. The rooms, furnished with heirlooms, enclose a Renaissance patio that is thought to be by Vandelvira.

Parador de Úbeda

Jaén. **Road map** E3. Plaza Vázquez de Molina 1, 23400. ▮ *(953) 75 03 45.* ▮ *75 12 59. Rooms: 31.* ▮ ▮
▮ ▮ ▮ ▮ ▮ ▮ ▮ *AE, DC, MC, V.* ⓟⓟⓟⓟ

Presiding over the monumental square in the center of Úbeda, this parador is in a former aristocratic residence dating back to the 16th century. One of the main sights of the town *(see p150)*, it has a delightful courtyard half-covered with blue-and-white tiles and set with tables and chairs.

CADIZ AND MALAGA

ARCOS DE LA FRONTERA

Cortijo Faín

Cádiz. **Road map** B4. Ctra de Algar km 3, 11630. ▮ *(956) 70 11 67.* ▮ *70 11 67. Rooms: 8.* ▮ ▮ ▮ ▮ ▮
▮ ▮ ▮ ▮ *AE, MC, V.* ⓟⓟⓟ

This whitewashed, 17th-century farmhouse stands majestically in an estate of olive trees, amid which the swimming pool is hidden. The rooms are furnished with antiques and many of them have wonderful old iron or brass bed frames.

Parador de Arcos de la Frontera

Cádiz. **Road map** B4. Plaza de España, 11630. ▮ *(956) 70 05 00.* ▮ *70 11 16. Rooms: 24.* ▮ ▮ ▮ ▮ ▮ ▮
▮ ▮ *AE, DC, MC, V.* ⓟⓟⓟⓟ

This parador occupies a fine white mansion, formerly a magistrate's house, on the main square at the top of the town. A terrace, perched on the edge of a precipice, offers spectacular views over the town and the plains below. It is a good base from which to visit Jerez de la Frontera *(see p158)* nearby.

BENAOJÁN

Molino del Santo

Málaga. **Road map** C4. Calle Barriada Estación s/n, 29370. ▮ *(95) 216 71 51.* ▮ *216 71 51. Rooms: 12.* ▮ ▮
▮ ▮ ▮ ▮ ▮ *DC, MC, V.* ⓟⓟ

This old, converted water mill in the hills near Ronda is a relaxing and popular suntrap, centered on an attractive swimming pool. The owners are a useful mine of local tourist information. They also rent out mountain bikes to guests.

CASTELLAR DE LA FRONTERA

Casa Convento La Almoraima

Málaga. **Road map** C5. Finca la Almoraima, 11350. ▮ *(956) 69 30 02.* ▮ *69 32 14. Rooms: 17.* ▮ ▮
▮ ▮ ▮ ▮ ▮ ▮ *AE, DC, V.* ⓟⓟⓟ

This house is on one of Europe's largest country estates (now in public ownership). Built by the dukes of Medinaceli in the 17th century, it was used by them as a hunting lodge. The public rooms include a billiard room and have the atmosphere of a stately home.

GIBRALTAR

The Rock

Road map C5. 3 Europa Road. ▮ *(350) 730 00.* ▮ *735 13. Rooms: 141.* ▮ ▮ ▮ ▮ ▮ ▮ ▮ ▮
▮ *AE, DC, MC, V.* ⓟⓟⓟⓟⓟ

Still trading on its old-fashioned colonial style and service, Gibraltar's first five-star hotel is elevated above the town and harbor and enjoys views across the bay. Many celebrities have stayed here.

MÁLAGA

Don Curro

Málaga. **Road map** D4. Calle Sancha de Lara 7, 29015. ▮ *(95) 222 72 00.* ▮ *221 59 46. Rooms: 105.* ▮ ▮
▮ ▮ ▮ ▮ ▮ ▮ *AE, DC, MC, V.* ⓟⓟⓟ

The exterior may not be attractive, but this hotel is charming inside and comfortably appointed. The owners take pride in constantly upgrading the fixtures and decorations, and the hotel has a friendly, welcoming atmosphere.

MARBELLA

El Fuerte

Málaga. **Road map** C4. Avenida El Fuerte s/n, 29600. ☎ (95) 286 15 00. 🖷 282 44 11. **Rooms**: 263. 🛏 ⬜ 🏊 📺 ⬜ 🅿 🍴 ⬜ AE, DC, MC, V. ⓇⓇⓇⓇ

El Fuerte was the first hotel built in Marbella, and it is still one of the best in the resort. All of the rooms are spacious and elegant: a few have mountain views and others look to the sea. The hotel has a heated, glass-enclosed pool and a health center with a gym.

Marbella Club Hotel

Málaga. **Road map** C4. Bulevar Príncipe Alfonso von Hohenlohe s/n, 29600. ☎ (95) 282 22 11. 🖷 282 98 84. **Rooms**: 139. 🛏 ⬜ 🏊 📺 ⬜ 🏊 🦽 🅿 🍴 ⬜ AE, DC, MC, V. ⓇⓇⓇⓇ

This exclusive, low-level, beach-side complex is between Marbella and Puerto Banús. Subtropical gardens encompass a choice of places to eat and relax. This hotel has two pools, one of them indoors.

NERJA

Hostal Avalón

Málaga. **Road map** D4. Urbanización Punta Lara, 29780. ☎ (95) 252 06 98. **Rooms**: 8. 🛏 🏊 🅿 ⬜ Ⓡ

This small, friendly hotel above the coast road just outside Nerja makes a welcome alternative to the budget package-vacation hotels of the Costa del Sol. The bedrooms are clean and comfortable, and all but one of them have a balcony with a sea view. The very informal main sitting-room area has a number of comfortable sofas and a selection of well-thumbed novels.

PRADO DEL REY

Cortijo Huerta Dorotea

Cádiz. **Road map** BC4. Carretera Villamartín-Ubrique km 12, 11660. ☎ (956) 72 42 91. 🖷 72 42 89. **Rooms**: 7. 🛏 ⬜ 🏊 📺 🏊 🅿 🍴 ⬜ AE, DC, MC, V. Ⓡ

On a hill surrounded by olive trees, near the white town of Prado del Rey, is this new hotel, run by a co-operative. Guests have a choice of staying in rooms or log cabins. The management takes great pains to make guests feel at home. Horses are also available for avid riders.

EL PUERTO DE SANTA MARÍA

Monasterio San Miguel

Cádiz. **Road map** B4. Calle Larga 27, 11500. ☎ (956) 54 04 40. 🖷 54 26 04. **Rooms**: 169. 🛏 ⬜ 🏊 📺 ⬜ 🏊 🦽 🌳 🅿 🍴 ⬜ AE, DC, MC, V. ⓇⓇⓇⓇ

A cool, elegant, rather plush hotel, well placed for visits to Cádiz and Jerez de la Frontera. It is pervaded by a faintly monastic atmosphere, reminiscent of the former function of this Baroque building.

RONDA

Hotel Reina Victoria

Málaga. **Road map** C4. Calle Jerez 25, 29400. ☎ (95) 287 12 40. 🖷 287 10 75. **Rooms**: 89. 🛏 ⬜ 🏊 📺 ⬜ 🏊 🦽 🌳 🅿 🍴 ⬜ AE, DC, MC, V. ⓇⓇⓇⓇ

Reina Victoria is perched on a cliff edge and has spectacular views. It was once Ronda's grand hotel but the parador is now more popular.

Parador de Ronda

Málaga. **Road map** C4. Plaza España s/n, 29400. ☎ (95) 287 75 00. 🖷 287 81 88. **Rooms**: 79. 🛏 ⬜ 🏊 📺 ⬜ 🏊 🦽 🌳 🅿 🍴 ⬜ AE, DC, MC, V. ⓇⓇⓇⓇ

Edging up to Ronda's famous cliff, yet close to the town center, this modern, custom-built parador has stunning views over the gorge, especially from the top-floor suites.

SANLÚCAR DE BARRAMEDA

Hotel Los Helechos

Cádiz. **Road map** B4. Plaza Madre de Dios 9, 11540. ☎ (956) 36 13 49. 🖷 36 96 50. **Rooms**: 56. 🛏 ⬜ 🏊 ⬜ 🅿 ⬜ AE, DC, MC, V. ⓇⓇ

Decorated with tiles and plants, Los Helechos is a stylish, relaxing hideaway. Visits to Coto Doñana (see pp126–7) can be arranged.

TARIFA

Hotel Hurricane

Cádiz. **Road map** B5. Carretera Nacional 340 km 77, 11380. ☎ (956) 68 49 19. 🖷 68 03 29. **Rooms**: 33. 🛏 ⬜ 🏊 🏊 🅿 ⬜ AE, DC, MC, V. ⓇⓇⓇ

Tarifa is a mecca for windsurfers, and the Hurricane is a temple to the sport and to physical fitness in general. An imaginative open-plan building in subtropical gardens, it also offers views of Africa.

TORREMOLINOS

Hotel Miami

Málaga. **Road map** D4. Calle Aladino 14, 29620. ☎ (95) 238 52 55. **Rooms**: 26. 🛏 ⬜ 🏊 🅿 Ⓡ

The Miami, between Torremolinos and Málaga, gives welcome respite on this overdeveloped coast. It has whitewashed walls, tiles, iron grilles, balconies, and plants.

GRANADA AND ALMERIA

ALMERÍA

Torreluz IV

Almería. **Road map** F4. Plaza Flores 5, 04001. ☎ (950) 23 47 99. 🖷 23 47 99. **Rooms**: 105. 🛏 ⬜ 🏊 📺 ⬜ 🏊 🌳 🅿 🍴 ⬜ AE, DC, MC, V. ⓇⓇⓇⓇ

This is a stylish city-center hotel with a spiral staircase and a swimming pool on the roof. The management also runs the adjacent and more economical Torreluz II and III.

BUBIÓN

Villa Turística de Bubión

Granada. **Road map** E4. C/ Barrio Alto s/n, 18412. ☎ (958) 76 31 11. 🖷 76 31 36. **Rooms**: 43. 🛏 ⬜ 🏊 📺 🦽 🅿 🍴 ⬜ AE, DC, MC, V. ⓇⓇ

This mini-village with flat roofs and tall chimneys is in the Alpujarra style. You can cook in your kitchen and eat in the informal restaurant. Horseback riding and guided hikes can be arranged.

DÚRCAL

Cortijo la Solana

Granada. **Road map** E4. Apartado de Correos 43, La Solana Alta 3, 18650. ☎ (958) 78 05 75. 🖷 78 05 75. **Rooms**: 4. ⬜ 🏊 Ⓡ

A country bed-and-breakfast hotel built in a little-known valley in the mountains of Granada. Its main attraction is its extensive grounds.

GRANADA

Hotel América

Granada. **Road map** D4. Calle Real de la Alhambra 53, 18009. 📞 *(958) 22 74 71.* **FAX** *22 74 70.* **Rooms:** 13. 🛏 🚪 🎯 🍴 🆎 *AE, MC, V.* 🅟🅟

This cozy, affordable, family-run hotel is beside the Alhambra on the same street as Granada's parador. In summer good home cooking is served in a delightful, plant-filled courtyard. This is a very popular hotel, so book well in advance.

Reina Cristina

Granada. **Road map** D4. C/ Tablas 4, 18002. 📞 *(958) 25 32 11.* **FAX** *25 57 28.* **Rooms:** 42. 🛏 🚪 🎯 📺 🍴 🆎 🅿 🍴 🆎 *AE, DC, MC, V.* 🅟🅟

An original glass-covered courtyard and a handsome balustrade have been preserved in this 19th-century mansion, which was one of the last hiding places of poet García Lorca *(see p53).* The rooms are small, simply furnished, and comfortable. The atmosphere is friendly.

Alhambra Palace

Granada. **Road map** D4. Calle Peña Partida 2 & 4, 18009. 📞 *(958) 22 14 68.* **FAX** *22 64 04.* **Rooms:** 140. 🛏 🚪 🎯 📺 🍴 🆎 🅿 🍴 🆎 *AE, DC, MC, V.* 🅟🅟🅟🅟

A gloriously kitsch mock-Moorish building occupying the same hill as the Alhambra *(see pp186–7).* It has a superb terrace with views over one of the city's old quarters.

Parador de Granada

Granada. **Road map** D4. Calle Real de la Alhambra s/n, 18009. 📞 *(958) 22 14 40.* **FAX** *22 22 64.* **Rooms:** 35. 🛏 🚪 🎯 📺 🍴 🆎 🅿 🍴 🆎 *AE, DC, MC, V.* 🅟🅟🅟🅟🅟

This elegant parador located in the gardens of the Alhambra used to be a convent. For a room in such a privileged spot you often have to book months in advance.

GUALCHOS

La Posada

Granada. **Road map** E4. Plaza de la Constitución 3 & 4, 18614. 📞 *(958) 65 60 34.* **FAX** *65 60 34.* **Rooms:** 9. 🛏 🚪 🍴 🆎 *MC, V.* 🅟🅟🅟

This is primarily a restaurant, with a few cozy rooms scattered around an interesting old building. It is on the square of an unspoiled village in the hills above Granada's coast.

LOJA

La Bobadilla

Granada. **Road map** D4. Finca La Bobadilla, 18300. 📞 *(958) 32 18 61.* **FAX** *32 18 10.* **Rooms:** 60. 🛏 🚪 🎯 📺 🍴 🅿 🍴 🆎 *AE, DC, MC, V.* 🅟🅟🅟🅟🅟

Looking rather like a labyrinthine Andalusian village, this hotel, in its own estate, has been said to be one of the best in Europe. It is certainly luxurious. A wide variety of sports and activities is available.

MOJÁCAR

Parador de Mojácar

Almería. **Road map** F4. Mojácar 04638. 📞 *(950) 47 82 50.* **FAX** *47 81 83.* **Rooms:** 98. 🛏 🚪 🎯 📺 🍴 🏊 🆎 🅿 🍴 🆎 *AE, DC, MC, V.* 🅟🅟🅟🅟

The architecture of this modern, custom-built parador on the dry, sunny coast of Almería echoes that of the white cubic houses in the nearby town of Mojácar *(see p195).* Various water sports are available.

ORGIVA

Taray

Granada. **Road map** E4. Carretera Tablate-Albuñol km 18.5, 18400. 📞 *(958) 78 45 25.* **FAX** *78 45 31.* **Rooms:** 15. 🛏 🚪 🎯 📺 🍴 🆎 🅿 🍴 🆎 *AE, DC, MC, V.* 🅟🅟

This hotel is set in a garden of lawns, olive and orange trees, and a pond. The rooms are very large, almost small apartments. The smaller and more intimate of the hotel's two restaurants is used for long lunches. The surrounding area is good walking country, and the hotel organizes horseback riding.

PECHINA

Balneario de Sierra Alhamilla

Almería. **Road map** F4. Calle Pechina, 04259. 📞 *(950) 31 74 13.* **FAX** *16 02 57.* **Rooms:** 24. 🛏 🚪 🎯 📺 🍴 🆎 🅿 🍴 🆎 *AE, MC, V.* 🅟🅟🅟

This spa hotel amid peaceful but barren hills has now been restored to its 18th-century glory. There are Roman baths in the basement and, nearby, the hotel's naturally heated swimming pool. This spot makes a suitable base from which to visit the city or province of Almería.

PINOS GENIL

La Bella María

Granada. **Road map** E4. Carretera Sierra Nevada km 8.2, 18191. 📞 *(958) 48 87 46.* **FAX** *48 87 26.* **Rooms:** 24. 🛏 🚪 🎯 🍴 🆎 🅿 🍴 🆎 *AE, DC, MC, V.* 🅟🅟

A modern, family-run hotel just outside Granada, it is well placed for visiting the city or the nearby Sierra Nevada. The rooms are comfortable and airy; some are large enough to accommodate a family of four.

SAN JOSÉ

San José

Almería. **Road map** F4. Calle Correo s/n, 04118. 📞 *(950) 38 01 16.* **FAX** *38 00 02.* **Rooms:** 8. 🛏 🚪 🎯 📺 🍴 🆎 *AE, V.* 🅟🅟🅟🅟

A gaudy color scheme, eccentric furnishings, and a parrot lend charm to this hotel. It is located near the beach in a small, developing resort and is close to the Parque Natural de Cabo de Gata *(see p194).*

TREVÉLEZ

Mesón la Fragua

Granada. **Road map** E4. Calle San Antonio 4 18417. 📞 *(958) 85 86 26.* **FAX** *85 86 14.* **Rooms:** 14. 🛏 🚪 🎯 📺 🍴 🆎 *MC, V.* 🅟

This *mesón* is located in what some say is the highest village in Spain. There are great views of the valley from the rooftop terrace. Rooms vary greatly in size and character.

TURRE

Finca Listonero

Almería. **Road map** F4. Cortijo Grande, 04639. 📞 *(950) 47 90 94.* **FAX** *47 90 94.* **Rooms:** 5. 🛏 🚪 🎯 🍴 🆎 *MC, V.* 🅟🅟

This hotel is a restored farmhouse in the countryside near Mojácar. Breakfast is generous; home-grown vegetables are served at meals.

El Nacimiento

Almería. **Road map** F4. Calle Cortijo El Nacimiento, 04639. 📞 *(950) 52 80 90.* **Rooms:** 4. 🚪 🎯 🅿 🍴 🆎

This lovely old house in a remote setting is run by a young couple as an inexpensive bed-and-breakfast. They serve organic produce from their own farm.

RESTAURANTS, CAFÉS, AND BARS

ONE OF THE JOYS of eating out in this region is the sheer sociability of the Andalusians. Family and friends, often with children in tow, start early with tapas and usually continue eating until after midnight. The food has a regional bias – the best restaurants have

Sign advertising house specialties

grown from taverns and tapas bars serving food based on fresh produce and home cooking. The restaurants listed on pages 216–21 have been selected for food and conviviality. Tapas bars and a glossary are listed on pages 222–3, and pages 212–15 show what to eat and drink.

The dining room of El Churrasco restaurant, Córdoba *(see p218)*

ANDALUSIAN CUISINE

THE FOOD of Andalusia falls into two categories: coastal and inland. Five of Andalusia's eight provinces have stretches of coastline and a sixth, Seville, has a tidal river and a seaport. The cooking of the coastal regions is distinguished by a huge variety of fish and shellfish. The most famous of the many fish dishes of Andalusia is *pesca'ito frito* (fried fish).

Inland, rich stews with hams and sausages, and game, pork, lamb, and chicken dishes are served. Vegetables and salads are excellent, as is Andalusia's signature dish, gazpacho, made from vine-ripened tomatoes.

Andalusia is the world's largest producer of olive oil. Its flavor is basic to the region's cooking. However, because good olive oil can be expensive, cheaper vegetable oils are used in the kitchens of many restaurants.

MEAL HOURS

IN SPAIN, breakfast, or *desayuno*, is eaten twice. The first is a light breakfast, often toasted bread with olive oil, or butter and jam and *café con leche* (milky coffee).

A more substantial breakfast follows between 10 and 11am, perhaps in a café: a *bocadillo* or *mollete* (a sandwich or muffin) with ham, sausage, or cheese; a thick slice of *tortilla de patatas* (potato omelette); or a *suizo* or *torta de aceite* (sweet rolls). *Churros* (fried dough strips) are sold mainly from stalls. Coffee, fruit juice, or beer accompany this breakfast.

By 1pm, some people will have stopped in a bar for a beer or a *copa* of wine with

Standing up, enjoying a tapa

tapas. By 1:30 or 2pm offices and business close for *la comida* (lunch), the main meal of the day, eaten between 2 and 3pm, followed by a *siesta* hour. By 5:30 or 6pm cafés, *salones de té* (tea rooms), and *pastelerías* (pastry shops) fill up for *la merienda* (tea): pastries, cakes, and sandwiches with coffee, tea, or juice. By 7pm tapas bars are becoming busy.

La cena (supper), is eaten from about 9pm, although some places begin service earlier for tourists. In summer people eat as late as midnight. Spaniards tend to eat lunch out on weekdays and dine out on weekends. Sunday lunch is a family affair.

HOW TO DRESS

WHILE A JACKET AND TIE are rarely required, Spaniards dress stylishly, especially in city restaurants. In the beach resorts dress is casual, although shorts are frowned on at night.

READING THE MENU

THE SPANISH FOR MENU is *la carta*. The Spanish *menú* means a fixed-price menu-of-the-day. Some finer restaurants offer a *menú de degustación*, which allows you to sample six or seven of the chef's special dishes. The day's specialties are often chalked on a board or clipped to the menu.

La carta will start with *sopas* (soups), *ensaladas* (salads), *entremeses* (hors d'oeuvres), *huevos y tortillas* (eggs and omelettes), and *verduras y legumbres* (vegetable dishes).

Bar in Calle Gerona, behind the Iglesia de Santa Catalina *(see p89)*, Seville

Among the vegetable, salad, and egg dishes, some may be suitable for vegetarians, though some of these may contain a few pieces of ham, so ask first.

Main courses are *pescados y mariscos* (fish and shellfish) and *carnes y aves* (meat and poultry). Paella and other rice dishes often come as the first course. Follow rice with meat, or start with *serrano* ham or salad and follow with paella.

Desserts are listed as *postres*, but fresh fruit is often the preferred choice for desserts in Andalusia.

CHILDREN

CHILDREN ARE generally very welcome in restaurants, but there are seldom special facilities for them. *Ventas (see p223)* are the exception; they often have play areas.

SMOKING

FINE RESTAURANTS will have a selection of *puros* (cigars), which are offered with coffee and brandy. Nonsmoking areas are very rare in Spain.

WHEELCHAIR ACCESS

SINCE RESTAURANTS are rarely designed for wheelchairs, you (or hotel staff) should call to book and to discuss access to restaurant and toilets.

Stylish dining room of the exclusive Egaña Oriza, Seville *(see p217)*

WINE CHOICES

DRY FINO WINES are perfect with shellfish, *serrano* ham, olives, soups, and first courses. Wines with meals are usually from Ribera del Duero, Rioja, Navarra, or Penedés. A tapas bar might serve Valdepeñas, or La Mancha wines. *Oloroso* wines are often drunk as a digestif. *(See also What to Drink pp214–15 and The Land of Sherry pp28–9.)*

WHAT IT COSTS

THE CHEAPEST PLACES to eat are usually tapas bars and smaller, family-run establishments (*bar-restaurantes*).

A *menú del día* is offered in the majority of restaurants. It is usually three courses and priced well below choices from *la carta*.

Ordering from *la carta* in a restaurant can push your final check way above average, especially if you choose items like *ibérico* ham and fresh sea-food. If you find "bargain prices" for swordfish, hake, sole, and other fish, then it is probably frozen. Expect shell-fish such as lobster and large shrimp, and fish such as sea bass and bream, to be priced by weight.

The check *(la cuenta)* includes service charges and often a small cover charge. Prices on the menus do not include six percent *IVA* (VAT), which, as a rule, is added when the bill is totaled. Tipping is just that, a discretionary gratuity. The Spanish rarely tip more than five percent, often just rounding up the check.

Credit cards are accepted in restaurants everywhere, but do not expect to pay by credit card in a tapas bar or café.

Relaxed ambience at the Manolo Bar in the Parque María Luisa *(see pp96–7)*, Seville

Key to the symbols in the restaurant listings on pages 216–21.

USING THE LISTINGS

- open
- closed
- fixed-price menu
- outdoor eating
- wheelchair access
- jacket and tie required
- nonsmoking section
- air-conditioning
- excellent wine list
- credit cards accepted
- AE American Express
- MC Mastercard
- DC Diners Club
- V Visa

Price categories for a three-course evening meal for one, including a half-bottle of house wine, cover charge, tax, and service:
- ₧ under 3,000 ptas
- ₧₧ 3,000–4,500 ptas
- ₧₧₧ 4,500–6,000 ptas
- ₧₧₧₧ over 6,000 ptas

What to Eat in Andalusia

ANDALUSIA PRODUCES over 20 percent of the world's olive oil *(aceite de oliva)*. It is used in the region's cooking in a huge variety of ways – to fry fish and as an ingredient in quite a few dishes, including gazpacho (cold soup). Summer fare is light: gazpacho (including a white variation called *ajo blanco)*, salads, and grilled fish and meat. Winter sees the preparation of hearty soups and stews *(sopa, puchero, estofado, cocido, potaje)* with sausages and beans.

A snack of fried *churros* and hot chocolate

Tostada con Aceite
A thick slice of toasted bread, spread with olive oil, is a typical breakfast.

Jamón ibérico **(cured ham)**

Huevos rellenos **(eggs stuffed with tuna)**

Boquerones al natural **(marinated anchovies)**

Gambas al ajillo **(garlic-fried shrimp)**

Albóndigas **(meatballs)**

Chorizo **(spicy garlic sausage)**

Soldaditos de pavía **(codfish fritters)**

Salchichón **(pork sausage)**

Morcilla **(blood sausage)**

Aceitunas **(olives)**

TAPAS

Tapas *(see pp222–3)* are bite-sized servings of food, which are usually offered as an accompaniment to an apéritif such as wine, beer, or *fino (see p214)*. They include fish and shellfish, morsels of meat or chicken in a sauce, spicy sausages, olives, and, perhaps best of all, cured Iberian ham.

Squid · Shrimp · Fried cubes of bread · Diced pepper · Diced cucumber · Hake

Fritura de Pescados
Squid, fresh hake, and a variety of other fish are deep fried and served as a mixed fish fry.

Gazpacho
An archetypal Andalusian dish, this cold soup is made from ripe tomatoes, bread, garlic, and olive oil. It is usually garnished with diced peppers and cucumber, and fried cubes of bread.

Tortilla de Patatas
Potato is the main ingredient in this omelette, often served with beans or wild asparagus.

Rabo de Toro
Braised bull's tail in a sauce flavored with paprika is typical of Córdoba and Seville.

Pollo al Ajillo
Chicken is sautéed in oil with lots of garlic. A touch of sherry is also added.

Clam

Dublin Bay shrimp

Mayonnaise made with olive oil

Garlic and parsley sauce

Squid

Shrimp

Pescado a la Sal
Whole fish is baked in a thick coating of salt. The salt is removed with the skin and the moist flesh served with sauces.

Cazuela de Arroz con Mariscos
In this Andalusian version of paella, saffron-flavored rice is served in a large, flat dish with an assortment of fish and shellfish.

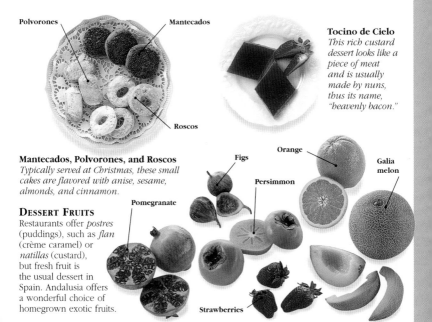

Polvorones

Mantecados

Roscos

Mantecados, Polvorones, and Roscos
Typically served at Christmas, these small cakes are flavored with anise, sesame, almonds, and cinnamon.

Tocino de Cielo
This rich custard dessert looks like a piece of meat and is usually made by nuns, thus its name, "heavenly bacon."

DESSERT FRUITS
Restaurants offer *postres* (puddings), such as *flan* (crème caramel) or *natillas* (custard), but fresh fruit is the usual dessert in Spain. Andalusia offers a wonderful choice of homegrown exotic fruits.

Figs

Orange

Galia melon

Persimmon

Pomegranate

Strawberries

What to Drink in Andalusia

Andalusia is the third largest of Spain's wine regions and produces some of the world's best-known wines, particularly sherry *(see pp28–9)*. Wine is such a large part of the culture that festivals celebrating the *vendimia* (grape harvest) are held all over the region *(see p34)*. Bars and cafés are institutions in Andalusia, and much public life takes place over morning coffee. Start the day with coffee

A jug of sangría

at the counter in a café, have sherry or beer at midday, wine with lunch, and finish lunch or dinner with coffee and a *copa* of brandy.

Autumn grape harvest or *vendimia* celebrated all over Andalusia

Fino from Jerez

Manzanilla from Sanlúcar

Fino from Montilla

FINO

Fino is Andalusia's signature drink. Ask for *un fino* or *una copa de vino fino*. Depending on where you are, you may be served a dry, pale sherry from Jerez de la Frontera *(see p158)*, a dry Montilla-Moriles wine from Córdoba province, or a dry Manzanilla, a sherry from Sanlúcar de Barrameda *(see p158)*. You can also ask for *fino* by name: for instance, Tío Pepe, a sherry from the González Byass *bodega* in Jerez; Gran Barquero, which comes from Montilla *(see p143)*; or Solear, a Manzanilla from the Barbadillo *bodega* in Sanlúcar. Manzanilla is the favored drink during the Feria de Abril in Seville *(see p36)*.

Fino wine is fortified, meaning that it has a higher degree of alcohol than table wines (around 15 percent). When drunk, it should have a fresh aroma and be slightly chilled. It is usually served in a small-stemmed glass with a rim narrower than its base. (Hold it by the base, not around the middle.) However, in some rustic bars, *fino* comes in a tall straight glass, known as a *copita* or a *vasito*.

Fino is most often drunk with first courses and tapas, and its dry taste is a perfect accompaniment to dishes such as *jamón serrano* and *aceitunas aliñadas (see pp222–3)*.

WINE

Andalusia produces a few young white table wines, most notably Castillo de San Diego, Marqués de la Sierra, and wines from El Condado *(see p125)*. Most table wines – *tinto* (red), *blanco* (white), and *rosado* (rosé) – come from other parts of Spain. In more upscale establishments these tend to be Rioja, Ribera del Duero, Navarra, and Penedés. Look for the label showing the wine's *denominación de origen* (guarantee of origin and quality). Recent vintages, or *cosecha* wines, are least expensive; *crianza* and *reserva* wines are aged and more expensive. *Cava*, sparkling wines made by *méthode champenoise*, are usually from Catalonia.

The ordinary Valdepeñas and La Mancha wines are served in simpler restaurants and tapas bars. Don't be surprised to see people diluting these wines with some *gaseosa*, a slightly sweet lemon soda. The resulting mixture is actually very refreshing.

Castillo de San Diego

BEER

Several brands of lager beers are brewed in Andalusia. These all come in bottles, although quite a few of them are available on draft, too. People often drink draft beers with tapas, especially in summer. Ask for *una caña*. One very good local beer, among the best in Spain, is Cruz Campo. Another, which may perhaps be more familiar to non-Spaniards, is San Miguel.

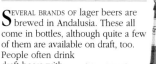

Una caña de cerveza

Cruz Campo in a bottle

**Anise brandy
(aguardiente)**

**Moscatel from
Málaga**

**Lepanto coñac
from Jerez**

COFFEE

IN THE MORNING, the Spanish tend to drink *café con leche,* half hot milk, half coffee, often served in a glass instead of a cup. Children and insomniacs might prefer to have a *sombra* instead, prepared with just a "shadow" of coffee and lots of hot milk. Another option is a *cortado,* which is mainly coffee with a tiny amount of milk. After dinner, you should drink *café solo,* a black espresso-style coffee, which is served in a tiny cup, though it sometimes comes in a short glass.

**Café con
leche**

Café solo

Spanish coffee is made in espresso machines from coffee beans dark-roasted *(torrefacto)* with a little sugar to give it a special flavor.

OTHER DRINKS

HERBAL TEAS or *infusiones* can be ordered in most bars and cafés. *Poleo-menta* (mint), *manzanilla* (chamomile), and *tila* (limeflower) are among the best. *Zumo de naranja natural* (freshly squeezed orange juice) is excellent but expensive and not always available. *Mosto* is grape juice. Tap water throughout Spain is safe to drink, but Andalusians are discerning about the taste of their water and buy it bottled from natural springs, such as Lanjarón *(see p181);* it can be bought either *sin gas* (still) or *con gas* (bubbly). Fresh goat's milk is also available in most villages.

**Mineral water
from Lanjarón**

**Fresh orange
juice**

**Chamomile tea
(manzanilla)**

OTHER APÉRITIFS AND DIGESTIFS

ANISE BRANDY, which is often called *aguardiente,* the name for any distilled spirit, can be sweet or dry. It is drunk from breakfast *(desayuno)* to late afternoon tea *(la merienda)* and is sometimes accompanied by little cakes, especially during festivities. It is also drunk after dinner as a digestif.

Tinto de verano is a summer drink of red wine with ice and *gaseosa. Sangría* is a red-wine punch with fruit.

With tapas, instead of *fino,* try one of the mellow apéritif wines, such as *amontillado, oloroso,* or *palo cortado (see p29),* made in Jerez and Montilla. With your dessert try a *moscatel;* the best known of these is a Málaga wine from Pedro Ximénez or muscatel grapes. Alternatively try a sweet "cream" sherry from Jerez. After dinner, have a brandy with coffee. Spanish brandy comes mainly from the sherry *bodegas* in Jerez and is called *coñac* in bars. Most *bodegas* produce at least three labels and price ranges, often displayed on shelves whose levels correspond to quality. A good middle-shelf brandy is Magno; top-shelf labels are Lepanto and Larios 1886.

If you are going on to a nightclub, it is customary to switch to tall drinks – Scotch with ice and water, gin and tonic, or rum and soda. Rum is made on the south coast, where sugar cane is grown.

**Amontillado from Jerez,
an apéritif wine**

HOT CHOCOLATE

Chocolate, originally from Mexico, was imported to Europe by conquistadors. *Tchocolatl,* a bitter, peppery drink made from cocoa, was drunk by the Aztec Indians during religious celebrations. Nuns, living in the colonies, adapted it by adding sugar to the cocoa, creating a sweeter drink more acceptable to European tastes. During the 16th century, chocolate became increasingly popular. Spain had a monopoly on the export of cocoa beans and the "formula" for chocolate was a state secret for over a century. In the 1830s the English writer Richard Ford described chocolate as "for the Spanish what tea is for the English." For many Spaniards this is still the case.

Hot chocolate

**Aztec making
*tchocolatl***

SEVILLE

City Center

Jamón Real

Calle Pastor y Landero 20. **Map** 3 B1
(5 B4). ◷ 11–4pm, 7pm–midnight
Wed–Mon. ⍟❘⬛❘⚲⬛❘☒ MC, V.
℗

Not much more than a hole-in-the-
wall, this eatery offers tasty hams,
olives, cheeses, honey, and the
country cooking of Extremadura. It
is perfectly all right to *chuparse los
dedos* – lick your fingers. Order a
board of *ibérico* ham and sausages,
or nine different cheeses.

Las Meninas

Calle Santo Tomás 3. **Map** 3 D1 (5 D4).
◖ (95) 422 62 26. ◷ 7am–7pm
Mon–Fri, 8am–7pm Sat, 9am–4pm
Sun. ⍟❘⬛❘⬛❘⚲⬛❘

Hearty food and good prices make
this place popular with students
and business people. A variety of
some of Seville's best dishes, such
as braised bull's tail, potage of
chickpeas and cod, and gazpacho
may be on the menu.

Bodegón Torre del Oro

Calle Santander 15. **Map** 3 B2 (5 C5).
◖ (95) 422 08 80. ◷ noon–
midnight daily. ⍟❘⬛❘⚲⬛❘⬛❘☒ AE,
DC, MC, V. ℗℗

Bar and dining room share one big
space, with barrels, ceramics, and
hams hanging from the beams for
decor. Specialties are *raciones (see
p222).* Try *garbanzos con espinacas*
(chickpeas with spinach), the tiny
grilled cuttlefish called *puntillitas,*
or *punta de solomillo* (fillet tip).

Casa Robles

Calle Alvarez Quintero 58. **Map** 3 C1
(6 D3). ◖ (95) 456 32 72. ◷ noon–
6pm, 8:30pm–1am daily. ⍟❘⬛❘
⬛❘⬛❘☒ AE, DC, MC, V. ℗℗

Right in the heart of Seville, this
lively place has three small dining
rooms behind the tapas bar. Fish is
a specialty – fried, baked, or with
rice. More than a dozen types of
shellfish are fresh daily. The meat
and tapas are good, and there are
emparedados (tiny sandwiches).

Corral del Agua

Callejón del Agua 6. **Map** 3 C2 (6 E5).
◖ (95) 422 48 41. ◷ noon–4pm,
8pm–midnight Mon–Sat. ⍟❘⬛❘
☒ AE, DC, MC, V. ℗℗

On a narrow street in the Barrio
Santa Cruz, in the lee of the Reales
Alcázares' gardens, this restaurant

offers the charm of dining on a
cool, vine-covered patio. The menu
emphasizes seasonal specialties,
carefully prepared and served.

Enrique Becerra

Calle Gamazo 2. **Map** 3 B1 (5 C4).
◖ (95) 421 30 49. ◷ 1–5pm,
8pm–midnight Mon–Sat. ⍟❘⬛❘
⬛❘☒ AE, DC, MC, V. ℗℗

This plush restaurant-bar near the
Ayuntamiento attracts well-heeled
customers for apéritifs and meals.
Besides a fine selection of fish and
meat dishes, the daily specials
feature Andalusian home cooking.

Hostería del Laurel

Plaza de los Venerables 5. **Map** 3 C2
(6 D4). ◖ (95) 422 02 95.
◷ noon–4pm, 7:30pm–midnight
daily. ⍟❘⬛❘⬛❘⚲⬛❘☒ AE, DC,
MC, V. ℗℗

Decorated in rustic style with
wooden barrels and colorful
wall tiles, this restaurant and bar
is reached through a labyrinth of
walkways around Santa Cruz *(see
pp70–71).* A fine lunch consists of
serrano ham, fat Seville olives, and
tortilla de patatas (potato omelette).

Mesón Casa Luciano

Calle Paraíso 3. **Map** 3 B3. ◖ (95)
427 37 59. ◷ 1–5pm, 8:30pm–1am,
daily. ⍟❘⬛❘⬛❘☒ AE, DC, MC, V.
℗℗

Best *ibérico* hams hang from the
wooden rafters and are a specialty
at this friendly restaurant-cum-
taberna. Charcoal-grilled beef, lamb,
and pork are also on the beams.
The homemade custard desserts
are highly recommended.

Mesón Don Raimundo

Calle Argote de Molina 26. **Map** 3 C1
(6 D4). ◖ (95) 422 33 55 or 421 29
25. ◷ noon–5pm, 7pm–midnight
daily. ⍟❘⬛❘⬛❘⚲⬛❘☒ AE, DC,
MC, V. ℗℗

Set in a 17th-century convent in
Santa Cruz, this restaurant could
double as a museum, with its old
ceramics, tapestries, and copper
utensils on the walls. Traditional
Andalusian food, based on wild
duck, rabbit, and partridge from
the Marismas of the Guadalquivir,
is served, as well as seafood dishes
such as clam soup with pine nuts.
The "ordinary" wine list is extremely
good and there is a *bodega* of
extraordinary *reserva* wines.

Río Grande

Calle Betis s/n. **Map** 3 B3 (5 B5).
◖ (95) 427 83 71. ◷ 1–5pm,
8pm–midnight daily. ⍟❘⬛❘⬛❘⚲⬛❘
⬛❘☒ AE, DC, MC, V. ℗℗

Tourists flock here because of the
terrific location on the banks of the
Guadalquivir. The restaurant terrace
is a fine place to eat, with the city
skyline visible across the river. The
gazpacho is good; the *rabo de toro*
(braised bull's tail) is excellent.

La Albahaca

Pl de Santa Cruz 12. **Map** 3 D2 (6 E4).
◖ (95) 422 07 14. ◷ 1–4pm, 8pm–
midnight Mon–Sat. ⍟❘⬛❘⚲⬛❘
⬛❘☒ AE, DC, MC, V. ℗℗℗

A 1920s mansion furnished with
17th-century antiques in a handsome setting on the lovely Plaza
Santa Cruz make this a special
place for dining. The restaurant
serves Basque-influenced food
with a modern touch. The menu
changes with the seasons.

El Burladero

Hotel Colón, Calle Canalejas 1.
Map 3 B1 (5 B3). ◖ (95) 422 29 00.
◷ 1:30– 4pm, 9pm–midnight daily.
⍟❘⬛❘⚲⬛❘☒ AE, DC, MC, V.
℗℗℗

Dining is refined in this Seville
landmark, where bullfighters
change into their "suits of lights"
before *corridas.* The restaurant,
full of bullfighting memorabilia,
is named after the *burladero,* the
inner barrier in the bullring. On
the menu, caviar and filet mignon
keep company with traditional
Seville dishes such as *puchero*
(meal-in-a-pot) and bull's tail.

El Giraldillo

Plaza Virgen de los Reyes 2. **Map** 3 C2
(6 D4). ◖ (95) 421 45 25.
◷ 11am–midnight daily. ⍟❘⬛❘
☒ DC, MC, V. ℗℗℗

Just a step off the plaza facing the
Giralda and cathedral, but still a
quiet corner for relaxed dining.
Andalusian paella, fried fish, and
fillet of *ibérico* pork are good.

La Isla

Calle Arfe 25. **Map** 3 B2 (5 C4).
◖ (95) 421 26 31 or 421 53 76
⟨FAX⟩ 456 2219. ◷ 1–4pm, 8pm–
midnight, Tue–Sun. ◑ Aug. ⬛❘
☒ AE, DC, MC, V. ℗℗℗

Right in the heart of town, this
attractive restaurant features
superb seafood: turbot, bream,
red mullet, bass, swordfish, plus
delicacies such as *percebes* (sea
barnacles). Prices are steep, but
quality and service are impeccable.

La Judería

Calle Cano y Cueto 13. **Map** 4 D2
(6 E4). ◖ (95) 441 20 52.
◷ 1–5pm, 7:30pm–1am daily. ⍟❘
⬛❘☒ AE, DC, MC, V. ℗℗℗

A pretty restaurant in the medieval Jewish quarter, with brick arches and terra-cotta floors. It offers a huge range of seafood and game in season. *Cazuela de arroz*, a rice casserole for two with lobster or shrimp, is especially good.

Ox's

Calle Betis 61. **Map** 3 B3 (5 B5). ((95) 427 62 75. ◯ 1:30–4pm, 8:30pm– midnight Mon–Sat; 1:30–4pm Sun. ▤ ▮ & ✦ AE, DC, MC, V ®®®

This small and intimate *asador* (grill room) specializes in charcoal-grilled meats, but the fish dishes are every bit as good. Clams with artichokes and *angulas* (tiny baby eels) are specialties of the house.

Egaña Oriza

Calle San Fernando 41. **Map** 3 C3 (6 D5). ((95) 422 72 11. ◯ 1:30–4pm, 9pm–midnight Mon–Fri; 9pm–midnight Sat. ▮◉▮ ▤ ▮ ✦ AE, DC, MC, V. ®®®

Tucked in a niche against the walls of the Alcázar Gardens, this is a light, airy, and stylish restaurant. The food, created by owner-chef José María Egaña, is Basque with Andalusian accents. Fish, such as *lomo de merluza en salsa verde* (center cut of hake in a green sauce) is a specialty. Meat dishes are excellent and the desserts are exceptional. This is Seville's most expensive restaurant, but worth it.

SEVILLE ENVIRONS

Jamaica

Calle Jamaica 16 (Heliopolis). **Road map** B3. ((95) 461 12 44. ◯ 1–5pm, 8:30–12:30am Mon–Sat; 1–5pm Sun. ▮◉▮ ▤ ▮ & ✦ AE, DC, MC, V. ®®

Jamaica occupies a private villa in Seville's suburb of Heliopolis. A good selection of fish and meat dishes are prepared with style, and game dishes are featured in season. The wine list is excellent.

Al-Mutamid

Calle Alfonso XI (Gran Plaza). **Road map** B3. ((95) 492 55 04. ◯ 1–5pm, 8:30pm–12:30am daily. ▮◉▮ ▤ ▮ ▦ ✦ AE, DC, MC, V. ®®®

Start your meal in the *bodega* with one of the extraordinary *reserva* wines or *cavas* cellared here. In the cool, elegant restaurant, the seafood in some 30 guises is the star, but there are enough fine meat entrées to keep carnivores happy. For dessert, try a traditional Sevillian sweet, *yemas*, made from egg yolks and sugar.

SEVILLA AND HUELVA

ALJARAQUE

Las Candelas

Huelva. **Road map** A4. Ctra Huelva–Punta Umbria. ((959) 31 84 33. ◯ 1–4:30pm, 9–11:30pm Mon–Sat. ▮◉▮ ▤ ▮ ✦ AE, DC, MC, V. ®®

About halfway between Huelva and the beach is this attractive restaurant with a rustic dining area and fireplace. The menu is equally divided between the fine local seafood and excellent meat dishes.

HUELVA

El Estero

Huelva. **Road map** A3. Avda Martín Alonso Pinzón 13. ((959) 25 65 72. ◯ 1–4pm, 8pm–midnight Mon–Sat. ▮◉▮ ▤ ▮ & ✦ AE, DC, MC, V. ®®

This is probably the best place to eat in Huelva's center. The food is traditional local fare, with *chocos con habas* (cuttlefish and beans), *raya en pimentón* (skate with paprika), sole stuffed with oysters, and *ibérico* pork fillet with herbs.

ISLA CRISTINA

Casa Rufino

Huelva. **Road map** A4. Avenida de la Playa s/n. ((959) 33 08 10. ◯ Jun–Sep: 1–4:30pm, 8pm–12:30am daily; Oct–May: 1–4:30pm Thu–Tue. ● Nov. ▮◉▮ & ▦ ✦ AE, DC, MC, V. ®

Right on the beach, Casa Rufino is popular in summer. In the *el tonteo* menu (for four), eight different fish are served in eight sauces; one is angler fish with raisin sauce.

JABUGO

Mesón Sánchez Romero Carvajal

Huelva. **Road map** A3. Carretera San Juan del Puerto s/n. ((959) 12 15 15. ◯ 1–4:30pm, 9–11:30pm daily. ▤ ▮ & ▦ ✦ V. ®

One of Andalusia's best hams is Jabugo. Fine hams are made at Sánchez Romero Carvajal, and the adjoining bar-restaurant is a good place to sample them. Besides dishes featuring ham and sausage, try the fresh *ibérico* pork dishes, such as *presa de paletilla al mesón*.

LA RÁBIDA

Hostería de la Rábida

Huelva. **Road map** A4. Paraje de la Rábida s/n. ((959) 35 03 12. ◯ 1–4pm, 8:30–10:30pm daily. ▤ ▮ ✦ MC, V. ®®

Christopher Columbus stayed at the 14th-century monastery of La Rábida beside this restaurant. With fish and seafood its specialty, it is a good place to dine.

SANLÚCAR LA MAYOR

La Alquería

Sevilla. **Road map** B3. Hacienda Benazuza. ((95) 570 33 44. ◯ 2–4pm; 9pm–midnight daily. ▮◉▮ ▤ ▮ ✦ AE, DC, MC, V. ®®®

Only 15 minutes' drive from Seville, this beautiful country hacienda has a restaurant in what were once stables. Chef Sergio Ruiz strikes a good balance between innovative and simple dishes based on quality produce. His kitchen deserves its reputation for outstanding dishes.

CORDOBA AND JAEN

BAEZA

Juanito

Jaén. **Road map** E3. Avenida Arca del Agua s/n. ((953) 74 00 40. ◯ 1–3:30pm, 8:30–11pm Tue–Sat; 1–3:30pm Sun–Mon. ▤ ▮ ▦ ✦ V. ®®

When Juanito Salcedo opened a *taberna* back in 1954, his wife Luisa provided popular home-style cooking. She still does, although the restaurant has become grander. Spinach casserole, cod dishes, and partridge paté with Jaén olive oil are some of the house specialties.

Andrés de Vandelvira

Jaén. **Road map** E3. Calle San Francisco 14. ((953) 74 81 30. ◯ 1–4pm, 8:30–11pm Tue –Sat; 1–4pm Sun. ▮◉▮ ▤ ▮ ✦ AE, DC, MC, V. ®®®

This restaurant is located in a restored 16th-century monastery, the work of Andrés de Vandelvira, Jaén's Renaissance architect. It is furnished with antiques. The food is typical of the region: partridge salad, casserole made with salt cod, and *cardos* or cardoons, a type of artichoke, in cream sauce.

For key to symbols see p211

BAILÉN

Zodíaco

Jaén. **Road map** D3. Ctra Madrid–
Cádiz km 294. **(** (953) 67 10 58.
○ 1–4pm, 8:30–11:30pm daily. **¶●¶**
▤ ▧ ⬤ AE, DC, MC, V. **®®**

This is a consistently good place
to eat. In summer there are cold
soups on the menu, including *ajo
blanco* (white garlic) with white
almonds. *Revuelto* (eggs scrambled
with ham, asparagus, shrimp, and
young eels) and partridge are
particular specialties.

CÓRDOBA

Federación de Peñas

Córdoba. **Road map** C3. Calle Conde
y Luque 8. **(** (957) 47 54 27.
○ 1–4pm, 8–11pm. **⬤** Jan 15–
Feb 15. **¶●¶ ▧ ▤ ⬤** MC, V. **®**

This cooperative restaurant, with a
patio, has inexpensive local food.
Cardos (cardoons) with clams is
an unusual dish. *Rabo de toro*
(braised bull's tail) is a specialty.

Almudaina

Córdoba. **Road map** C3. Jardines de
los Santos Mártires 1. **(** (957) 47
43 42. **○** 1–5pm daily; Jul & Aug:
1–5pm, 8:30pm–midnight Mon–Sat.
¶●¶ ▤ ▧ ⬤ AE, DC, MC, V. **®®**

In the 16th century this mansion
was the palace of Bishop Leopold
of Austria. There are seven dining
rooms, including a lovely brick-
walled patio. Food includes venison
and boar from the Sierra Morena.

El Churrasco

Córdoba. **Road map** C3. Calle Romero
16. **(** (957) 29 08 19. **○** 1–4pm,
8pm–midnight daily. **⬤** Aug.
▤ ▧ ▦ ⬤ AE, DC, MC, V. **®®**

Beef steaks, tiny lamb cutlets, thick
fish steaks, and fresh anchovies are
all displayed at the entrance. The
specialty is charcoal-grilled meat,
but dishes such as *salmorejo*, a
thick tomato cream served with
crisp wafers of fried eggplant, are
among the best. The wine cellars,
a few doors away, where you can
sip an apéritif, are among the
finest in Spain.

Taberna Pepe de la
Judería

Córdoba. **Road map** C3. Calle
Romero 1. **(** (957) 20 07 44.
○ noon–4:30pm, 7:30pm–midnight
daily. **⬤** Dec 24 & 31. **¶●¶ ▤ ▧**
▦ ⬤ AE, DC, MC, V. **®®**

This restaurant occupies the site of
a tavern that was first opened in
1930 by the original Pepe. Dining
rooms are festooned with photos
of bullfighters and other notables
who have passed through. The
gazpacho, available all year, and
flamenquín (fried rolls of veal and
ham) are specialties.

El Blasón

Córdoba. **Road map** C3. Calle José
Zorilla 11. **(** (957) 48 06 25.
○ noon–5pm , 8pm–midnight.
⬤ Dec 24. **¶●¶ ▤ ▧ ▦ ⬤** AE,
MC, V. **®®®**

Situated near Córdoba's main
shopping area, the ground-floor
bar and café in this charming old
house is fine for light meals. The
food upstairs is not very exciting.

Caballo Rojo

Córdoba. **Road map** C3. Calle
Cardenal Herrero 28. **(** (957) 47 53
75. **○** noon–5pm, 8pm–midnight
daily. **⬤** Dec 24. **¶●¶ ▤ ▧ ⬤**
⬤ AE, DC, MC, V. **®®®**

Just behind the Mezquita *(see
pp140–41)* is this lovely place to
dine. The menu offers traditional
foods, including many adapted from
Moorish and Sephardic dishes.
Try the lamb with honey, fish with
raisins and pine nuts, *Sefardi* salad
of wild mushrooms, asparagus,
roasted peppers, and salt cod. The
restaurant is fairly expensive but
well worth the price.

JAÉN

Casa Vicente

Jaén. **Road map** D3. Calle Francisco
Martín Mora 1. **(** (953) 23 28 16.
○ 1–4:30pm, 9pm–midnight
Mon–Sat; 1–4:30pm Sun. **¶●¶**
▤ ▧ ▦ ⬤ MC, V. **®®**

Located a few steps from the
cathedral, Vicente serves typical
jinense dishes – lamb stew, spinach
casserole, artichokes in sauce – in
a classic setting with a central patio.

PALMA DEL RÍO

Hospedería de San
Francisco

Córdoba. **Road map** C3. Avda Pío XII
35. **(** (957) 71 01 83. **○** 1:30–
4pm, 8:30–11pm Mon–Sat. **⬤** Aug.
¶●¶ ▤ ▧ ⬤ MC, V. **®®**

The food in this out-of-the-way
hostelry, a 15th-century monastery,
is exceptional. The restaurant is
accustomed to catering to groups
of politicians and business people.

CADIZ AND
MALAGA

ANTEQUERA

La Espuela

Málaga. **Road map** D4. Plaza de Toros.
((95) 270 26 76. **○** 1–4pm,
8:30–11:30pm daily. **¶●¶ ▧ ▦**
⬤ AE, DC, MC, V. **®**

This is probably the only restaurant
located in a bullring. Traditional
Andalusian dishes include partridge
and boar in season, and the town
specialty, *porra* (a thick gazpacho).

CÁDIZ

La Costera

Cádiz. **Road map** B4. Calle Dr
Fleming 8. **(** (956) 27 34 88. **○**
11am–4pm, 7pm–midnight daily. **▤**
▧ ▧ ▦ ⬤ AE, DC, MC, V. **®®**

A nautical theme prevails at this
seafront restaurant, but meat also
figures on the menu, including hake
with meat sauce. You can order
tapas at the bar or on the terrace.

Curro el Cojo

Cádiz. **Road map** B4. Paseo Marítimo
2. **(** (956) 25 31 86. **○** noon–5pm,
7:30pm–midnight daily. **⬤** Sep–May:
Tue. **¶●¶ ▤ ▧ ▦ ⬤** AE, DC, MC,
V. **®®**

This lively place is worth a visit for
its ambience. Most of the action is
at the bar, where you order tapas
from a lengthy list. Local seafood,
partridge, and lamb are specialties.

Ventorillo del Chato

Cádiz. **Road map** B4. Ctra Cádiz–
San Fernando km 684. **(** (956) 25 00
25. **○** 12:30–4:30pm, 8:30pm–
12:30am Mon–Sat. **¶●¶ ▤ ▧ ▧**
⬤ AE, DC, MC, V. **®®**

This rustic inn is over 200 years old
and claims to have catered to
Fernando VII during the Peninsular
Wars. The menu features seafood,
venison, and a daily "soup spoon"
special, such as *berza* (vegetable and
sausage stew) or *menudo* (tripe).

El Faro

Cádiz. **Road map** B4. Calle San Felix
15. **(** (956) 21 10 68. **○** 1–4pm,
8:30pm–midnight daily. **¶●¶ ▤ ▤**
▧ ⬤ AE, DC, MC, V. **®®®**

This Cádiz classic has been serving
good food since 1966. Today's
menu is a superb blend of modern
and traditional dishes based on the

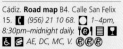

freshest of ingredients. Wooden beams and whitewashed walls give an atmosphere of warmth. The menu changes every day, but fish and shellfish from the Bay of Cádiz are always the star dishes. Sample the *tortillitas de camarones* (crisp fritters of tiny shrimps).

ESTEPONA

La Alborada

Málaga. **Road map** C5. Puerto Deportivo de Estepona. 【 (95) 280 20 47. ◷ noon–4pm, 8pm–midnight Thu–Tue. ◔ Nov. 🅰 🅱 🆑 AE, DC, MC, V.

This quayside eatery serves prize-winning paella and other rice dishes such as *arroz a banda* and *fideua* (pasta-paella), plus fish and steaks. Allow 30 minutes for paellas.

FUENGIROLA

Portofino

Málaga. **Road map** C4. Edificio Perla 1, Paseo Marítimo. 【 (95) 247 06 43. ◷ 1–3:30pm, 7–11pm Tue–Sun (closed for lunch in summer). 🅱 🅰 🅱 🆑 AE, DC, MC, V.

This restaurant faces the sea and is always packed. Resident foreigners love it for its good Italian food and friendly service. The fish and shellfish brochette is excellent.

JEREZ DE LA FRONTERA

Gaitán

Cádiz. **Road map** B4. Calle Gaitán 3. 【 (956) 34 58 59. ◷ 1–4:30pm, 8:30–11:30pm Mon–Sat; 1–4:30pm Sun. 🍴 🅱 🆑 🅰 🆑 AE, DC, MC, V.

Gaitán's innovative chef combines Basque and Andalusian influences. Turbot with mountain thyme, hake confit with roasted vegetables and laurel, and breast of chicken with *foie gras* and pine nuts are just a few of the possibilities.

La Mesa Redonda

Cádiz. **Road map** B4. Calle Manuel de la Quintana 3. 【 (956) 34 00 69. ◷ 1–4pm; 9pm–midnight Mon–Sat. ◔ public hols. 🍴 🅱 🅰 🅱 🆑 AE, DC, MC, V.

Sherry dynasty insiders run this charming small restaurant, where the dedication to fine cooking is very much in evidence. Sample *mojama* (cured tuna) as a starter.

LOS BARRIOS

Mesón El Copo

Cádiz. **Road map** C5. Calle Almadraba 2, Palmones. 【 (956) 67 77 10. ◷ 1:15–5pm, 8:30pm–midnight Mon–Sat. 🅱 🅰 🆑 AE, DC, MC, V.

At El Copo, with its fishnet decor and aquariums of live fish and shellfish, you will find superb seafood at competitive prices. Every day a choice of some 40 different dishes is available: from inexpensive fried anchovies to much pricier lobsters and sea bass, from sea nettles to clams and shrimp. Order three or four shellfish dishes *para picar* (to share as starters). Follow with the *dorada al borno* (bream baked in a casserole with potatoes).

MÁLAGA

Marisquería Santa Paula

Málaga. **Road map** D4. Avenida de los Guindos s/n, Barriada Santa Paula. 【 (95) 223 65 57. ◷ Feb–Sep: 6am–1am daily; Oct–Jan: 6am–midnight daily. 🍴 🅱 🅰 🅱 🆑 AE, DC, MC, V.

One of Málaga's traditional seafood bars, Santa Paula serves a great *fritura* (mixed fish fry) and a *mariscada* (selection of shellfish). It attracts families on weekends.

Mesón Astorga

Málaga. **Road map** D4. C/ Gerona 11. 【 (95) 234 68 32. ◷ 1–4:30pm, 8pm–midnight Mon–Sat. 🅱 🅰 🅱 🆑 AE, DC, MC, V.

Creative flair with Málaga's superb local produce makes this restaurant popular with the local restaurant cognoscenti. Try fried eggplant drizzled with molasses, angler fish mousse, or salad of fresh tuna with sherry vinegar dressing. The tapas bar is also a lively meeting place.

MANILVA

Macues

Málaga. **Road map** C5. Puerto de la Duquesa. 【 (95) 289 03 95. ◷ 1–3:30pm, 8pm–midnight Sat–Sun; 8pm–midnight Tue–Fri. ◔ Feb. 🅱 🅱 🅰 🅱 🆑 AE, DC, MC, V.

At this restaurant, with its deep, covered terrace overlooking the yacht harbor, your fish will be brought for inspection before it is cooked. Fish baked in salt is a specialty here – priced by weight – but the meat is fine too.

MARBELLA

Triana

Málaga. **Road map** C4. C/ Gloria 11. 【 (95) 277 99 62. ◷ 1:30–4pm, 7:30pm–midnight Tue–Sun. ◔ Jan 10–Mar 1. 🅱 🅰 🆑 AE, DC, MC, V.

Right in the center of Marbella's old town, this intimate restaurant specializes in Valencia-style rice dishes. Apart from paella, there are black rice, fish with rice on the side, *caldoso con langosta* (soupy rice with lobster), and *fideua* (a paella with pasta instead of rice).

Santiago

Málaga. **Road map** C4. Paseo Marítimo 5. 【 (95) 277 43 39. ◷ 1–5pm, 7pm–1am daily. ◔ Nov. 🍴 🅱 🅱 🅰 🅱 🆑 AE, DC, MC, V.

This is probably the best place for seafood on the Costa del Sol. In 1957 Santiago Domínguez turned a beach shack into a restaurant specializing in classic Spanish dishes. On any day, there might be 40–50 fish and shellfish dishes, including paella. If meat is your thing, enjoy well-prepared suckling pig and baby lamb. An extensive *bodega* has some 120,000 *reserva* wines. The attractive dining area opens onto the beach front.

Toni Dalli

Málaga. **Road map** C4. El Oasis, Ctra Cádiz km 176. 【 (95) 277 00 35. ◷ 8pm–1am daily. 🅱 🅰 🆑 AE, DC, MC, V.

A splendiferous white palace flanked by palms, right on the beach, Toni Dalli's restaurant makes for a great night out. The food has an Italian accent and live music is sometimes provided by Toni Dalli himself. Homemade pastas, *osso buco*, and meat or fish *carpaccio* are some of the specialties.

La Hacienda

Málaga. **Road map** C4. Urbanización Hacienda Las Chapas, Ctra Cádiz km 193. 【 (95) 283 12 67. ◷ Sep–Jun: 1–3:30pm, 8–11:30pm Wed–Sun; Jul–Aug: 8:30–12:30pm daily. ◔ mid-Nov–mid-Dec. 🍴 🅱 🅰 🅱 🆑 AE, DC, MC, V.

Set in a gracious villa in an exclusive residential area, the restaurant has gardens with views to the sea. The kitchen, capably managed by the founder's daughter, serves excellent food – the flavors are Andalusian with French touches. Specialties are a salmon and cod *torte* with basil, guinea fowl with raisin cream, and game in season.

For key to symbols *see p211*

La Meridiana

Málaga. **Road map** C4. Camino de la Cruz. ((95) 277 61 90. ◒ 1:30–3:30pm, 8:30–11:30pm Wed–Sun; 8:30–11:30pm Mon–Tue. ◓ Jan, Jun 15–Sep 30 for lunch. ⑂ 🖩 ▤ 🍷 🕭 🗓 🖪 🖃 *AE, DC, MC, V.* Ⓟ Ⓟ Ⓟ Ⓟ

La Meridiana, with its sleek decor, has become a Marbella classic. And so has the food. Situated in Marbella's rarefied heights, the restaurant has a canopied garden room and an adjoining patio bar. The menu features dishes such as swordfish *carpaccio*, artichokes with *foie gras*, and game in season.

MIJAS

El Mirador

Málaga. **Road map** C4. La Alcazaba, Plaza de la Constitución. ((95) 259 00 97. ◒ 12:30–3:30pm, 6:30–11pm Wed–Mon. ▤ 🕭 🗓 🖃 *AE, DC, MC, V.* Ⓟ Ⓟ

In this picturesque hill town there are regrettably few good restaurants. However, this one has great vistas to the sea and offers excellent meat dishes and Valencia-style paella.

EL PUERTO DE SANTA MARÍA

Las Bóvedas

Cádiz. **Road map** B4. Calle Larga 27. ((956) 54 04 40. ◒ 2–4pm, 9pm–midnight daily. ⑂ 🖩 ▤ 🍷 🕭 🗓 🖃 *AE, DC, MC, V.* Ⓟ Ⓟ

Dine in style under the vaulted brick ceilings of what was once a cloistered monastery. There is nothing monastic about the menu, but the restaurant maintains a reverent interpretation of fine local foods, especially fish and shellfish. One dessert, named *tocino de cielo* (heavenly bacon), is in its element here – nuns make it from egg yolks donated by nearby *bodegas*, who clarify sherry with the whites.

El Faro del Puerto

Cádiz. **Road map** B4. Carretera de Rota km 0.5. ((956) 87 09 52. ◒ 1–4:30pm, 9pm–midnight daily (Sep–Jun: closed Sun night). ⑂ 🖩 ▤ 🍷 🕭 🗓 🖃 *AE, DC, MC, V.* Ⓟ Ⓟ Ⓟ

An offshoot of the family-run El Faro in Cádiz, this restaurant has small dining rooms clustered around a skylighted atrium. The menu offers refined interpretations of regional dishes. Not to be missed are the desserts, especially homemade *oloroso* sherry ice cream.

RONDA

Pedro Romero

Málaga. **Road map** C4. Calle Virgen de la Paz 18. ((95) 287 11 10. ◒ 12:30–4:30pm, 7–11pm. ◓ Dec 24 & 31. ⑂ 🖩 ▤ 🍷 🕭 🗓 🖃 *AE, DC, MC, V.*

Facing Ronda's graceful bullring, this restaurant serves well-prepared, honest country food – rabbit with thyme, braised bull's tail, beans stewed with sausages. Wood-paneled walls are covered with pictures of famous bullfighters.

SAN FERNANDO

Venta Vargas

Cádiz. **Road map** B4. Avda Puente Zuazo s/n. ((956) 88 16 22. ◒ 1–5pm, 8:30pm–1am Tue–Sun. ◓ Nov. ⑂ 🖩 ▤ 🗓 🖃 *AE, MC, V.* Ⓟ Ⓟ

This popular small town eatery has lots of flamenco atmosphere. Order *raciones* of the classics – *patatas aliñadas* (potato salad), *lenguados de estero* (tiny soles from the Cádiz estuary), and *berza* (vegetable and meat stew) at midday. There are occasional flamenco evenings.

SAN ROQUE

Los Remos en Villa Victoria

Cádiz. **Road map** C5. Carretera Nacional San Roque–La Línea, Gibraltar Campamento. ((956) 69 84 12. ◒ 12:30–4:30pm, 8–11:30pm Mon–Sat. ⑂ 🖩 ▤ 🍷 🕭 🗓 🖃 *AE, DC, MC, V.* Ⓟ Ⓟ Ⓟ

Once a humble fisherman's tavern, Los Remos has relocated to a restored mansion with Mediterranean decor. The exquisite dishes, with a focus on first-rate seafood, are created by the owner, Alejandro Fernández. On a sampling menu of eight dishes are shrimp fritters, lobster croquettes, and sea nettles.

SANLÚCAR DE BARRAMEDA

Casa Bigote

Cádiz. **Road map** B4. Bajo de Guía. ((956) 36 26 96. ◒ 12:30–4pm, 8pm–midnight Mon–Sat. ⑂ 🖩 🕭 🗓 🖃 *AE, DC, MC, V.* Ⓟ Ⓟ

At the mouth of the Guadalquivir River, this typical sailor's *taberna* is the place to sample *langostinos de Sanlúcar* (large, sweet, striped shrimp) and fresh fish from the day's catch. Baby eels, poached corvina roe, and other specialties are recommended. Enjoy a glass of Manzanilla, dry sherry made only at Sanlúcar, as an apéritif.

TORREMOLINOS

Casa Juan

Málaga. **Road map** D4. Paseo Marítimo 29, La Carihuela. ((95) 238 56 56. ◒ 1–4pm, 7:30pm–midnight daily. ◓ Jan. ⑂ 🗓 🖃 *AE, DC, MC, V.* Ⓟ Ⓟ

Several beach front restaurants in the La Carihuela district are equally good for fish. This is one of the most popular. Fish baked in salt and *fritura malagueña* (mixed fish fry) are favorites. Gilthead bream in salt *(dorada a la sal)* comes with three sauces and potatoes.

Frutos

Málaga. **Road map** D4. Urbanización Los Alamos; Carretera Cádiz km 228. ((95) 238 14 50. ◒ 1– 4pm, 8pm–midnight daily (Oct–Jun: closed Sun night). ⑂ 🖩 ▤ 🍷 🗓 🖃 *AE, DC, MC, V.* Ⓟ Ⓟ

This "grande dame" of Costa del Sol restaurants, located between Torremolinos and Málaga, serves superb meat and fish – suckling pig, fish baked in a casserole – to a discerning clientele. Finish with *arroz con leche* (rice pudding).

GRANADA AND ALMERIA

ALMERÍA

Rincón de Juan Pedro

Almería. **Road map** F4. C/ Federico Castro 2. ((950) 23 58 19. ◒ 1–3:30pm, 8–11pm Tue–Sun. ⑂ 🖩 🍷 🗓 🖃 *AE, DC, MC, V.* Ⓟ

Juan Pedro's "corner" specializes in Andalusian meat and seafood and features local dishes such as *trigo a la cortijera*, a stew with wheat berries, meat, and sausage.

Bellavista

Almería. **Road map** F4. Calle Llanos del Alquián s/n. ((950) 29 71 56. ◒ 1–5pm, 8pm–midnight Tue–Sat; 1–5pm Sun. ◓ Oct 15–Nov 1. ▤ 🕭 🗓 🖃 *AE, DC, MC, V.* Ⓟ

This attractive restaurant outside the city has top quality fish and shellfish prepared in various ways. It is a good place to try baby kid.

Local dishes, such as *berza de trigo* (stew with wheat) and paella, can be ordered in advance. The fine *bodega* doubles as a dining room.

Club de Mar

Almería. **Road map** F4. Calle Muelle 1. 📞 *(950) 23 50 48.* ⏱ *1–4pm, 8pm– midnight Tue–Sun (Jul and Aug, daily).* 🍽🅿 ▤ ⚐ ⛢ ⚑ *AE, DC, V.* ⓅⓅ

At this restaurant fresh fish and shellfish can be enjoyed right on the seafront. The *bullabesa* (the Spanish bouillabaisse) and *fritura* (mixed fried fish) are specialties.

ALMUÑÉCAR

Playa Cotobro

Granada. **Road map** D4. Calle Bajada del Mar 1. 📞 *(958) 63 18 02.* ⏱ *1–4pm, 7:30–11pm Tue–Sun (summers, daily).* ● *last 2 weeks Nov.* 🍽🅿 ⚑ ⛢ *MC, V.* ⓅⓅ

The food here has a French touch, with specialties such as pastry with shrimp and leeks, and angler fish gratin with spinach. The sea-front terrace is open all year.

BUBIÓN

Villa Turística de Bubión

Granada. **Road map** E4. Barrio Alto s/n. 📞 *(958) 76 31 11.* ⏱ *8–11am, 1–3:30pm, 8–11pm, Mon–Sun.* 🍽🅿 ▤ ⛢ ⚑ ⛢ *AE, DC, MC, V.*

This restaurant in the Alpujarras *(see p190)* serves typical mountain food: *plato alpujarreño* (potatoes with egg, sausages, ham, and pork loin), and *choto al ajillo* (kid with garlic).

GRANADA

Las Brasas

Granada. **Road map** D4. Carretera de la Sierra 54, Cenes de la Vega. 📞 *(958) 48 60 35.* ⏱ *1–4pm, 8:30–11pm Fri–Sat; 1– 4pm Mon, Tue & Thu; 1–5pm Sun.* ● *Aug.* ⛢ ⓅⓅ

Besides charcoal-grilled steaks and ribs, try red and black sausages, *plato alpujarreño,* and *patatas a lo pobre,* a wonderful potato casserole.

Casa Bienvenido

Granada. **Road map** D4. Calle Cádiz–San José 1, Barrio de Monachil, Monachil. 📞 *(958) 50 05 03.* ⏱ *1:30–4:30pm, 8–11:30pm Tue–Sun (Oct–Apr: closed Sun nights).* 🍽🅿 ▤ ⛢ ⚑ ⛢ *DC, MC, V.* Ⓟ

Home-style cooking is served in this family restaurant, which has been open since 1948. Most of the vegetables and meat are grown on the farm, which also produces the famous *embutidos* (sausages). Every day there is a different rustic country dish, such as *cocido* (stew) and lentils with rice and sausages. Desserts are homemade.

Don Giovanni

Granada. **Road map** D4. Avenida de Cádiz Zaidin. ⏱ *noon–4:30pm, 8pm–12:30am Thu–Tue.* ● *5–30 Aug.* 🍽🅿 ⛢ ⚑ ⛢ *AE, DC, MC, V.* Ⓟ

It is hard to beat Don Giovanni's prices for pizzas made in the restaurant kitchens and baked in a clay oven, and good selection of pastas, meat dishes and salads.

Chikito

Granada. **Road map** D4. Plaza Campillo 9. 📞 *(958) 22 33 64.* ⏱ *1–4pm, 8–11:30pm Thu–Tue.* ● *Dec 24 & 25.* 🍽🅿 ▤ ⛢ ⛢ *AE, DC, MC, V.* ⛢

This was the site of a café where the poet Lorca, composer de Falla, and other artists used to meet. Though now entirely remodeled, the place maintains a rustic charm and a congenial atmosphere, which attract celebrities. Broad beans with ham and Sacromonte omelette are two specialties. Try the *piononos* (anise-flavored cake).

Mirador de Morayma

Granada. **Road map** D4. Calle Pianista Garcia Carillo 2. 📞 *(958) 22 82 90.* ⏱ *1:30–3:30pm, 8:30–11pm Mon–Sat; 1:30–3:30pm Sun.* ▤ ⚑ ⛢ *AE, MC, V.* ⓅⓅ

Such a romantic location! Situated in the Albaicín *(see pp184–5),* with views of the Alhambra, this restaurant is named after the wife of Spain's last Moorish king. The traditional dishes of Granada are the specialty, such as *remojón* (a salad of oranges and codfish) and kid fried with garlic, here known as *choto albaicinero.*

Velázquez

Granada. **Road map** D4. Calle Emilio Orozco 1. 📞 *(958) 28 01 09.* ⏱ *1–4pm, 8pm–midnight Mon–Sat.* ● *Aug.* 🍽🅿 ▤ ⛢ ⛢ *AE, DC, MC, V.* ⓅⓅ

The ambience here is warm and elegant. The food is imaginative, with modern interpretations of such Moorish dishes as *bstella* (a meat pastry with almonds and pine nuts), savory almond cream soup, and boned lamb shoulder with a *mozárabe* sauce with raisins.

Ruta del Veleta

Granada. **Road map** D4. Carretera Sierra Nevada 50, Cenes de la Vega. 📞 *(958) 48 61 34.* ⏱ *1–4:30pm, 8pm–midnight Mon–Sat; 1–4:30pm Sun.* 🍽🅿 ▤ ⛢ ⚑ *AE, DC, MC, V.* ⓅⓅⓅ

Located 6 km (3.7 miles) from Granada on the road to the Sierra Nevada, this restaurant, which grew from a simple *mesón,* is decorated with typical Alpujarran textiles and hundreds of ceramic jugs hung from the rafters. The food is traditional – roast baby kid, broad beans with ham, asparagus with mushrooms, good seafood – but the prices are as high as the nearby mountains. A second restaurant is at Solynieve, the ski area in the Sierra Nevada.

LOJA

La Finca

Granada. **Road map** D4. Hotel La Bobadilla, Autovía Granada–Seville, Exit Iznájar. 📞 *(958) 32 18 61.* ⏱ *2–4pm, 8:30–10:30pm daily.* 🍽🅿 ▤ ⛢ ⚑ ⛢ ⛢ *AE, DC, MC, V.* ⓅⓅⓅⓅ

Worth a detour off the *autovía,* La Finca, although pricey, is an exceptional restaurant, a place for fine dining. The chef makes creative use of good market produce, serving fresh greens, vegetables, superb capon and pork grown on the *finca* (farm), game when in season, and seafood.

MOTRIL

Tropical

Granada. **Road map** E4. Avenida Rodriguez Acosta 23. 📞 *(958) 60 04 50.* ⏱ *1–4pm, 8–11pm, Mon–Sat.* ● *Jun.* 🍽🅿 ▤ ⛢ *AE, DC, MC, V.* ⓅⓅ

Both seafood, such as bass with *ajo verde* (green garlic), and meat, such as *choto a la brasa* (roast baby kid), are specialties here.

VERA

Terraza Carmona

Almería. **Road map** F4. Calle Manuel Giménez 1. 📞 *(950) 39 07 60.* ⏱ *2–4:30pm, 8–11pm Tue–Sun.* ● *Sep 1–15.* 🍽🅿 ▤ ⛢ ⚑ ⛢ *AE, DC, MC, V.* ⓅⓅ

The specialties here are excellent seafood and unusual regional dishes – *gurullos con conejo* (pasta with rabbit) and *guiso de pelotas* (stewed corn meal dumplings).

For key to symbols *see p211*

Andalusia's Tapas Bars

TAPAS ARE MORE THAN JUST SNACKS. In Andalusia, where the custom of the *tapeo* (moving from bar to bar and sampling just one dish in each) was born, they are a way of life. The word *tapa* means a cover or lid. The term is thought to come from the habit of having a few nibbles with a drink to *tapar el apetito* ("put a lid on the appetite") before a meal – or from a bartenders' practice of covering *copas* (glasses) with a saucer, or *tapa*, to keep out flies. From there it was only a small step for a chunk of sausage or cheese, or a few olives, to be placed on the saucer. After that, the free market took over, with bars producing the tastiest tapas selling the most wine. In the old days – this happens only occasionally today – tapas were served free with every glass of wine.

Some bars will offer dozens of dishes; others just three or four specialties. The list may be displayed on a board or recited at great speed by a bartender. The check is sometimes chalked up on the bar.

WHERE TO EAT TAPAS

EVEN SMALL VILLAGES have a few bars where the locals go to enjoy a *copa* and tapas. On Sundays and holidays, the favorite places are packed with whole families enjoying the fare. In Seville, certain neighborhoods are popular for the *tapeo*. Close to the cathedral, and particularly in the Barrio Santa Cruz (*see pp68–81*), are clusters of lively tapas bars. Another great spot is across the river in Triana (*see pp100–101*) on Calle Betis and the streets radiating from it. There are lots of other tapas bars throughout the city and visitors should not feel shy about trying them. As well as the tapas bars that are listed in the directory, there are likely to be good bars attached to many of the restaurants listed on pages 216–21.

EATING TAPAS

AN INTEGRAL PART of Spain's culture, tapas are usually eaten with a drink, often with sherry (*see p214*). This wine is fortified – its alcohol content is higher than that of table wine, sometimes more than 15 percent. Eating one or two tapas with a glass will enhance the taste experience and also slow down the effect of the alcohol. Some people prefer beer or table wine (*see p214*) with tapas, especially in summer. If you do not drink alcohol, ask for mineral water.

You can sample tapas in bars, *tascas* and *tabernas,* and in many cafés. You can eat tapas at just one bar, but it is more customary to move from bar to bar sampling the specialties of each. Each tapa is really just a bite. You can sample two or three before dinner, or you can make a meal of them by ordering *raciones*, larger portions. Tapas *de cocina* (from the kitchen) are served from 1 to 3pm and from 7 to 10pm.

Tapas are generally eaten standing at the bar rather than sitting at a table, for which a surcharge is often payable.

TAPAS BARS

SEVILLE

El Bacalao
Plaza Ponce de León 15.
Map 2 E5 (6 E2).

Becerrita
Calle Hernando Colón 1.
Map 3 C1 (6 E4).

Bodega la Albariza
Calle Betis 6.
Map 3 A2 (5 A4).

Casa Manolo
Calle San Jorge 16.
Map 3 A2 (5 A4).

Casa Omana
Pl de los Venerables 1 (by Hospital de los Venerables).
Map 3 C2 (5 D4).

La Estrella
Calle Estrella 3 (leading into Argote de Molina).
Map 3 C1 (6 D3).

La Giralda
Calle Mateos Gago 1.
Map 3 C2 (6 E4).

Kiosko de las Flores
Plaza del Altozano.
Map 3 A2 (5 A4).

Mariscos Emilio
Ronda de Capuchinos 2.
Map 2 E4.
Calle Génova 1. **Map** 3 B3.

Modesto
Calle Cano y Cueto.
Map 4 D2 (6 E4).

Quitapesares
Plaza Padre Jerónimo de Córdoba 2.
Map 2 E5 (6 E2).

El Rinconcillo
Calle Gerona 2.
Map 2 D5 (6 E2).

Sol y Sombra
Calle Castilla 151 (Triana).

Las Teresas
Calle Santa Teresa 2.
Map 4 D2 (6 E4).

Toboso
Gran Plaza 9.

GRANADA

Las Copas
Calle Navas.

La Gaviota
Avda Andalucía 2, Local 1.

Los Manueles
Calle Zaragoza 2.

Sibari
Plaza Nueva 34.

Taberna Carmen
Plaza Menorca s/n.

CÓRDOBA

Bar Santos "La Tortilla"
Calle Magistral González Francés 3.

Taberna de Bodegas Campos
Calle de los Lineros 32.

Taberna Chico Medina
Calle Cruz Conde 3.

Taberna San Miguel "Casa El Pisto"
Plaza San Miguel 1.

MÁLAGA

Antigua Casa Guardia
Alameda Principal 18.

Antigua Venta de Alfarnate
Alfarnate (NE of Málaga).

El Chinitas
Plaza el Chinitas.

Lo Güeno
Calle Marín García 11.

El Malagueto
Avenida Cánovas del Castillo 12.

La Tasca
Calle Marín García 12.

OTHER SNACKS

B ESIDES TAPAS BARS, other popular eating places are *ventas*, country or roadside restaurants; *chiringuitos* and *merenderos* are similar but are found at the beach. The *freidurías* sell fried fish, and shellfish are sold at *cocederos*. *Ventas*, some of which are old stagecoach houses, offer fairly rustic dishes such as chicken or rabbit fried in lots of garlic, occasionally venison, or *potajes* (stews) of sausages, beans, and legumes. Because of their locations on mountain-sides and riverbanks, *ventas* tend to attract large crowds on Sunday outings from the cities. *Chiringuitos* used to be humble beach shacks where the fishermen's catch was served – for example, *espetones* are fresh sardines grilled over a driftwood fire and marvelous to taste. These days, however, the stricter regulations that now govern Andalusia's coasts have caused most to become real (and, as an inevitable result, pricier) restaurants.

TAPAS GLOSSARY

T HE SHEER range of food available as tapas can seem overwhelming to the visitor, especially if a waiter is reciting a list of them. This glossary covers most that you will encounter in Andalusia. Some common tapas are shown on pages 212–13.

HAMS AND SAUSAGES

Chorizo, morcilla, morcón, salchichón: red and black sausages in many varieties.
Jamón ibérico: salt-cured ham from small pigs fed on acorns; sometimes called *pata negra* because of their black hoofs. Very expensive.
Jamón serrano: salt-cured ham dried in mountain air.

OLIVES

Aceitunas aliñadas: home-cured olives; slightly bitter and redolent of garlic and thyme.
Alcaparrones: large, pickled capers.
Manzanilla, gordal: two varieties of fat Seville olives; *manzanilla* olives also come pitted and stuffed with anchovies, almonds, or pimiento.

SALADS AND COLD DISHES

Campera: potato salad with chunks of canned tuna.
Huevas: fresh fish roe, poached and dressed with oil and lemon.
Pimientos asados: salad of roasted sweet peppers.
Remojón: salad of oranges, onions, olives, and codfish.
Salpicón: chopped tomatoes, peppers, and onions, with a medley of shellfish, marinated overnight in vinaigrette.

SHELLFISH

Calamares: fried squid rings.
Caracoles; cabrillas: snails stewed in an herb sauce.
Cazuela Tío Diego:. shrimp, mushrooms, and ham served in clay dishes.
Chocos con habas: cuttlefish stewed with fava beans.
Cigalas: Dublin Bay shrimp, boiled in seawater.
Coquinas a la marinera: tiny clams cooked with wine, garlic, and parsley.
Gambas al ajillo: peeled shrimp fried with garlic.
Gambas a la plancha: grilled unpeeled shrimp.
Gambas rebozadas: batter-fried shrimp.
Langostinos de Sanlúcar: big striped prawns, usually cooked in their shells.
Navajas: grilled razor-shell clams; tastes a little like squid.
Puntillitas: the tiniest cuttle-fish, crisply fried.
Tigres: stuffed mussels, breaded and fried.
Tortillitas de camarones: fritters of tiny shrimp.

EGGS

Huevos a la flamenca: eggs baked with ham, asparagus, peas, and tomatoes.
Huevos rellenos: eggs stuffed with tuna.
Revuelto de setas; de ajetes; de espárragos: scrambled eggs with wild mushrooms, green garlic, or wild asparagus.
Tortilla de patatas: thick potato omelette.

SOUPS

Caldo: hot broth in a cup.
Gazpacho: cold soup, served in a glass (as a tapa, without the accompanying garnishes).
Salmorejo: thick cream of tomato with ham and egg.

VEGETABLES

Alcauciles rellenos: stuffed globe artichokes.
Berenjenas rebozadas: eggplant fried in olive oil.
Espinacas con garbanzos: stewed spinach and chick peas.
Habas con jamón: fava beans with chopped ham.

FISH

Atún encebollado: fresh tuna cooked with onions.
Boquerones al natural: fresh anchovies, marinated.
Cazón en adobo: marinated, fried cubes of shark.
Pescado en amarillo: fish braised in saffron and wine.
Pez espada a la plancha: tiny grilled swordfish steaks.
Soldaditos de pavía: codfish fritters.

MEAT AND POULTRY

Albóndigas: meatballs, in almond or tomato sauce.
Caldereta de cordero: stew of lamb, pepper, and onion.
Estofado de ternera: veal hot-pot; often flavored with mint.
Flamenquines: veal, ham, and cheese rolls, crisply fried.
Lomo en adobo: marinated pork loin.
Menudo, callos:. tripe stew.
Pajaritos: tiny birds, cooked in wine and served whole.
Pinchitos morunos: spicy kebabs, usually of pork.
Pollo al ajillo: chicken fried with garlic. Also with rabbit.
Pringá: chopped meat and fat from the pot, served on bread.
Punta del solomillo: grilled pork sirloin tips.
Rabo de toro: braised bull's tail in paprika flavored sauce.
Riñones al jerez: kidneys in a sherry sauce.
Ternera mechada: veal roast with stuffed olives and ham.

SHOPS AND MARKETS

SHOPPING IN ANDALUSIA is a highly pleasurable business, particularly if you approach it in a typically Spanish manner. Here, shopping fits in with the climate, always respects the siesta, and is meant to be an unhurried, leisurely activity, punctuated with frequent coffee breaks, tapas, and afternoon tea.

Although a number of European chain stores and franchises are beginning to appear all over Spain, the towns and villages of the south are refreshingly full of shops and businesses that are unique to the area. The region is

Traditional polka-dot flamenco dress

renowned for its high-quality, traditional arts and crafts, and there is an overwhelming choice of ceramics, leather goods, marquetry, silver-filigree jewelry, and candy and cookies.

World-famous wines can be had from the *bodegas* of Jerez, Montilla, Málaga, and Sanlúcar de Barrameda. A visit to a *bodega*, an experience in itself, is the best way to become familiar with the variety of wines offered.

Many shops still provide personal service. Although few salespeople speak English, most are very obliging.

Calle de las Sierpes, one of the busiest shopping streets in Seville

WHEN TO SHOP

SPANISH SHOPS tend to close during the afternoon siesta (except for department stores and touristy souvenir stores in the large towns). Most stores open at 9:30am and close at 1:30pm. They usually reopen about 4:30pm or 5pm, and stay open until around 8pm. These times will obviously vary from store to store; boutiques, for example, rarely open before 10am. Times also tend to vary during summer – some stores close altogether in the afternoon heat, while others will stay open later than usual, in order to take full advantage of the large numbers of visitors.

Many stores – especially if they are in small towns – close on Saturday afternoons. This practice, however, is now gradually disappearing.

Sales generally take place in January and July, though stores may also sometimes offer pre-Christmas discounts or start their sales in late December.

HOW TO PAY

IT IS STILL CUSTOMARY among Spaniards to pay in cash. While many shops, especially larger ones, now accept major credit cards, few take traveler's checks.

You are entitled to exchange goods if you can produce a receipt, although this does not apply to items bought in a sale. Large shops and department stores tend to give credit slips rather than cash refunds. It is a good idea to check the store's policy with a salesperson before you buy anything.

One of several styles of plates made in Seville

VAT EXEMPTION

VISITORS TO SPAIN who come from countries outside the European Union can claim a 15 percent refund of sales tax (*IVA*, pronounced "eeva" in Spanish) on items bought at large department stores such as **Cortefiel** and **El Corte Inglés**. For each item that you purchase costing more than 15,000 pesetas, you need to get a form from the store's central cash register. You should have this stamped both as you leave Spain and on reentering your own country. You then need to return the stamped form to the store where the purchase was made, which, in turn, will send you a check for 15 percent of the value of the articles.

An array of fans at Díaz, Calle de las Sierpes, Seville

Stylish hats from Sombrerería Hermanos de J Russi in Córdoba

SHOPPING IN SEVILLE

SEVILLE IS A CHARMING CITY in which to shop, offering the buyer a unique mix of old-style regional crafts and good modern design.

The district that surrounds Calle Tetuán and the pedestrianized Calle de las Sierpes *(see p72)* is the place to visit for the best of Seville's old and new shops. This is a stylish area of bustling streets, where you will find an eclectic range of goods. These include shoes (**Sierpes Ochentaydos** and **Pineda** are two of the best), and typically Andalusian items such as elaborate fans from **Diaz**, top-quality *cordobés* hats from **Maquedano** and some fabulous, hand-embroidered shawls from **Foronda**.

Clothes that have a distinctly Andalusian style are displayed at the designers **Vittorio & Lucchino**, and stylish **Loewe** makes exquisite luggage and leather goods, clothes, and accessories in striking colors.

The streets around the Plaza Nueva are full of shops such as **Tony Benítez** and **Marisa Martín**, selling chic, tailored clothes, and quaint shops that sell religious objects. Among these are **Casa Rodríguez** and **Velasco**, which specialize in trimmings for church robes and religious images. For the most exquisite baby clothes, head for **Marco y Ana**.

Around the Barrio de Santa Cruz there are some interesting shops for browsing. By the Giralda *(see p76)* is **Agua de Sevilla**, a fragrant shop selling only jasmine-scented eau de toilette. The Calle Hernando Colón has a few curious shops for collectors of everything from old children's toys to stamps, while **El Postigo** is an arts and crafts center with a good selection of hand-made items for sale.

Sevillarte, close to Reales Alcázares *(see pp80–81)*, and **Martián** sell attractive ceramics. **Esquivel** is the place to look for ceramic clocks.

For some of Andalusia's finest ceramics, however, head for Triana *(see p100)*. Watch out especially for **Cerámica Santa Ana**, **Antonio Campos** and the many small workshops along the Calle Covadonga.

Triana is also a good area for purchasing flamenco outfits, while at **Juan Osete** you can buy a marvelous range of *feria* accessories.

Any serious collector of fine antiques must stop at **Antigüedades Angel Luis Friazza**, which specializes in classic Spanish furniture, or **Londres Desván**, which deals in imported, traditional English pieces.

At **La Trinidad** glass factory Seville's famous blue glass is much less expensive than that in the city's gift shops.

Muebles Ceballos on the busy Calle de la Feria is one of several shops specializing in traditionally made wickerwork items.

La Trinidad, makers of Seville's characteristic blue glassware

CÓRDOBA

CÓRDOBA PRESENTS plenty of options for the shopper. Perhaps the most fascinating shopping area is within the old narrow streets of the Judería *(see p136)*. Here the **Zoco Municipal** runs an interesting selection of crafts workshops making Córdoban specialties such as filigree silver jewelry, hand-painted ceramics, leatherware, and wonderful, award-winning painted masks.

Nearby is **Artesanía Jesús Marquéz**, where you may be offered a glass of *fino (see p214)* while browsing around the wide-ranging selection of ceramics, jewelry, glassware, and assorted gifts.

The area surrounding the Mezquita *(see p140)* is packed with souvenir shops, which apart from the expected tourist trinkets, sell a range of fine handicrafts. Of these, **Meryan** specializes in embossed leather goods.

At the guitar workshop of **Manuel Reyes Maldonado** you can purchase custom-built guitars of the very highest quality, many of which end up in the hands of internationally renowned musicians. The busy **Miguel Rodríguez** workshop also produces finely crafted, world-class guitars.

One of the most celebrated hat makers in the whole of Spain is the **Sombrerería Hermanos de J Russi**. You can purchase a typical, flat-topped *córdobes* hat here for a great deal less than the price that would be asked of you in either Madrid or Seville.

Manuel Reyes Maldonado in his guitar workshop in Córdoba

Marquetry in the making in a Granada workshop

GRANADA

THE CHARACTERISTICALLY cold winters ensure that stores in Granada keep a good range of stylish winter clothes and shoes. **Julio Callejón** has an original collection of shoes, and **Cortefiel** is a quality department store that specializes in clothing. With the Sierra Nevada so close by, skiwear is sold in most stores as well as in many specialty shops.

The city center is full of surprises, among them the **Mercado Arabe**, a long gallery packed with shops that sell Moroccan-inspired clothing and accessories. **Miguel Laguna, Taller de Taracea**, is a shop-cum-workshop where you can watch the ancient art of marquetry in progress.

Tienda La Victoria has a superb selection of old prints, curios, and furniture; and in the streets around the Gran Vía are some wonderful *platerías* – stylish shops selling silverware.

ANDALUSIA

IN ANDALUSIA people frequently make special trips to towns famed for one particular item, such as olive oil, wine, rugs, or furniture. If you have time to explore, the whole region offers countless local, hand-made specialties.

The finest virgin olive oils come from Baena *(see p143)* and Segura de la Sierra *(see p152)*. Some of the best olive oil in Sevilla province is sold in the village of Ginés. Many monasteries make and sell their own candy and cookies, which can be unusual gifts.

There are several *bodegas* that are worth a visit, namely those in Jerez *(see p158)*, in Sanlúcar de Barrameda *(see p158)*, in Montilla *(see p143)* and in Málaga town *(see p172)*.

Botijos – spouted ceramic drinking jugs – are a local specialty of the town of La Rambla, 30 km (19 miles) south of Córdoba. In Córdoba province, Lucena *(see p143)* is a good place to buy ceramics and wrought ironwork.

Ronda *(see p168)* has a few shops shops selling rustic-style furniture. In Guarromán, in Jaén province, antique furniture is sold at **Trastos Viejos**, which is an old *cortijo* (farmhouse).

In Granada province, the villages of Las Alpujarras *(see p190)* are famous for *jarapas* (rag rugs), basketwork, and locally grown medicinal herbs.

Basketware from Alhama de Granada

Fruit and vegetable market in Vélez Blanco (see p191)

Just north of Granada, in the small village of Jún, **Cerámica Miguel Ruiz** collects and sells some of the finest ceramics made all over Andalusia.

Exquisite hand-embroidered shawls are sold by **Angeles Espinar** in Villamanrique de Condesa, outside Seville.

MARKETS

THE MARKETS HELD in most Andalusian towns offer a wonderful opportunity to try local food specialties, including a wide range of sausages, cheeses, and cured ham.

Most markets tend to sell a little of everything. However, Seville does have a few specialized markets. These include an antiques and bric-a-brac market, which is held in Calle Feria on Thursdays.

On Sundays, Los Pájaros pet market takes place in Plaza del Alfalfa, and stamps and coins are traded at Plaza del Cabildo. On Sunday mornings, all manner of bric-a-brac are sold on Alameda de Hércules *(see p86)*, and a bigger *rastro* (flea market) is held in the Parque Alcosa, northeast of the center.

The food markets in Plaza de la Encarnación and El Arenal are both very good.

Córdoba has an absorbing flea market on Saturdays and Sundays at the 16th-century, arcaded Plaza de la Corredera.

On the Costa del Sol, bric-a-brac markets and car trunk sales are popular. The best of these is held on Saturday morning beside the bullring at Puerto Banús, just outside Marbella.

Pottery stall at the Plaza de la Corredera market in Córdoba

DIRECTORY

SEVILLE

Department Stores
El Corte Inglés
Pl Duque de la Victoria 10.
Map 1 C5 (5 C2).
((95) 422 09 31.

**Fashion and
Accessories**
El Caballo
Calle Sauceda 3.
Map 5 C2.
((95) 422 4448.

Loewe
Plaza Nueva 12.
Map 3 B1 (5 C3).
((95) 422 52 53.

Maquedano
Calle de las Sierpes 40.
Map 3 C1 (5 C3).
((95) 456 47 71.

Marisa Martín
C/ Argote de Molina 21.
Map 4 C1 (6 D4).
((95) 456 25 21.

Tony Benítez
Calle Placentines 1.
Map 3 C1 (6 D4).
((95) 456 37 62.

Vittorio & Lucchino
Calle de las Sierpes 87.
Map 3 C1 (5 C3).
((95) 422 79 51.

Children's Clothes
Marco y Ana
Calle Francos 34.
Map 4 C1 (6 D3).
((95) 421 30 38.

Shoes
Calzados Mayo
Plaza del Alfalfa 2.
Map 3 C1 (6 D3).
((95) 422 55 55.

Pineda
Plaza Nueva 12.
Map 3 B1 (5 C3).
((95) 456 42 49.

Sierpes Ochentaydos
Calle de las Sierpes 82.
Map 3 C1 (5 C3).
((95) 422 46 99.

Flamenco
Díaz
Calle de las Sierpes 71.
Map 3 C1 (5 C3).
((95) 422 81 02.

Foronda
Calle de las Sierpes 67.
Map 3 C1 (5 C3).
((95) 422 17 27.

Juan Osete
Calle Castilla 12.
Map 3 A1.
((95) 434 33 31.

Perfume
Agua de Sevilla
Calle Rodrigo Cano 3 (off
Calle Mateos Gago).
Map 3 C2 (6 E4).
((95) 456 24 74.

Religious Objects
Casa Rodríguez
Calle Francos 35.
Map 3 C1 (6 D3).
((95) 422 78 42.

Velasco
Calle Chapineros 4 (off
Calle Francos).
Map 3 C1 (6 D3).
((95) 431 83 38.

Arts and Crafts
Antonio Campos
Calle Alfarería 22, Triana.
Map 3 A2.
((95) 434 33 04.

Cerámica Santa Ana
Calle San Jorge 31,
Triana.
Map 3 A2 (5 A4).
((95) 433 39 90.

Esquivel
Pasaje Marqués de Esquivel
11 (off Pacheco y Núñez del
Prado).
Map 2 D3.
((95) 490 27 95.

Martián
Calle de las Sierpes 74.
Map 3 C1 (5 C3).
((95) 421 34 13.

Muebles Ceballos
Calle de la Feria 58
(near Calle de Relator).
Map 2 D4.
((95) 438 18 15.

El Postigo
Calle Arfe s/n.
Map 3 B2 (5 C4).
((95) 421 39 76.

Sevillarte
Calle Vida 13.
Map 3 C2 (6 D5).
((95) 456 29 45.

La Trinidad
Avda de Miraflores 18–20
(off Ronda de Capuchinos).
Map 2 F4.
((95) 435 31 00.

Art and Antiques
Antigüedades Angel
Luis Friazza
Calle Zaragoza 48.
Map 3 B1 (5 B3).
((95) 422 35 67.

Londres Desván
C/ Virgen de la Cinta 19.
Map 3 B4.
((95) 428 41 28.

Food and Wine
Convento de
Santa Paula
Calle Santa Paula.
Map 2 E5 (6 F1).

Hornos de
Buenaventura
Calle Carlos Cañal 28.
Map 3 B1 (5 B3).
((95) 422 33 72.

Tierras Nobles
Calle Constancia 41.
Map 3 A3.
((95) 445 21 19.

El Torno
Plaza del Cabildo s/n.
Map 3 C2 (5 C4).
((95) 421 91 90.

CÓRDOBA

Fashion
Mango
Calle Cruz Conde 15.
((957) 48 84 09.

Arts and Crafts
Artesanía Jesús Márquez
Calle Tomás Conde 5.
((957) 29 39 25.

Manuel Reyes
Maldonado
Calle Armas 4.
((957) 47 91 16.

Meryan
Calleja de las Flores 2.
((957) 47 59 02.

Miguel Rodríguez
Calle Alfaros 15.
((957) 47 13 22.

Sombrerería Hermanos
de J Russi
C/ Ambrosio de Morales 1.
((957) 47 79 53.

Zoco Municipal
Calle Judíos s/n.
((957) 29 05 75.

GRANADA

**Fashion, Shoes,
and Accessories**
Adolfo Domínguez
Calle Mesones 57.
((958) 52 13 32.

Centro Aliatar
Calle Recogidas 2.
((958) 26 19 84.

Cortefiel
Gran Vía de Colón 1.
((958) 22 93 99.

Julio Callejón
Calle Mesones 36.
((958) 25 87 74.

Arts and Crafts
Francisco Rienda
Cuesta del Chapiz 6.
((958) 22 42 75.

Mercado Arabe
La Alcaicería.

Miguel Laguna,
Taller de Taracea
Real de la Alhambra 30.
((958) 22 90 19.

Antiques and Gifts
Tienda La Victoria
Calle Zacatín 21.
((958) 22 23 47.

Food and Wine
Flor y Nata
Calle Mesones 51.
((958) 26 68 39.

Vinoteca Maese Pio
Calle Obispo Hurtado,
Callejón Prosperidad s/n.
((958) 52 09 41.

ANDALUSIA

Angeles Espinar
Calle Pascual Márquez 8,
Villamanrique de
Condesa, Sevilla.
((95) 475 51 20.

Cerámica Miguel Ruiz
Camino Viejo de Jún s/n,
Jún, Granada.
((958) 42 61 77.

Trastos Viejos
Autovía E5 km 280, Aldea
de los Rios, Guarromán,
Jaén.
((953) 61 51 26.

What to Buy in Andalusia

Filigree silver bracelet

THE STRONG AND VIBRANT CULTURE of Andalusia is reflected in the items available in the region's markets and shops. Andalusia has a long tradition of arts and crafts, so its towns and villages produce a surprising range of unique, often exquisite, handmade goods. Many towns have their own specialties; for example, Granada is famous for marquetry and Moorish-style painted ceramics; Seville for fans and *mantillas*; Jerez, Montilla, and Málaga for their renowned wines. While Córdoba specializes in filigree silver, leather work, and guitars.

Traditional glazed earthenware pots from Úbeda *(see pp150–51)* **in the province of Jaén**

THE CERAMICS OF ANDALUSIA

The rich, clay soil of Andalusia has been utilized for centuries in the creation of practical and decorative ceramics. The variety encompasses simple earthenware cooking dishes *(cazuelas)*, drinking jugs *(botijos)*, pots *(tinajas)*, decorative painted tiles *(azulejos)*, and kitchen and tableware. You can buy them from workshops or, less expensively, from local markets.

Ceramic plate painted in traditional colors

Plate from Ronda spattered in blue and green

Bowl from Córdoba in a traditional design

Replicas of 18th-century tiles from Triana *(see p100)*

Rugs
Andalusian rug-making skills have developed over centuries. The most famous rug-making area is in the Alpujarras (see pp190–91), where rugs are made of various fibers, including cotton and wool, and in color schemes in which earth tones and blues predominate.

Leather Goods
Leather goods such as bags and belts can be bought all over Andalusia. Embossed leather, however, is a specialty of the city of Córdoba (see pp136–42).

Inlaid Boxes
Marquetry is produced in Granada (see pp182–8). Craftsmen make furniture, boxes, and other items inlaid with ivory and colored woods in Moorish designs.

Handmade Fans

A classic souvenir from Andalusia, a fan is useful in the searing heat. The most exclusive are wooden, carved and painted by hand.

Castanets

Castanets, a classic flamenco musical instrument, can be bought in a variety of sizes, made of wood or plastic.

Guitars

In the land of flamenco, guitars are a specialty. Workshops in Córdoba produce top-quality, custom-made guitars, many of which are destined for famous guitarists.

Mantillas

A mantilla is a headdress of lace draped over a large and ornate comb which is crafted from wood or made in plastic.

THE FLAVORS OF ANDALUSIA

Andalusian gastronomy reflects locally grown produce. An astonishing range of olive oils is available, and the region's grapes are made into sherry vinegars, as well as some of Spain's most distinctive wines *(see p214)*. Almonds are used to make delicious candy, such as *turrón*, a type of nougat.

Olive oil from the provinces of Córdoba and Sevilla

Sherry wine vinegars produced by sherry *bodegas*

Yemas, candy produced by nuns in the Convento de San Leandro *(see p75)*

Marmalade from the Convento de Santa Paula *(see p88)* in Seville

HERBS AND SPICES

Almost 800 years of Moorish occupation in Andalusia left a distinctive mark on the region's cuisine. Many dishes are flavored with fragrant spices once imported from the East, such as cumin, coriander, paprika, and strands of saffron. Markets are the best place to buy exotic spices and locally grown herbs, which are sold loose by weight.

Saffron threads

Pimentón (paprika)   **Coriander seeds**   **Cumin seeds**

ENTERTAINMENT IN ANDALUSIA

I N ANDALUSIA life takes place on the streets. The *paseo*, *tapeo*, and dressing up for a night on the town are all an integral part of a day. Southern Spain is also a land of *fiestas* and *ferias (see pp36– 7)*, and at certain times of the year a constant stream of music, singing, and excited voices fills the air.

With temperatures soaring to 45° C (113° F), summer days are organized around enjoying the cool of the

Poster for dance festival at Itálica

night. Evenings out begin late and go on until dawn; many of the cultural events and concerts start at around midnight.

Seville sets the pace for the whole region, and the stylish *sevillanos* are fiercely proud of their beautiful city and of their reputation as all-night revelers. A thriving center for art, fashion, and flamenco, Seville is also an excellent place to see bullfights and to watch or participate in sports.

Flamenco guitarist playing at a festival in Teatro de la Maestranza, Seville

PRACTICAL INFORMATION

E VENTS are normally advertised on posters all around town, especially in Seville. *El Giraldillo* is a monthly listings magazine featuring everything from the arts to bars, clubs, and sports. On Fridays, the *Diario 16*, a national newspaper, publishes a regional listings supplement. Granada has its own monthly listings magazine, which is called *Guía de Ocio*. (See also p245.)

BOOKING TICKETS

I T IS USUALLY POSSIBLE to book tickets in advance for major sports events, opera, concerts, and festivals. Your hotel or nearest tourist information office should have details on

where to purchase them. Soccer is always immensely popular, so ensure that you start lining up early for tickets to important matches. Bear in mind that even major events are often set up hurriedly, so that customers have little advance notice.

FLAMENCO

F LAMENCO embraces a broad spectrum, and in Seville it can be found in all its expressions. The *tablaos* (flamenco bars) in the Barrio de Santa Cruz *(see p68)* are aimed at tourists, yet they still provide high-quality performances. Soul-stirring outbursts of song known as *cante jondo* are sung in the gypsy bars of Triana, and in Calle Salado there are bars where the public can dance *sevillanas*, upbeat folk dances popular with, and danced by, virtually everyone in Andalusia. **El Patio Sevillano** is a *tablao* with traditional Andalusian patios. Nearby is the **Buque "El Patio,"** moored on the river opposite the bullring, which takes revelers out on flamenco river parties.

One of the best-known flamenco places in the city of Granada is in the gypsy caves of Sacromonte *(see p185)* on the city outskirts.

Flamenco festivals and competitions are held frequently, all over Andalusia *(see pp32–4)*. Among these is the prestigious Festival de la Guitarra in Córdoba,

which also features classical guitarists. Another important festival is the **Bienal de Arte Flamenco**, held in Seville. In Córdoba, the crafts market **El Zoco Municipal** and **La Posada del Potro** sometimes put on live flamenco shows.

THEATER

M AKING A VISIT to the theater in Andalusia and mixing with the perfectly groomed *andaluces* decked out in their finery is a true occasion.

In Seville, the **Teatro de la Maestranza** *(see p66)* and the **Teatro Lope de Vega** *(see p95)* are the leading places for a grand evening out. On Isla de la Cartuja *(see p102)*, the openair stage **El Auditorio** is also another fine place for theater.

In May, sometimes running on into early June, the Festival Internacional de Teatro y Danza *(see p36)* is held at the **Teatro de la Maestranza** in Seville.

Córdoba also boasts its own highly respected season of theater at the **Gran Teatro**.

Gran Teatro, Córdoba, one of the city's leading spots for theater

Rosario Flores, the famous Andalusian singing star, performing at one of her concerts

OPERA AND CLASSICAL MUSIC

SEVILLE, THE SETTING of Bizet's *Carmen* and Rossini's *The Barber of Seville*, is a city of opera lovers. Most operas, including those by prestigious international companies, are performed either in the Post-Modern setting of **El Auditorio** on Isla de la Cartuja *(see p102)* or at the elegant **Teatro de la Maestranza** *(see p66)*.

Classical music is also performed at the **Teatro Lope de Vega** *(see p95)*, at the old **Conservatorio Superior de Música Manuel Castillo**, and at the cathedral *(see pp76–7)*.

Several classical music festivals are held in Andalusia *(see pp32–4)*. Among them, Sevilla en Otoño provides a rich and varied musical program from October to February. In June and July, Granada hosts the Festival Internacional de Música y Danza *(see p33)*, one of the most prestigious events in Andalusia, when concerts are held against the backdrop of the Generalife *(see p188)*.

FOLK

OCCASIONALLY, lively groups of minstrels with lutes and mandolins, known as *la tuna*, perform in Andalusia. In Seville on the eve of the feast of the Inmaculada Concepción *(see p35)*, December 8, *la tuna* play and sing in honor of the Virgin in front of her statue at Plaza del Triunfo *(see p78)*.

ROCK, POP, AND JAZZ

FEW INTERNATIONAL rock stars make it to Seville, as Madrid and Barcelona monopolize the market. Large concerts are sometimes held at **Estadio Ramón Sánchez Pijuán**, or at the open-air **El Auditorio** on Isla de la Cartuja. However, there are plans to hold more international concerts in Seville in the future.

Some of Spain's most popular groups are from Andalusia, particularly those in the flamenco pop genre, for example Ketama or Rosario Flores.

International jazz festivals *(see p34)* are held in Seville and Granada. In Seville, there are two main spots for jazz throughout the year: the **Blue Moon Jazz Café**, northeast of the Barrio de Santa Cruz, and the classic **El Sol Jazz Club**, which is in the town center.

La tuna, traditional singers in Santa Cruz, Seville

NIGHTLIFE

THE NIGHTLIFE of Seville offers an endless array of possibilities. Timing, however, is important. The early meeting bars are typically traditional cafés or tapas bars, while the late bars have a different decor, ambience, music, and clientele.

Virtually all nightclubs in town have free entrance.

Seville's Plaza del Alfalfa overflows with young revelers, while the Calle Reina Mercedes near the university is a favorite hangout for students. Calle Mateos Gago, and particularly **Bar Giralda**, around the corner from the Giralda *(see p76)*, is packed on weekends. The city also has a number of unusual nightspots, including **Bar Garlochi**, which is decorated with kitsch effigies of the Virgin. Some of Seville's clubs are only just getting going at 3am. Head off to **Catedral** late, to experience a club with a novel ecclesiastical theme.

In Granada, one of the great social hubs is the area around the cathedral. **Cunini** is a wonderful place in which to enjoy wine, champagne, and oysters. After dinner, Paseo de los Tristes, overlooked by the Alhambra *(see pp186–7)*, offers bohemian bars with music and a warm, artsy ambience.

In Córdoba, the *tapeo (see p222)* is the dominant element in the city's nightlife. **Taberna San Miguel** is a classic bar off Plaza Tendillas. The Judería *(see p136)* is an attractive area for enjoyable drinking.

A display of flamenco dancing in a bar in Seville

Real Escuela Andaluza de Arte Ecuestre, Jerez de la Frontera

BULLFIGHTING

THE MAESTRANZA bullring in Seville is legendary among fans of bullfighting, and some of the most important bullfights in Spain are held here during the Feria de Abril *(see p36)*. Most towns in Andalusia have their own bullrings; Ronda, Córdoba and Granada are among the other famous spots.

Generally, the bullfighting season runs from April to October. Booking tickets in advance is essential if the matadors are well known, and advisable if you want to be seated in the shade *(sombra)*. It may be easier to get tickets for *novilladas*, fights which involve matadors who are not yet fully qualified. Tickets are sold at the *taquilla* (booking office) at the bullring.

Tile for Seville's Betis football club

SPECTATOR SPORTS

SOCCER IS hugely popular. Seville has two rival teams, FC Sevilla, who are based at the **Estadio Ramón Sánchez Pizjuán**, and Betis, who play at the **Estadio de Benito Villamarín**. Matches are played on Sunday afternoons from September to May. Also very popular, particularly in Seville, is basketball *(baloncesto)*. The main Seville team is the Caja de San Fernando, which often competes against international teams at **Complejo Deportivo San Pablo**.

GOLF

GOLF IS A MAJOR sport in Andalusia, and a spectacular range of courses is available on the Costa del Sol *(see p174)*. Seville and Jerez both also have a few excellent courses. Greens fees range from 3,500–15,000 pesetas a round. Only the few most exclusive clubs require membership. Advance booking is advisable at Easter and in the autumn.

EQUESTRIAN SPORTS

THE HORSE IS an integral part of life in Andalusia, as is demonstrated during Seville's Feria de Abril *(see p36)*. The undoubted equestrian capital of Andalusia, however, is Jerez de la Frontera *(see p158)*. The Feria del Caballo (International Horse Week) *(see p32)* is held here in May, and horses form an important part of the local *fiestas* celebrated in September and October. Dancing horses perform in spectacular shows at the **Real Escuela Andaluza de Arte Ecuestre** *(see p158)*. Andalusians also have a great interest in horse racing. A day at the races is considered to be quite a chic occasion.

Horse trekking is a splendid way in which to get to know the often rugged countryside of Andalusia. Several riding schools, among them **Hípica Puerta Príncipe**, offer lessons in the area around Seville.

WATER SPORTS

WATER-SPORTS facilities are available at most resorts along the coast. Tarifa has ideal conditions for windsurfing. In Seville, windsurfing, canoeing, and rowing on the Río Guadalquivir are popular. East of the city is the **Guadalpark**, an outdoor swimming pool complex open from June to September.

SKIING

THE SIERRA NEVADA *(see p189)* is the southernmost skiing region in Europe. **Solynieve**, its only resort, has the facilities to accommodate up to 30,000 skiers. The season starts late – mid to late December – but may run on until May.

In 1996, **Solynieve** played host to the World Ski Championships, thereby raising the profile of the Sierra Nevada as a skiing vacation destination.

Skiers enjoying the Solynieve ski resort in the Sierra Nevada

DIRECTORY

FLAMENCO

Seville
Bienal de Arte Flamenco
*(festival held every other
year: 1986, 1988, etc.)*
(95) 421 72 50.

Buque "El Patio"
Po de A M Contadero s/n.
Map 3 B2 (5 B5).
(95) 421 38 36.

Corazón de Triana
(sevillanas)
Calle de la Pureza 118.
Map 3 B2 (5 B5).

Los Gallos
Plaza de Santa Cruz 11.
Map 4 D2 (6 E4).
(95) 421 69 81.

El Patio Sevillano
Po de Cristóbal Colón 11a.
Map 3 B2 (5 C5).
(95) 421 41 20.

Granada
Jardines Neptuno
Calle Arabia s/n.
(958) 25 20 50.

La Reina Mora
Mirador de San Cristóbal,
Carretera Murcia.
(958) 27 82 28.

Córdoba
**Mesón Flamenco La
Bulería**
Calle Pedro López 3.
(957) 48 38 39.

La Posada del Potro
Plaza del Potro.

El Zoco Municipal
Calle Judíos s/n.

THEATER

Seville
El Auditorio
Camino del Descubrimiento
s/n, Isla de la Cartuja.
Map 1 B4.
(95) 446 07 48.

Teatro Alameda
Calle Crédito 13.
Map 2 D4.
(95) 438 83 12.

Teatro Lope de Vega
Avenida María Luisa s/n.
Map 3 C3.
(95) 459 08 53.

Teatro de la Maestranza
Paseo de Cristóbal
Colón 22.
Map 3 B2 (5 C5).
(95) 421 69 81.

Granada
Teatro Isabel La Católica
Acera del Casino 9.
(958) 22 02 69.

Córdoba
Gran Teatro
Avenida Gran Capitán 3.
(957) 48 02 37.

OPERA AND CLASSICAL MUSIC

Seville
El Auditorio
Camino del Descubrimiento
s/n, Isla de la Cartuja.
Map 1 B4.
(95) 446 07 48.

**Conservatorio
Superior de Música
Manuel Castillo**
C/ Jesús del Gran Poder 49.
Map 1 C4.
(95) 438 10 09.

Teatro Lope de Vega
Avenida María Luisa s/n.
Map 3 C3.
(95) 459 08 53.

Teatro de la Maestranza
Po de Cristóbal Colón 22–3.
Map 3 B2 (5 C5).
(95) 422 33 44.

Córdoba
**Conservatorio Superior
de Música**
C/ Ángel de Saavedra 1.
(957) 47 39 09.

ROCK, POP, AND JAZZ

Seville
El Auditorio
Camino del Descubrimiento
s/n, Isla de la Cartuja.
Map 1 B4.
(95) 446 07 48.

Blue Moon Jazz Café
Calle Juan Antonio
Cavestany s/n.
Map 4 E1.
(95) 442 69 06.

El Sol Jazz Club
Calle Sol 40.
Map 2 E5 (6 F1).

NIGHTLIFE

Seville
Bar Antigüedades
Calle Argote de Molina.
Map 3 C1 (6 D4).

Bar Garlochi
Calle Boteros 26.
Map 3 C1 (6 E3).

Bar Giralda
Calle Mateos Gago 2.
Map 3 C2 (6 E4).

La Carbonería
Calle Levíes 18.
Map 4 D1 (6 E4).

Catedral
Calle Cuesta del Rosario.
Map 3 B1 (5 C3).

El Coto
Meliá Lebreros Hotel,
Calle Luis Montoto 118.
Map 4 E1.
(95) 458 31 88.

Granada
Cunini
Plaza de Pescadería 14.
(958) 25 07 77.

Granada 10
Calle de Cárcel Baja 10.

Córdoba
Cafetería Gaudí
Avda Gran Capitán 22.
(957) 47 17 36.

Taberna San Miguel
Plaza San Miguel 1.
(957) 47 01 66.

BULLFIGHTING

Seville
**Plaza de Toros de la
Maestranza**
Paseo de Cristóbal Colón
12. **Map** 3 B2 (5 B4).
(95) 422 35 06

Granada
Plaza de Toros
Avenida Doctor Oloriz 25.
(958) 22 22 72.

Córdoba
Plaza de Toros
Avda de Gran Vía Parque.
(957) 23 25 07.

SPECTATOR SPORTS

**Estadio de Benito
Villamarín**
Avenida Heliópolis s/n,
Seville.
(95) 461 03 40.

**Estadio Ramón Sánchez
Pizjuán (Sevilla FC)**
Calle Luis de Morales s/n,
Seville.
Map 4 F2.
(95) 453 53 53.

**Complejo Deportivo
San Pablo**
Avda Kansas City, Seville.
(95) 467 67 00.

GOLF

Seville
**Real Club de Golf de
Seville**
Ctra Sevilla–Utrera km 3,
Montequinto.
(95) 412 43 01.

Costa del Sol
Club de Golf Valderrama
Avenida Cortijos s/n,
Sotogrande.
(956) 79 57 75.

Mijas Golf Internacional
Apto 145, Fuengirola.
(95) 247 68 43.

Golf La Dama de Noche
Carretera Istan, Río Verde,
Nueva Andalucía.
(95) 281 81 50.

EQUESTRIAN SPORTS

Seville
Hípica Puerta Príncipe
Ctra Sevilla-Utrera km 11.5.
(95) 595 08 48.

**Hipódromo Real Club
Pineda**
Avenida de Jerez s/n.
(95) 461 33 99.

Jerez de la Frontera
**Real Escuela Andaluza
de Arte Ecuestre**
Avenida Duque de
Abrantes s/n.
(956) 33 11 11.

WATER SPORTS

Guadalpark
Polígono Aeropuerto.
Sevilla-Este.
(95) 440 66 22.

SKIING

Solynieve
Sierra Nevada (Granada).
(958) 24 91 00 (info);
(958) 24 91 11 (booking).

Survival Guide

PRACTICAL INFORMATION

THE ECONOMY of Andalusia is heavily dependent on tourism. The rich variety of natural attractions and its cultural heritage draw visitors to the area throughout the year. Many have even settled in this evocative region, home of all things quintessentially Spanish: rich terra-cotta landscapes, olive groves, flamenco dancing, and *corridas* (bullfights).

Junta de Andalucía tourist office logo

Events such as Expo '92 in Seville, the 500th anniversary of Columbus, the Sierra Nevada Ski Championships, and the cultural tours created for the Legado Andalusi in 1995 have led to an increase in the number of tourist facilities and an improved infrastructure. The Junta de Andalucía has tourist offices across the region, offering a wealth of helpful brochures, maps, and leaflets.

Try not to do too much at once, but savor the particular delights of one or two places. Adjust to the slower pace and, in summer, do your sightseeing early in the day before the heat becomes unbearable.

Tickets for Hospital de los Venerables, Seville *(see p79)*

Leaflets on Andalusian culture, published by Junta de Andalucía

TOURIST INFORMATION

MOST OF THE major cities of Andalusia have several Oficinas de Turismo (tourist offices). Turespaña provides tourist information on Spain at a national level, while offices run by the Junta de Andalucía cover Andalusia as a region. Local tourist offices, found also in small towns, usually have details only of their environs.

Most tourist offices are well organized, offering brochures covering monuments, trips, emergency services, and places to stay, among other services. They have a range of leaflets listing local festivals and can also offer suggestions on nightlife, theaters, and flamenco shows. If you require more detailed information on sports, exhibitions, and concerts, check the listings in local papers *(see p245)*.

If you wish to hire a tour guide while staying in a major city, the tourist office will be able to direct you to a number of multilingual agencies.

El Legado Andalusi ("The Legacy of Andalus"), a project organized in 1995, highlights Andalusia's Moorish heritage through exhibitions and self-guided cultural tours. These are accompanied by leaflets and a guidebook.

ADMISSION CHARGES

SOME MONUMENTS and museums offer free entry to Spanish residents and members of the European Union. Others charge a moderate fee (children up to 12 years pay half price). Large groups may be offered a 50 percent discount on tickets. Payments must be made in cash and not by credit card.

OPENING HOURS

HOURS KEPT BY monuments and museums can vary considerably, so it is always best to check them before your visit. From October until March, most museums open between 9:30 and 10am and close for the siesta at 1:30 or 2pm. They open again from

Foreign visitors on a guided tour of Seville

◁ **Plaza de la Corredera market, Córdoba**

Flamenco street performers entertaining visitors outside a bar

DIRECTORY

TOURIST INFORMATION

Oficinas de Turismo
Avenida de la Constitución 21,
Seville. **Map** 3 C2 (5 C4).
((95) 422 14 04.
Paseo de las Delicias 9, Seville.
Map 3 C4.
((95) 423 44 65.
Calle Torrijos 10, Córdoba.
((957) 47 12 35.
C/ Mariana Pineda s/n, Granada.
((958) 22 59 90.

Tourist Office of Spain
US
665 Fifth Ave,
New York, NY 10022.
((212) 759-8822.

RELIGIOUS SERVICES

Catholic in English
Iglesia del Señor
Calle San José 25, Seville.
Map 4 D1 (6 E4).
((95) 422 03 19.

Jewish
Sinagoga
Urbanización el Real km 184,
Marbella.
((952) 277 40 74.

Muslim
Mezquita
Carretera de Cádiz km 178,
Marbella.
((952) 277 41 43.

around 4:30pm and then close at 6 or 8pm. Most close on Sunday afternoons. However, during the tourist season many museums stay open all day.

Most churches open only for Mass, but in small towns a caretaker will often let visitors in between religious services.

VISITING CHURCHES

MASS IS HELD every hour on Sundays, and at about 7–9pm on weekdays. In most churches, tourists are welcome in the church during a service as long as they are quiet.

Dress codes are not as strict as in other Catholic countries, but avoid skimpy shorts and bare arms. There is usually no admission charge, although a donation may be expected.

ETIQUETTE

THE OPEN, FRIENDLY character of the Spanish means that strangers usually greet each other with a ¡Hola!, ¡Buenos días!, or ¡Buenas tardes! on meeting in doorways or elevators – and even when passing on the street in small towns. It is also considered polite for people who know each other to shake hands each time they meet, and for women to kiss each other on both cheeks.

Smoking is prohibited in movie theaters, elevators, and public transportation, but other no-smoking areas are rare.

Spaniards rarely drink alcohol without nibbles until after dinner. It is not thought polite to share the price of a round of drinks except with people you know very well.

While totally accepted on the Costa del Sol, topless sunbathing is frowned upon in many small coastal places.

TIPPING

OWING TO THE RISING cost of living, tipping tends to be an issue of discretion in Spain. A service charge (servicio) is usually included (see p211) in checks, but it is common to tip up to 10 percent in addition and to give small change to taxi drivers, movie ushers, and doormen.

COMPLAINTS BOOK

IF YOU ARE NOT HAPPY with a service, particularly in a restaurant or hotel, you are entitled to ask for the Libro de Reclamaciones. This is an official complaints book at the disposal of customers, which

Sign indicating the establishment has a Libro de Reclamaciones

is inspected periodically by the local authorities. Only use it for very unsatisfactory affairs, or threaten to use it if you suspect you are being cheated.

TOILETS

PUBLIC TOILETS are scarce. However, there is a bar on virtually every corner and most do not object to passers-by using the servicios. In fact, they are legally bound to allow you to use them. A "D" on the door stands for Damas (ladies), and a "C" indicates Caballeros (gentlemen).

Toilets are rarely money operated, except in some new buildings. Where there is an attendant, it is customary to leave some small change.

Foreign student relaxing by a fountain in Seville

IMMIGRATION AND CUSTOMS

V ISITORS FROM the US and those from the European Union (EU) and New Zealand do not need a visa for stays of up to 90 days. If your visit is for more than three months, you will need to apply for a permit *(visado)* from your Spanish Consulate several weeks before going. Citizens of Canada and Australia will need a visa whatever their length of stay.

On arriving in Spain, getting through customs is generally easy. It is not necessary to register with the local police once there, but your hotel will take your passport details. Vaccination certificates are not needed to enter the country.

A sales tax *(IVA)* refund system is available in large Spanish department stores *(see p224)*. It is applicable to all except members of the EU.

EMBASSIES AND CONSULATES

I N THE EVENT of losing your passport or needing legal advice or other help, contact your national embassy or consulate. Most sizable towns have volunteer interpreters, usually found at local police stations *(see p240)*. On the

Costa del Sol, the Foreigners' Department of the Ayuntamiento (Departamento de Extranjeros) can help.

USEFUL ADDRESSES

American Embassy
Serrano 75, 28006 Madrid.
(*(91) 577 40 00.*

British Consulate
Plaza Nueva 8B, 41001 Seville.
Map 3 B1 (5 C3).
(*(95) 422 88 75.*
Calle Duquesa de Parcent 8, Málaga.
(*(95) 221 75 71.*

Canadian Consulate
Avenida de la Constitución 30, 2nd Floor, 41001 Seville. **Map** 3 C2 (5 C4).
(*(95) 422 94 13.*

DISABLED TRAVELERS

M ODERN BUILDINGS generally have adequate provisions for people with disabilities, with elevators, ramps, and special toilet facilities. However, entry to some historical monuments may be restricted. Local tourist offices, or the staff, can provide information about wheelchair access.

The **Society for the Advancement of Travel for the Handicapped, Inc.** provides travel information for the disabled. **Servi-COCEMFE** in Madrid advises on hotels that are equipped for disabled travelers *(see p201)*.

STUDENT INFORMATION

S EVILLE, GRANADA, and Córdoba attract large numbers of students, many of whom come to Andalusia to learn Spanish. Most large towns have a **Centro de Documentación e Información Juvenil**, which provides information for students and young people. A valid International Student Identification Card (ISIC card) entitles you to some price reductions, including museum entrance fees and travel.

SPECIAL-INTEREST TRIPS

T HERE IS AMPLE opportunity to study Spanish language and culture in Andalusia. The universities of Seville *(see p94)* and **Granada** run various courses throughout the year and there are also several private organizations. Contact **AEEA** (Asociación Empresarial de Escuelas de Español para

Horseback riding in the Granada countryside

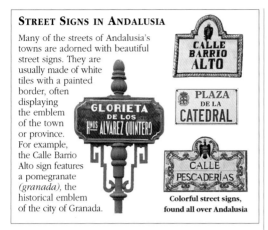

Street Signs in Andalusia

Many of the streets of Andalusia's towns are adorned with beautiful street signs. They are usually made of white tiles with a painted border, often displaying the emblem of the town or province. For example, the Calle Barrio Alto sign features a pomegranate *(granada),* the historical emblem of the city of Granada.

Colorful street signs, found all over Andalusia

Extranjeros de Andalucía) or the **Instituto Cervantes** (Spanish Institute) for a list of Spanish language courses.

For more details on cooking courses, wine, and painting vacations contact **Learning for Pleasure**. There is also plenty offered for the nature lover and for golf, horseback riding, and water-sport fans *(see p232).* More information on alternative and special-interest vacations can be found at Spanish tourist offices at home and in Spain *(see p237).*

ELECTRICAL ADAPTERS

THE CURRENT IN SPAIN is 220v-AC with two-pin, round-pronged plugs. Adapters can be found in many hypermarkets, supermarkets, and also some electrical stores. If you can, take one with you to be on the safe side. Most hotels and *pensiones* have electrical outlets for hair dryers and shavers in all the bedrooms. Many now use the key/card system for switching on the electricity supply in rooms.

ADDRESSES

IN SPEECH, on maps, and in written information, the Spaniards often drop the *Calle* in street names, so that Calle Mateos Gago becomes Mateos Gago. Other terms, such as *Plaza, Callejón, Carretera,* and *Avenida,* do not change.

In addresses, a *s/n (sin número)* after the street name indicates that the building has

no number. Outside towns, an address may say "Carretera Córdoba–Málaga km 47" – the site is on the highway near the kilometer sign.

SPANISH TIME

SPAIN IS SIX HOURS AHEAD of Eastern Standard Time (EST) and Eastern Daylight Time. The time difference between Seville and other cities is: New York -6 hours, London -1, Perth +7, Auckland +12, Tokyo +8. These figures may vary for brief periods in spring and autumn when clock changes are not synchronized.

The 24-hour clock is used in listings and for official purposes but not in speech. The morning (am) is referred to as *por la mañana* and the afternoon (pm), *por la tarde.* Afternoon does not start at midday, but rather after siesta time, at around 4 or 5pm.

CONVERSION CHART

US Standard to Metric
1 inch = 2.54 centimeters
1 foot = 30 centimeters
1 mile = 1.6 kilometers
1 ounce = 28 grams
1 pound = 454 grams
1 US quart = 0.946 liter
1 US gallon = 3.79 liters

Metric to US Standard
1 centimeter = 0.4 inch
1 meter = 3 feet, 3 inches
1 kilometer = 0.6 mile
1 gram = 0.04 ounce
1 kilogram = 2.2 pounds
1 liter = 1.1 US quarts

Personal Security and Health

ANDALUSIA IS, BY AND LARGE, a safe place for visitors. Women traveling alone tend not to be hassled, but may have to put up with so-called compliments from men of all ages. Pickpockets and purse-snatchers, however, are very common, especially in Seville, so it is best to be careful in popular tourist spots and on crowded buses. Try to avoid carrying valuable items and, if possible, wear a money belt. If you become ill during your stay, go to the nearest pharmacy, where someone should be able to advise you. Organize your travel insurance before leaving for Spain since it is difficult to get and more expensive once there.

Officer of the *Policía Nacional*

Mounted police officers from the *Policía Nacional*

PROTECTING YOUR PROPERTY

PICKPOCKETS ARE COMMON in crowded areas, especially outside monuments and at markets. Be particularly wary of people asking you the time, since they are probably trying to distract you while someone else attempts to snatch your purse or wallet. Also, if you have a scooter, make sure that it is securely chained, especially in Seville and Málaga.

Use traveler's checks rather than cash, and carry a photocopy of your passport, leaving the original in the hotel safe. If you have a car, do not leave valuables in view, and try to leave it in a security-controlled parking lot.

In the event of being robbed or attacked, report the incident to the police (*poner una denuncia*) as soon as possible (at least within 24 hours). This is extremely important if you wish to obtain a statement (*denuncia*) to make an insurance claim.

PERSONAL SAFETY

THE ABUNDANCE of street-life means that you will rarely find yourself alone or in a position to be harassed. However, women may be intimidated by men making comments as they walk by, or even following them. This pastime, known as *piropo*, is common and not meant as a serious threat.

There are no particularly notorious areas of Seville to be avoided. Just act street-wise: do not use maps late at night and try to look like you know where you're going.

When visiting the Sacromonte caves in Granada to see gypsy families perform flamenco (*see p185*), it is a good idea to go in a group and keep an eye on your belongings.

Make sure that you take official taxis displaying a license number and avoid public transportation at night if alone. Any cab driver soliciting business is likely to be illegal.

POLICE

THERE ARE BASICALLY three types of police in Spain – the *Guardia Civil*, the *Policía Nacional*, and the *Policía Local*. When approaching the police remember that it is illegal to be without ID.

Out of the main towns you will usually encounter the green-uniformed *Guardia Civil*. They patrol the country highways and, although they have a mean reputation, they will help if your car breaks down (*see p253*).

The *Policía Nacional*, who wear a blue uniform, are the best to turn to, especially when reporting a crime. They have many different responsibilities, including dealing with visitors' permits and documentation. In the bigger cities the *Policía Nacional* also guard many important establishments, such as government buildings, embassies, and barracks.

The *Policía Local* take care of the day-to-day policing of small towns and villages.

Marked car of the *Policía Nacional*

Policía Local patrol car, mainly seen in small towns

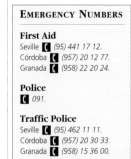

EMERGENCY NUMBERS

First Aid
Seville ☎ (95) 441 17 12.
Córdoba ☎ (957) 20 12 77.
Granada ☎ (958) 22 20 24.

Police
☎ 091.

Traffic Police
Seville ☎ (95) 462 11 11.
Córdoba ☎ (957) 20 30 33.
Granada ☎ (958) 15 36 00.

PHARMACIES

FOR MINOR COMPLAINTS, visit a pharmacy *(farmacia),* where pharmacists are highly trained. They dispense a wide range of medication over the counter, including antibiotics.

Farmacias have a green or red neon cross outside, usually flashing, and are found in most villages and towns. They keep the same hours as most other stores (9:30am–1:30pm and 4–8pm). At least one will be *de guardia*

Spanish pharmacy signs

– ready to dispatch at off-hours, at night, and on Sunday. The schedule is posted on the door of all *farmacias* and you will also be able to find it listed in local newspapers.

MEDICAL TREATMENT

IF IN NEED of urgent medical assistance, go to the nearest *Urgencias* – the emergency room of a hospital or clinic.

All the cities have several hospitals each, while the Costa del Sol has a hospital situated on the main coastal highway (N340) just east of Marbella. Most hospitals have volunteer interpreters who speak English and occasionally also other languages.

A Red Cross ambulance

The Cruz Roja (Red Cross) has an extensive network throughout Spain and runs an ambulance service.

Visitors from the US should check with their insurance companies before leaving home to be sure they are covered if medical care is needed. Many medical facilities will require that you pay for your treatment in full at the time of service. Be sure to get an itemized bill to submit to your insurance company. In some cases, insurance companies require that you provide an official translation

before they will reimburse you. Travelers may wish to take out additional, private travel insurance against the cost of any emergency hospital care, doctor's fees, and returning you to the US. If you have private travel insurance, make sure you have your policy on you when requesting medical assistance. Depending on which insurance company you use, you may be expected to pay for treatment and be reimbursed at a later date.

HEALTH PRECAUTIONS

BEWARE OF THE SUN, particularly from May to October when temperatures can reach up to 45° C (113° F). Try to avoid walking in the midday sun, and stay in the shade whenever possible. Drink plenty of bottled mineral water.

It is advisable to wear sunglasses, sunscreen, and a hat when you are out sightseeing. When in the countryside, you may see signs showing a bull or saying *Toro bravo* (fighting bull). These signs should be taken seriously since these bulls are extremely dangerous and by no means should be approached.

LEGAL ASSISTANCE

IF YOU ARE INVOLVED in an incident that requires a lawyer, ask your Embassy or Consulate *(see p238)* for the name of a reputable one. However, do not expect all lawyers to speak English. Police stations can sometimes provide volunteer interpreters *(intérpretes)* to help visitors from other countries. Otherwise it may be necessary to hire an interpreter to state your case clearly. *Traductores Oficiales* or *Jurados* are qualified to undertake most types of legal or official work.

DIRECTORY

LOST PROPERTY

Seville
Oficina de Objetos Perdidos, Calle Almansa 21. **Map** 3 B1 (5 B3). [(95) 421 18 00.

Córdoba
Comisaría de Policía, Avenida Doctor Fleming. [(957) 47 75 00.

Granada
Ayuntamiento, Plaza del Carmen s/n. [(958) 22 75 68.

MISSING TRAVELER'S CHECKS OR CREDIT CARDS

VISA Freefone [900 94 11 18.

Thomas Cook [(91) 411 20 19.

American Express [(91) 570 77 77.

Diners Club [(91) 574 40 00.

MEDICAL TREATMENT

Cruz Roja
Hospital Victoria Eugenia, Avenida de la Cruz Roja, Seville. **Map** 2 E4. [(95) 435 01 35.

Hospital Costa del Sol
Carretera Nacional 340 km 187, Marbella, Málaga. [(958) 286 27 48.

Hospital General
Avenida de la Constitución s/n, Granada. [(958) 27 64 00.

Hospital Nuestra Señora de Valme
Carretera de Cádiz, Seville. [(95) 459 60 00.

Hospital Reina Sofía
Avenida Menéndez Pidal s/n, Córdoba. [(957) 21 70 00.

LEGAL ASSISTANCE

Asociación Profesional de Traductores e Intérpretes
[(91) 221 1055. *Will supply details of local interpreters.*

Banking and Local Currency

CHANGING MONEY IN SPAIN can often be quite time-consuming. Finding exchange facilities is not a problem, however. There are usually one or two banks even in small towns (but not necessarily in villages). Other options for changing traveler's checks and currency include *casas de cambio*, hotels, and travel agents. Alternatively, credit cards and Eurocheques are widely accepted in larger stores, hotels, and restaurants. And, bank or credit cards can be used at ATMs to get cash.

If you bring money worth over one million pesetas to Spain, you must declare it on entry.

24-hour cash machine, accepting major credit cards

CHANGING MONEY

YOU CAN CHANGE money and cash traveler's checks at *casas de cambio* (bureaux de change), banks, and *cajas de ahorros* (building societies). Travel agents and hotels also change money. Málaga airport has 24-hour exchange facilities and Seville airport has a bank open at the usual times.

It is better to buy enough pesetas for your initial needs before traveling, and to shop around for the best rates at your leisure after you arrive. Hotels and travel agents do not give good exchange rates, and commissions charged on foreign currency transactions also vary. They are higher than average at the airports.

It is compulsory to show your passport or driver's license when changing money or traveler's checks.

Bureau de change, found in small towns all over Andalusia

USING BANKS

BE PATIENT when using banks in Andalusia. You will generally find that there are very few bank clerks

waiting on the public and that lines can be endless. In larger banks you may find that some staff speak English, but only a few words.

In some banks you must fill in a few forms at the *cambio* (exchange desk) before going to the *caja* (cash desk) to line up for your money. It is best to choose one of the bigger banks, such as the BBV (Banco Bilbao Vizcaya) or the Banco Central Hispano. These will have branches throughout Andalusia and you often have to line up just once for your money.

Many banks now have electronically operated double doors. First you must press the button to open the outer door. Once inside, wait until you see the green light (which comes on when the outer door closes) and the second door will then open automatically.

BANKING HOURS

BANKS IN ANDALUSIA are open for business from 8:30am to 2pm Monday to Friday but only from 8:30am to 1pm on Saturdays during the winter. From May to September they do not open on Saturdays.

Banks are never open on public holidays (*see p35*), and during a town's annual *feria* week (*see pp36–7*) the banks will open for just three hours from 9am to noon. This is to allow the staff to join in the general merrymaking.

Logos for BBV and Banco de Grananda

CREDIT CARDS

CREDIT CARDS such as VISA, American Express, and Mastercard (Access) are widely accepted all over Spain. Some establishments may require identification such as a passport or driving license. Major banks will give cash on credit cards, and if your card is linked to your home bank account, you can also use it with your PIN number to withdraw money from cash machines.

Instructions are given on the display in several languages. Standard bank cards bearing the Cirrus logo can also be used widely to withdraw money from cash machines or, as at home, as debit cards to purchase goods.

TRAVELER'S CHECKS

MOST TYPES of traveler's checks are accepted in Spanish banks. It is probably best to choose US dollars or British pounds, but most currencies are acceptable. American Express offices do not charge any commission on their own checks.

If you wish to cash checks larger than 500,000 pesetas, you must give the bank 24 hours' notice. Also, if you draw more than 100,000 pesetas on traveler's checks, you will probably be asked to produce the purchase certificate.

EUROCHEQUES

IF YOU HAVE a European bank account, you can write checks in Spanish pesetas using Eurocheques, or use them to get cash at a bank. Be prepared to show your Eurocard and passport.

CURRENCY

THE CURRENCY of Spain is the peseta, usually abbreviated to "ptas." In popular speech it is common to speak of *duros* (one *duro* is equal to 5 pese-

tas). *Cinco duros* equals 25 pesetas and *mil* (1,000) *duros* equals 5,000 pesetas. When giving change, sales clerks often round the figure up or down to the nearest 5 pesetas.

Spanish coins are often a source of confusion. For only nine denominations 58 different coins are in circulation. However, many of these are now being phased out and from January 1997 only coins minted after 1986 will be in use. (The almost worthless 1- and 2-peseta coins will be removed from circulation.)

The seven denominations of coin that will be in circulation after 1997 will be easy to distinguish by shape and color, but the prints will still vary from year to year. Thus, a 200-peseta coin from 1992 shows King Juan Carlos I and his son Prince Felipe on one side and a famous Madrid statue on the other; in the 1994 version, both sides are dedicated to famous Spanish paintings. A 2,000-peseta coin has been minted, but so far is available as a collectors' item only.

1,000 pesetas

2,000 pesetas

Bank Notes
Spanish bank notes comes in four different denominations. The smallest is the 1,000-ptas bill (two types, both green), followed by the 2,000-ptas bill (pink), the 5,000-ptas bill (ocher with brown and purple) and the 10,000-ptas bill (blue).

5,000 pesetas

10,000 pesetas

Coins
Spanish coins, shown here at actual size, are in denominations of 5 ptas, 10 ptas, 25 ptas, 50 ptas, 100 ptas, 200 ptas, and 500 ptas. The 500-ptas, 100-ptas, 25-ptas, and 5-ptas coins are a dull gold color. The 200-ptas, 50-ptas, and 10-ptas coins are silver.

5 pesetas   **10 pesetas**   **25 pesetas**

50 pesetas   **100 pesetas**   **200 pesetas**   **500 pesetas**

Communications

Post office (correos) sign

THE TELEPHONE SYSTEM in Spain is run by Telefónica. It is efficient, but is said to be the most expensive in Europe. Most lines abroad are very good and there is no shortage of public telephones.

Spain's postal service is notoriously inefficient but letters posted at central post offices will not take too long. Radio and television are very popular with Spaniards, and there are a great number of local radio stations. Regional newspapers have gained popularity in Andalusia, but sales are still below the Spanish average.

TELEPHONING IN ANDALUSIA

SPANIARDS LOVE to talk, so there are plenty of phone booths (*cabinas telefónicas*) on the streets, and most bars have public phones. There are public telephone offices (*locutorios*), where you make a call and pay for it afterward, and also private bureaus with phones and faxes.

Public phones use coins and phone-

cards (*tarjetas telefónicas*). *Cabinas* are often positioned in pairs on the streets, one accepting coins and one cards. To call from a pay phone you must insert 25 pesetas at least. You can buy phonecards from tobacconists (*estancos*) and newsstands. They are priced according to their value in units.

It is easiest to make long-distance calls (*conferencias interurbanas*) at *locutorios*. A call made from a *cabina telefónica* or

Telefónica's modern, blue and green public telephones

locutorio costs 35 percent more than from a private phone. In a bar the cost can be prohibitive, since many bars install phone meters and some charge very high rates. Calling abroad is cheapest between 10pm and 8am daily.

Logo of Spanish telecom system, Telefónica

USING A COIN AND CARD TELEPHONE

1 Lift the receiver, wait for dial tone and for the display to show "*Inserte monedas o tarjeta.*"

2 Insert either coins (*monedas*) or a card (*tarjeta*).

3 Key in the number (firmly, but not too fast – Spanish phones prefer you to pause between digits).

4 As you press the digits, the number you are dialing will show on the display. You will also be able to see how much money or units are left and when to insert more coins.

5 When your call is finished, replace the receiver. A phonecard then re-emerges automatically. Any excess coins inserted will also be returned.

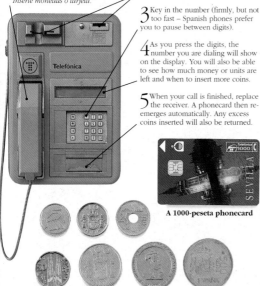

A 1000-peseta phonecard

Denominations of pesetas accepted in coin-operated telephones

USING A PUBLIC TELEPHONE

MOST OF the new public phone booths have a visual display to guide users. Illustrated instructions on how to use the phone, and lists of local and national dialing codes, are posted in most booths in cities and tourist areas. Some phones are designed so that users may change the language of the instructions by pressing a button with a flag symbol.

Expect some public phones in streets to be out of order. If you call from an open booth, watch your purse, wallet, and bags as you are an obvious target for pickpockets.

SENDING LETTERS

THE SPANISH POSTAL SERVICE is accurately known as slow and unreliable. Service between cities is fairly efficient, but mail to or from smaller towns can be very slow. Postcards can take more than a month, particularly in the summer. Letters

Distinctive yellow Spanish mailbox *(buzón)*

Standard issue stamps with a portrait of King Juan Carlos I

REACHING THE RIGHT NUMBER

• Area codes for the different provinces are: Seville and Málaga 95 (+ 7-digit number); Córdoba 957, Granada 958, Cádiz 956, Huelva 959, Jaén 953, Almería 950 (all + 6-digit number). Drop the first 9 when phoning from abroad.
• International calls: dial 07, wait for tone, dial country and area codes and number.
• National directory inquiries: dial 003.

• International directory inquiries are on 025.
• Operator assistance for calls to Europe and North Africa is on 9198. For the rest of the world, dial 9191. If you want to know the cost, ask the operator beforehand.
• To connect directly with the operator in your country dial 900 followed by 990061 (Australia); 990015 (Canada); 990011 (US); or 990044 for the United Kingdom.

mailed at a central post office will usually arrive in reasonable time, but mailboxes *(buzones)* may not be emptied for days, even in large towns and cities.

Send important or urgent mail by *certificado* (registered) and *urgente* (express) mail. It should arrive anywhere in Spain on the following day and in towns in the US in three to five days.

When sending a package, be sure it is securely tied with string. If you fail to do so, you may be asked to have it sealed at a cost of 50 pesetas. You will also have to fill out a form stating the contents and destination of the package.

Buy stamps *(sellos)* at post offices and *estancos* (state-run tobacconists) displaying a distinctive yellow and red sign. Main post offices open 8am–9pm Monday to Friday, 9am–7pm Saturday; local post offices 9am–2pm Monday to Friday, 9am–1pm Saturday.

POSTE RESTANTE

IN MOST LARGE TOWNS a *poste restante* service is available. A letter should be addressed to the relevant person, *"Lista de Correos,"* the town name and region. Letters are kept at the town's main post office, where they can be picked up. A passport or other form of identification is needed but there is no collection fee.

TV AND RADIO

THERE ARE TWO state channels in Spain, TVE1 and TVE2, plus stations Antena 3 and Telecinco (5). In addition, Andalusia has its own, very popular, Canal Sur. Canal Plus is a cable television company that features mainly films, sports, and documentaries. Subtitled foreign films are indicated in TV listings by the letters V.O. *(Versión Original).*

The best radio news programs are broadcast on Radio Nacional de España. BBC World Service frequencies and listings can be found in its monthly *Worldwide* magazine for English language listening.

Canal Sur, the local broadcasting station

Socialist Government), *ABC* (conservative), and *El Mundo* (independent). Local papers such as *Ideal* in Granada, the Córdoba *Diario*, or the Málaga *Sur* have more extensive listings of local cultural and sporting activities. An English version of *Sur* is distributed free in Málaga on Fridays. The local listings magazines are the *Giraldillo* in Seville and the *Guía del Ocio* in Granada *(see p230). La Tribuna*, Córdoba's weekly newsletter, publishes useful practical information.

A selection of national and regional Spanish newspapers

NEWSPAPERS AND MAGAZINES

THE MOST IMPORTANT national papers are *El País* (which prints an Andalusian version daily and is linked to the

---

TRAVEL INFORMATION

ANDALUSIA is well served by a wide range of transportation. Each year thousands of charter and scheduled flights arrive, mostly from European countries. Most flights from beyond Europe stop in Madrid or Barcelona, requiring a changeover before arriving at Andalusia's busiest airport, Málaga. Located only a few miles from Morocco, Málaga serves as a gateway to Africa. Seville airport also handles international flights. Seville has good rail connections, and the AVE high-speed train

Iberia Airlines aircraft

between Seville and major cities – such as Córdoba and Madrid – is often faster than flying (if you include check-in time). There are buses from northern Europe and regional services throughout Andalusia, and ferries sail from the United Kingdom to Santander and Bilbao; from here it is about a ten-hour drive to Andalusia. However, driving is not recommended in summer when there is a mass exodus from Madrid to the Costa del Sol and the number of cars on the roads is at its greatest.

Seville Airport, conveniently situated just outside the city

ARRIVING BY AIR

MOST OF EUROPE'S major airlines run scheduled flights to Málaga, Andalusia's main airport. The majority of air traffic, however, is made up of cheap charter flights, which bring in thousands of vacationers at all hours of the day and night. Seville airport is much less busy and is convenient for travelers staying inland. There are no direct scheduled flights from the US to Málaga or Seville. Travelers must therefore fly to Madrid and take Iberia Airlines from there.

PACKAGE VACATIONS

ALMOST ALL package deals to Andalusia focus on beach vacations. However, one or two tour operators also offer city visits. Some offer a tour of a number of cities, starting in Málaga (you can fly there from Madrid), then following an itinerary, traveling by bus,

along the Costa del Sol, to Seville, Córdoba, Granada, and Cádiz.

SEVILLE AIRPORT

SEVILLE AIRPORT is useful for travelers who are staying away from the coast. Located just 4 km (2.5 miles) out of the city center, on the NIV road to Córdoba and Madrid, it is modern, easily manageable, and very convenient.

There are scheduled flights daily to and from London, Paris, and Frankfurt. As well as cities such as Madrid, Barcelona, and Santiago de Compostela, the internal destinations include Palma de Mallorca and Tenerife. Charter flights also operate out of Seville, but only at certain times of the year. There is no public transporta-

Iberia Airlines ticket machine

tion to or from the airport, but a taxi ride is quick and inexpensive. Airport services include gift shops, a newsstand, and a timesaving machine for buying internal Iberia tickets.

MÁLAGA AIRPORT

THE BUSY AIRPORT at Málaga receives around 6 million passengers a year and has links to about 90 international destinations. Eighty percent of international traffic is chartered flights, mostly from the UK. The airport is busy all year, but particularly so from June to September. If you are intent on traveling to Málaga by charter, be sure to book well in advance. Obtaining scheduled flights is easier; in the US and Canada they are available from **Iberia**.

The airport terminal at Málaga is vast and can be tiresome to walk around, particularly for the elderly or infirm. Electronic buggies can be ordered, and there are electronic walkways too. Airport facilities include gift shops, jewelers, photographic stores, a pharmacy, and a multidenominational chapel.

There are plenty of car rental companies, but it is advisable to book well in advance.

The *tren de cercanías (see p248)* runs into Málaga and to the Costa del Sol as far as Fuengirola, every 20 minutes from 6am to 11pm.

By car it takes 20 minutes into Málaga. Taxis are available 24 hours, with set fees. The No. 19 bus, which runs every 30 minutes from 6:30am to midnight, also goes to Málaga.

Logo for Iberia Airlines

GRANADA AIRPORT

GRANADA'S AIRPORT is 17 km (10.5 miles) southeast of the city on the main road to Málaga. There are plans to expand the flight network but at present the airport handles internal flights only. Facilities are also fairly limited: there is a newsstand, and a gift shop, a café, and a restaurant. There are regular flights to Palma de Mallorca, Tenerife, and Las Palmas, as well as to major Spanish cities – Barcelona, Madrid, and Valencia. The airport opens from 8:30am to 8:30pm and there are car rental facilities in the terminal.

GIBRALTAR AIRPORT

THIS AIRPORT, located on the famous British rock, can be a useful arrival point for people visiting the west of Andalusia. Flights are operated exclusively by **GB Airways** from Britain (Gatwick, Heathrow, and Manchester) and North Africa. The airport itself is small and manageable, but has few amenities.

AIRPORT CAR RENTAL

THE MAJOR AIRPORTS are well served with international car rental companies such as **AVIS**, **Hertz**, and **Europcar**, as well as a range of local companies. It is advisable to book a car prior to your visit, particularly during the tourist-season summer months.

Many travel agents are able to organize fly-drive deals. These usually offer discounts on car rental arranged from abroad before traveling.

USEFUL NUMBERS

American Airlines
(800) 433-7300.

Delta Airlines
(800) 221-1212.

GB Airways
Cloister Building, Gibraltar.
(9567) 79300.

Iberia
Calle Almirante Lobo 2, Seville.
Map 3 C2 (5 C5).
(95) 422 89 01 (Seville);
(800) 772-4642 (US).

Airport Information
Seville (95) 451 61 11.
Málaga (95) 221 63 24.
Granada (958) 44 64 11.
Gibraltar (9567) 44737.

AVIS
Seville (900 13 57 90.
Málaga (95) 223 08 55.
Granada (958) 44 64 55.

Europcar
Seville (95) 425 42 98.
Málaga (95) 223 72 18.

Hertz
Málaga (95) 223 16 59.

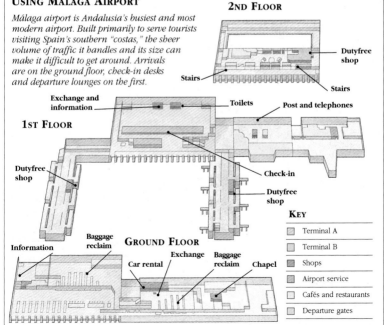

USING MÁLAGA AIRPORT

Málaga airport is Andalusia's busiest and most modern airport. Built primarily to serve tourists visiting Spain's southern "costas," the sheer volume of traffic it handles and its size can make it difficult to get around. Arrivals are on the ground floor, check-in desks and departure lounges on the first.

2ND FLOOR

Dutyfree shop

Stairs

Stairs

Exchange and information

Toilets

Post and telephones

1ST FLOOR

Dutyfree shop

Check-in

Dutyfree shop

KEY

Information

Baggage reclaim

GROUND FLOOR

Car rental

Exchange

Baggage reclaim

Chapel

☐	Terminal A
☐	Terminal B
☐	Shops
☐	Airport service
☐	Cafés and restaurants
☐	Departure gates

Traveling by Train

Logo for AVE high-speed trains

OWING TO the natural bottleneck of the Pyrenees, train connections between Spain and the rest of Europe are a little restricted. **Iberail**, however, a subsidiary of Spain's national network, RENFE, runs a service that links Madrid and Barcelona to France, Italy, Austria, and Switzerland. **RENFE** offers routes throughout the country, on a variety of trains, at a high level of service. The high-speed AVE *(Tren de Alta Velocidad Española)* linking Seville, Córdoba, and Madrid has cut down travel times by almost half and is extremely efficient.

AVE high-speed trains at Estación de Santa Justa, Seville

ARRIVING BY TRAIN

TRAINS COMING from other European countries to Spain terminate in either Madrid or Barcelona. From Barcelona it is nine hours to Seville; from Madrid it takes around three hours traveling by AVE.

Andalusia's most important station is Santa Justa *(see p250)* in Seville. It has connections with major Andalusian towns and with Barcelona and Madrid (including 11 AVE high-speed trains running daily).

European and American rail passes, including EurRail and Inter-Rail, are accepted on the RENFE network, subject to the usual conditions. However, on certain trains you may find a supplement is payable.

TRAIN TRAVEL IN SPAIN

THE TRAIN NETWORK in Spain is very extensive and there are services designed to suit every pocket. Traveling on the AVE is expensive, but fast. There is also a money-back guarantee that the train will

reach its destination no more than five minutes late.

Other long distance services, known as *largo recorrido*, are divided into *diurnos* (daytime) and *nocturnos* (nighttime). *Intercity* is the name given to standard daytime trains. *Talgos* are slightly more luxurious and more expensive. Night trains include *Expresos* and *Talgo cama* (*cama* means bed). *Regionales* run daytime from

city to city within a limited area. *Cercanías* are commuter trains running from large towns to their surrounding suburbs, towns, and villages.

BOOKINGS AND RESERVATIONS

IT IS ADVISABLE to book long-distance trips in advance, essential if you travel on public holidays *(días festivos)* or long weekends *(puentes)*. You can book a ticket from a station up to 60 days in advance and collect it up to 24 hours before traveling. It can also be sent to your hotel *(servicio a domicilio)*. Tickets for *regionales* cannot be booked in advance. Most staff are helpful, although few speak English. RENFE agents in travel agencies are often more willing to discuss the available options.

TICKETS

TRAIN TRAVEL IN SPAIN is fairly reasonably priced. *Largo recorrido* and *regionales* have first and second class *(primera/ segunda clase)*. The pricing for AVE trains and the Talgo 200 from Málaga to Madrid is worked out on a class system – *turista* (low), *preferente* (medium), and *club* (high) – and also by how busy trains are at certain times – *valle* (low), *plano* (middle), and *punta* (high). Thus, the most expensive tickets are *club punta* and the cheapest are *turista valle*. The tickets on Spanish trains always show a number for your seat (or bed

AL ANDALUS EXPRESO

The Al Andalus Expreso is a luxurious and evocative way to see Andalusia in style. This magnificent train is Spain's version of the Orient Express. Pulling 14 original carriages, all built between 1900–30, the Al Andalus provides the splendor of turn-of-the-century travel accompanied by all the comforts of modern-day living.

Short, leisurely paced trips around the cities of Andalusia operate from April to October. On each trip, visits are scheduled to Seville, Córdoba, Jerez, Granada, and Ronda.

Al Andalus Expreso, interior

SPAIN'S PRINCIPAL RENFE NETWORK

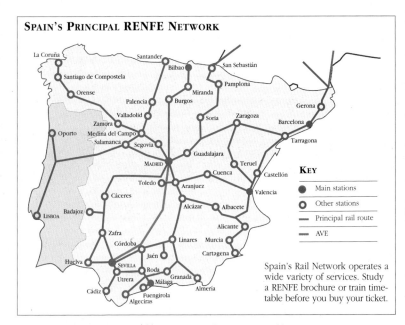

KEY

⬤ Main stations
◯ Other stations
━ Principal rail route
━ AVE

Spain's Rail Network operates a wide variety of services. Study a RENFE brochure or train timetable before you buy your ticket.

on sleepers). Tickets for long trips are sold at main line stations, at the RENFE offices, and some *cercanías* stations. Credit cards are accepted at the main stations, but not at the smaller or *cercanías* stations. You can change the date of a ticket twice, but you pay an extra 10–15 percent. If further changes are then required, the ticket is reissued at full fare.

TICKETS FOR CERCANÍAS AND REGIONAL TRAINS

On REGIONAL LINES and on *cercanías* you can buy a ticket, or *bono*, covering ten trips, which offers a saving of as much as 40 percent of the standard price. When entering a station, you pass the *bono* through a slot in the automatic barrier leading to the platform.

TIMETABLES

THE PUNCTUALITY RATING of trains in Andalusia is quite high, particularly for the AVE. Brochures with price scales and timetables are distributed free of charge and are easy to follow. Information for *laborables* (weekdays) and *sábados, domingos, y festivos* (Saturdays, Sundays, and public holidays) is generally displayed at the bottom of the timetable.

USEFUL NUMBERS

Booking Agents for RENFE
Seville
La Campana 7. **Map** 5 C2.
📞 *(95) 422 50 27.*

Córdoba
Ronda de los Tejares 11.
📞 *(957) 47 78 35.*

Granada
Avenida de Madrid 3.
📞 *(958) 28 25 00.*

Málaga
Calle Trinidad Grund 2.
📞 *(95) 221 81 91.*

Iberail
Estación de Santa Justa, Avenida Kansas City s/n, Seville. **Map** 4 F1.
📞 *(95) 453 72 27.*

Al Andalus Expreso
📞 *(91) 571 58 15.*

USING A TICKET MACHINE

Ticket machines for *cercanías* and regional lines are easy to use. A green flashing light guides you through the instructions printed on the front of the machine until you complete them and your ticket is dispatched.

Ticket

1 Select your destination from panel on left.

2 Select ticket type; *sencillo* (single), *ida y vuelta* (return), or *tarjeta dorada* (for retirees).

3 Insert money (1,000 ptas bills or 500, 200, 100, 50, 25, or 5 ptas coins). The machine will return your change.

4 If it says *Solo Monedas*, only coins are accepted.

5 Take your ticket.

The ultramodern façade of Seville's Santa Justa railroad station, built in 1992

SEVILLE, SANTA JUSTA

MODERN and user-friendly, Santa Justa is one of Andalusia's most recent landmarks. Even when busy, it seems spacious and safe, although visitors should look out for pickpockets during the summer months.

It is an easy station to use, and trains and platforms are visible through huge windows in the center of the building.

Near the ticket office there are large notices featuring schedules for AVE and other long-distance train services. Self-service ticket machines are available for regional journeys and journeys by *cercanías* (see pp248–9).

Electronic departures board at Santa Justa railroad station

Ticket counter at Santa Justa railroad station

The station has a large self-service restaurant, gift shops, newsstands, cash machines, and money-changing facilities. For lost property, go to the office marked *Atención al Cliente*. At the front of the station you will find a large taxi stand and a spacious parking lot. The station is open from 4am to midnight and, although it is located in a slightly drab suburb, it is only about five minutes by car or bus from the city center.

RENFE logo

CÓRDOBA

CÓRDOBA HAS A GRAND, new station, which opened in October 1994. Located in the northwest of the city, it is just a few minutes by car or taxi to the city center. Like Santa Justa, it is large, efficiently run, and easy to find one's way around. Trains run to Madrid, Málaga, Barcelona, Seville, Jaén, and Bilbao. The AVE to Madrid takes just 2 hours; to Seville 45 minutes. The station is well served with cafés, shops, and ticket offices. Lockers for storing luggage are available.

GRANADA

SMALL AND PROVINCIAL, the station in Granada is more fitting to a village than a city. It is housed in an old building and has few amenities. There is a small café-cum-restaurant and a taxi stand outside. Most trains

that pass through are regional or *cercanías*, but long-distance trains do run to Madrid, Seville, the Costa Blanca, Barcelona, Almería, Córdoba, and Málaga.

Exterior of Granada station

MÁLAGA

THE STATION IN MALAGA is quite small and is only busy at times when trains are due to depart or arrive. Connected by a *cercanías* to the coast as far as Fuengirola, it is convenient for visitors to the Costa del Sol. Trains also leave regularly for Madrid, Barcelona, Seville, Córdoba, and Cádiz. There is a taxi stand outside.

TRAIN STATIONS

Seville, Santa Justa
Avenida Kansas City. **Map** 2 F5 & 4 F1.
((95) 441 47 00.

Granada
Avenida Andaluces s/n.
((958) 27 12 72.

Córdoba
Avenida de América.
((957) 49 02 02.

Málaga
Plaza de la Estación.
((95) 236 02 02.

Traveling by Bus

THE MAJOR BUS LINKS between Andalusia and the rest of Europe are with France, Holland, Belgium, Switzerland, and Austria. Within the region itself, bus travel is very popular and has improved enormously in recent years. Most buses now have air-conditioning, a video, bar, and toilet. Traveling by bus in Andalusia is very economical, and thanks to the recent improvements in roads, it can be quick and enjoyable. However, around the many holidays in the Spanish festive calendar, traveling can be difficult: bus stations tend to be over-crowded, buses slow to depart, and the roads busy.

Regional bus operated by the Alsina Graells company

ARRIVING BY BUS

THE MAJOR BUS STATIONS in Andalusia are in Seville, Granada, Córdoba, and Málaga. However, some individual companies have a policy of avoiding central bus stations for departures and arrivals, particularly in Granada where there are a number of different companies in operation.

Buses run frequently between major cities and towns and can sometimes provide the only way of getting to and from small villages. Traveling on these routes will certainly give you an experience of the region's local color.

SEVILLE

SEVILLE's main bus station is located in the center of town at the Plaza de Armas. It is a modern, user-friendly building with plenty of ticket windows, an information desk, and a shopping mall. From here the Alsa bus company operates routes to destinations all over Spain as well as to France and Switzerland.

CÓRDOBA

THE MAIN BUS STATION in Córdoba is run by the Alsina Graells bus company. It is small and basic, consisting just a small waiting area with a café and a newsstand.

Buses depart regularly from this point for Granada, Murcia, Almería, Málaga, Algeciras, Cádiz, and Seville.

GRANADA

IN GRANADA, bus travelers may be confused by the choice of bus companies, each of which deals with a variety of different destinations. The largest is Alsina Graells Sur, and its station is what is normally referred to as the central bus station. Dirty and overcrowded, it is not an attractive place to linger, and it is advisable to buy your ticket in advance and turn up at the bus station a few minutes before departure. This bus station offers routes all over Murcia and Andalusia. Buses for Madrid leave from outside the main train station in Avenida Andaluces.

MÁLAGA

MÁLAGA BUS STATION is located in the center of town. From here you can take buses daily to a variety of locations all over Spain including Madrid, Barcelona, Valencia, and Alicante, as well as the eight provincial capitals of Andalusia. Julia Tours and Lineabus operate buses to Belgium, Holland, Switzerland, and Germany from Málaga. Eurolines and Iberbus operate lines to the United Kingdom via Madrid and Paris.

BUS STATIONS

Seville
Estación Plaza de Armas
Calle Arjona. **Map** 1 B5 & 5 A2.
C *(95) 441 71 11.*

Córdoba
Terminal Alsina Graells
Avenida Medina Azahara 29.
C *(957) 23 64 74.*

Granada
Terminal Alsina Graells Sur
Camino de Ronda 97, Granada.
C *(958) 25 13 50.*

Málaga
Estación de Autobuses
Paseo de los Tilos.
C *(95) 235 00 61.*

The main departure hall of Plaza de Armas bus station in Seville

Driving in Andalusia

Logo of a leading chain of gas stations

M ANY OF THE MAIN ROADS and highways in Andalusia are new and in very good condition. However, as a result of the rapid expansion of the road network in recent years, some road maps are out-of-date, so be sure to buy one that was published recently. You should also bear in mind that the number of accidents on Spanish roads is the second highest in Europe. Always drive with caution, but particularly in July and August when the roads are packed with vacationers who do not know the area. When visiting towns and villages, it is generally best to park away from the center and then walk in.

Typically narrow Andalusian street blocked by a parked car

Arriving by Car

V ISITORS DRIVING vehicles from other countries need no special documentation in Spain. You should just make sure you have all the relevant papers from your country of origin: your driver's license, vehicle registration document, and insurance. Your insurance company should be able to arrange an overseas extension of your car insurance. To rent a car in Spain you need to show only a current driver's license, however, it is generally recommended that you obtain an international driver's license to facilitate dealing with traffic officials in case problems develop.

Most Spanish highways are well equipped with an SOS network of telephones, which provide instant access to the emergency services. Ask for *auxilio en carretera*.

Rules of the Road

I N SPAIN PEOPLE DRIVE on the right, so you must give way to the right. At traffic circles you should yield to cars already in the traffic circle – but be extremely careful when in a circle; do not expect oncoming cars to stop. Some will disregard you and drive straight on.

The speed limits are 50 kmh (30mph) in built-up areas; 90– 100 kmh (55–60 mph) outside them, and 120 kph (75 mph) on highways. Seat belts are required both in the back and

front; motorcyclists must wear helmets. Drivers must always carry a warning triangle and can be fined by the traffic police for not being equipped with a first-aid kit.

Road Signs

T HE STANDARD EUROPEAN road signs are used on the roads in Andalusia. However, signs are often confusing and inconsistent, so you need to be especially attentive when navigating in or out of cities. When leaving a town, scan the road for direction signs to other towns. Some are rather small and easily missed.

If you find yourself on the wrong road and need to change direction, look for signs that say *Cambio de Sentido*. They generally lead to bridges or underpasses where you can turn around.

Local Drivers

M ANY DRIVERS in Andalusia ignore road signs and most speed up at yellow traffic lights instead of stopping.

It is common for drivers to tailgate the car in front to

Road Signs in Andalusia

Watch for the following road signs: *Peligro*, indicating danger; *Obras*, meaning roadworks ahead; *Ceda el Paso*, showing that you should yield; and *Cuidado*, advising caution.

Overhead sign indicating the road is a highway

A road sign showing major routes at a crossroads

Be alert to the fact that bulls may be on the road

Warning of the likelihood of snow or ice

signal that they want to overtake. Vehicles overtaking may signal with an arm for you to let them pass.

Indicators are not necessarily used by Spanish drivers, so be alert and try to anticipate the movements of nearby vehicles.

HIGHWAYS

IN ANDALUSIA almost all the highways are free; they are called *autovías* and they are often revamped pre-existing routes. An *autopista* (toll highway), the A4 (*Autopista Mare Nostrum*) connects Seville and Cádiz.

As you approach the *autopista*, drive into one of the lanes to the booths, move up when a green light comes on, and take the ticket that is given. You pay when you leave the *autopista* for the distance you have traveled, so take care not to lose your ticket.

DRIVING IN THE COUNTRYSIDE

ONLY HEAD OFF the major "N" roads (*rutas nacionales*) if you are not in any hurry. The "N" roads are usually very good, but some of the minor roads in Andalusia wind and climb, and their surfaces will often be in poor condition. In addition, although diversions may be marked, when you take them you may find they are inadequately or confusingly signposted. You could add hours to a trip by taking a minor road.

BUYING GAS

MORE THAN HALF of the gas stations in Andalusia still have attendants, although this is changing. There are many gas stations out of town, and the larger ones tend to remain open 24 hours a day.

At self-service stations you generally have to pay for the gas before it is dispensed. S*uper* (four-star), *gasoil* (diesel), and *sin plomo* (unleaded) are usually available. Credit cards are widely accepted.

DRIVING IN TOWN

DRIVING IN THE TOWNS and cities of Andalusia can be difficult. The centers of Seville (in particular around Santa Cruz) and Córdoba (near the Mezquita) have streets that are narrow, labyrinthine, and hard to negotiate in a car.

When this is coupled with the fast, often inconsiderate driving of the residents, it can be stressful to drive in town. If you arrive by car, you are advised to garage it and use public transportation until you are familiar with the area.

A parking attendant

PARKING

AS LONG AS you try to avoid Santa Cruz, the parking situation in Seville is usually not too bad. There are no official areas with parking meters (known as *zonasazules* in other parts of Spain), but quite a few convenient underground garages.

In some streets or squares, however, there are parking attendants. They operate unofficially but most of them are honest. For a tip they will help you into a space and then watch your car until you return.

It is very difficult to park in Córdoba center, but you may find space in the underground garage beside the Mezquita.

Granada is reasonably well provided with parking spaces

and with indoor garages. The charge for parking is about 200 pesetas an hour.

CYCLING

SPAIN IS NOT a bike-friendly country. There are no bike lanes in Andalusia's cities, and cars tend to treat cyclists as a nuisance. A certain amount of sexual harassment also tends to afflict female cyclists. The traffic in the cities is usually too fast and chaotic to allow enjoyable or safe cycling, so it is generally best to stick to excursions into the country on mountain bikes.

Driving in the Sierra Nevada along one of the highest roads in Europe

Getting Around on Foot and by Bus

MANY OF ANDALUSIA'S TOWNS and villages have small, historic centers, characterized by narrow streets and tiny squares. Walking is an excellent and practical way of getting around the sights, especially as entry by car is restricted to residents only in parts of many towns. For the same reason, city buses are generally not much good for traveling between monuments, but they are useful to get to shopping areas or from your hotel into the center of town. Buses are inexpensive, clean, and safe, and generally only crowded during rush hour.

Route numbers | **Bus routes, with**
for *circulares* | **stops shown**

WALKING

IN MANY ANDALUSIAN TOWNS major sights are often only a short walk from where you are likely to be staying – at most just a short bus or taxi ride away.

In Seville the tourist offices have a brochure, *Paseando por Sevilla* (strolling around Seville), which lists the city's interesting walks. However, one of the joys of Andalusia's cities is to lose yourself in their narrow streets and to stumble upon the sights as you go.

There are plenty of organized walking groups that make excursions to the countryside. Look them up in the listings magazine *Giraldillo (see p245)* under *Deportes* (Sports).

The evening *paseo*, or stroll, is an institution. Groups of friends, couples, and families dress up and take to the streets to shop, drink coffee, and see and be seen, before stopping for dinner around 10pm.

CROSSING ROADS

DRIVERS IN SPAIN tend not to respect pedestrians, even where pedestrians have the right of way. It is very rare for a driver to stop at crosswalks. Crossings with pedestrian signals often have only a flashing yellow light for oncoming drivers, even when the signal pedestrians see shows a green man; it is advisable to be very cautious when crossing if you can see any traffic approaching.

Red signal for wait; green for walk with care

CITY BUSES

BUSES IN SPAIN are all single-decker. Get on at the front and either pay the driver, show your travel card, or punch your *bonobus* (ticket) in the machine at the front of the bus. When getting off, press the button to request your stop and, if the bus is crowded, remember to give yourself plenty of time to get off at the side exit.

Orange, singledecker Tussam city bus, operating in Seville

Seville's air-conditioned buses are controlled mainly by the company **Autobuses Urbanos Tussam**. The most useful lines for visitors are the *circulares*, numbered C1 to C4, which run around the city center. Buses run from 6am on weekdays and Saturdays (from 7am on Sundays and public holidays), until 11:30pm in winter and 12:30am in summer. After these times, night buses take over, running on the hour until 2am.

A great way to see the major sights in Seville is by **Sevirama City Tour**, an open-topped double-decker bus. It goes from the Torre del Oro *(see p67)* or Plaza de España *(see p96)*.

The buses are less useful in Granada, as most of the sights are in pedestrian areas. One useful bus route is the No. 2, which runs from the center of the city to the Alhambra.

In Córdoba the center of town is again geared toward pedestrians. The No. 12 takes passengers from the Mezquita area to the newer, commercial center of the city.

CITY BUS COMPANIES

Autobuses Urbanos Tussam
C/ Diego de Riaño 2, Seville. **Map** 4 D3.
📞 (95) 442 00 11.

Sevirama City Tour
Paseo de las Delicias 1, Seville.
Map 3 C3. 📞 (95) 456 06 93.

Sevillanos enjoying the Spanish national institution of the *paseo*

Horse-Drawn Carriages

There is no better way to soak up the ambience of Andalusia's fine cities than from the seat of an old-fashioned, horse-drawn carriage. The official tariffs are usually posted by the places where the drivers wait in line with their carriages; for example, near the Giralda *(see p76)* in Seville or the Mezquita *(see pp140–41)* in Córdoba. The price is usually a few thousand pesetas, although you will find that the drivers are sometimes willing to negotiate a less expensive fare. The carriages can seat up to four passengers.

Horse-drawn carriage by the cathedral in Seville

Tickets and Travel Cards

In Seville, a *billete sencillo* or *univiaje* (one-way ticket) can be purchased on the buses. Make sure, however, that you

Tussam kiosk selling *bono-buses* and *tarjetas turísticas*

have enough small change, since a driver who cannot change a large bill may ask you to get off at the next stop.

A *bonobus* ticket, valid for ten trips, costs half of the price of ten one-way tickets. A *bonobus con derecho a transbordo* is similar, but it allows you to switch buses to continue a trip, if you do so within an hour. It is slightly more expensive.

Also a good value, if you make more than five bus trips in a day, is a *tarjeta turística* (a three- or seven-day tourist bus pass), which gives you unlimited bus travel. This can be bought from Tussam kiosks, newsstands, and tobacconists.

For visitors staying longer in Seville, a *bono mensual* (a one-month pass) is a good value. To buy one you need a photo-card, which you can have made at the Tussam central office.

Taxis

Spanish towns and cities are generously supplied with taxis, so there is not usually a problem finding one, day or night. Taxis are always white and have a logo on the doors, which displays their official number. Drivers rarely speak any English, so learn enough Spanish to explain where you are going and to negotiate the fare. The meter marks up the basic fare; however, supplements may be added for *tarifa nocturna* (nighttime driving), *maletas* (luggage), or *días festivos* (public holidays). If in doubt of the correct price, ask for the *tarifas* (tariff list).

Taxi meter, displaying the fare and the tariff band

Standard, white Seville taxi, with its logo and official number

Taxi Booking Numbers

Seville
[(95) 496 00 00.

Córdoba
[(957) 45 00 00.

Granada
[(958) 13 23 23.

Using a Ticket Stamping Machine

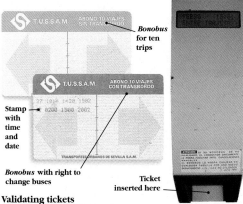

Bonobus for ten trips

Stamp with time and date

Bonobus with right to change buses

Ticket inserted here

Ticket-stamping machine

Validating tickets
Ten tickets (bonobus)*, bought in advance, are valid when stamped.*

General Index

Acknowledgments

DORLING KINDERSLEY would like to thank the following people whose contributions and assistance have made the preparation of this book possible.

MAIN CONTRIBUTORS

DAVID BAIRD, resident in Andalusia from 1971 to 1995, has written many articles and books on Spain, including *Inside Andalusia*.

MARTIN SYMINGTON is a travel journalist and author who has written extensively on Spain. He is a contributor to *The Daily Telegraph* and also worked on the *Eyewitness Travel Guide to Great Britain*.

NIGEL TISDALL, contributor to the *Eyewitness Travel Guide to France*, is the author of many travel publications, including the *Insight Pocket Guide to Seville*.

ADDITIONAL CONTRIBUTORS

Louise Cook, Josefina Fernández, Adam Hopkins, Nick Inman, Janet Mendel, Steve Miller, Javier Gómez Morata, Clara Villanueva.

ADDITIONAL ILLUSTRATIONS

Richard Bonson, Brian Cracker, Roy Flooks, Jared Gilbey, Paul Guest, Christian Hook, Mike Lake, Maltings Partnership, John Woodcock.

ADDITIONAL CARTOGRAPHY

James Anderson, DK Cartography.

DESIGN AND EDITORIAL ASSISTANCE

Greta Britton, Maggie Crowley, Cathy Day, Tim Hollis, Colin Loughrey, Francesca Machiavelli, Susan Mennell, Michael Osborne, Olivia Shepherd, Michael T. Wise.

INDEX

Hilary Bird.

ADDITIONAL PHOTOGRAPHY

Patrick Llewelyn-Davies, David Murray, Martin Norris, Clive Streeter.

PHOTOGRAPHIC AND ARTWORK REFERENCE

Concha Moreno at Aeropuerto Málaga; Fanny de Carranza at the Area de Cultura del Ayuntamiento, Málaga; Tere González at Oficina de Turismo, Ayuntamiento, Cádiz; and staff at Castillo San Marcos, El Puerto de Santa María, Itálica, Seville cathedral and the Museo Bellas Artes, Seville.

SPECIAL ASSISTANCE

DORLING KINDERSLEY would like to thank all the regional and local tourist offices, *ayuntamientos* and *diputaciones* in Andalusia for their valuable help, and especially the Oficina de Turismo de Sevilla de Junta de Andalucía and other departments of the Junta de Andalucía. Particular thanks also to: Javier Morata, Jose Luis de Andrés de Colsa and Isidoro González-Adalid Cabezas at

Acanto Arquitectura y Urbanismo, Madrid; Juan Fernández at Aguilar for his helpful comments; Robert op de Beek at Alvear, Montilla; Francisco Benavent at Fundación Andaluza de Flamenco, Jerez de la Frontera; staff at the Locutorio, Granada; Paul Montegrifo; Amanda Corbett at Patronato Provincial de Turismo de Sevilla; José Pérez de Ayala at the Parque Nacional de Coto Doñana; Gabinete de Prensa, RENFE, Sevilla; Graham Hines and Rachel Taylor at the Sherry Institute of Spain, London; Dr. David Stone; Joaquín Sendra at Turismo Andaluz SA; *6 Toros 6* magazine, Madrid.

PHOTOGRAPHY PERMISSIONS

THE PUBLISHER would like to thank all those who gave permission to photograph at various *ayuntamientos*, cathedrals, churches, galleries, hotels, museums, restaurants, shops, transport services and other establishments too numerous to thank individually.

PICTURE CREDITS

t = top; tl = top left; tc = top center; tr = top right; cla = center left above; ca = center above; cra = center right above; cl = center left; c = center; cr = center right; clb = center left below; cb = center below; crb = center right below; bl = bottom left; b = bottom; bc = bottom center; br = bottom right; d = detail.

Every effort has been made to trace the copyright holders and we apologize in advance for any unintentional omissions. We would be pleased to insert the appropriate acknowledgments in any subsequent edition of this publication.

Works of art have been reproduced with the permission of the following copyright holders: © DACS London 1996: 52clb, 53ca; © PATRIMONIO NACIONAL MADRID: 43br, 46cl, 46cb, 47ca, 50bl.

Photos taken with the assistance of AL-ANDALUS, IBERRAIL SA, Madrid: 248b; CASA-MUSEO FG LORCA, Fuentevaqueros, Granada: 195b; TEATRO DE LA MAESTANZA, Seville: 230t; CANAL SUR, Sevilla: 245cr.

The publisher would like to thank the following individuals, companies and picture libraries for permission to reproduce their photographs:

AISA ARCHIVO ICONOGRÁFICO, Barcelona: 4t, 21b, 21cr, *Juanita Cruz*, A Beltrane (1934) 24bl (d); Biblioteca Nacional Madrid/Museo Universal, *La Spange de C Davillier*, Gustavo Doré 26cl (d); 39t, 40tl, 40c, 40br, 41cr, 42ca; Cathedral, Seville, *San Isidoro y San Leandro*, Ignacio de Ries (17th century) 43crb; Universidad de Barcelona, *La Corte de Abderramán*, Dionisio Baixeres (1885) 44cr–45cl; 45tc, 45bl, 46bl, 46br, 47bl, 48bl; Museo Naval Madrid, *Retrato de Magallanes*, 48br; 50cl; Casón del Buen Retiro, *La Rendición de Bailén*, J Casado del Alisal (1864) 51t; Greenwich Museum, *Battle of Trafalgar*, G Chamberg 51ca (d);

50cr–51cl, 53br, 117bl; Museo-Casa de los Tiros, *Gitanos Bailando el Vito*, Anonymous 185br (d); Algar 42bl, 44clb; Servicio Histórico Nacional, *Alfonso XII*, R de Madrazo 51br (d); 53ca; © DACS 1996 Museo Nacional del Teatro, Almagro, Ciudad Real, poster "Yerma" (FG Lorca) by José Caballero y Juan Antonio Morales (1934) 53cb; D Baird 34b, 37c; Bevilacqua 43bl, 47c; JD Dallet 40clb; Dulevant 48clb; J Lorman 31tc; M Ángeles Sánchez 36t; Sevillano 37t; ARENAS FOTOGRAFÍA ARTÍSTICA, Seville: 47cr, 116cl, Monasterio de la Rábida, Huelva, *Partida de Colón*, Manuel Cabral Bejarano 123b (d).

LA BELLE AURORE, Steve Davey & Juliet Coombe: 17c, 244clb; BRIDGEMAN ART LIBRARY/INDEX: *The Life and Times of Don Quixote y Saavedra* (1608), Biblioteca Universidad Barcelona 49bl.

CEPHAS: Mick Rock 18tr, 28tr, 28cl, 29cr, 29br, 155; Roy Stedall 29tr; CNES, 1987 DISTRIBUTION SPOT IMAGE: 11t; BRUCE COLEMAN: Hans Reinhard 19crb; Konrad Wothe 153crb; DEE CONWAY: 27ca, 27cr; GIANCARLO COSTA, MILAN: 25bc (d), 39b.

JD DALLET, MÁLAGA: 16bl, 30tl, 30clb, 30br, 33b, 34t, 126tl, 142cr, 154, 198t.

AGENCIA EFE, MADRID: 54clb, 54b, 55b, 55crb; EQUIPO 28, SEVILLE: 27tl; MARY EVANS PICTURE LIBRARY: 9 (inset), 26tl, 57 (inset), 67b, 94b, 115 (inset), 169b (d), 235 (inset).

THE ROLAND GRANT ARCHIVE: *"For a Few Dollars More,"* United Artists 194t; GIRAUDON, PARIS: 40cr, Flammarion-Giraudon 41c; JOSÉ M GUTIERREZ GUILLÉN, SEVILLE: 82.

ROBERT HARDING PICTURE LIBRARY: Sheila Terry 47br, 56–57; HULTON DEUTSCH: 52cr–53cl, AM/Keystone 55tl, 163b.

IBERIA ARCHIVES: 246t; INCAFO ARCHIVO FOTOGRÁFICO, MADRID: 153t, 153ca; A Camoyán 153cra, 153cb; JL Glez Grande 153cla; Candy Lopesino/Juan Hidalgo 153clb; JL Muñoz 153b; INDEX, BARCELONA: 41cb, 42br, 44cla, 44bl, 44br, 45cb, 50tl, 50br, 51crb, 51clb (d), 51bl, 187cra; Image/Index 52tl, Private Collection, *Sucesos de Casaviejas*, Saenz Tejada 53tl, 197 (inset); Iranzo 42clb; THE IMAGE BANK: © Chasan 59b; Stockphotos inc © Terry Williams 176; IMAGES: 4b, 14, 18b, 19tl, 19bl, 30tr, 32b; AGE Fotostock, 11b, 15t, 24tr, 24clb, 25c, 26br, 29cl, 35t, 35b, 36b, 133t, 153c, 214tr, 232t; Horizon/Michele Paggetta 24c–25c.

PABLO JULIÁ, SEVILLE: 231b.

ANTHONY KING: 19tr.

LIFE FILE PHOTOGRAPHIC LIBRARY/Emma Lee 28tl, 144bl; JOSÉ LUCAS, SEVILLE: 230c, 232c; NEIL LUKAS: 126cb, 126b.

ARXIU MAS, BARCELONA: 24br; Museo Taurino, Madrid, poster for a bullfight featuring Rodolfo Gaona, H Colmenero 25bl; 43tc, 44tl, 46tl, 46c, 46cr–47cl; Museo América, Madrid, *View of Seville*, Sánchez Coello 48cr–49cl; © Patrimonio Nacional Madrid 43br, 46cl, 46cb, 47ca; MAGNUM/Jean Gaumy 55cb.

NATURPRESS, MADRID: Jose Luis G Grande 127b; Francisco Márquez 19br, 127c; NETWORK PHOTOGRAPHERS: 29tl; Rapho/Hans Silvester 32c.

ORONOZ ARCHIVO FOTOGRÁFICO, MADRID: Private Collection, *La Feria* (Seville), J Domínguez Bécquer (1855) 8–9; 24ca, Private Collection *Reyes Presidiendo a una Corrida de Toros* (1862), Anonymous 25br, Banco Urquijo *Cartel Anunciador Feria de Sevilla* (1903), J Aranda 32t, 36c, 40b, 41tl, 41tc, 41cl, 41crb, 41br, 42tl, 43tl; María Novella Church, Florence, *Detail of Averroes*, Andrea Bonainti 45tl; 45crb, 45br, 47tl, Diputación de Granada, *Salida de Boabdil de la Alhambra*, Manuel Gómez Moreno 47clb; 48tl, 48cla; Museo del Prado, *Cristo Crucificado*, Diego Velázquez 49c (d); Museo de Prado, *Expulsión de los Moriscos*, Vicent Carducho 49cb (d); Musée du Louvre, Paris, *Joven Mendigo*, Bartolomé Murillo 49br (d); © Patrimonio Nacional Madrid, Palacio Real, Riofrio, Segovia, *Carlos III Vestido de Cazador*, F Liani 50bl; © DACS London 1996, Sternberg Palace, Prague, *Self-Portrait*, Pablo Picasso 52clb; Private Collection, Madrid, *Soldados del Ejército Español en la Guerra de Cuba* 52br; 53crb, 53bl, 54tl, 55tc, 70bl, 81b, 139t, 140c; Private Collection, Madrid, *Patio Andaluz*, Garcia Rodríguez 142cl; 160tl; Museo de Bellas Artes, Cádiz, *San Bruno en Éxtasis*, Zurbarán 160tr; 185bl, 215br.

EDUARDO PAEZ, GRANADA: *Porte de la Justice*, Baron de Taylor 38; PAISAJES ESPAÑOLES, MADRID: 87t; JOSE M PEREZ DE AYALA, DOÑANA: 126tr, 126cl, 127t, 127ca; PICTURES: 37b; PRISMA, BARCELONA: 49tl, 55bl, 131b; Museo Lázaro Galdiano, Madrid, *Lope de Vega*, F Pacheco 134b; 137t; *Vista desde el Puerto* Nicolás Chapny (1884) 175t; 231t, 232b; Ferreras 238b, Hans Lohr 157b; Anna N 166c; Sonsoles Prada 41bl.

M ÁNGELES SÁNCHEZ, MADRID: 228tr, 228tc; TONY STONE IMAGES: Robert Everts 80cla.

6 TOROS 6, MADRID: 25crb.

VISIONS OF ANDALUCÍA SLIDE LIBRARY, MÁLAGA: M Almarza 19cr; Michelle Chaplow 17br; 26cr–27cl, 158b, 249b; A Navarro 34cl.

PETER WILSON: 1, 2–3, 33t, 59cb, 141t, 166t, 166b, 171t.

Front endpaper: all commissioned photography with the exception of JD DALLET, MÁLAGA: bc; THE IMAGE BANK: Stockphotos inc © Terry Williams br; JOSE M GUTIERREZ GUILLÉN, SEVILLE: tc.

Jacket: all commissioned photography with the exception of NEIL LUKAS: front left; INCAFO: JJ Blassi front tr.

Phrase Book

In Emergency

Help!	**¡Socorro!**	soh-**koh**-roh
Stop!	**¡Pare!**	**pah**-reh
Call a doctor!	**¡Llame a un médico!**	**yah**-meh ah **oon meh**-dee-koh
Call an ambulance!	**¡Llame a una ambulancia!**	**yah**-meh ah **oonah** ahm-boo-**lahn**-*thee-ah*
Call the police!	**¡Llame a la policía!**	**yah**-meh ah lah poh-lee-**thee**-ah
Call the fire department!	**¡Llame a los bomberos!**	**yah**-meh ah lohs bohm-**beh**-rohs
Where is the nearest telephone?	**Dónde está el teléfono más próximo?**	**dohn**-deh ehs-**tah** ehl teh-**leh**-foh-noh **mahs prohx**-ee-moh
Where is the nearest hospital?	**Dónde está el hospital más próximo?**	**dohn**-deh ehs-**tah** ehl ohs-pee-**tahl mahs prohx**-ee-moh

Communication Essentials

Yes	**Sí**	see
No	**No**	noh
Please	**Por favor**	pohr fah-**vohr**
Thank you	**Gracias**	**grah**-thee-ahs
Excuse me	**Perdone**	pehr-**doh**-neh
Hello	**Hola**	**oh**-lah
Goodbye	**Adiós**	ah-dee-**ohs**
Good night	**Buenas noches**	**bweh**-nahs **noh**-chehs
Morning	**La mañana**	lah mah-**nyah**-nah
Afternoon	**La tarde**	lah **tahr**-deh
Evening	**La tarde**	lah **tahr**-deh
Yesterday	**Ayer**	ah-**yehr**
Today	**Hoy**	oy
Tomorrow	**Mañana**	mah-**nyah**-nah
Here	**Aquí**	ah-**kee**
There	**Allí**	ah-**yee**
What?	**¿Qué?**	**keh**
When?	**¿Cuándo?**	**kwahn**-doh
Why?	**¿Por qué?**	pohr-**keh**
Where?	**¿Dónde?**	**dohn**-deh

Useful Phrases

How are you?	**¿Cómo está usted?**	**koh**-moh ehs-**tah** oos-**tehd**
Very well, thank you.	**Muy bien, gracias.**	mwee bee-**yehn grah**-thee-ahs
Pleased to meet you.	**Encantado de conocerle.**	ehn-kahn-**tah**-doh deh koh-noh-**thehr**-leh
See you soon.	**Hasta pronto.**	ahs-tah **prohn**-toh
That's fine.	**Está bien.**	ehs-**tah** bee-**yehn**
Where is/are . . .?	**¿Dónde está/están . . .?**	**dohn**-deh ehs-**tah**/ehs-**tahn**
How far is it to . . .?	**Cuántos metros/kilómetros hay de aquí a . . .?**	**kwahn**-tohs **meh**-trohs/kee-**loh**-meh-trohs **eye** deh ah-**kee** ah
Which way to . . .?	**¿Por dónde se va a . . .?**	pohr **dohn**-deh seh **vah** ah
Do you speak English?	**¿Habla inglés?**	**ah**-blah een-**glehs**
I don't understand	**No comprendo**	noh kohm-**prehn**-doh
Could you speak slowly please?	**¿Puede hablar más despacio por favor?**	pweh-deh ah-**blahr mahs** dehs-pah-thee-oh pohr fah-**vohr**
I'm sorry.	**Lo siento.**	loh see-**ehn**-toh

Useful Words

big	**grande**	**grahn**-deh
small	**pequeño**	peh-**keh**-nyoh
hot	**caliente**	kah-lee-**ehn**-teh
cold	**frío**	**free**-oh
good	**bueno**	**bweh**-noh
bad	**malo**	**mah**-loh
enough	**bastante**	bahs-**tahn**-teh
well	**bien**	bee-**yehn**
open	**abierto**	ah-bee-**ehr**-toh
closed	**cerrado**	thehr-**rah**-doh
left	**izquierda**	eeth-key-**ehr**-dah
right	**derecha**	deh-**reh**-chah
ahead	**todo recto**	toh-doh **rehk**-toh
near	**cerca**	**thehr**-kah
far	**lejos**	**leh**-hohs
up	**arriba**	ah-**ree**-bah
down	**abajo**	ah-**bah**-hoh
early	**temprano**	tehm-**prah**-noh
late	**tarde**	**tahr**-deh
entrance	**entrada**	ehn-**trah**-dah
exit	**salida**	sah-**lee**-dah
toilet	**lavabos, servicios**	lah-**vah**-bohs sehr-**vee**-thee-ohs
more	**más**	**mahs**
less	**menos**	**meh**-nohs

Shopping

How much does this cost?	**¿Cuánto cuesta esto?**	**kwahn**-toh **kwehs**-tah **ehs**-toh
I would like . . .	**Me gustaría . . .**	meh goos-tah-**ree**-ah
Do you have?	**¿Tienen?**	tee-**yeh**-nehn
I'm just looking.	**Sólo estoy mirando, gracias.**	**soh**-loh ehs-**toy** mee-**rahn**-doh **grah**-thee-ahs
Do you take credit cards?	**¿Aceptan tarjetas de crédito?**	ah-**thehp**-tahn tahr-**heh**-tahs deh **kreh**-dee-toh
What time do you open?	**¿A qué hora abren?**	ah **keh** oh-rah **ah**-brehn
What time do you close?	**¿A qué hora cierran?**	ah keh oh-rah thee-**yehr**-rahn
This one.	**Este**	**ehs**-teh
That one.	**Ese**	**eh**-seh
expensive	**caro**	**kahr**-oh
cheap	**barato**	bah-**rah**-toh
size, clothes	**talla**	***tah**-yah*
size, shoes	**número**	**noo**-mehr-oh
white	**blanco**	**blahn**-koh
black	**negro**	**neh**-groh
red	**rojo**	**roh**-hoh
yellow	**amarillo**	ah-mah-**ree**-yoh
green	**verde**	**vehr**-deh
blue	**azul**	ah-**thool**
antique shop	**la tienda de antigüedades**	lah tee-**yehn**-dah deh ahn-tee-gweh-**dah**-dehs
bakery	**la panadería**	lah pah-nah-deh **ree**-ah
bank	**el banco**	ehl **bahn**-koh
bookstore	**la librería**	lah lee-breh-**ree**-ah
butcher	**la carnicería**	lah kahr-nee-theh-**ree**-ah
drugstore	**la farmacia**	lah fahr-**mah**-thee-ah
fish market	**la pescadería**	lah pehs-kah-deh-**ree**-ah
greengrocer	**la frutería**	lah froo-teh-**ree**-ah
grocery	**la tienda de comestibles**	lah tee-**yehn**-dah deh koh-mehs-**tee**-blehs
hairdresser	**la peluquería**	lah peh-loo-keh-**ree**-ah
market	**el mercado**	ehl mehr-**kah**-doh
newsstand	**el kiosko de prensa**	ehl kee-**yohs**-koh deh **prehn**-sah
pastry shop	**la pastelería**	lah pahs-teh-leh-**ree**-ah
post office	**la oficina de correos**	lah oh-fee-**thee**-nah deh kohr-**reh**-ohs
shoe shop	**la zapatería**	lah thah-pah-teh-**ree**-ah
supermarket	**el supermercado**	ehl soo-pehr-mehr-**kah**-doh
tobacco shop	**el estanco**	ehl ehs-**tahn**-koh
travel agency	**la agencia de viajes**	lah ah-**hehn**-thee-ah deh vee-**ah**-hehs

Sightseeing

art gallery	**el museo de arte**	ehl moo-**seh**-oh deh **ahr**-teh
cathedral	**la catedral**	lah kah-teh-**drahl**
church	**la iglesia**	lah ee-**gleh**-see-yah
	la basílica	lah bah-**see**-lee-kah
garden	**el jardín**	ehl hahr-**deen**
library	**la biblioteca**	lah bee-blee-yoh-**teh**-kah
museum	**el museo**	ehl moo-**seh**-oh
tourist information office	**la oficina de información turística**	lah oh-fee-**thee**-nah deh een-fohr-mah-cee-**yohn** too-**rees**-tee-kah
town hall	**el ayuntamiento**	ehl ah-yoon-tah-mee-**yehn**-toh
closed for vacation	**cerrado por vacaciones**	thehr-**rah**-doh pohr vah-kah-cee-**yoh**-nehs
bus station	**la estación de autobuses**	lah ehs-tah-ee-**yohn** deh owtoh-**boo**-sehs
train station	**la estación de trenes**	lah ehs-tah-thee-**ohn** deh **treh**-nehs

STAYING IN A HOTEL

Do you have a vacant room?	¿Tiene una habitación libre?	tee-**yeh**-neh **oo**-nah ah-bee-tah-thee-**yohn** lee-breh
double room	habitación doble	ah-bee-tah-thee-**yohn doh**-bleh
with double bed	con cama de matrimonio	kohn **kah**-mah deh mah-tree-**moh**-nee-oh
twin room	habitación con dos camas	ah-bee-tah-thee-**yohn** kohn dohs **kah**-mahs
single room	habitación individual	ah-bee-tah-thee-**yohn** een-dee-vee-doo-**ahl**
room with a bath, shower	habitación con baño, ducha	ah-bee-tah-thee-**yohn** kohn bah-nyoh, **doo**-chah
porter	el botones	ehl boh-**toh**-nehs
key	la llave	lah **yah**-veh
I have a reservation.	Tengo una habitación reservada.	tehn-goh **oo**-na ah-bee-tah-thee-**yohn** reh-sehr-**vah**-dah

EATING OUT

Have you got a table for . . .?	¿Tienen mesa para . . .?	tee-**yeh**-nehn meh-sah pah-**rah**
I want to reserve a table.	Quiero reservar una mesa.	kee-yeh-roh reh-sehr-**vahr oo**-nah **meh**-sah
The check please.	La cuenta por favor.	lah **kwehn**-tah pohr fah-**vohr**
I am a vegetarian	Soy vegetariano/a	soy beh-heh-tah-ree-**yah**-no/na
Waitress/ waiter	Camarera/ camarero	kah-mah-**reh**-rah kah-mah-**reh**-roh
menu	la carta	lah **kahr**-tah
fixed-price menu	menú del día	meh-**noo** dehl **dee**-ah
wine list	la carta de vinos	lah **kahr**-tah deh **bee**-nohs
glass	un vaso	oon **vah**-soh
bottle	una botella	oo-nah boh-**teh**-yah
knife	un cuchillo	oon koo-**chee**-yoh
fork	un tenedor	oon teh-neh-**dohr**
spoon	una cuchara	oo-nah koo-**chah**-rah
breakfast	el desayuno	ehl deh-sah-**yoo**-noh
lunch	la comida	lah koh-**mee**-dah
	el almuerzo	ehl ahl-**mwehr**-thoh
dinner	la cena	lah **theh**-nah
main course	el primer plato	ehl pree-**mehr plah**-toh
appetizers	los entremeses	lohs ehn-treh-**meh**-sehs
dish of the day	el plato del día	ehl **plah**-toh dehl **dee**-ah
coffee	el café	ehl kah-**feh**
rare	poco hecho	**poh**-koh **eh**-choh
medium	medio hecho	**meh**-dee-yoh **eh**-choh
well done	muy hecho	mwee **eh**-choh

MENU DECODER

al horno	ahl **ohr**-noh	baked
asado	ah-**sah**-doh	roast
el aceite	ah-**theh**-ee-teh	oil
las aceitunas	ah-theh-**toon**-ahs	olives
el agua mineral	ah-gwa mee-neh-**rahl**	mineral water
el ajo	**ah**-hoh	garlic
el arroz	ahr-**rohth**	rice
el azúcar	ah-**thoo**-kahr	sugar
la carne	**kahr**-neh	meat
la cebolla	theh-**boh**-yah	onion
la cerveza	thehr-**veh**-thah	beer
el cerdo	**therh**-doh	pork
el chocolate	choh-koh-**lah**-teh	chocolate
el chorizo	choh-**ree**-thoh	red sausage
el cordero	kohr-**deh**-roh	lamb
el fiambre	fee-**ahm**-breh	cold meat
frito	**free**-toh	fried
la fruta	**froo**-tah	fruit
los frutos secos	froo-tohs seh-kohs	nuts
las gambas	**gahm**-bahs	shrimp
el helado	eh-**lah**-doh	ice cream
el huevo	oo-**eh**-voh	egg
el jamón serrano	hah-**mohn** sehr-**rah**-noh	cured ham

el jerez	heh-**rehz**	sherry
la langosta	lahn-**gohs**-tah	lobster
la leche	**leh**-cheh	milk
el limón	lee-**mohn**	lemon
la limonada	lee-moh-**nah**-dah	lemonade
la mantequilla	mahn-teh-**kee**-yah	butter
la manzana	mahn-**thah**-nah	apple
los mariscos	mah-**rees**-kohs	seafood
la menestra	meh-**nehs**-trah	vegetable stew
la naranja	nah-**rahn**-hah	orange
el pan	pahn	bread
el pastel	pahs-**tehl**	cake
las patatas	pah-**tah**-tahs	potatoes
el pescado	pehs-**kah**-doh	fish
la pimienta	pee-mee-**yehn**-tah	pepper
el plátano	**plah**-tah-noh	banana
el pollo	**poh**-yoh	chicken
el postre	**pohs**-treh	dessert
el queso	**keh**-soh	cheese
la sal	sahl	salt
las salchichas	sahl-**chee**-chahs	sausages
la salsa	**sahl**-sah	sauce
seco	**seh**-koh	dry
el solomillo	soh-loh-**mee**-yoh	sirloin
la sopa	**soh**-pah	soup
la tarta	**tahr**-tah	pie/cake
el té	teh	tea
la ternera	tehr-**neh**-rah	beef
las tostadas	tohs-**tah**-dahs	toast
el vinagre	bee-**nah**-greh	vinegar
el vino blanco	**bee**-noh **blahn**-koh	white wine
el vino rosado	**bee**-noh roh-**sah**-doh	rosé wine
el vino tinto	**bee**-noh **teen**-toh	red wine

NUMBERS

0	cero	**theh**-roh
1	uno	**oo**-noh
2	dos	dohs
3	tres	trehs
4	cuatro	**kwa**-troh
5	cinco	**theen**-koh
6	seis	says
7	siete	**see**-yeh-teh
8	ocho	**oh**-choh
9	nueve	**nweh**-veh
10	diez	dee-**yehz**
11	once	**ohn**-theh
12	doce	**doh**-theh
13	trece	**treh**-theh
14	catorce	kah-**tohr**-theh
15	quince	**keen**-theh
16	dieciséis	dee-eh-thee-**seh**-ees
17	diecisiete	dee-eh-thee-see-**yeh**-teh
18	dieciocho	dee-eh-thee-**oh**-choh
19	diecinueve	dee-eh-thee-**nweh**-veh
20	veinte	**beh**-yeen-teh
21	veintiuno	beh-yeen-tee-**oo**-noh
22	veintidós	beh-yeen-tee-**dohs**
30	treinta	**treh**-yeen-tah
31	treinta y uno	treh-yeen-tah ee **oo**-noh
40	cuarenta	kwah-**rehn**-tah
50	cincuenta	theen-**kwehn**-tah
60	sesenta	seh-**sehn**-tah
70	setenta	seh-**tehn**-tah
80	ochenta	oh-**chehn**-tah
90	noventa	noh-**behn**-tah
100	cien	thee-**yehn**
101	ciento uno	thee-**yehn**-toh **oo**-noh
102	ciento dos	thee-**yehn**-toh **dohs**
200	doscientos	dohs-thee-**yehn**-tohs
500	quinientos	khee-nee-**yehn**-tohs
700	setecientos	seh-teh-thee-**yehn**-tohs
900	novecientos	noh-veh-thee-**yehn**-tohs
1,000	mil	meel
1,001	mil uno	meel **oo**-noh

TIME

one minute	un minuto	oon mee-**noo**-toh
one hour	una hora	oo-na **oh**-rah
half an hour	media hora	**meh**-dee-a **oh**-rah
Monday	lunes	**loo**-nehs
Tuesday	martes	**mahr**-tehs
Wednesday	miércoles	mee-**ehr**-koh-lehs
Thursday	jueves	**hweh**-vehs
Friday	viernes	bee-**yehr**-nehs
Saturday	sábado	**sah**-bah-doh
Sunday	domingo	doh-**meen**-goh

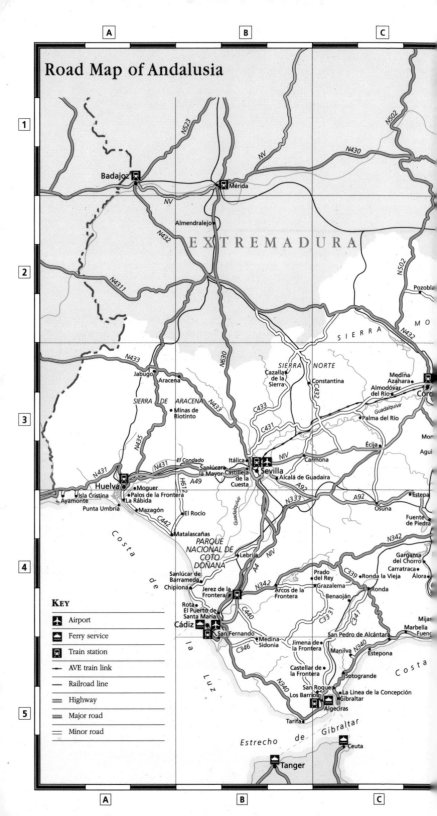